KINGDOM
in the
WEST

The Mormons and the American Frontier

Will Bagley, series editor

VOLUME 6

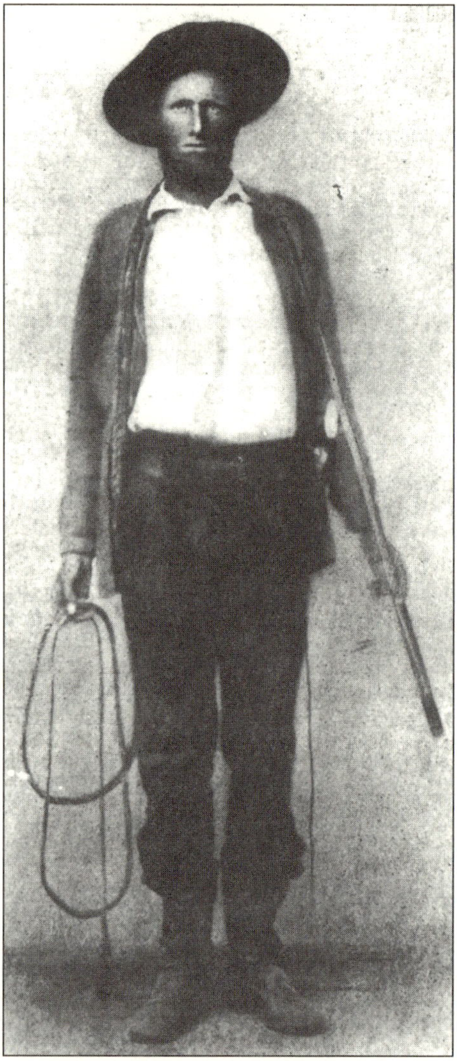

Lewis W. Shurtliff, shown at about the age when he began his adventures as a hired hand at Fort Limhi. He made hazardous winter journeys, pursued Indians, and almost married a chief's daughter as a religious duty. He would later become one of northern Utah's most respected citizens. *Used by permission, Utah State Historical Society, all rights reserved.*

Fort Limhi

The Mormon Adventure in Oregon Territory 1855–1858

by
David L. Bigler

THE ARTHUR H. CLARK COMPANY
Spokane, Washington
2003

Library of Congress Catalog Card Number 2003010556
ISBN 0-87062-324-9
ISBN-0-87062-274-9 (entire series)

Library of Congress Cataloging-in-Publication Data

Bigler, David L., 1927-
Fort Limhi : the Mormon adventure in Oregon territory, 1855/1858 / by David L. Bigler.
p. cm. -- (Kingdom in the West ; v. 6)
Includes bibliographical references and index.
ISBN 0-87062-324-9 (hard cover : alk. paper)
1. Fort Lemhi (Idaho)--History. 2. Mormon pioneers--Idaho--Lemhi County--History. 3. Mormon missionaries--Idaho--Lemhi County--History. 4. Frontier and pioneer life--Idaho--Lemhi County. 5. Indians of North America--Missions--Idaho--Lemhi County--History--19th century. 6. Mormon Church--Missions--Idaho--Lemhi County--History--19th century. 7. Lemhi County (Idaho)--History--19th century. 8. Oregon--History--To 1859. I. Title. II. Series.
F754.F68B54 2003
979.6'78--dc21

2003010556

For Evah
who was there in the beginning

Contents

Illustrations

Acknowledgments

The author wishes to recognize with appreciation some of the associates whose support made this work possible. Foremost of these is series editor Will Bagley, whose research and suggestions made an indispensable contribution. Ross Goddard of Tendoy, Idaho, and Stephen Mahaffey, the current and former owners of the property on which Fort Limhi was located, have allowed ready access to the site and supplied useful information about the area. William P. MacKinnon of Bloomfield Hills, Mich., the leading authority on the 1857 Utah War, generously provided his knowledge of this antebellum conflict, and historian John D. Nash of Oakdale, Calif., author of some of the best papers and articles on Fort Limhi, kindly shared his resources, knowledge, and insights on the mission. Ardis Parshall, a truly remarkable scholar, generously shared a wealth of material from nineteenth-century newspapers and documents. Brigham Madsen, former tribal historian for the Shoshone Nation and a pioneering expert on trails to Idaho and Montana, reviewed and commented on a draft of this work, while Peter H. DeLafosse, an astute observer of Latter-day Saint culture and a fine editorial critic, read the finished manuscript and made a number of improvements.

Others making especially helpful contributions to this work include Ann Buttars, Merrill Library, Utah State University; Doug Misner, Utah State Historical Society; David A. Kingma, archivist, The Oregon Province of the Society of Jesus, Gonzaga University; Brian Shovers, Montana Historical Society; Larry R. Jones, Idaho State Historical Society; Drufilla Gould, American Indian Studies, Idaho State University; Otis Halfmoon, Nez Percé National Historic Park; Jeff Johnson, Utah State Archives; and Dennis Baird, University of Idaho. Jean Schurman of Victor, Montana, provided us with the previously unpublished portrait of Richard Grant.

Finally, the author will ever value and never take for granted the kindness and professionalism of the archivists and historians at the LDS Historical Department; Utah State Historical Society; Harold B. Lee Library, Brigham Young University; Marriott Library, University of Utah; Stewart Library, Weber State University; and Preston Library, Virginia Military Institute.

Editorial Procedures

In preparing this work, the author has relied almost exclusively on primary sources, the many journals, diaries, letters, and reminiscences of the men and women who either served at Fort Limhi or played significant roles in the story of the mission during its three-year existence.

By far the most important of these sources is the Salmon River Mission Journal kept by David Moore, mission clerk, and Jacob Miller and Benjamin Franklin Cummings, who acted as scribes in his absence. As indicated in the Introduction, there are two versions of this document, an edited account on microfilm, accessible at Bancroft Library and the Archives of the Church of Jesus Christ of Latter-day Saints (cited here as "LDS Archives"), and the original journal, located at LDS Archives. A photocopy of the holograph manuscript recently became available at Merrill Library, Utah State University. The author has taken quotations from both, citing them in footnotes as a single source. When entries are the same, he has chosen the edited version because it is easier to follow. A reader can readily identify passages from the original journal that are not found in the edited version by their phonetic spelling and inconsistent punctuation and grammar.

In presenting the Salmon River Mission Journal and other original sources, the only changes the author has made has been to capitalize the first word of sentences and add periods at the end. Phonetically spelled words are usually given in their original form with brackets and *sics* added sparingly. Otherwise, to preserve the excitement and flavor of these first-person accounts, the author has undertaken to set the stage but tell the story of Fort Limhi in the words of those who lived the adventure.

Foreword

The history of the Mormons in the American West is so sweeping it is easy to ignore episodes that, for one reason or another, found no place in the traditional annals of the region. Few Americans recall that several hundred Mormon soldiers marched from Santa Fe to San Diego the year before Brigham Young first saw the Salt Lake Valley, and even fewer recall (or care) that San Francisco was once, as H. H. Bancroft observed, "very largely a Mormon town." Such events are often overlooked in the standard histories of the West and simply do not fit into the popular mythology. The pioneering incursion of the Mormons into the remote backcountry of Oregon Territory in the mid-1850s is an excellent example. Enterprises like this provide powerful reminders that the Mormons (or Latter-day Saints, as they prefer to be known) achieved much and dreamed of accomplishing much more in the West than merely establishing the oddest state in the American Republic. Considering such important but obscure undertakings often provides a better understanding of what happened in the antebellum West—and why it happened. Doing so requires looking closely at the record, questioning the accepted history, and seeking to unravel the contradictions, eliminate the inconsistencies, and solve the mysteries that bedevil the accepted story. To step outside this historical box requires a creative and courageous scholar.

David L. Bigler is such a historian.

In his latest contribution to Western history, Mr. Bigler completes a project he began almost forty years ago. As an executive for U.S. Steel, he became interested in the conflict between the federal government and the "theo-democracy" the Mormons established in Utah Territory. The traditional telling of the story simply did not make sense—it was contradictory, avoided analyzing significant events, ignored contemporary evidence, and came to a happy ending that, given the suffering and sacrifice it imposed on the Mormon people, seemed more imaginary than real. In his *History of Idaho,* the respected historian Leonard J. Arrington seemed baffled about why Brigham Young visited Fort Limhi while the fires of the Mormon Reformation burned in Utah and as the territory's relationship with the federal government was collapsing. Arrington concluded the trip was "a pioneer equivalent of a vacation to 'see the country': the only known occasion when Brigham Young and his associates took along their families and friends with the primary purpose of enjoying the scenery."

The president of the United States, who was squaring off against Brigham Young while the Mormon prophet and some 150 of his closest associates were on vacation in 1857, would have questioned such a benign interpretation. When the president interviewed Utah congressional delegate John M. Bernhisel in spring 1858, he told the Mormon diplomat that some of Brigham Young's speeches in the *Deseret News* "were terrible" and had convinced him "Gov. Young intended to establish an Independent Government and had been preparing for this for years." The president "spoke of the report of [the Mormons] being about to remove to the British possessions" and asked pointedly "where Gov. Young went last Spring." Clearly, James Buchanan did not believe Utah's *de facto* Indian superintendent left his post and traveled almost eight hundred miles merely to take in the scenery.

"Some 100 men were called to go with the President, this coming spring, to the settlement on Salmon River on an exploring expedition," Judge Elias Smith wrote to George A. Smith on 1 March 1857. "All the men that can tell a piece of chalk, from rock ore, of any kind, will have a chance to display their knowledge of mineralogy during the trip or after their return." Smith's description of this "exploring expedition" suggests it was at least a working vacation.

As he surveyed the sources, Bigler became convinced of the pivotal role the Salmon River Indian Mission played in the resolution of the Utah War of 1857–1858, and how the catastrophe that ended the colony at Fort Limhi brought Utah back from the very brink of war with the United States. To understand what took place at the Mormon outpost in Oregon, Bigler began gathering eyewitness accounts from the descendants of the Salmon River settlers and searching out their stories in libraries and archives. The result of his work, *Fort Limhi: The Mormon Adventure in Oregon Territory,* is an innovative look at a fascinating but forgotten story.

The word "adventure" in David L. Bigler's latest title is appropriate. While many documentary histories are tedious collections of the Works of Famous Men, right down to their laundry lists, *Fort Limhi* lets ordinary western folk who survived an extraordinary exploit tell their stories in their own words, and these narratives are dramatic, compelling, ironic, enlightening, and downright fun. With its astonishing fish stories, desperate Indian battles, life-threatening chases, and heroic rides to rescue a terrified and helpless outpost, this work has all the elements of a great frontier novel. It even tells of the star-crossed love of Lewis Shurtliff and Louisa Moore, whose romance, like the story of Fort Limhi, came to a tragic ending.

The Mormon stalwarts who pioneered today's Idaho remind us that early, ordinary Latter-day Saints were not only much-married polygamists but resourceful people of fortitude, determination, and considerable courage. "Colonel" Thomas S. Smith, Fort Limhi's resolute and hardheaded leader, provided his missionaries with an example of stalwart determination. Clerk David Moore, who with Jacob Miller created a detailed record of the outpost's story, proved himself a writer and historian of noteworthy talent. The explorations of B. F. "Frank" Cummings, a resourceful operative and scout, supplement the exploits of Baldwin Watts and Ezra Barnard, the heroic couriers whose message saved Fort Limhi and ended what would have been a horrific religious civil war.

David Bigler's masterful study reveals dozens of new or ignored primary sources about the Indians of the Pacific Northwest during the 1850s, a time when eyewitness accounts of this remarkable region are surprisingly few. The Mormon missionaries who settled among Sacagawea's kin intentionally selected a spot that put them at the crossroads of ancient trails used by Nez Percé, Shoshone, Bannock, and Flathead bands as they battled each other and pursued their annual pilgrimages to trade, harvest salmon, and hunt buffalo. The sophisticated leaders of these nations reveal a much deeper understanding of the Mormons than the missionaries who sought to redeem the souls of the "Lamanites" had of their prospective converts. As historian Martin Ridge observed in his essay, "Mormon 'Deliverance' and the Closing of the Frontier," "The Indians refused to be what Mormon theology said they were."

Fort Limhi provides new material on the obscure fur-trade veterans and misfits who called themselves "mountaineers" (the contemporary term for that "majority of scoundrels" now known as the fearless "Mountain Men") and sheds light on their contentious relations with their Mormon neighbors. From their initial encounters in 1847 and 1848, the Mormons and their only white neighbors had an uneasy relationship. Beginning in 1853 "Deseret" waged war with the mountaineers for control of the lucrative overland trade in the Green River Valley. Despite their reputation as fearless frontiersmen, these seasoned veterans of the fur trade soon developed a healthy respect for, if not downright fear of, their millennialist rivals. When a Mormon posse that included Sheriff James Ferguson, Bill Hickman, Ephraim Hanks, and Andrew Cunningham confronted Jim Bridger, he abandoned his post to these hard-cases. "Old Gabe" chose to hide in the bushes and watch the "Saints" destroy his stock of rum "one dram at a time" rather than rally his Shoshone kinsmen to fight back. And when the hardboiled first citizens of today's Montana came to believe that Mormon bees would soon swarm into the Bitterroot Valley, the news threw many of these bold mountaineers into a panic.

A remarkable cast of characters assumes supporting roles in the story of the first attempt to establish a farming settlement in today's Idaho. The towering Bannock Chief Shou-woo-koo, known to the Mormons as Rock-e-kay (their phonetic rendition of the nickname French trappers gave to *Le Grand Coquin*), shows why he was known as "The Big Rogue." Edward "Ned" Williamson, who was famous for his survival skills, his role in the discovery of gold in Montana, and his adventures in its vigilante movement, survived to guide Gen. John Gibbon's column in the Sioux Campaign of 1876 before he disappeared. The Grants were a rugged Scots family headed by Richard Grant, the Hudson's Bay Company chieftain at Fort Hall whose pivotal role in the opening of the Oregon and California trails in the 1840s is unjustly uncelebrated. His son John Francis, notorious and beloved by his fellow Montana pioneers as

"Johnny," had a singular talent for skirting "very close to trouble" but somehow always emerged with his skin and scalp intact. The Grants' many Indian wives and their beautiful daughters are less well known but every bit as intriguing. And it would be hard to find two more colorful frontiersmen than John W. Powell and B. F. Ficklin, who hardly deserve their unsung obscurity.

David Bigler is a native son of Utah who knows the rivers, mountains, deserts, and valleys of the Great Basin and the old Oregon Territory intimately. Coupled with five decades of creative, persistent research in primary sources, his practical understanding of the land, people, and trails of the West brings to life a forgotten past that deserves to be remembered. Working on *Fort Limhi: The Mormon Adventure in Oregon Territory* has been the most enjoyable editorial task of my life. I owe a great debt to my friend and mentor, whose work continues the chronicle of the Kingdom in the West with a masterful telling of a colorful story that reveals how the influence of the Mormons in the West extended far beyond the borders of Utah.

WILL BAGLEY
Salt Lake City, Utah

Introduction

Few historians have appreciated the importance of Brigham Young's journey into Oregon Territory in spring 1857 to visit Fort Limhi on the east fork of Salmon River, the northern-most outpost of the vast empire the enterprising LDS president had established in the American West. A military showdown between the Mormon theocracy and the United States, known as the Utah War, was imminent. Young's excursion to the Northern Indian Mission was undertaken shortly after yet another batch of federal officials had fled the Mormon Kingdom, and just weeks before President James Buchanan ordered the U.S. Army to impose the national government's authority over Utah Territory. After Young's overland treks in the 1840s, his trip to Salmon River would be the longest sojourn of his career in the West.

Only Andrew Love Neff saw that while the Mormon leader never visited other far-off outposts of his faith, he spent thirty-three days on the tour to the northern settlement, near present Salmon, Idaho, "in anticipation, perhaps, of filling it with Mormon colonists." The respected Utah historian thought Young's actions to expand the colony and establish "intermediate connecting stations" to it were "foiled by the Utah War."[1] Like others, he failed to consider the likelihood that Young's 1857 journey to Fort Limhi and subsequent measures to strengthen the settlement were undertaken because he anticipated the coming confrontation with the United States.

The Mormon leader hardly needed the gift of prophecy to see the storm clouds gathering to the East. The millennial doctrines of his faith and his establishment of God's Kingdom as an earthly dominion in the American West, prior to Christ's imminent return, made such a conflict

---

[1]Neff, *History of Utah, 1847 to 1869*, 235–36.

probable, even unavoidable. He and his people believed the fledgling theocracy, ruled from heaven through inspired men on earth, was the stone the prophet Daniel envisioned, "cut out of the mountain without hands."[2] Its purpose, "to reduce all nations and creeds to one political and religious standard," was a revolutionary one.[3] The destiny of the Kingdom of God was to replace all man-made realms, including its parent republic. Its very nature compelled it to prevail over lesser systems, not compromise or coexist with or under them. And divine support made its ultimate victory certain.

Eight years after his 1847 arrival in Salt Lake Valley, then within the Republic of Mexico, Brigham Young told his followers, "The Kingdom of God is actually organized and the inhabitants of the earth do not know it." And he proclaimed in 1855 the mission of the millennial religion, as foretold by Old Testament prophets and their counterparts in the Last Days. "We will roll on the Kingdom of our God, gather out the seed of Abraham, build the cities and temples of Zion, and establish the Kingdom of God to bear rule over all the earth," said he.[4]

But by that year, events unforeseen by prophets, ancient or modern, had already overtaken his Kingdom and placed it on a collision course with the most dynamic society on earth. At Sutter's Mill in California on 24 January 1848, Mormon Battalion veteran Henry W. Bigler wrote the words that raised hopes more worldly in nature than millennial: "This day some kind of mettle was found in the tail race that looks like goald."[5] Just ten days later, the United States, under the the terms of the Treaty of Guadalupe Hidalgo ending the Mexican War, expanded its continental domain by the addition of much of the interior American West, including the states of Utah, California, New Mexico, Arizona, and Nevada, plus large parts of Wyoming and Colorado.

One cannot overstate the impact of these events on Mormon history. The nation's second-largest land acquisition after the Louisiana Purchase placed the Kingdom right back in the United States, from whence

[2]Dan. 3:45.

[3]Pratt, *Proclamation of the Twelve Apostles of the Church of Jesus Christ of Latter-day Saints to All the Kings of the World, to the President of the United States of America; to the Governors of the Several States, and to the Rulers and People of All Nations.*

[4]Remarks by Brigham Young, July 1855, *Journal of Discourses,* 2:310, 317.

[5]Paul, *The California Gold Discovery: Sources, Documents, Accounts and Memoirs Relating to the Discovery of Gold at Sutter's Mill,* 63.

it came, while the gold discovery positioned it squarely in the path of a great population shift to the West, the mass migration known in the beginning as the Gold Rush. Occurring only days apart, the acquisition of the American Southwest and the discovery of gold brought cheek to jowl two incompatible forms of government: one a theocracy, ruled from on high by God through inspired men, the other a democratic republic, governed from below by its people. The struggle between these two great powers for supremacy would continue for the next half-century and transform a revolutionary millennial faith into the respected pillar of traditional American values that it is today.

In 1849 Mormon leaders moved to reach a temporary accommodation with the United States, when they established the State of Deseret as a "free and independent government" and petitioned Congress for statehood.[6] For its population of fewer than ten thousand, the vastness of Deseret was impressive. The new sovereign state, including a seaport at San Diego, was about twice the area of Texas, or about fifty square miles per inhabitant. Its projected size reflected the church's expectation to populate this region with a flood of Abraham's progeny, who would come from the nations of earth to redeem Zion in the Last Days. Its name, Deseret, was a synonym for the Kingdom of God.

Unaware of such lofty aspirations and obsessed with the debate over slavery, Congress ignored the bid for statehood and instead created a new territory under the Compromise of 1850. Federal lawmakers thought that the word "Deseret," so cherished by the builders of Zion, sounded too much like "desert," so they bestowed on it an unwanted name in honor of its native inhabitants.[7] They also cut its size back sharply. Even then, the borders of Utah Territory encompassed over 220,000 square miles, making it some two and a half times larger than today's state. From east to west its limits ran from the Continental Divide to the crest of California's Sierra Nevada, and its borders encompassed present Utah, nearly all of Nevada, the western slope of Colorado, and the southwestern corner of Wyoming, including Fort Bridger and today's Evanston.

Regardless of its size, however, it was far from certain that Mormon leaders would accept this new dominion that President Millard Fillmore

[6]Morgan, *The State of Deseret*, 27.

[7]The name Deseret comes from *The Book of Mormon* and means "honey bee."

signed into existence on 9 September 1850. A territorial form of government would force them to surrender the right to rule themselves, which they viewed as bestowed by heavenly authority, to political favorites and carpetbaggers chosen by the president. At this imagined affront, Brigham Young characteristically made his feelings plain: "I am the governor of the state of Deseret, I was elected for life, and no other person shall hold that office here while I live," he reportedly said. "If they send a governor here, he will be glad to black my boots for me."[8] A crisis was avoided when Fillmore astutely appointed Young himself governor, but three of the six other territorial offices went to outsiders not of his faith, creating a source of continuing controversy.

Lt. John W. Gunnison, a young Army officer who spent 1849 and 1850 in Deseret with the Stansbury Expedition, described its people as "being satisfied to abide their time, in accession of strength by numbers, when they may be deemed fit to take a sovereign position."[9] But the creation of Utah Territory upset this plan. Even with Young as governor, the unwanted form of government placed God's Kingdom under Washington's thumb, as represented by self-seeking outsiders and prying bureaucrats, who imposed intolerable interference onto divine rule. Before the new territory celebrated its first anniversary, the leaders of Deseret opened a campaign to throw off the federal yoke and adopt a position independent from the American republic, either as a sovereign state or, preferably, as an independent nation-state in the American West. Only then could the Kingdom begin its ascendancy to world rule.

The church's actions to assert Zion's sovereignty included: the rejection of non-Mormon officials; the outlawing of traditional American legal processes and adoption of a separate court system; the acceleration of immigration from overseas (which led to the 1856 handcart disaster); the great Reformation that same year to cleanse the body of Israel and make the people worthy of divine intervention when the probable confrontation with the United States came; and the creation of a military force far larger than required for defense. An especially revealing sign that God's Kingdom had opened its march to universal dominion was the call of hundreds of Indian missionaries, starting in 1854, to forge alliances with North American tribes.

---

[8]Bigler, ed., *A Winter with the Mormons: The 1852 Letters of Jotham Goodell,* 50.

[9]Gunnison, *The Mormons, or Latter-day Saints,* 23.

Among those sent to carry the gospel of their Hebrew forbears to the native peoples they called "Remnants of Israel" or "Lamanites" in the Northwest were 116 men, women, and children, known as the Salmon River mission, who from 1855 to 1858 pushed the northern limits of the Kingdom into what was then Oregon Territory and is now in eastern Idaho.[10] They named their outpost Fort Limhi after King Limhi from *The Book of Mormon,* who had preserved a colony of his people in the wilderness. Later misspelled, his name lives on today in the name of Lemhi County, where the settlement was located, and in such other familiar Idaho place names as Lemhi River, Lemhi Pass, and Lemhi Range.

The author discovered their story some years ago when the late historian and journalist Harold Schindler, then writing his classic biography of Orrin Porter Rockwell, asked for information about the early bishop of Nephi, an ancestor. Jacob Bigler testified as a defense witness in the 1878 trial of Sylvanus Collett for the murder twenty-one years earlier of John Aiken. Witnesses also implicated Rockwell and Bigler himself in the 1857 killing of some Californians, known as the Aiken party.[11]

Collett's alibi was convincing and unbreakable. The Englishman said that he was hundreds of miles from the scene of the crime as an Indian missionary at Fort Limhi. At his trial, Thomas S. Smith, former president of the Salmon River mission and a man known for his forthright honesty, confirmed in detail Collett's story. Also swearing to its truthfulness were many of the defendant's former Fort Limhi companions, all respected members of their communities. A mixed jury found Collett innocent and the case is now forgotten—except for one thing. Evidence has surfaced revealing that these men, all of unquestioned good character, all committed perjury in an orchestrated performance. No doubt good men did this because they believed the cause they served justified their lying under oath.[12]

Nor was this the only case of moral relativism the author found after he became interested in the Fort Limhi story. On the east bench that overlooks the ruins of the fort's corral stands a handsome monument dedi-

[10]See Appendix A, "A Comprehensive List of the Missionaries, Family Members, and Hired Hands Who Served at Fort Limhi from May 1855 to April 1858."

[11]For the story of this episode, see Schindler, *Orrin Porter Rockwell: Man of God, Son of Thunder,* 268–81.

[12]For evidence that has come to light since the trial, see Chapter 8.

cated on 13 May 1950. A brass plaque carries an impressive quote by Brigham Young, as provided by the late distinguished historian Merrill D. Beal, author of the prize-winning work, *"I will fight no more forever": Chief Joseph and the Nez Perce War,* and over two dozen books on Mormon and Idaho history. According to him, Young said: "Go into the Salmon River country, Oregon Territory. Many tribes converge upon that area to fish and hunt. Choose an appropriate location and found a mission. Teach them the arts of husbandry and peace according to our gospel plan . . ."[13]

This quotation "does not figure to be correct," thought John D. Nash in 1966, and the professor of history at Modesto Junior College asked Beal about it.[14] Much to Nash's "surprise and chagrin," Beal responded that he had written the statement himself "in the manner of 'poetic license' for placement upon a plaque at the Salmon River monument" because he thought it conformed "nicely with the spirit and intent of the Mission Call."[15] Young's alleged injunction no doubt touched the hearts and faith of those who attended the dedication, as it was apparently meant to do, but it subtly distorted the mission's role and the beliefs of those who founded it. Nash's own excellent paper on Fort Limhi, prepared for the Fourth Annual Idaho Historical Conference and published as "The Salmon River Mission of 1855," offers a better example of how history should be made.[16]

Far more harmful than false quotes on historical markers has been the restricted access to critical sources imposed on historians like Nash, who have tried to write the Fort Limhi story honestly. For no apparent reason, LDS church officials long kept under wraps the original Salmon River Mission Journal, as recorded by David Moore and Jacob Miller from 6 April 1855 to 11 April 1858. Nash told then Church Historian Leonard J. Arrington in 1974 that he had been unable to see this document. Arrington replied that he could "think of no reason why you might have been denied seeing it, except that it was in pretty ragged condition" and promised to have it microfilmed and made available for researchers.[17] But other officials continued to withhold it. Historians,

[13]*Souvenir Program for the Dedication of the LDS Idaho Pioneer Monument at Fort Limhi.*

[14]Nash to Bigler, 1966. Unfortunately the first page of this letter with the exact date has been lost.

[15]Beal to Nash, 25 July 1966.

[16]See Nash, "The Salmon River Mission of 1855," 22–31.

[17]Arrington to Nash, 30 August 1974.

except for a select few, had to work from microfilm copies of an edited version, written by a single hand during the nineteenth century for historian H. H. Bancroft, now located at the church's Salt Lake City archives and the Bancroft Library, University of California at Berkeley. But the absence of entries for critical periods, not to mention excellent handwriting, spelling, and grammar, reveals that while it is useful, it is a revised version.

Now, thanks to Arrington, researchers enjoy access to a photocopy of the original Salmon River Mission Journal in the collection named after this distinguished Mormon scholar at Merrill Library, Utah State University. In addition, the original journal is now available to researchers at LDS Archives. In comparing it with the edited version one finds that the differences mainly relate to punctuation and spelling or to questions of no real importance. For example, the following italicized words have been erased from the edited journal. "The old Nezperce chief rose very early this morning and came to [mission president] Col. Smith and wished to have a smoke with him, *his wish was gratified by the Col. taking a good smoke with him,* which made the old chief feel in fine spirits."[18] Also deleted was the mission head's rebuke that the unbecoming behavior of the missionaries, "such as pitching quotes [quoits] & gambling for supplies," was the cause of Indian trouble.[19]

More significant are the deletions that show the mission traded ammunition and firearms to the natives, as charged by U.S. Army officers in the Northwest, although the practice does not appear to have been systematic or widespread. Nor will one discover in this expurgated version any mention that during Brigham Young's 1857 visit to Fort Limhi, Mormon leaders told the missionaries "to marry the native women, that the marrige [*sic*] tie was the strongest tie of friendship that existed," a policy made possible by the practice of polygamy.[20]

Especially harmful to a real understanding of this period, the editor of the revised journal struck from that record all evidence that the Mormon theocracy in 1857 planned to cut its ties with the United States and take an independent position. One illustration of this unfortunate

[18]Salmon River Mission Journal, 23 June 1855.
[19]Ibid., 1 November 1857.
[20]Ibid., 10 May 1857

practice is the following entry from the original journal on 22 September 1857: "Pres. Brigham Young has declared in the name of Isreals [*sic*] God that the Saints shall be free from all gentile Government [and] has also said the Soldiers shall not come to the valley. Different companies have ~~not~~ gone to meet them and if they (the Soldiers) turn not back blood has been shed ere this."[21]

Fortunately, Brigham Young's Nauvoo Legion and the U.S. Army did not engage in hostilities that resulted in casualties. Happily, too, the original Salmon River Mission Journal can now be added to the growing evidence that refutes the old and unwarranted slander that it was "Buchanan's blunder" when the American president ordered the U.S. Army to assert federal authority over a secessionist territory.[22] Moreover, this invaluable source and the many others that have become available in recent years provide a largely unexploited wealth of information about native history and culture in eastern Idaho. They further cast light on little-known trails followed by Indians, mountaineers, and emigrants in this region. Perhaps most significant, they are a remarkable collection of personal documents that describe the adventures, trials and triumphs, and the loves and losses of an extraordinary sampling of frontier Americans whose lives should not be forgotten.

Above all, the narratives point up the importance of the settlement on Salmon River, both as an Indian mission, dedicated to redeem the "remnants of the House of Jacob," and as a location of highest strategic value in the pre-Civil War military confrontation between the Mormon theocracy and the United States. To give the story of Fort Limhi the attention it deserves in the history of Idaho and Montana, to provide insights into the role of Mormons in the West and their Indian relations, to explain some long-standing puzzles about the Utah War of 1857–1858, and to do so without bias, is the purpose of this work.

---

[21]Ibid., 22 September 1857.

[22]For the author's use of both the revised and original Salmon River Mission Journal, see Editorial Procedures.

Chapter I

Sound an Alarm

At once, I saw that something had transpired which occasioned a stir in the community, and soon learned that news had been received of a massacre of the Saints at Salmon River. — *Thomas L. Kane*

Two men, exhausted and drawn from six days and nights of winter travel, led their worn-out horses into Barnard's Fort, a Mormon outpost on Malad River, some four miles south of the northern border of Utah Territory and five miles north of today's Plymouth. It was Saturday, 6 March 1858, and their need for fresh mounts overrode their own fatigue and hunger. Baldwin Watts and Ezra Barnard had arrived at the northern outskirts of the settlements of Utah bearing an urgent alarm that had to be carried to Great Salt Lake City immediately.

Theirs had been a desperate journey. On 28 February the two missionaries to the Indians of Oregon at Fort Limhi, four hundred miles to the north, had mounted the only two good horses remaining after a sudden and fatal attack on the small settlement. They quietly had slipped out of the stockade at night to begin their long ride to Salt Lake City bearing an urgent cry for help. While the settlers in the besieged fort feared every moment to hear the darkness torn by gunfire, the riders had stolen past the Indian camps along the river and slapped leather for Mormon settlements far to the south, closely pursued during the first hundred miles of their journey. For the last forty-eight hours of the six-day, late-winter dash they had no food and only one able horse between them.

Stitched into Barnard's coat lining by one of the women at Fort Limhi was a dispatch to Brigham Young from Thomas S. Smith, the grizzled president of the Salmon River colony in Oregon Territory. It described a fateful turn of events.

Attack on Fort Limhi

Virtually without warning, on the morning of 25 February 1858 some 250 Bannock and Shoshone warriors attacked the northernmost Mormon outpost and Indian mission.[1] Fort Limhi was located just west of present Lemhi Pass over the Continental Divide, crossed fifty years before by Lewis and Clark. It was about nineteen miles southeast of today's Salmon, Idaho, on the east fork of Salmon River, now Lemhi River, near the birthplace of the Shoshone woman, Sacagawea, who had accompanied Lewis and Clark.

The Indians surprised the missionaries who were working in widely separated locations, killing two and wounding five in scattered fighting before the heavily outnumbered defenders retreated to the safety of their log stockade. Among those injured was their forty-year-old leader, Smith himself, fortunately just grazed on the arm by a burst of fire that shot off his hat and cut his suspenders.

The attackers seized the target of their incursion: almost the entire mission herd, numbering well over two hundred cattle, thirty or more horses, and other animals. But this loss, serious enough, paled alongside a heavier blow delivered to Mormon plans for their very survival in the American West. Great Salt Lake and the surrounding settlements were facing the imminent arrival of the United States Army, and Brigham Young had publicly resolved to treat "every army and every armed company that attempts to come here as a mob."[2] Unexpectedly eliminated by the Indian raid was this vital halfway base of supply and refitting in a projected movement of the faith north from Salt Lake over the Rocky Mountains to the headwaters of the Missouri River, then northwest to the Bitterroot Valley and, if necessary, into Canada.

Since any chance to make this move rested on the goodwill of the region's native inhabitants, the report that many of the Indian attackers themselves were members of the millennial faith, baptized by Mormon Indian missionaries over the previous three years, was especially alarming. In a revealing test of influence, "gentile" mountain men, a group

[1]For the best works on the Bannock and Northern Shoshone nations, see Brigham D. Madsen's *The Bannock of Idaho* and *The Northern Shoshoni*. Madsen used the tribe's preferred spelling for "Shoshoni" in his title, but the tribe has now adopted the more commonly used "Shoshone."

[2]Brigham Young, 13 September 1857, *Journal of Discourses*, 4:232.

Ezra Jacob Wycoff Barnard
He and Baldwin H. Watts, both in their twenties, performed one of the heroic feats of the 1857 Utah War when they rode nearly four hundred miles in mid-winter with no spare horses to report the Indian attack on Fort Limhi. *Courtesy, Barnard family.*

who had been troublesome for Mormons in the past, had apparently talked their Indian friends out of their new religion and into a raid on the mission herd. The outcome was a cruel setback at a critical hour, but as with similar catastrophes in the church's short history, there was rarely time for lamentation.

Immediate action was needed against the peril that threatened nearly seventy Mormon settlers on the Salmon River, many of them women and children, cut off and facing possible death in the wilderness. When the two messengers had escaped south, the settlers were stiffening their courage and defenses for a last stand, hammering their scythes into spears at the blacksmith shop. The men still able to resist were outnumbered by as many as ten to one. But just eight days later, on 8 March, these odds began to shift as their brethren far to the south prepared to enter the contest.

"An Armed Mercenary Mob"

The mild south wind that began to blow moisture from communal "big fields" at Mormon settlements on the western slope of the Wasatch Mountains on Monday, 8 March 1858, warned of changes in the weather, a break in a string of mild days. The eleventh spring since the Mormons had arrived in the valley of the Great Salt Lake was about to open. But for the first time the settlers looked to their fields without a sense of hope for the future.

By that March day, their thoughts bore a blanket of late winter reflection that had smothered the instinctive anticipation farmers felt at the coming of a new growing season. Withered, too, was the emotional conflagration ignited by the great spiritual revival known as the Reformation in 1856 and 1857 that was to prepare God's people for an inevitable confrontation with the American republic. Gone as well was the boastful defiance of the year before. Out of sight, if not out of mind, on the other side of the Wasatch Range near Fort Bridger, was the reason for apprehension. And it had a familiar threatening look.

In its twenty-seven year history, the controversial millennial movement known as the Church of Jesus Christ of Latter-day Saints, commonly called Mormons, had aroused violent opposition from its neighbors in New York, Ohio, Missouri, and Illinois. Early forms of democracy on the American frontier had proved incapable of protecting believers who moved as one in all things, according to the dictates of heaven through a modern prophet. The young religion's enemies had taken many forms: sheriffs' posses, judges, state militias, and angry rabble best described as mobs in the true sense of the word. Now, at last, came soldiers of the United States, sent by an American president.

A small but highly motivated American army stood poised on the Great Basin theocracy's eastern border like a frozen sword, waiting for spring to open the trail to Salt Lake Valley and allow a frontal assault on the Mormon stronghold. President James Buchanan had ordered the military force to Utah the year before. Its purpose was to escort a new governor to replace Brigham Young, leader of both the LDS church and the civil government in the territory, and assert federal authority in a territory considered to be in a state of rebellion. As if to confirm the president's opinion, Young had branded the U.S. Army expedition "an armed mercenary mob" and mobilized his faith's military arm, the Nauvoo Legion, ostensibly known as the territorial militia, to repel the "threatened invasion."[3]

[3]Brigham Young, "Proclamation by the Governor," 15 September 1857.

American military commanders recognized that the president had launched the Utah Expedition so late in the season as to court disaster, and fast-moving mounted companies of the Legion had burned the expedition's supply wagons on Big Sandy and Green rivers while other Legion forces had fortified Echo Canyon. Fortune smiled on the Mormon forces when an early winter stopped the Army's advance toward Salt Lake Valley at James Bridger's trading post.

Now the 2,500 officers and men of the Army of Utah under the Second U.S. Cavalry's Col. Albert S. Johnston stamped the ground on Blacks Fork to keep their feet warm and waited impatiently for spring to open the trail to Salt Lake Valley. They looked anxiously to the east for much-needed supplies and reinforcements. And in the nation's capital, an aroused American government at last moved to support its embarrassed and isolated expedition in present southwestern Wyoming, sent to put down promptly an attempt by one of its territories to establish its independence from the United States.

By late winter the temper of the nation also provided good reason for Mormon leaders at Great Salt Lake City to at last face up realistically to the deadly seriousness of a confrontation wrought by millennial expectations and imagined fulfillment of Old Testament prophecy.[4] Silent on this day was the inflammatory rhetoric of the 1856 Reformation and the emotional voices that a few months before had called for the hosts of Israel to dispatch the so-called "mob" of armed "gentiles." If forced to fight, Brigham Young had then told his people, they would do so "in the strength of Israel's God" when "one will chase a thousand, and two will put ten thousand to flight."[5] "Good God!" Apostle Heber C. Kimball had said, "I have wives enough to whip out the United States."[6]

But in the event such predictions of victory failed, authorities of the religious movement meant no longer to suffer rule by corrupt carpetbaggers sent by a government that had refused to protect their constitutional rights and religious freedom in years past. With time and the season now favoring their enemies, they made plans to abandon the

[4]At this time Mormons believed that they had established the Kingdom of God as an earthly state in western America in literal fulfillment of Daniel's prophecy that a stone would be cut out of the mountain without hands that would consume all other kingdoms and stand forever. See Dan. 2:28-45.

[5]Brigham Young, 13 September 1857, *Journal of Discourses*, 4:229. Also see Deut. 32:30.

[6]*Deseret News*, 12 August 1857, 172.

Great Basin settlements in which their people had built their homes and farms over the past decade. Nor would this be the first time they had packed up and left cherished homes rather than coexist with institutions built by man or unfriendly neighbors. As they had done in 1846 when leaving the City of Nauvoo on the Mississippi River, Mormon leaders screened their possible exodus behind a curtain of rumors and false clues that implied the direction of their latest migration would be to the south. They planned instead to go the other way—north to the headwaters of the Missouri River, Bitterroot Valley, and perhaps beyond.

Meanwhile, on 8 March the shifting wind from the south and serious faces in Brigham Young's Lion House were not the only omens of change for the Kingdom of God in western America. That day, thirty-five-year-old Thomas L. Kane, the son of a prominent Philadelphia judge and benefactor of the Mormons during the Nauvoo exodus, prepared to leave Utah's capital and go to the U.S. Army's winter encampment on Blacks Fork. Two weeks before, the self-appointed peacemaker had reached Great Salt Lake over the Spanish Trail from Los Angeles. On arrival he urged Brigham Young to authorize him to offer food to the hungry American soldiers in the mountains as an olive branch. But he now prepared to ride north the next morning to seek peace talks with federal officers at Camp Scott with nothing to show for his efforts, despite the warm reception the Mormon leaders had given to an old friend.

This is how it was on Monday, 8 March 1858—mild and windy in the Great Basin, a day that opened like others before it, yet one stirring with unforeseen events that would shape the future. For it was on this day that shocking news came like an icy blast from out of the north, ending the immediate dream of a sovereign Mormon state in western America and putting on hold its envisioned march to universal dominion.

The Alarm Sounds

The rolling drumbeat early on 9 March 1858 snapped heads up in fields, hills, and nearby canyons. The local militia's traditional alert from the main gate of the adobe wall around the settlement of Lehi at the north end of Utah Valley notified men of the town to put aside their plows and hammers and prepare for war. After weeks of uncertainty the call to action was almost welcome. An express from Legion headquarters at Great Salt Lake City had arrived shortly before at the fort on Dry Creek. It carried shocking, unexpected news and military orders "from Fort Limhi on Salmon River . . . Indains [*sic*] he[a]ded by some mountaineers . . . attacted the bretheren . . . killed 2 also wounded 5 . . . stole most of their cattle."[7]

The steady drum roll from the gate sounded an unintentional salute to the men of Lehi's mounted company. Horsemen from the settlement had won their standing in action against War Chief Walkara's Indian band in 1853 and 1854 and battling Chief Tintic's proud Utah warriors almost on the outskirts of their town in 1856. Lehi's cavalrymen had upheld their reputation in 1857 in action against the U.S. Army, patrolling the ramparts of the Mormon kingdom until late December. Not by accident did the commander of the Nauvoo Legion, Lt. Gen. Daniel H. Wells, order these tested veterans to join with other Mormon forces being called up for this emergency mission. In any Indian fight the Lehi command could be counted on to give strong support to the two additional companies called out from Weber and Davis counties north of the capital.

One of the least likely to be impressed by the one-sided and potentially futile opposition at Fort Limhi was David Evans, the fifty-three-year-old bishop of Lehi. Evans was an early convert to the Latter-day Saints, a veteran of Zion's Camp in Missouri some two decades earlier who had served as commander of the Mormon forces that were massacred at Haun's Mill. His experience fighting enemies there and later in Illinois served him well in his role as bishop of the settlement. This high calling in the Mormon theocracy encompassed the offices of mayor, representative to the territorial legislature, probate judge, and district commander of the Nauvoo Legion. In keeping with his authority was David Evans's appearance. The bishop's bulldog face, wide-open eyes, set jaw, and flat nose announced a servant of God incapable of suffering slackers or human tabernacles that housed apostate spirits. And while the years had gently loosened his waistline, advancing age had only hardened a mind and will that were unbending to start with.

[7]Samuel Pitchforth Journal, 1857–1868, 10 March 1858.

And in the end, one thing was certain. Whenever Bishop Evans ordered out the mounted company from his settlement, the response was always the same: everyone who could go, went. At the same time, in sending the men of Lehi on a hazardous late winter round trip of some eight hundred miles, there was no need for Evans to whip a few laggards with his practiced tongue. Almost every man well enough to saddle and stay on his horse was ready to go.

As the Lehi company prepared to ride, the express carrying the news about Fort Limhi continued south on the muddy wagon road that loosely connected the Mormon settlements in Utah Valley. The cry for help brought by Watts and Barnard from the besieged fort far to the north was spreading through the small settlements of Utah, dampening even further the hopes of a people facing invasion and war.

Army of Israel to the Rescue

Placed in command of the expedition to Salmon River was Andrew Cunningham, a forty-one-year-old Virginian who had been appointed only two days before as colonel in the newly created Standing Army of Israel. (Patterned after the Continental Army, this full-time military force was organized in 1858 to defend the right to autonomous rule and supported by subscription of the people.) Andrew Cunningham in earlier months had taken a leading role in the cause of his faith. The preceding January, he and four others had signed "An Address from the people of Great Salt Lake City" to Congress. This rehearsal of Mormon grievances since the 1830 founding of their church concluded, "we will no longer wear your cursed yoke of unconstitutional requirements." Of the United States, the address said: "The young Hercules has found an adder in his path, his once manly frame is feeble and emaciated . . ."[8]

Even more significant had been the colonel's assignment in the autumn of 1857 to establish relief stations northward along the projected route of the Mormon exodus, should all else fail. Shortly after

---

[8]*Deseret News,* 27 January 1858, 370–71. An apparent reference to the Sons of Dan, or Danites, a secret Mormon order created during the 1838 Missouri War to punish apostates and execute vengeance against enemies of the faith. See Gen. 49:17: "Dan shall be a serpent by the way, an adder in the path, that biteth the horse heels . . ."

directing the faithful in outlying settlements in Carson Valley and San Bernardino to sell their property and return to Utah, Brigham Young had ordered a company of fifty to build a new settlement near present Blackfoot, Idaho, not far from the intersection of the trail to Fort Limhi and the Oregon Trail. That fall Mormons abandoning Carson Valley told westbound emigrants they were heading for the Salmon River to found a settlement "extending north into the Russian possessions."[9]

Cunningham's newly appointed second in command, Maj. Marcellus Monroe, had marched out that previous fall with a smaller party to deliver to Indian chiefs on Bear River what he called the "necessary instructions."[10] While Monroe did not spell these out, directives to other Mormon officers at that time instructed them to tell the natives that "*our* enemies, are also *their* enemies."[11]

Finally, of the two companies from Weber and Davis counties in the mobilizing expedition, the one best equipped and first ready to take the field was a unit of the Standing Army of Israel, which unlike the militias of other states and territories was a unique, full-time regular military force created within the borders of the United States made up of between one thousand and twelve hundred mounted riflemen.[12]

By eight P.M. on Tuesday, 9 March, the mobilization of Mormon forces was well underway to save, if possible, those in peril far to the north. Only then did Brigham Young swallow his pride and disappointment and dictate a letter to Thomas Kane. He dispatched it "by my son, Joseph A." and George Stringham, with instructions to overtake the peacemaker before he reached the U.S. Army forces at Camp Scott. Young's letter opened by noting that he had just learned from the "southern Indians" that "the troops are very destitute of provisions." With the option to escape to the north country now lost, the Mormon leader went on to offer his enemies in the mountains something to eat.[13]

[9]"Interesting from Carson Valley," *Alta California*, 8 October 1857, 1.

[10]Marcellus Monroe, "Report of a Party of Observation," 18 August 1857, Utah Militia Records.

[11]Adjutant General, Nauvoo Legion, to Col. W. B. Pace, 13 August 1857, Utah Militia Records.

[12]Horton D. Haight, "Captain Horton D. Haight's Company that served in the Salmon River Expedition, 1858." The author has been unable to locate other militia records relating to the 1858 expedition to Salmon River cited in his 1967 article, "The Crisis at Fort Limhi, 1858."

[13]Young to Kane, Sen. Exec. Doc. 1 (35-2), 1858, 87, 88. Young's letter is also published in Hafen and Hafen, *The Utah Expedition, 1857–1858, A Documentary Account of the United States Military Movement under Colonel Albert Sidney Johnston, and the Resistance by Brigham Young and the Mormon Nauvoo Legion*, 269–70.

"FRANK" CUMMINGS RIDES NORTH

Ahead of the main column, ten picked men rode north from Ogden under the command of a veteran officer who knew the route. Their orders were to break through to Fort Limhi with a dispatch that help was on the way. The success of this assignment and the survival of those entrusted to carry it out depended on speed and surprise alone.

Benjamin Franklin Cummings had just celebrated his thirty-seventh birthday when a rider from Nauvoo Legion headquarters at Great Salt Lake arrived on Tuesday, 9 March, at his Ogden home. "Early in the morning got orders to prepare myself to go to Salmon River on horse back to start the next morning at 10 A M," Cummings said. "[I] did what I could to get ready." Before noon the next day, the Mormon major swung into the saddle as leader of the advance company of ten hurrying north to the besieged fort on Salmon River. His orders were to "go through as quick as we could."[14]

Cummings had played an important role in locating Fort Limhi three years earlier. He and two others from the fort had explored north in November 1856 and reported to Brigham Young regarding the country surrounding the headwaters of the Missouri River and the Bitterroot Valley. For this service, Cummings had received "permission to stay at home for a season."[15] But hardly had he returned to Ogden before he again was ordered north. This time he led an infantry battalion of Mormon soldiers to Soda Springs on the Oregon Trail to block a half-hearted attempt by Col. Edmund Alexander, acting commander of the U.S. Army's Utah Expedition, to follow the Oregon Trail along Bear River and enter Salt Lake Valley from the north.

Past performance on the Mormon theocracy's northern ramparts had now earned Cummings an assignment more dangerous than any he had previously attempted. Riding with him were the men he had chosen. They included five other Salmon River missionaries: Baldwin Harvey Watts, called "B. H." or "Baldy," one of the pair who had ridden from Fort Limhi for help two weeks before; thirty-six-year-old Ohioan George Washington Hill; Mormon Battalion veteran Thomas Bingham, thirty-

[14]Biography and Journals of Benjamin Franklin Cummings, 1821–1878, 10 March 1858.
[15]Ibid., entry in June 1857.

BENJAMIN FRANKLIN CUMMINGS
Relying on speed and surprise, the dependable Salmon River missionary and Nauvoo Legion major led a mounted company of ten through late winter storms to carry word to Fort Limhi settlers that a rescue expedition was coming.
Used by permission, Utah State Historical Society, all rights reserved.

three; William Bailey Lake, thirty-two; and Fort Limhi mail rider Abraham Zundel, twenty-two. The others were Benjamin Cutler, Thomas Bloxham, Thomas Workman, John Hammer, and George Munson.

Following the wagon road to Fort Hall, the little command on 10 and 11 March rode north through Brigham City, crossed Bear River at or near present Deweyville, Utah, and headed up the valley of Malad River, a sweep of sagebrush between the Malad Mountains on the east and the barren West Hills opposite. As they urged their horses up the open valley, the mild gusts from the south of recent days suddenly reversed with chilling effect to a cold wind from the northwest and the skies lowered.

Ignoring these omens, the riders pushed steadily forward and by Thursday night, 11 March, gained a camp on Henderson Creek, near present Woodruff, Idaho, some seventy miles north of Ogden. Pinned down by a snowstorm heavy enough to blot out the trail and landmarks, they fretted the next precious day away. As they waited the colonel jotted a terse account of the journey.

Biography and Journals of
Benjamin Franklin Cummings, March 1858.

> Sat 13th Crossed over the east mt and camped on a small creek about 2 miles from Marsh Creek. Severe storm. Traveled down Marsh crossed over and continued on down a few miles and struck up on to the bench and down on to Portniff and crossed over about 7 miles above the mouth of Marsh creek. Traveled down about 5 miles and camped. Stormy all day and cold.

The day dawned late with no sign of clearing weather. Not willing to delay longer, Cummings decided to go on. Instead of staying on the Fort Hall Road along Little Malad River, he gambled to make up lost time and followed a little-traveled shortcut north over the Malad Divide to Marsh Creek on the line followed after 1862 by the Montana Trail and today by I-15 from Malad City, Idaho, to Pocatello.[16] Men and horses drove into the mountains on dangerous footing, heads down, shrouded with snow, their visibility cut almost to zero by a falling blanket of white.

Sunday opened cold and gray to find the little company pushing more slowly through deep powder snow. Without pause or much conversation, they advanced down Marsh Creek to pick up and follow Portneuf River, camping for the night near the southern outskirts of today's Pocatello, Idaho.

> Mon. 15th. Started 8 a m. Continue on down the Canyon about 10 miles and came out into an arm of the valley about 8 miles and stop[p]ed for noon 12-1/2 p m. Started at 2 p m and camp at the Black Foot creek mission.

The gamble had paid off. Cummings and his half-frozen little party emerged from the mountains into the kinder climate of Snake River Valley. Heading now to the northeast, they rested at midday near the intersection of the Oregon Trail, then rode on. That night they camped in the comfort of the cabins built on Blackfoot River between Ferry Butte and present Blackfoot, Idaho, by Andrew Cunningham's company late in 1857. At this point, they had covered about 180 miles, or nearly half of their journey. If someone knew where to find the food cached by Cunningham a few months before, that night they may have enjoyed their first full meal in days. The following day they would take advantage of the new crossing of Snake River that Cunningham had located the previous year.

---

[16]For more on this route, see Madsen and Madsen, *North to Montana! Jehus, Bullwhackers, and Mule Skinners on the Montana Trail.*

Tues. 16th Cross the river and travel up about 35 miles and camped.

On the seventh day, the riders crossed Snake River by the ford above the Blackfoot and headed northeast along the north bank at a faster pace on the Flathead Trail used by Indians and traders between Fort Hall and the Bitterroot Valley.[17] On their right hand, the tributary of the Columbia River curved its way through the valley. On their left, a waterless carpet of black lava rock and sagebrush, as much as fifty miles across, discouraged a direct approach to the mountains beyond.

> Wed. 17th. Continue on left Snake river at the Big Slough. Stop[p]ed at the mouth of Camash creek 2 P M to let our horses eat. Found the tracks of a number of ponies and mules in the road near the place where we stopped. Supposed to [be] the Indians who had pursued the Brethern who came in with the express. 4 P M start on for Spring Creek where we arrived about I o'clock at night.

At the marshy bend in the Snake River, known to mountaineers as "the market" for its abundance of waterfowl and to travelers today as Market Lake, some twenty miles north of present Idaho Falls, the party turned sharply away from the river bearing northwest toward Mud Lake, a milky body in a barren region. They pulled up in the early afternoon on Camas Creek, near the parting of the Fort Limhi route from the Flathead Trail, where Watts pointed to the tracks perhaps made by the Bannock war party that had pursued the twenty-two-year-old and his companion less than three weeks before. As the hoofprints warned, Cummings and his men had paused on the very brink of peril.

Prior to Indian hostilities, the distance from this point to Fort Limhi and the Lewis and Clark Pass over the Continental Divide had the appearance of a divinely laid out escape route, a covered corridor through the mountains to fertile lands beyond. "Bro Snow hinted plain about the presidency going to find a place of safety for this people and related the following dream," wrote Samuel Pitchforth at Nephi. "Bro Brigham said look to the west for they where [were] on the east side of a plain and on the west side was high mountains with perpendicular

[17]The Flathead Trail crossed the Continental Divide on the line of present I-15 at Monida, Montana, and went to the Beaverhead and Big Hole regions on the Upper Missouri, near today's Dillon, Montana. From here it recrossed the great divide to the Columbia River drainage at Deer Lodge Pass, following Clark Fork, earlier named Hell Gate River, to the north end of Bitterroot Valley at present Missoula. A branch led down the valley of Big Hole River to cross the Continental Divide at Gibbons Pass and entered Ross' Hole at the south end of Bitterroot Valley.

Rocks about 600 ft high. Bro Brigham [said] Bro Snow do you see where that creek comes out[?] He said yes he then said there is room for one man to pass in at a time."[18]

But the dream of one Mormon leader had been drastically reversed by the Indian attack on Fort Limhi. No longer was the route from Camas Creek to the Salmon River settlement the envisioned corridor to safety and peaceful valleys. Now it was a potential trail of death through a region apparently designed by a native landscape artist as an ideal setting for his favored war tactic.

The first leg, some thirty-five miles from Camas Creek to the stream Cummings called Spring Creek, now named Birch Creek, at the narrow entry in the mountains, was virtually an invitation to be ambushed. The naked approach to the mountains beckoned the unwary to cross a sloping tableland of low brush and lava gravel unbroken by a shred of cover or protecting ravine. A lookout in the mountains ahead could see anyone coming across this flat wasteland for miles.

The rest of the way to the mission was an eighty-mile gauntlet through a narrow valley ranging in width from a few thousand feet to eight miles, hemmed on both sides for almost the entire distance by impassable mountains.[19] To the west, the Lemhi Range soared over 10,000 feet. Only a shade less rugged, the Beaverhead Mountains and the Continental Divide guarded against any entry from the east. Between these imposing barriers, the wagon road wound to the northwest along birch-lined creeks, over broken benches of sagebrush and through a maze of side canyons and dry creek beds.

For Cummings and his little command, Fort Limhi was no haven of safety and rest in a covered alley to freedom. Instead, the northernmost Mormon colony had the look of a compelling piece of live bait at the far end of a native bushwhacker's favorite landscape.[20]

To avoid detection from the mountains, Cummings wisely timed the start of his exposed approach to this stretch for late afternoon. By the first hour of morning, the party gained the cover of the birch willows and brush near the sink of Birch Creek, still a few miles short of their

[18]Samuel Pitchforth Journal, 1857–1868, 19 February 1857.

[19]This route is generally followed today by Idaho State Highway 28 from Mud Lake to Salmon.

[20]Brigham Young, who had a military eye for terrain, made a similar comment on his first and only visit to the region in May 1857.

entry point into the mountains. Stiff and cold from riding into a hard, freezing wind that blew up shortly after dark, the men worked their horses down into the heavy cover along the creek where a small fire would be unseen for more than a few hundred feet. In this shelter, they hunkered down, thawed out, and dozed until first dawn when they moved on.

> Thur. 18th. Wind continues very strong from the north which we had to face. Started about 6-1/2 A M and traveled 14 miles up the creek and turned into a small Kanyon on the right opposite the first crossing [of] the creek about 10 A M. Found good feed and little wind.

After pushing ahead into a driving wind and blowing snow, the riders by midmorning that day passed the narrow entrance between the mountain ranges. From here on they would stay away from the exposed trail in the lower valley, keep as much as possible to the protective benches that hugged the east mountain, and travel mainly at night and early morning.

> Fri. 19th. Wind continue[d] very high. Start 9 A M. Travel up to the mouth of Bear Creek Kanyon and camp.[21] Wind blow hard all day but ceased about Sunset. Considerable snow.

The Mormon horsemen girded now for a final push of about sixty miles with brief stops only long enough to rest their animals. The last section of their journey led over a low divide between Birch Creek and Eighteenmile Creek, a headwater of Salmon River, then along the latter stream to the east fork of Salmon River, and another two dozen miles down the river to their destination near present Tendoy, Idaho.

> Sat. 20th. Start 7 A M. Crossed the divide. Snow very bad crusted in many places so as to bear the horses.

From the snow-covered divide, their goal came within striking distance, downhill the rest of the way. With restored spirit, the men pushed their tired horses forward, kept their rifles checked, and scanned carefully every hill and ravine as they traveled for any sign of Indians. It was after dark that day when the trouble that Cummings so long had expected at last came.

The eleven horsemen reined up suddenly at the glow of native sentinel fires on high ground that commanded a narrowing in the valley

[21]Properly named Bare Creek Canyon, east of present Kaufman, Idaho.

ahead. After a short whispered council, Cummings again elected to gamble, this time on the chance that his hard-riding company had reached this point undetected and he would not lead his men into an ambush on the far side of the flickering beacons. Throwing caution to the wind, they spurred their horses and drove straight into and past the threat, while surprised lookouts tried in vain to arouse a sleeping encampment. Speed and boldness delivered the little command when its moment of greatest danger arrived.

Shortly after 1 A.M. on Sunday, 21 March, near the end of their eleventh day on the march, Maj. Benjamin Franklin Cummings and his tired but jubilant company of ten rode up to the log stockade on the east bank of the river, shouting to the guard to hold his fire and open the gate. To tears of joy and shouts of welcome, they charged into the fort and were pulled off their horses into the arms of the friends they had come to rescue, all of them still alive.

"Col. Andrew Cunningham and company arrived with ten baggage wagons and about 100 men," rejoiced David Moore at the mission on 23 March 1858. Two days later, "Captain Haight and company of 50 from Davis County arrived having five baggage wagons and some extra horses and sets of harness."[22] Behind Hector Haight's regular soldiers of the Standing Army came Bishop Evans's veteran fighters from Lehi.

Even before the Nauvoo Legion command arrived, the Mormon colonists on east fork of Salmon River had followed orders delivered by Cummings and begun to pack up their belongings and prepare to permanently abandon the earliest white community in present Idaho. The evacuation would close a significant chapter of Mormon settlement in the Northwest, yet one that had lasted less than three years.

As the sixty-seven men, women, and children loaded the wagons for the long, cold journey home, Maj. "Frank" Cummings and nine men, seven of them members of his arriving company, saddled their horses. On Friday, 26 March, they rode out ahead of the rest to deliver Andrew Cunningham's report on the successful rescue to Brigham Young.[23]

On the ride north, the Nauvoo Legion officer from New England at

[22]Salmon River Mission Journal, 23 March 1858.

[23]Besides Cummings, the return company included George Hill, B. H. Watts, Thomas Bingham, Bailey Lake, Benjamin Cutler, George Barber, Thomas Bloxham, John Blanchard, Jr., and Thomas Workman.

least twice had weighed unfavorable odds, then chosen to gamble. Both times his luck had held. But good fortune and the size of the friendly forces now between his little company and the earlier point of danger may have tempted him to become overconfident. On the return trip, with no need to gamble, Cummings took another chance. And this time his luck ran out.

The consequence was a bloody footnote to a pivotal but little-known chapter in the history of the Mormon theocracy in the American West, known as Deseret, or Utah Territory. This fatal confrontation gave a tragic ending to a story that had opened only three years before with high millennial hopes and the expectation that the Kingdom of God on earth was about to roll forth and prepare the way for the return of Jesus Christ to reign in righteousness.

Chapter 2

To the Remnants of Jacob

We're called by Brother Brigham
And sent forth by God's command
To spy out the Flat Head nation
Passing through the Bannock land.
We'll search them from the hills and mountains
And the rocks and caves and dens
Passing by the river fountains
Till we hunt out Laman's men.

— *Israel J. Clark*
"Indian Mission Song"

It began in 1855, the year of the Lamanite. For the children of Israel in the Last Days, this was a portentous moment. After more than two thousand years, events foretold by prophets of the Old Testament and *The Book of Mormon* were about to unfold. The last seconds of the fifty-ninth minute of the final hour were at hand, moments in the annals of humankind rich with millennial promise. The time had at last arrived "when these remnants of Jacob shall flock into the kingdom, and that purifying process commence, which will make them a white and delightsome people," prior to return of the Lord.[1]

On 6 April that year, the twenty-fifth anniversary of the founding of the Church of Jesus Christ of Latter-day Saints, thousands gathered on Temple Square at Great Salt Lake City for the faith's annual general conference. They filled the open bowery, then under construction just north of the adobe first tabernacle. Spacious enough to accommodate such a large turnout, the brush-roofed framework gave little protection from a fresh spring wind. Shivers were forgotten, however, in the excitement of an unexpected announcement:

---

[1] *Latter-day Saints' Millennial Star,* 17:34, 25 August 1855, 536–38.

Prest. Young said the day has come to turn the key of the Gospel against the Gentiles, and open it to the remnants of Israel, the people shouted, Amen, and the feeling was such that most present could realize, but few describe.[2]

The time had finally come for the "remnant of Jacob," believed under the doctrines of Mormonism to be the American Indians, to hear the gospel of their fathers and return to build New Jerusalem in Jackson County, Missouri. The announcement meant that the stone envisioned by the prophet Daniel, symbolizing the Great Basin theocracy, was ready to roll forth from the mountains and break to pieces the kingdoms of this world before the Second Coming of Jesus Christ opened His millennial reign.[3]

An essential Mormon scripture, *The Book of Mormon* is accepted by members of the faith as the record of the followers of a God-fearing man, named Lehi, led by God in about 600 B.C. from Jerusalem to the New World, just before the City of David fell to the Babylonians. In America these descendants of Jacob from the tribe of Manasseh became divided into two great peoples, the Nephites, named after Lehi's righteous son, Nephi, and Lamanites, descendants of his sons, Laman and Lemuel, whom God cursed with a dark skin because of their wickedness. For centuries they waged war against each other.

The history of the two branches of Israel in the Americas before the fifth century A.D. was allegedly preserved on gold plates, which were delivered by a resurrected Nephite prophet to Joseph Smith, founder of this distinctive American religion, who said that he translated the ancient record with the aid of the urim and thummim.[4] Published as *The Book of Mormon* in 1830, Smith's translation tells how the Lamanites eventually destroyed their white cousins and went on to become the American Indians, a remnant of Israel in the New World.

But they were not alone in this Hebrew family tree. Smith's followers believed they, too, literally shared this lineage, according to a revelation to their prophet, "Ye are the children of Israel, and of the seed of Abraham."[5] Most considered themselves to be descendants of Ephraim, Manasseh's younger brother, who also fathered a tribe of Israel. They

[2]Brooks, ed., *Journal of the Southern Indian Mission, Diary of Thomas D. Brown*, 21 April 1855.

[3]See Dan. 2:31–45.

[4]Possibly seer stones that were placed in the breastplate of the high priest in Old Testament times. See Ex. 28:30 and Lev. 8:8.

[5]Smith, *History of the Church*, 2:36-39, February 1834.

accordingly referred to outsiders as "gentiles," a term that carried all of the unfavorable connotations reflected in the Bible.

Thus, the natives of the Western Hemisphere and the earliest white settlers of the Great Basin shared an important bond. Under Mormon belief, they were both descendants of Abraham through Isaac, Jacob, and Joseph, the eleventh of Jacob's twelve sons, who was sold by his brothers into slavery in Egypt. They were cousins by blood.

The Book of Mormon foretold that Jacob's native descendants in the New World would one day learn of God's promise to His people, unite with their white cousins in building New Jerusalem, and become once again "a white and delightsome people."[6] To fulfill this prelude to Christ's return, within months of the church's founding at Manchester, New York, Mormon missionaries had headed into Indian territory to show the natives "what great things the Lord hath done for their fathers . . . that they might know the covenants of the Lord."[7]

Brigham Young expressed these beliefs soon after arriving in Salt Lake Valley in 1847. He told his followers that "our people would be connected with every tribe of Indians throughout America & our people would yet take their squaws wash & dress them up teach them our language & learn them to labor & learn them the gospel of their forefathers." They would "raise up children by them," he went on, and "not many generations hence they will become A white & delightsome people."[8]

Now the time had come to gather the American Indians, known as Lamanites, and begin their transformation. At the April conference, some 160 missionaries were called to leave their new homes and go out into the wilderness to seek out their native cousins. They would be the first of hundreds sent out over the next three years to the Crows, Lakotas, Cherokees, Choctaws, Moquis (Hopis), Mojaves, Nez Percés, Delawares, Utahs, Shoshones, Goshutes, Navahos, Shawnees, Bannocks, Paiutes, Omahas, Flatheads, and many other tribes of North America.

Among those called were twenty-seven men, most from settlements north of Great Salt Lake City, who were "set apart for the Northern Mission to the Remnants of the House of Jacob, which inhabit the

[6] *The Book of Mormon,* 2 Nephi 30:6. The original "white and delightsome" was later changed to "pure and delightsome."

[7] Ibid., Title Page.

[8] Kenney, ed., *Wilford Woodruff's Journal,* 3:241.

Mountain Regions Known as the Rocky Mountains."[9] They were: Ira Ames, Jr., Ezra Jacob Wyckoff Barnard, William H. Batchelor, Gilbert Belnap, John W. Browning, William L. Brundage, William Burch, William Burgess, Jr., Thomas Butterfield, Israel Justus Clark, Benjamin Franklin Cummings, Charles Dalton, Francillo Durfee, John Galliher, George Roberts Grant, George Washington Hill, Nathaniel Leavitt, Everet Lish, Charles Aron McGary, David Moore, Joseph Parry, Isaac Monroe Shepard, Thomas Sasson Smith, David Henderson Stephens, Pleasant Green Taylor, Baldwin Harvey Watts, and Abraham Zundel.

The Kingdom of God's new emissaries to the tribes of Oregon Territory were told "to go North as far as Flathead Country if the Missionaries thought it wisdom to do so."[10] In carrying out this mandate, they would plant the northernmost early colony of their faith and one of present Idaho's earliest white settlements.

The sudden upsurge in Indian proselytizing followed the success of some twenty-one Mormon missionaries who had gone out the year before to the Southern Paiutes, whom they called Piedes, along the tributaries of the Colorado River in present southern Utah and Nevada. There they had taught the poor desert Indians to farm and protected them from their predatory kinsmen of the Utah tribe (now known as the Utes) to the north, who kidnapped their children and sold them to slave traders from New Mexico for horses. In return, hundreds of Southern Paiutes along the Santa Clara, Virgin, and Muddy rivers had gone down to the waters of baptism.

Fortified Mormon Outposts

This abundant harvest was considered a clear sign that the offspring of Israel in the New World were ready to receive the message of ancient prophets and fulfill their destiny to establish God's Kingdom on the American continent. It produced the call by late 1857 of at least three hundred missionaries to preach to the tribes in their own languages, singly, in pairs, or from newly built mission forts or stations. By then, fortified Mormon outposts had sprung up at distant points on almost

[9] Salmon River Mission Journal, 6 April 1855.

[10] Compiled writings of David Moore, Journal and Life History, April 1855.

every trail or wagon road approaching the Great Basin theocracy from any direction.

Besides Fort Limhi, they included Fort Louisa (soon renamed Parowan); Fort Harmony, near present Cedar City, Utah; Las Vegas Springs at today's Las Vegas, Nevada, on the Spanish Trail; Mormon Station in Carson Valley, Nevada, on the California Trail; Fort Malad, or Barnard's Fort, on the Malad River near today's Utah-Idaho border and on the Fort Hall Road and cutoffs of the California Trail; Deer Creek Station, near present Douglas, Wyoming; Fort Supply, near Fort Bridger on the Oregon-California-Mormon Trail; and Elk Mountain Mission at present Moab, Utah, on the Spanish Trail.[11]

Related to this expansion was Brigham Young's offer in 1856 to purchase Fort Hall, near present Pocatello, from Hudson's Bay Company and the construction the next year of a separate fort on Snake River, near today's Blackfoot, Idaho. These outposts overlooked at various times the Oregon Trail, the California Trail and its several cutoffs, the Spanish Trail, John C. Frémont's trails of 1845 and 1854, John W. Gunnison's route of 1853, and the Fort Hall Road.

Their location on the main avenues of travel during the flood tide of America's western migration bore sobering implications when viewed in relation to other Mormon doctrines regarding American Indians. The Old Testament prophet Micah said in the Last Days, when Israel was redeemed, "the remnant of Jacob shall be among the Gentiles in the midst of many people as a lion among the beasts of the forest, as a young lion among the flocks of sheep." A *Book of Mormon* prophet repeated this warning, pointedly adding, "if the Gentiles do not repent."[12]

Echoing these forecasts, a patriarchal blessing given to John Borrowman in 1846 included the promise that "when the remnants of Jacob go through the Gentiles like a lion among the beasts of the forest, as the prophets have spoken, thou shalt be in their midst and shall be a captain of hundreds."[13] Some Mormon emissaries to the tribes considered their

---

[11]Ostensibly, the Deer Creek outpost and other locations in Nebraska Territory were among the mail stations Brigham Young established in 1857 under a federal contract awarded in 1856 to Mormon Hiram Kimball and later revoked. The size of these colonies, however, reveals that their primary purpose related more to the Mormon frontier expansion of 1855–1856 than to mail delivery.

[12]Mic. 5:8; *The Book of Mormon,* 3 Nephi 20:15, 16. Also see. Pratt, *The Essential Parley P. Pratt,* 23, 24.

[13]Journal of John Borrowman, 1846–1860.

native cousins to be "the battle axe of the lord."[14] Beliefs like these were hardly a source of comfort for settlers who lived in isolated cabins when Mormon missionaries visited nearby tribes. From the earliest days of the faith, claims like these had been a source of trouble on the frontier.

Perhaps this was why a new U.S. Indian agent to the Utah tribe became alarmed at the great 1855 call of Indian missionaries. Garland Hurt of Virginia fired off a confidential report to alert the commissioner of Indian Affairs at Washington, D.C., to this development. He described the missionaries as "a class of rude and lawless young men" and warned "there is perhaps not a tribe on the continent that will not be visited by one or more of them."[15]

Moreover, less than six months after coming to Utah, Hurt had come to believe that Mormons were encouraging the natives to think there was a difference between themselves and other Americans, "that cannot act otherwise than prejudicial to the latter." He urged the commissioner of Indian Affairs to alert "all superintendents, agents, and sub-agents, and all other loyal citizens" in the Indian country to ensure that federal laws to preserve peace on the frontiers "would be properly enforced."[16] His warning touched off many reports over the next few years of Mormon tampering with the Indians.[17]

The Gospel Net

Unaware of any national alarm they might be causing, the twenty-seven newly-called missionaries to the Indians of Oregon Territory began to assemble on 15 May 1855 on the western slope of the Wasatch Mountains, a few miles north of Ogden. It seemed the worst of times to entrust the care of their families to others and go on an Indian mission, a dangerous profession by itself. For the fields in which they bedded down showed no sign of spring, having been ravished by drought and its voracious ally, the so-called Mormon cricket, or grasshopper.

Two days later, still short six members, the little company and its ten wagons moved slowly north on Hensley's Salt Lake Cutoff, a segment of

[14]Brooks, ed., *Journal of The Southern Indians Mission,* 14 May 1854.

[15]Hurt to Manypenny, 2 May 1855, House Exec. Doc. 71 (35-1), 176–77.

[16]Ibid.

[17]For examples, see Bigler, "Garland Hurt, the American Friend of the Utahs," 156n28.

the California Trail.[18] At Willow Creek, now Willard, they picked up two more members and another wagon before going on to camp at Grover's Spring, north of present Brigham City, where the last four members of the new Northern Indian Mission caught up from Ogden.

The gospel net gathered all kinds, Brigham Young sometimes said, "gars, sharks, sheepheads, lamper-eels and every other," and the company that assembled on Bear River was a typical haul of the Almighty's seine.[19] Although they ranged in age from eighteen-year-old Ira Ames to Isaac Shepard, forty-eight, most were tested members of the faith whose age averaged over thirty-two. Francillo Durfee from Vermont, forty-three, had marched some two thousand miles with the Mormon Battalion in 1846 to claim California for the United States during the War with Mexico.

At a time of hardship in Mormon settlements, most of the Indian missionaries had left wives and children in the care of others. Several followed the marriage doctrine of polygamy allegedly revealed to the founding prophet of the movement and made public in 1852, and had more than one wife and family to worry about. The most recent to wed was William Batchelor from England, now single in name only, who said goodbye to a new bride of less than a week.

Two of the four Canadians in the party illustrated the contrast found among those who had chosen to follow an American prophet. Black-bearded Gilbert Belnap, age thirty-three, was a former revolutionist and ex-sergeant in the light horse rangers of the "Patriot Army," led by Louis Joseph Papineau, that revolted in 1837 against British rule in Canada. His cause defeated, Belnap found himself in a Toronto prison, chained to "60 pounds of iron," for nearly a year before his deportation to the United States in 1839.[20] He then joined the Mormons at Nauvoo, Illinois, and spied on the faith's enemies in Hancock County. After coming to Utah, he had served as the marshal at Ogden, where he arrested an

[18]Samuel J. Hensley, an 1843 California pioneer and officer in John C. Frémont's California Battalion, opened this route with a ten-man pack party in 1848 on his return home after testifying at Frémont's court martial. Heavily traveled during the Gold Rush, it followed the Fort Hall road to the crossings of Bear River, north of Brigham City, then headed northwest on the line of today's I-84 and Utah Highway 30 to join the California Trail in the Silent City of Rocks, near Almo, Idaho. For more on this route, see Bagley, "Hensley's Salt Lake Cutoff" in DeLafosse, ed., *Trailing the Pioneers: A Guide to Utah's Emigrant Trails, 1829–1869*, 93–109; Bagley, ed., *A Road From El Dorado: The 1848 Trail Journal of Ephraim Green*; and Flemming and Standing, "The Road to 'Fortune': The Salt Lake Cutoff," 248–71.

[19]*Deseret News*, 12 March 1856, 2. Also see Matt. 13:47.

[20]Autobiography of Gilbert Belnap.

emigrant for "traducing the character of Brigham Young."[21] Belnap was a quiet man with a strong sense of justice and a "lion's passion" that raged whenever the helpless suffered at the hands of arbitrary authority.

The other Canadian, thirty-six-year-old David Moore, was a fighter, too, but not always on the same side as his former countryman. As a teenager Moore had joined loyalist forces and fought against Papineau's revolt, which he believed was trumped up under "the pretence of oppression from the British Government." At Nauvoo he had guarded Brigham Young and in 1844 served as a "bishop" in the Mormon city-state's police force, commanding thirteen men. Each of them carried a "large hickory cane and a toothpick (a huge knife) . . . to whittle Rascals out of town."[22]

Almost as distinctive were the backgrounds of the twenty-one Americans in the party who hailed from ten states, reflecting the rapid spread of the millennial movement. Seven, the largest number from any one state, came from the Lake Ontario region of New York, a hotbed of the religious innovation that produced the faith's founding prophet. Four more hailed from New England, home of Brigham Young. Benjamin Franklin Cummings and Thomas Butterfield were born in the same town, Farmington, Maine.

Of three Ohioans, George Washington Hill, age thirty-three, would become one of the most prolific missionaries of any faith to the tribes on the American frontier. From the same state was Ira Ames, Jr., the only company member born into the faith at Kirtland, Ohio, on Lake Erie, location of its first temple. Two Pennsylvanians, Charles Dalton and Abraham Zundel, and single sons of Kentucky, Mississippi, Tennessee, and Illinois journeyed north with the missionary company. The party also included two Englishmen, thirty-year-old Joseph Parry and William Batchelor.

Set apart as president of Zion's emissaries to the Lamanites of the Northwest was thirty-seven-year-old New Yorker Thomas Sasson Smith, a member of the Iron Mission to southern Utah in 1851. His ordination by the laying on of hands empowered him to receive divine guidance in directing all affairs of the mission and its members. This authority rested on such absolute grounds that it emptied of substance the outwardly democratic processes followed by his company.

[21]Ibid.

[22]Journal and Life History of David Moore.

Thomas Sasson Smith as he appeared later in life. The veteran Mormon colonizer was thirty-seven when he was set apart as head of the mission "to the remnants of the House of Jacob," the Shoshone, Bannock, Flathead, Nez Perce, and other tribes. *Courtesy of the Church Archives, The Church of Jesus Christ of Latter-day Saints.*

If the first missionaries to the northern tribes were a mixed company, they were all alike in one respect. None had volunteered for this assignment and few, if any, wanted to go. At best, the lot of an Indian missionary was hard and dangerous, with little hope of any earthly reward or early return to loved ones whose survival rested on the support of others. Moreover, it seemed the worst of times to go. The specter of hunger lay across fields due to the lack of moisture in the preceding winter, and the California gulls failed to destroy the ravenous invading grasshoppers and rescue the settlers as they had done in 1848. Personal sacrifices were more than offset, however, by the hope of a great spiritual reward. "Brigham Young promised us that if we were faithful we should . . . have the privilege of seeing one of the three Nephite Apostles," said twenty-eight-year-old Kentuckian Pleasant Green Taylor, a company member.[23] According to *The Book of Mormon,* Jesus Christ had granted the wish of this trio of white-skinned disciples in the New World to "never taste of death . . . until all things shall be fulfilled."[24]

[23]Autobiography of Pleasant Green Taylor, 1855 entry.
[24]*The Book of Mormon,* 3 Nephi 28:1–6.

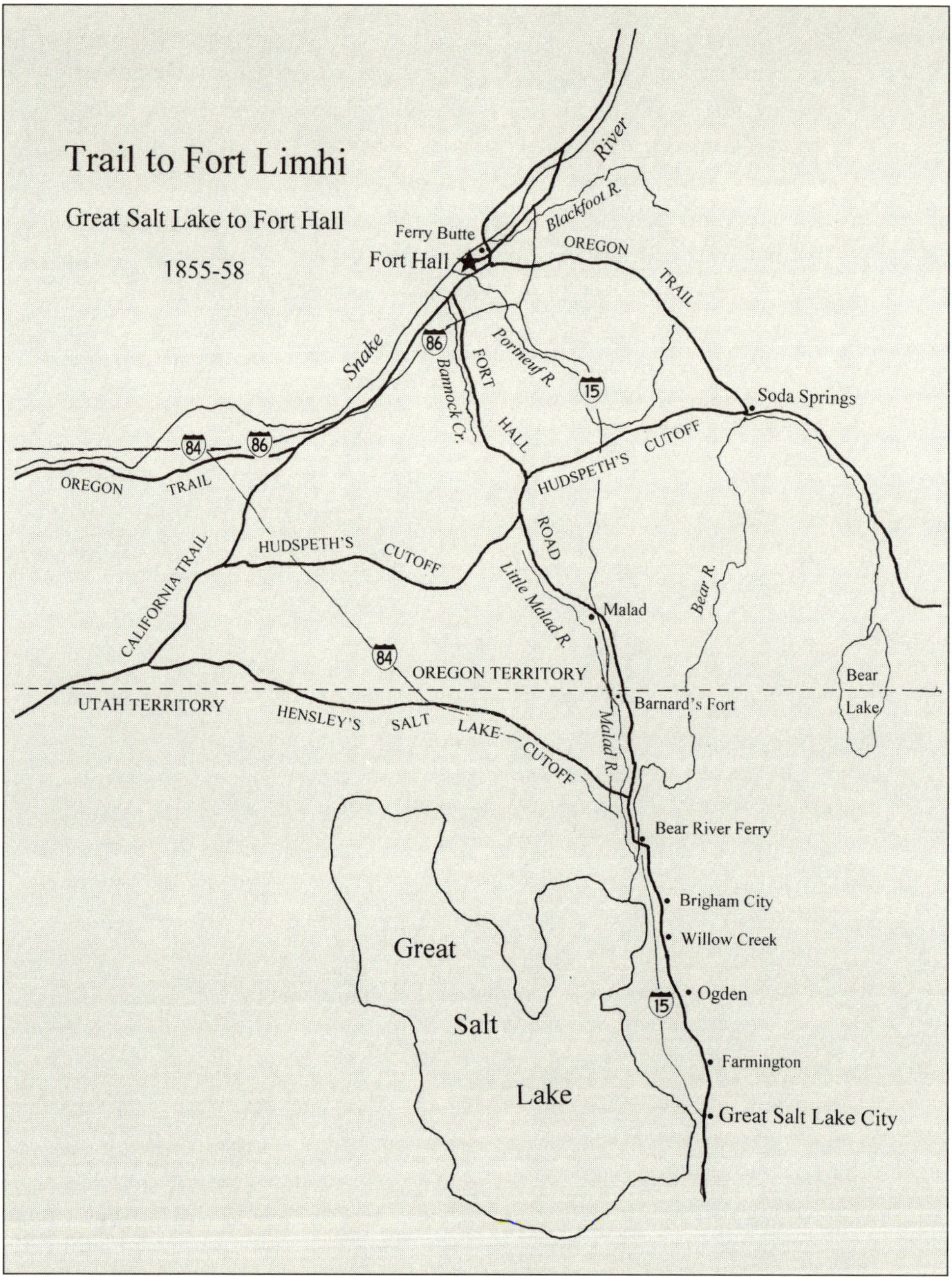

Trail to Fort Limhi
Great Salt Lake to Fort Hall
1855-58
Ferry Butte
Fort Hall
River
Blackfoot R.
OREGON
TRAIL
Snake
86
Bannock Cr.
FORT
HALL
ROAD
Portneuf R.
15
Soda Springs
84
86
OREGON
TRAIL
HUDSPETH'S
CUTOFF
HUDSPETH'S
CUTOFF
CALIFORNIA TRAIL
Little Malad R.
Malad
Bear R.
84
OREGON TERRITORY
Bear
Lake
UTAH TERRITORY
HENSLEY'S
SALT
LAKE
CUTOFF
Barnard's Fort
Malad R.
Bear River Ferry
Brigham City
Willow Creek
Great
Salt
Lake
Ogden
15
Farmington
Great Salt Lake City

The Trail North

Heartened by such promises, the party traveled to the Bear River ferry on 19 May, just north of present Honeyville, Utah, where the operator, William J. Simpson, ferried the wagons over the river while members swam their cattle across a short distance upstream. That afternoon another Mormon company on its way to Carson Valley under Apostle Orson Hyde came up and camped with them on the west bank of the river about three miles north of today's Bear River City.[25]

The next day, a Sunday, Thomas Smith organized the company. He named as captain Mormon Battalion veteran Francillo Durfee, forty-three, and appointed thirty-three-year-old William Burgess lieutenant; B. F. "Frank" Cummings, thirty-four, sergeant; and David Moore, thirty-six, clerk and historian. An inventory of their resources added up to eleven wagons, forty-six oxen, twenty-one cows, three calves, one bull, seven horses, three dogs, and "7554 lbs. of flour, 14 bushels 37 lbs. Wheat, 1 bu, 4 qrts. Corn, about $250.00 worth of tools, 19 guns, 11 revolvers and 5 pistols."[26] They journeyed about ten miles up Bear River to camp near present Plymouth, Utah.

From here they followed a clearly marked trail to Fort Hall, a distance of nearly 115 miles, opened by traders from the Snake River trading post to the Indians in Salt Lake and Utah valleys. John C. Frémont followed the trail north in 1843 on his way from Great Salt Lake to Fort Vancouver. Capt. Howard Stansbury, Corps of Topographical Engineers, investigated the suitability of the route for a wagon road during his expedition to survey Great Salt Lake and Utah valleys in 1849.[27]

From the last Bear River crossing, this avenue took them north up the east bank of Malad River on the line of present I-15 to the western outskirts of present Malad, Idaho, where it left today's main highway and

[25]The Utah legislature commissioned Apostle Hyde, Associate Justice George P. Stiles, a Nauvoo Mormon, and Territorial Marshal Joseph L. Heywood to meet with California officials and establish the boundary in Carson Valley between California and Utah Territory. The party also included missionaries identified by Hosea Stout as "a guard of some 25 men, under pay at 4 dollars pr day for man & horses," in an apparent attempt to apply costs of the expedition to federal accounts. But Stout expressed "douts about govt paying." See Brooks, ed., *On The Mormon Frontier: The Diary of Hosea Stout, 1844–1861*, 2:555.

[26]Salmon River Mission Journal, 21 May 1855.

[27]For descriptions of this route, see Stansbury's report and Brigham D. Madsen's detailed notes in Madsen, ed., *Exploring the Great Salt Lake: The Stansbury Expedition of 1849–50*, 157–88. Also see "The Bannock Mountain Road," 10–15.

continued north along Little Malad River. At the crossing of Wright Creek, near Daniels, Idaho, the company struck Hudspeth's Cutoff of the California Trail, described by Cummings as "hard and well beaten."[28] They had climbed in three days more than a thousand feet in elevation and covered more than a hundred miles.

"The camp attended prayers, morning and evening, since they were organized on Bear River, and peace and union prevailed," Clerk David Moore dutifully recorded.[29]

Backtracking Hudspeth's Cutoff, they journeyed up Dairy Creek and crossed the divide between the Great Basin and Columbia River drainage to Hawkins Basin, a scenic mountain bowl, where a sudden spring snowstorm on 25 May pinned them down. That afternoon Taylor, Moore, Belnap, and Hill ventured "to the Great Divide, between the waters of Great Salt Lake Basin and the Pacific and examined the road over the divide, then went along the divide farther north and found a much better road."[30] Leaving Hudspeth's shortcut to Raft River, they crossed the ridge between the Portneuf River and Bannock Creek drainages and traveled down winding Rattlesnake Creek, "over 20 miles of the worst road they had yet experienced," to its junction with Bannock Creek, where they camped."[31]

Now in more open country, they journeyed down the latter stream to the bank of Portneuf River, less than a half-dozen miles from Fort Hall.[32] There, at sundown, two young Bannock warriors "of fine and

[28]Hudspeth's Cutoff left the Oregon Trail at Soda Springs and joined the California Trail on Raft River, near present Malta, Idaho. It provided a more direct route than did the old trail via Fort Hall, and when it opened in 1849, the cutoff essentially terminated the post's role in overland trade. Although blazing this important route has long been credited to John J. Myers and Benoni Hudspeth, the diary of William John Clarke, Jr., describes setting out from Bear River on "the Emigrants Cut-off" on 10 June 1849, more than five weeks before Myers and Hudspeth did on 19 July. See William John Clarke, Jr., Diary, 10 June 1849.

[29]Salmon River Mission Journal, 23 May 1855.

[30]Ibid., 25 May 1855. The party actually crossed the rim of the Great Basin the day before between the head of Dairy Creek, a tributary of Malad River, and Hawkins Basin, which drains into Portneuf River. The divide the four explored separated the waters of the Portneuf and Bannock Creek. The Great Basin is a vast region of high-altitude deserts and north-south mountain ranges, encompassing parts of six western states, from which no water flows to any ocean. Rivers within its rim end in sinks, such as Humboldt Sinks, near Lovelock, Nevada, or briny lakes without outlets, such as Great Salt Lake.

[31]Ibid., 26 May 1855.

[32]The Fort Hall Road from Malad, Idaho, followed the West Daniels Road up Little Malad River to Daniels Reservoir, the Dairy Creek Road to Hawkins Basin, the Rattlesnake Creek Road and Bannock Creek Road to Portneuf River.

intelligent appearance" swam their horses over the river and rode into camp.[33] "We gave them something to eat after which they wished to stay all night with us," Moore said. "They were made welcome by all and they put their horses with ours & camped."[34] For one member of the company the dramatic arrival of the young Indians had special meaning.

Son of an Ohio stonemason, George Washington Hill had managed to convert himself to Mormonism, without outside help, by debating what little he knew about its doctrines against a Campbellite preacher. But other than his outgoing personality and a pleasure in talking, he was probably unaware that he possessed any exceptional gifts before he was called in 1855 on his first Indian mission. That year, it was "sealed on my head that I should see them in the Distance . . . that they would come to me by the hundred."[35]

At the Portneuf River crossing, he saw them, as promised—the two Bannock braves from Fort Hall boldly swimming their horses across the river toward the Mormon camp. Hill sang out, "There come some of my children and that I was going to Baptize them." His announcement "created some merriment among the Boys but on they came." The Ohioan's first native candidates for baptism "got off their horses and shook hands with us and stoped with us," Hill said, "when I went to talking to them as well as I could telling them who we were and what our Business was."[36] From this unexceptional beginning, the irresistible George Washington Hill went on to become one of the most fruitful missionaries to the Indians on America's frontier. For by the hundreds they did indeed come to him, even by the thousands.

David Moore: The Fort Is Kept Very Neat & Clean

Finding its waters too swift and deep to ford, the party looked for another way to cross Portneuf River whose banks were filled by the spring runoff. And not just out of curiosity did David Moore, B. F. Cummings, and Charles McGary seize the opportunity to inspect Fort

[33]Biography and Journals of Benjamin Franklin Cummings, 28 May 1855.

[34]Salmon River Mission Journal, 27 May 1855.

[35]Autobiography and Indian Mission Journals of George Washington Hill, 1.

[36]Ibid.

Hall. Although it was virtually abandoned, Brigham Young would later reveal he had taken an interest in the strategically located fort on Snake River that overlooked the Oregon Trail. Meanwhile, Recorder Moore described the fur-trading post founded by Nathaniel Wyeth twenty-one years before and acquired in 1837 by Hudson's Bay Company.

SALMON RIVER MISSION JOURNAL.

Monday May 28. Camp all well. The Portliff [Portneuf] being too high to ford the President considered it best to go by way of McArthurs Bridge. Accordingly the Company moved on [to] said Bridge which was some 6 or 7 miles travel. Arived there about 10 o'clock a.m. and concluded to lay by for the day.[37] Got the privilege of crossing the Bridge for 11 eleven dollars which was only one dollar per wagon. $7.50 of the amt. was settled by J. W. Browning & $3.50 by the rest of the Company. N. Leavitt Traded his mare here with McArthur for 3 head of Indian Ponies & Br G. R. Grant traded a Cow for a Bull with said McA. 2 oclock P.M. B. F. Cummings, D. Moore & Chas. McGary left the Camp in Co with Myette a Frenchman & a mountaineer, for the purpose of visiting Fort Hall. We had to cross no less than five streams, two of them quite as large as Ogden River, some 60 feet across & quite deep besides a number of muddy and swampy land & sloughs.

Fort Hall is situated on the Bank of Snake River and is built of adobies on a square of about one hundred feet. The north side is composed of Buildings two stories high fronting inwards. The other three sides consists also of rooms one story high fronting inside. The outside wall is about 2 feet thick & is raised above the roofs of the rooms last named, about 3 feet, which is intended for a breast work in case of trouble with the Indians. The Gate is on the south side of the Fort. The fort is kept very neat & clean under the care of Mr. Sinclair the Clerk of the Post.

We were recd. By Mr. Sinclair, on our arrival at the fort, with the greatest of courtesy.[38]

The Soil here and round about as far as we could see is of a very cold appearance wet & swampy on the bottom land & dry sandy & barren on the bench lands with one continual swamp of wild sage and but very little timber in sight on the mountains.

[37] At the toll bridge upstream they found the operator, Hudson's Bay trader Neil McArthur and his young partner, Louis R. Maillet, spelled "Myette" by Moore. The bridge was located just northwest of present Pocatello to serve travelers on Oregon Trail cutoffs, which bypassed Fort Hall along the eastern bluff. For more on Maillet and McArthur and their encounters with Mormons, see Maillet, "Historical Sketch of Louis R. Maillet," 197–228.

[38] William Sinclair was the son-in-law of Hudson's Bay Company chief trader Richard Grant.

Fort Hall in about 1855, just before Hudson's Bay Company abandoned the Snake River trading post, near present Pocatello, Idaho. Its strategic location on the Oregon Trail and north-south lines of communication and travel attracted the interest of a rising theocracy in the West.
Courtesy of the Idaho State Historical Society, Photo No. 1254-C.

David Moore: The Mountaineers All Seemed Very Anxious to Find Out What Was Up

On 29 May the missionaries broke camp at Portneuf Bridge and rolled some ten miles to the bridge on Ross Fork in today's town of Fort Hall on the Fort Hall Indian Reservation. They then headed northwest on the Oregon Trail's Jeffrey/Goodale Cutoff, opened in 1852, and went on to Snake River at Ferry Butte, less than a mile below the mouth of Blackfoot River. Like the Portneuf, the river was too high to ford, and the ferry was not in operation so early in the emigration season, but McArthur showed them a flatboat he owned and "gave us the right to Repair & use it if we wished," Moore said.[39] The Hudson's Bay agent's kindness failed to reflect the mutual mistrust that existed between Mormons and mountaineers. And here after talking incessantly for three days, George Hill fulfilled the vow he made, when he first saw the two young Bannocks coming toward him at Portneuf River, and chalked up his first native conquests.

Salmon River Mission Journal.

Wednesday 30th. Camp still laying by. President Smith sent D. Moore, G. W. Hill & Ezra J. Barnard up to examine the ford on Blackfoot fork where the old Flathead trail crosses it, which is some 7 miles from camp.[40] They examined the ford & found [it] nearly six feet deep. B. H. Watts & others were searching the River near camp while the afore named 3 were absent but could not find any ford the watter [*sic*] being too high in Snake River.

President Smith then concluded to repair the flat boat & accordingly sent B. F. Cummings & J. W. Browning back to Fort Hall for some calking tools for to Repair the said boat with. Meanwhile the Co turned the Boat over & got it ready for repairing. The two Bannack Indians that camped with us 3 nights past accompanied by another Bannack came by our camp this afternoon one of them having his wife and Child with him. G. W. Hill Preached to them. Showing the Book of Mormon & told them what [it] was a Record of & after which they offered themselves for Baptism.

6 oclock P.M. The President called the camp together when a hymn was sang and all then repaired to the watter where we all knelt in solemn prayer. G. W. Hill then Baptized all three of the men (the Squaw not wishing to be Baptized at that time).

---

[39] Salmon River Mission Journal, 29 May 1855.

[40] The Flathead Trail ford was located between the mouth of Blackfoot River and present Blackfoot, Idaho.

Their names are,
Warra hoop
Jock ick
Chu mi

They were confirmed under the hands of B. F. Cummings, I. J. Clark & N. Leavitt. After which they Blessed Warra hoop's little Boy Ion-ish a child about 12 or 14 months old. Warrahoop is the first Baptism on the Northern Mission. He is young, tall, and good looking. The other two are about middle size and also have a good & inteligent appearance.

Thursday May 31st. Weather pleasant and beautiful. The 3 Bannacks are still in camp with us. They seem in the best of Spirrits, & very much pleased with the principles of Mormonism.

Got the Boat done by one oclock & launched it, and took it up the River about a mile to where there was a good place to ferry. Some of the Co then crossed over & examined the other side of the River and finding it also good. President Smith thought best to ferry at that place as the main channel was much narrower than any other place to be found near by.

Mr. Hugo & one man came up from Fort Hall again today but soon returned again he having lost one of his dogs.

Mr. McArthur & Myette & another man came from the [Portneuf] Bridge again to see us & how we progressed with the ferry. They arrived shortly after Hugo left.

Hugo's Boy also came to cam & tried to persuade Warrahoop and the other Bannacks to leave us and go away but they would not, but thought that the boy might as well leave.

The Mountaineers all seemed very anxious to find out what was up with those Bannacks but could not get any satisfaction.

On 1 June they crossed the river, swimming many of the cattle to the north shore without the loss of a single head. Then, in a typical display of bovine wrong-headedness, "one cow swam back over the river again." It was a frustrating sight. But as they watched, the Bannock warrior Warra-hoop, a splendid horseman, raced after the wayward animal, urged his pony across the stream, "and soon had the Cow back in the herd." After crossing the wagons, "a part of the Company made a raft and took [it] over with the flat boat to the other side of the River, leaving the boat there, returned on the raft," Moore said.[41]

Early next morning the Mormon party "travelled ahead breaking our road through the sage without the aid of an Indian trail" and skirting

[41]Salmon River Mission Journal, 1 June 1855.

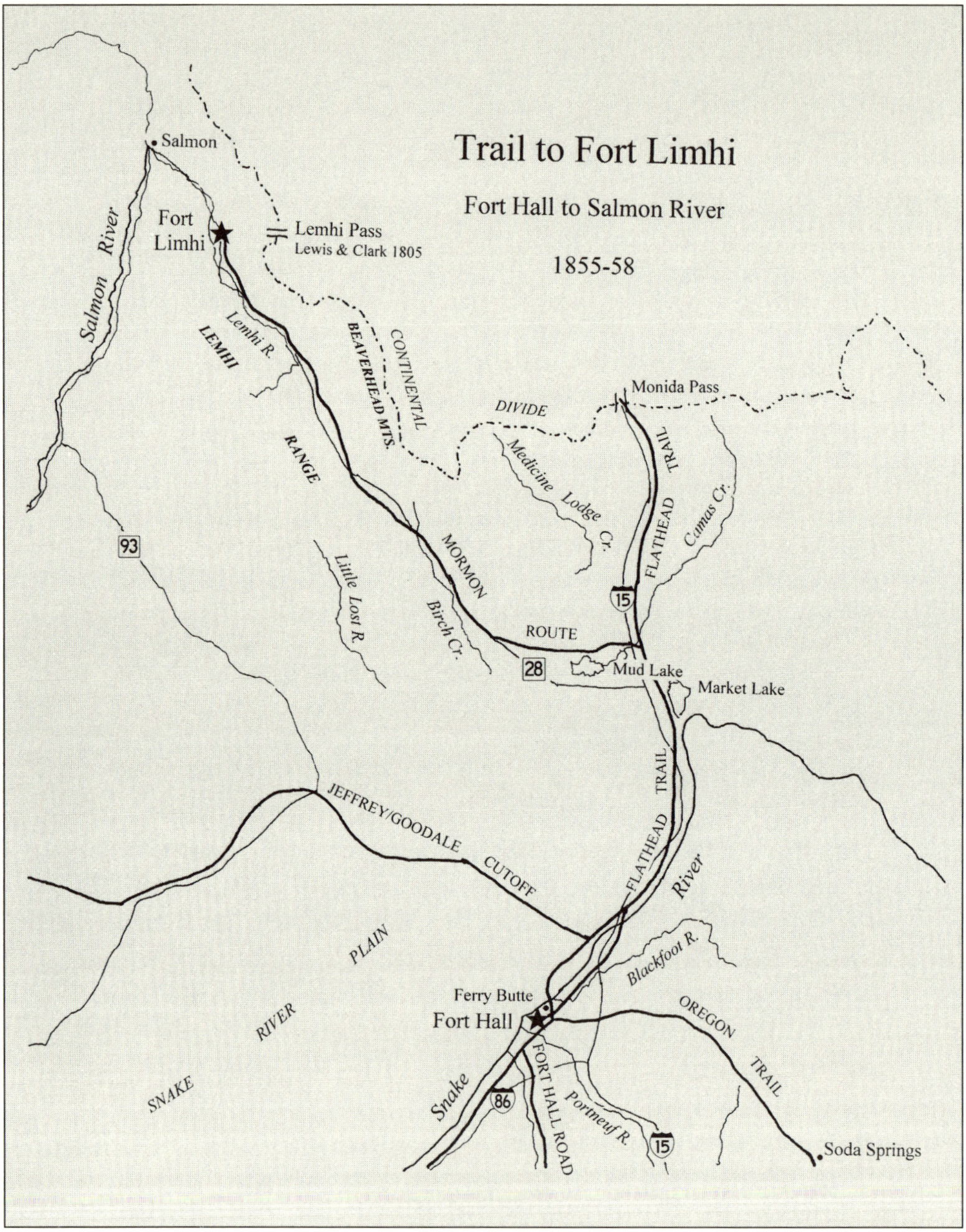

Trail to Fort Limhi
Fort Hall to Salmon River
1855-58
Salmon
Fort Limhi
Lemhi Pass
Lewis & Clark 1805
Salmon River
Lemhi R.
LEMHI
RANGE
BEAVERHEAD MTS.
CONTINENTAL
DIVIDE
Monida Pass
Medicine Lodge Cr.
FLATHEAD TRAIL
Camas Cr.
93
Little Lost R.
MORMON
ROUTE
Birch Cr.
15
28
Mud Lake
Market Lake
JEFFREY/GOODALE
CUTOFF
FLATHEAD TRAIL
River
PLAIN
Blackfoot R.
Ferry Butte
Fort Hall
OREGON
TRAIL
RIVER
SNAKE
Snake
86
FORT HALL ROAD
Portneuf R.
15
Soda Springs

the waterless spread of crumbling lava rock that blocked a direct route to the mountains. Some of the company suffered for want of water, "but on arriving at the bank of Snake River we soon refreshed ourselves & then travelled up Snake River some five or six miles farther and encamped for night on the old Flathead trail about a mile above the ford on Snake River," Moore noted.[42] Opposite the Snake River ford, just above today's Blackfoot, Idaho, they struck the Flathead Trail from Bitterroot Valley and the Beaverhead country of present Montana to Fort Hall. The distance from starting point to camp that day was fifteen miles.

For the next three days they marched on the line of present I-15 up Snake River to its great bend near present Roberts, Idaho. The land they passed over was "one continual barren waste of sage plain," with nothing to break the sameness of the landscape but four antelope. On 4 June they camped at Eagle Rock, which they named Black Rock, now Idaho Falls, and acquired some company. "About dark Mattigan, a Bannak, and his wife and one child, with two other Bannack Indians came into camp," Moore said. "They were on their way to Salmon River and said they would accompany us for a day or so."[43] Mattigan was friendly, but the next two years would witness a change in his attitude. On 6 June 1855 he guided the missionaries across the lava rocks and sagebrush north of Market Lake, a prairie basin some five or six miles across, filled in wet years by the flooding Snake River, near its big bend.

North of Market Lake they left the Flathead Trail and began the arduous task of breaking a wagon road for a hundred miles on the line of today's Idaho Highway 28 to their destination.[44] The first stop was Mud Lake, a monotonous pond worthy of its name, barren of trees, "about ten miles from east to west, by about five or six miles wide."[45] Here they faced a long waterless stretch to the nearest stream from the

[42]Ibid., 2 June 1855.

[43]Ibid., 4 June 1855.

[44]After the Battle of Big Hole in 1877, the Nez Percé escaped from the U.S. Army via Bannock Pass and struck what the National Park Service calls "the old Mormon Missionary Road" near Leadore, Idaho. They followed the road Smith's party blazed in 1855 south to Camas Creek, defeating Gen. O. O. Howard's troops in skirmishes at Birch Creek and Camas Meadow before escaping to the east around the foot of the Lemhi Range. Surviving traces of the Mormon wagon road parallel Highway 28 in the Lemhi-Birch Creek Valley and are now part of the Nez Percé Nee-Me-Poo National Historic Trail.

[45]Salmon River Mission Journal, 7 June 1855.

mountains in the distance. To cross it in a single day with oxen and wagons, the company on 8 June broke camp just after sunrise and moved out. Cummings and Moore rode ahead to scout the shortest way to today's Birch Creek, a willow-lined stream that flowed from the first valley on the Columbia River side of the Continental Divide to end abruptly in a sink on the Snake River Plain. In the heat of the day the trek put physical endurance and faith to a severe test.

"The teams were almost tired down while the men were almost choked for want of water, they having drank all the water and sweet and sour milk they had, before they had passed three fourths of the way across, the whole distance being some 20 miles without even an Indian trail, and about four miles being on continuous sage plain, with some five miles of heavy sand and large sage" said Moore.[46] George R. Grant and William Burgess collapsed from heat and thirst before the men and livestock pitched headlong together into the cool mountain water of Birch Creek, which they called Spring Creek, in late afternoon.

Renewed by rest and water, the missionaries opened the twenty-fourth day of their journey by advancing up the stream between the Beaverhead Mountains and the Lemhi Range toward the low divide between the waters of Snake River and the east fork of Salmon River, now named Lemhi River. Their plan was to follow the latter stream to the trail leading east to present Lemhi Pass, where Lewis and Clark crossed the Continental Divide in 1805, near the birthplace of Sacagawea. At this location on Lemhi River the Bannocks, a branch of the Northern Paiutes, fished the mountain stream for salmon. Here too the horse trails joined to funnel hunting parties of other intended converts, Shoshone, Flathead, and Nez Percé Indians, over the great divide for swift forays east into the rich buffalo hunting ground on Horse Prairie Creek, a headwater of the Missouri River. The trails from north and south allowed hunters from west of the Beaverhead Mountains to enter lands controlled by the Blackfeet without alerting their feared enemies in advance.

Nearing this point, the company on 11 June proceeded up the valley and crossed the seven-thousand-foot divide that opened on the highest waters of Salmon River's eastern tributary. The wagons rolled down

[46]Ibid., 8 June 1855.

Eighteenmile Creek through a sagebrush-covered valley from three to twelve miles wide that offered only rocks to dispute the farmer's plow, but little topsoil. The mountains on each side grew in majesty, their shoulders more heavily burdened with pine, their crests more than ten thousand feet above sea level.

Out of this majestic setting suddenly appeared an equally impressive Indian, borne by a powerful horse. In his moccasins, he stood inches over six feet tall, weighed some 275 pounds, and dwarfed all the white newcomers. With his wife and child the native had ridden nearly seventy-five miles up Lemhi River to meet the emissaries of the Mormon kingdom on 12 June at the head of the river. Shou-woo-koo, chief of the Bannocks, "appeared to be very glad to see the camp and told them that they were welcome," Moore said, "and he was very glad that they had come to open up farms and show the Indians how to work, as they were in a suffering condition for want of food, the traders not being allowed to trade them any ammunition."[47]

Friendly for the moment, the Bannock chief was better known among the mountain men, for reasons the missionaries would one day discover, as Le Grand Coquin, or "the Great Rogue," a fitting appellation bestowed by Hudson's Bay chief trader Richard Grant. Unlettered in French, the Mormons painfully wrote it down the way it sounded to them, "Grow-kre-kaw," later shortened in their daily usage to Rock-e-kay.[48]

Eager for possible rewards, the Bannock chief welcomed the newcomers and invited them to settle among his people. He encouraged them to stay by offering "any land that they might select for farming purposes."[49] Like other natives before, he would one day suffer a change of mind about his new neighbors. Now he escorted them personally down the river to a sheltered place in the cottonwoods along the stream, where most of the party hunted or fixed their wagons while the chief led Smith, Cummings, Durfee, Moore, and Leavitt north another thirty miles to seek a spread of soil large enough to farm.

Their journey was uneventful until, just before dark, six or seven Indians appeared suddenly, coming toward them. Fearing they were Black-

[47]Ibid., 12 June 1855.

[48]Variations of this name by others include Rock-e-kah, Took-oor-I-ka, and Ar-ro-ka-kee. Hereafter called Shou-woo-koo, or Grand Coquin.

[49]Salmon River Mission Journal, 12 June 1855.

feet, Shou-woo-koo prepared to ride for his life. The Mormons laughed at the chief's fright, taking too lightly his respect for the warlike tribe from the upper Missouri River. Were they "not afraid?" he said. They replied "in the negative." Then, he challenged, "Ride as fast as you can until you come up to them." Taking the dare, they spurred their horses and discovered to their renewed merriment that the imagined invaders belonged to the chief's own band. Even more embarrassing, they were all women. The huge chief was "some little chagrined when he saw his mistake," said Moore.[50]

In a more sober mood the advance party continued to the north down today's Lemhi River on 15 June, looking for a place to settle, and soon found it. Splashing across a swift mountain stream from the east, now named Pattee Creek, they "immediately came to a large tract of good farming land also a meadow adjoining it." Their long journey was over. Thirty days and nearly four hundred miles after setting out, they "examined the land . . . and selected a site for the fort."[51]

Elated by their success, the five scouts headed back up the river to bring their companions to the site they had chosen below present Lemhi Pass, where Lewis and Clark had crossed the Continental Divide a half-century before, not far from the spot where Sacagawea had been reunited with her family. As they went, another Indian overtook the scouts and "presented a recommend given him by McArthur stating that he was a friend to the whites and was willing to assist them." The native's name was Tin-go-sho, a Bannock, who rode with them back to the main camp.[52]

David Moore: A Very Handsome Piece of Table Land

On 17 June the reunited company rode eighteen miles down the east side of Salmon River's east fork and camped "near McArthur's old corral." The next day they "passed over the little mountain and down to the second creek to the place selected for their fort," a distance of about twelve miles, arriving there at about noon.[53] The rest of the day was

[50]Ibid., 14 June 1855.

[51]Biography and journals of Benjamin Franklin Cummings, 15 June 1855. The site is at present Tendoy, Idaho, about nineteen miles southeast of Salmon on Idaho Highway 28.

[52]Salmon River Mission Journal, 16 June 1855.

[53]Ibid., 18 June 1855.

The valley of Salmon River's east fork, now named Lemhi River, looks much the same today as it did in 1855 when the first party of Mormon Indian missionaries selected the scenic location, near Salmon, Idaho, as the site of Fort Limhi. *Photo by Steve Berlin.*

spent inspecting the ground for their new home. The next day mission recorder Moore described what they saw.

SALMON RIVER MISSION JOURNAL.

Salmon River runs a little west of north here, but sweeps farther west a few miles below. The valley is not very wide, and keeps about a uniform width for about seven or eight miles—that is to say about four miles up the river and some three or four miles down the river from the camp location.

Timber is plentiful on the river banks and along the small creeks that run down from the mountains to the river. Cottonwood, aspen, tag-elder, willow and chokecherry grow on the river and creeks with now and then a little birch.

The meadow is the effects of an old beaver dam or pond, which has been drained off some years past, and now is covered with a thick stout flat grass, which will afford quite an amount of hay every year.

The bench or table lands are very much broken by ravines or small canyons. They are covered with small bunch or mountain grass for several

> miles from the river on the east and west. The mountain sides and in several of the canyons there are groves of pine but some of them not near so good as further up the river.
>
> The site that Col. Smith has selected is on the north of the second creek below the small mountain. It is a very handsome piece of table land about twelve or fifteen feet higher than the bottom land. There is another bench a few rods further back, which is a good many feet higher than the place selected for the fort, and so the table lands continue to rise until they get to the highest mountain.
>
> There is considerable of sage on the higher portions of the bottom lands, some places there is wheat grass which grows very tall. There is also some blue grass and in the wet low ground here as well as on the divide above white clover is found.
>
> The fruit is the gooseberry, currants, red respberries, choke cherries, and service berries.

With a sense of discovery, he concluded, "this little valley might sustain a large number of inhabitants."[54] But the place they had chosen had already been inhabited for centuries before Moore and his companions arrived. The valley of Salmon River's east fork was a crossroads of native peoples, not all friendly toward each other. From all directions they came, from the south Shoshones and Bannocks, from the west Nez Percés, from Bitterroot Valley to the north the Flatheads and other Salish Indians, and from the east the Blackfeet slipped over the Continental Divide to prey on anyone not of their kind. They would all play a part in the Fort Limhi story.

---

[54]Ibid.

Chapter 3

A Piece of Ground for a Preacher

A preacher came to us. He made a farm and raised grain and bought our stock, as though there were two in one, one a preacher and the other a trader . . . I do not wish another preacher to come, and be both a trader and a preacher in one. A piece of ground for a preacher, big enough for his own use, is all that is necessary for him.
— *Eagle from the Light*[1]

Hardly had the first Mormon missionaries to the tribes of the Pacific Northwest unloaded their wagons and begun to build a blacksmith shop when a preeminent native chieftain arrived on 21 June 1855 from the country between the Clearwater and Salmon rivers in present western Idaho. He was the noted Nez Percé chief "Eagle from the Light" (Tip-pee-il-lan-ah-cow-pook) who came with his followers from Walla Walla Valley where he had eloquently addressed a great Indian conclave that year.[2] Convened by Governor Isaac I. Stevens, the council near the abandoned Whitman Mission had broken up only ten days before.[3]

[1]Remarks by Nez Percé Chief Eagle from the Light, 4 June 1855, before the 1855 Walla Walla Council, Minutes of the Official Proceedings which culminated in the Stevens Treaty of 1855, U.S. Bureau of Indian Affairs. For a true copy of this document, see *Kate and Sue McBeth, Missionary Teachers to the Nez Perce.*

[2]For the probable identity of the Nez Percé leader, the author is indebted to Otis Halfmoon of the Nez Perce National Historic Park who advised: "In our history, there is one Chief that fits this description. This being Eagle from the Light. He was a buffalo hunter type of Nez Percé that spent a lot of time with the Salish & Lemhis. He was one of our main leaders during the 1855 Treaty Council. He was also very much opposed to the Rev. Henry Harmon Spalding and his belief. I believe that the influences of the Salish and the Black Robes made an impression on him to eventually follow the belief of the Catholics." Dennis Baird, Nez Percé authority at University of Idaho Library, independently confirmed this identification.

[3]At the Walla Walla Council, which closed on 11 June 1855, Stevens coerced tribes from east of the Cascade Mountains, including the Nez Percé, Cayuse, Umatilla, Walla Walla, and Yakima, into signing treaties that extinguished the Indian claim and established reservations on about sixty thousand square miles of native homeland for an average payment of about three cents an acre. The Nez Percé, the largest tribe and among the most friendly, won the most favorable terms, a reservation nearly equal in size to Connecticut, plus payments or improvements totaling about $260,000. See Stevens, *The Life of Isaac Ingalls Stevens*, 2:16–65. Also see Kip, *The Indian Council in the Valley of the Walla Walla.*

SALMON RIVER MISSION JOURNAL, 21 JUNE 1855.

About noon some twenty one or twenty two lodges of the Nezpercies came in from the east and camped near by. They have three or four hundred head of horses with them. Some of the horses are very heavy and well made.

At evening the head chief of the Nezpercies came into camp from the Nezpercie country. He is quite a fine looking man of about fifty years of age and is very strict in his religion, which is of the Roman Catholic order.

Friday 22nd. Quite a number of the Red Skinned Brethren in Camp this morning all greeting us as they come with Sinty wah, i.e. Friend. They all seemed much pleased with us being here and were much taken up with seeing the white men labor.

The old Nezpercie Chief seems to feel in the best of Sp[i]rits this morning, although he cannot speak any English or Sho,sho,ne, but talks to us by means of a half Breed (French & Snake) by the name of Allexsee that he brought along with him. This half breed has a Nezpercie Squaw for a wife and can speak the French, Sho,sho,ne, Flathead & Nezpercies Tongues.[4]

The old Chief talks of returning to his home tomorrow and bringing a number of his people to see us and have a good talk with us.

He made Col Smith a present of some venison. Today Shou.woo.koo the old Bannack Chief arrived in camp this evening with his family. They were camped below the forks of the River.

Saturday 23rd. The old Nezpercie Chief rose very early this morning. Came to Col Smith and wishes to have a smoke with him. His wish was gratified by the Col. taking a good smoke with him which made the old Chief feel in fine Spirits.

The natives almost universally received the company with the best of feelings, yet they were not asleep, for they had already undertaken to prove the chastity of the men by offering them their females, but in this they failed to bring any into transgression.

The old Nezpercie Chief and his little company left this afternoon for his own country, but returned again at evening not quite satisfied with leaving the camp so.

When the brethren met for prayer the old chief and the Bannock chief also met with them and united their voices in keeping time with the time of the hymn sung, and during the time of prayer they observed the utmost attention and silence.

---

[4]John Owen in 1856 at Bitterroot Valley apparently referred to the chief's interpreter as Elecssie and Elissel. See Dunbar and Phillips, eds., *The Journals and Letters of Major John Owen, Pioneer of the Northwest, 1850–1871*, 1:127, 128.

The Building of Fort Limhi

Spurred by approaching winter, the Mormon newcomers soon wrought surprising changes in a region where for centuries the proof of human presence was limited to such evidence as Indian trails and an abandoned mountaineer's corral. Nearly fifty years later, those still alive from the first company would remember their labors that summer and autumn as the most arduous of their lifetimes.[5] The valley's native inhabitants watched with astonishment as a new settlement took shape before their eyes. But as it did, an ugly enemy of Mormon settlers in the Great Basin began to move northward from the Snake River plain.

Unaware of the threat, Zion's workmen in only one week opened roads to the canyons, where they cut logs and hauled them four miles to finish a new blacksmith shop and a corral some two hundred feet square for their livestock. In that time, they also built irrigation dams on the nearby creeks, dug ditches, and cleared and plowed almost a dozen acres of land along the river. While some fenced the field, others "planted corn, potatoes, beans, peas, and a variety of other vegetables."[6] As they worked, the Bannocks gathered for the summer buffalo hunt.

On 9 July the Bannock chief "kindled his assembly fire on the top of the mountain west of the camp, and about sundown a small band came in from below and camped with the old chief," Moore said. "The Bannacks are leaving in small bands for their Buffalo hunt," he added four days later. "They trouble us very much about trading." To some the lure of trade with the Indians in violation of mission rules, which restricted such dealing to Thomas Smith, was hard to resist. When twenty-nine-year-old Everet Lish succumbed to the temptation, Thomas Smith called him before the Sunday meeting "for trading a gun to an Indian contrary to his order." The offender's companions "spoke on the case highly reproveing Lish for taking the course he did." When Lish still refused to admit his error, the mission president motioned that "he have until next Sunday to make full satisfaction or be dealt with accordingly."[7]

---

[5]Bluth, "The Salmon River Mission: An Account of Its Origin, Purpose, Growth and Abandonment," 3:11, September 1900, 807.

[6]Autobiography of Gilbert Belnap, July 1855.

[7]Salmon River Mission Journal, entries on 9, 13, and 15 July 1855.

Before Lish "Got up and made a Confession of his error in trading the Gun," his companions had turned to "cutting and hauling house logs to build our houses." Within a week they had six cabins under construction, "some 14 by 16 feet square, others 16 by 16 and one 16 x 18." They built their cabins in a hollow square fourteen rods in width, or 231 feet measured from the perimeters, with the fronts facing inward to form an inner court of nearly four thousand square feet. Claiming the largest cabin, Thomas Smith and his "mess" took possession on 19 July. Three days later most of the others moved into their own tight quarters.[8] Outside, tender sprouts of corn and beans had already pushed above ground.

Work began on 23 July to build a stockade around the hollow square of cabins. Unlike the rock and adobe walls that encircled Mormon settlements at this time in Utah Territory, the palisade duplicated forts on the American frontier and a design from *The Book of Mormon.* This was a square fence of upright logs, "a breastwork of timbers,"[9] sixteen rods, or 264 feet, long on each side with a space between the wall and cabins of one rod, or 16.5 feet. The logs were twelve feet long with three feet below ground, nine above.

For the number of workmen involved, the project was no modest undertaking. To enclose the cabins required each man to build forty feet of stockade. The entire job would take "a large amount of logs," Moore said, at least five hundred, cut and hauled from the canyons. They also had to dig more than a thousand feet of footing ditch, three feet deep, "through cobble stone and white cement," and raise the logs in a row, tie them together, and pack the footings.[10] The fort's main gate, "ten feet wide and nine feet high and made of timbers well fitted together and four inches thick" faced east toward the Continental Divide. A smaller gate opposite opened toward the river.[11]

The design of the fort revealed the awareness that "Lamanites" were not always friendly, but the spot chosen to build it, a few hundred feet from the river, "just below a high bench on the east," was hardly well suited for defense.[12] The fort was close enough to the river for attackers

---

[8]Ibid., entries on 16, 19, 21, and 22 July 1855.

[9]For a description of the stockade, see *The Book of Mormon,* Alma 53:4.

[10]Salmon River Mission Journal, 30 July 1855.

[11]Ibid., 19 August 1855.

[12]Journal and Life History of David Moore, 19 June 1855.

to hide their approach in the trees and willows along the stream but too far away for those inside safely to get water. The steep bench on the east, covered with sagebrush, presented a more immediate threat. It was an elevated firing platform for a hidden enemy to shoot over the stockade wall directly into the fort.

For these weaknesses the responsibility rested on Thomas Smith, whose lack of concern over possible Indian trouble would surely not win the approval of the one man he most wanted to please. The eyes of Brigham Young always looked first to defense. David Moore, a Nauvoo Legion officer and veteran of fights with Mormon enemies and Indians, appeared to anticipate a rebuke by his outspoken leader when he observed: "The location is not as commanding as we would desire but is the best we could find."[13]

Certain it was that no stockade or wall could keep out the invaders that arrived as the missionaries began work on the wall. On 26 July, Moore said, "The grain looks well although the grasshoppers are beginning to come in upon the valley." Just two days later, he added, "The Grass hoppers continue to come in countless numbers, and are taking our little Crop of potatoes, corn, beans, pease, and turnips, as they pass and the whole air and face of the Earth are literally covered and filled with Grasshoppers."[14] Within a week the intruders "destroyed the company's prospects for a crop this season." They even stripped "young branches off the young cottonwood brush, and are destroying the fruit, such as choke cherries, serviceberries, currants, etc.," said the mission clerk.[15]

Even so, the repulsive invaders failed to delay work on the stockade walls, which were virtually completed in the remarkably short time of fifteen days. As the rest finished their share of the wall, some trusted members of the company, including David Moore and B. F. Cummings, rode north twenty miles to the mouth of Lemhi River on the Salmon River, the site of present Salmon, Idaho, to check out Indian stories about shining material in the water. "They found no place on the west side of the upper branch of Salmon River that is as well adapted for

[13]Ibid.

[14]Known as the "Mormon Cricket," but actually a wingless grasshopper, the destructive creature and its relatives for many years caused vast damage to crops in Utah despite the intervention of California gulls in 1848.

[15]Salmon River Mission Journal, 31 July 1855.

their purposes as at the Fort where they are already located," they reported back. "The water of the west fork has a very bad taste."[16] But the men kept silent on what else they found until Brigham Young himself had been notified.

Meanwhile the "four or five lodges of Shoshones," who came upstream and camped near Fort Limhi on 20 July before moving on up the river, were strangers in the valley.[17] They had followed Salmon River from the south on the line of present U.S. Highway 93 to its junction with Lemhi River, called "the forks" by missionaries, and up the latter stream to the mission. From the remote region between Snake River on the north and Humboldt River to the south, the Tosowitch, a Shoshone band "known as the White knives" or "Snake Diggers," often attacked small emigrant parties on the Oregon and California trails.[18] As events would soon reveal, the native newcomers had flown to Salmon River's eastern tributary to elude a U.S. Army force pursuing the perpetrators of a bloody massacre the year before near Fort Boise.

The hospitality afforded these visitors reflected the scriptural origins of the missionaries' activity. Four days later they named their new settlement Fort Limhi, after *The Book of Mormon* king who allegedly reigned on the American continent in 121 B.C.[19] According to this Mormon scripture, good King Limhi ruled over a colony of fair-skinned Nephites deep in the land of the Lamanites, ancestors of American Indians. Like Jeremiah, he instructed his people to obey God and get along with a stronger enemy until the hour of redemption. The parallel, however, was less than exact since Mormon scripture foretold that American Indians, held to be a remnant of Jacob, were destined to become partners with their millennial-minded cousins.

At first the prospects for such an alliance seemed bright. The many native visitors received the newcomers as friends without a sign of distrust or fear. "The Indians here are the noblest race I have seen in the

---

[16]Ibid., 4 August 1855. An apparent reference to the main Salmon River that flows north to its junction with its east fork, now named Lemhi River, at present Salmon, Idaho.

[17]Ibid., 20 July 1855.

[18]Wool to Thomas, 4 September 1855, Annual Report of Secretary of War, House Exec. Doc. 1 (34-1), 1856; and Madsen, *The Shoshoni Frontier and the Bear River Massacre*, 49, 91, 147, 214. This band is identified as both Bannock and Shoshone and appears not to have been closely associated with either tribe.

[19]The name Limhi is now misspelled Lemhi in such Idaho place names as Lemhi River, Lemhi Range, Lemhi Valley, and Lemhi County.

west," William Burgess, Jr., reported. "When we wash we sometimes let our clothes hang days let our tools lay around anyway," he told Apostle George A. Smith, but "not one thing has been stolen yet." He wished Christians were this honest.[20]

David Moore: A Trap to Catch Them In

Indians from four tribes came that summer to catch the fat ocean salmon that crowded Salmon River's east fork in numbers so large that "their backs would be out of the water" as they struggled upstream to spawn.[21] Marveled Burgess: "This is a great fish country in the season. The salmon come up in July in great quantities. They are the best fish I ever saw, I think. The herring come up here in September, red spotted trout come up in August and stay until cold weather."[22] The mission clerk described the techniques the natives employed that summer to catch salmon.

Salmon River Mission Journal, 1 July 1855.

The salmon are commencing to run up the river quite lively. The Indians are making a trap to catch them in as they run up. This is done by putting a kind of frame across the river in two places about two or three rods apart and leaving small doorways in the small willow work of the lower frame to allow the fish to pass; the small willows are placed against two poles that are lashed on the upper side of the frame, so that the big end of them rests on the bottom of the river. Those small willows are finally woven together with bark and then set along in webs. The upper frame work and willows are aimed to be so tight that the fish cannot get through, at the same time giving ample room for the water to pass between the willows. The willows of the upper rack are cut shorter than those of the lower rack, and stand sloping down stream, which allows the salmon to leap over the top of them and fall into a basket, where they are sure to remain. The Indians also take a great many by means of large hooks tied to a pole in such a manner that the hook will pull off the pole as soon as jerked into a fish, but is still held by the cord that fastens it to the pole and admits of the fish making some desperate plunges in the water until he is completely wearied, after which he is taken to the shore, where he is saluted by a squaw taking off a large piece of his tail, which seems to be a choice part of the fish with all the Indians.

---

[20]Burgess to Smith, 9 October 1855.

[21]Salmon River Mission Journal, 12 June 1855.

[22]Burgess to Smith, 9 October 1855.

George Washington Hill: Knocked Down as Dead

When Shou-woo-koo gave George Hill a personal indoctrination in Indian fishing methods, the Bannock chief had no idea it would prove fatal for one of his followers. The giant native leader, called "Rock-e-kay," asked the Ohioan "to take some men and teams and get some large timbers for a fish trap" while his followers "would make the wicket work." There would then be plenty of fish for everyone, the chief said, "and we would all fish together."[23] Thomas Smith approved the cooperative project, so the sociable Hill and others cut the timbers and helped build the trap. He later described what happened next.

Incidents in the Life of George Washington Hill, 1855.

When the trap was finished the Chief told me to come earley [*sic*] the next morning for the fish was already there and the Indians were hungry. Accordingly I went up to the trap as soon as it was Light taking Br B F Cummings with me as he had requested me to call him when I went.

When we got there there was about fifty Indians waiting on the bank of the river for me to come. The Chief chided me for being late saying the Indians were very hungry and they were not allowed to ketch anything untill I have caught the first fish then they could ketch but not before. So the Chief and me fixed our hooks and step[p]ed out on the platform the Chief waiting for me to catch the first before he was allowed to katch any. I had a Large Pole about 12 feet long for my fish pole with hook about four inches across and a soc[k]et to run my pole into with a piece of Lariett tied to my hook in sutch a man[n]er as to allow my hook to pull off of my pole and then the fish would hang by the Lariett and could not break my pole. The Bull pen as I called it was full of fish some of them from three to four feet in Length [next word crossed out] I got ready there was four very large ones swiming close to me so I made a grab at one and caught him in the side but he was so Large and I jerked so hard that I tore him for very nigh a foot and my hook came out so sudden that the end of my pole caught an Indian that was standing behind me right by the side of his nose and and [*sic*] knocked [him] down as dead to all appearences as if a Cannon ball had struck him while in the excitement I did not know I had hit any thing but as I was fixing my hook to try again the Chief sayes to me Look at that Indian you have killed. I Looked and saw him lying there sure enough. I asked the Chief what killed him he said I hit him in the eye. I went and examined him I saw I had hit him by the side of his nose. I felt of his pulse but he had none so I went to

[23]Incidents in the Life of George Washington Hill, 1855.

GEORGE W. HILL
The outgoing Ohioan baptized the first Bannock near Fort Hall and went on to become one of the most prolific missionaries of any faith to the tribes. Among his native friends was the professed son of William Clark by a Nez Percé woman.
Courtesy of the Church Archives, The Church of Jesus Christ of Latter-day Saints.

work Chapeing [*sic*] him but seemingly all to no purpose for some time. Finally he came to and I went back to my fishing but Br Cummings was very uneasy and kept insisting that we must go but I would not go untill I had caught five. Br Cummings Declareing he would not help to carry more than two and when I quit fishing and got a pole to hang them on he would not allow but two to be put on the Pole he was in sutch a hurry to get away for fear of the Indians.

So I gave three that I had caught to the Chief and left my hook with him for him to fish with as it was better than his and told the Chief when the Indian got smart enough to tell him to come up and I would make him some presents as I did not want to hurt him and did not want him to feel bad. He said he should not feel bad that he had no business behind me that I had no eyes in the back of my head. In three or four days after this the Indian came to see me and I gave him some presents and the Indians being about to start to the buffalo country I advised him to stay with us telling him that I would take care of him untill he would get well that I was afraid that if he went to the buffalo country I was afraid that so mutch traveling on horse back would kill him as the Bones were all broke clear through his head but he thought he could stand it but he could not and died in a few days out.

William Clark's Son

Fortunately, the Indians "never had any ill feelings towards me about it not in the least degree knowing it was purely accidental," Hill said.[24] Not only did they have no bad feelings toward him, the natives of every tribe were so drawn to the outgoing Ohioan that everything he did found approval in their eyes.

"We had a great ma[n]y Nez Perces [come] to visit us that summer and they all took quite a likeing to me," Hill said. "There was one in Particular named Clark a half Breed son of Clark of Clark and Louis Journall with Bright red hair blue eyes and [as] thin skin as you would see on any man.[25] He always called me his Little Brother because I was of the same Complection [*sic*] as he was and he was a little older. He would always come and stay with me when they would be there and take all the Pains immaginable [*sic*] with me to learn me the Nez per[c]es Language and I made wondefull progress in the Language while they would be with us."[26]

Whether Hill's new admirer was indeed a son of the redheaded William Clark of the legendary Lewis and Clark Expedition and a Nez Percé or Flathead woman, some five decades before, is not known. But such friendships did tend to conceal underlying causes of trouble to come. One portent of conflict with the natives was that missionaries began to see the valley of Salmon River's east fork as more than just a good location for an Indian mission. William Burgess spoke for more than just himself when he wrote:

"We have explored considerable since our last mail and find that there is more land here than we expected. It is our opinion that this valley would be sufficient to sustain as big a population as Davis county in Utah. It is a good country to raise stock, as there is a plenty of grass, and the Indians say not much snow here. The valley is from one to five miles wide, 60 or 70 miles long."[27]

---

[24]Ibid.

[25]According to Flathead historian Peter Ronan, William Clark fathered a son by a Flathead woman when the explorers remained two days and nights, 4 and 5 September 1805, with the tribe at Ross' Hole on the headwaters of the Bitterroot River. He said the son was baptized by Jesuit missionaries and named Peteter [*sic*] Clark. See Ronan, *Historical Sketch of the Flathead Indian Nation*, reprinted as *History of the Flathead Indians*, 44.

[26]Incidents in the Life of George Washington Hill, 1855.

[27]Burgess to Smith, 9 October 1855.

While some of the men began to think about moving their families to the region, they would first have to depend on the main Mormon settlements in the Great Basin to carry them over the winter. To make up for losses to grasshoppers and cut the number of mouths to feed, Thomas Smith on 5 August named Francillo Durfee, Ezra Barnard, William Brundage, Israel Clark, Gilbert Belnap, Charles McGary, and George R. Grant to return to northern Utah with ox teams for supplies. They took five horses. Soon after, he ordered a second party of five, Nathaniel Leavitt, Pleasant Green Taylor, David Moore, John Browning, and Everet Lish, to deliver eight horses to Utah and return with the supply wagons.

Including the mail riders, who left first on 13 August, returning parties rode or delivered at least sixteen horses to Salt Lake Valley, nine more than the seven with which the whole company started out. Nathaniel Leavitt, who had left Utah with one horse, owned seven of the animals, according to Moore. These numbers do not take in the horses that were left at the mission. They indicate that the missionaries, Thomas Smith or individually, had engaged in more than evangelism with their "Lamanite" cousins. The question is, did these missionary horse traders know whether the horses they had acquired from the natives had been stolen from emigrants on the overland trails?

For the coveted assignment of carrying the mail to Salt Lake Valley and returning with letters from home, Smith picked B. F. Cummings, whose wife Catharine was about to give birth to their second child, and John Galliher. More important, they were charged to deliver a letter from Smith to Brigham Young and inform him about the discovery the mission's scouts had made near the forks of the river. "The Ox teams and the mail to start Mon 13th and the horsemen to start Wed. 15th," Cummings said.[28] The first parties left on schedule early 13 August, but the five men, who delivered eight horses to Utah, found it expedient to leave a day early. At noon 14 August, they took off just ahead of an unexpected visitor to the region.

The reason they left a day early may be found in the sudden appearance of 1st Lt. Edward H. Day, 3rd Artillery, U.S. Army, and forty soldiers who had traveled north from Salmon Falls on Snake River, west of

[28]Biography and Journals of Benjamin Franklin Cummings, 7–9 August 1855.

present Twin Falls, Idaho, and followed Salmon River to the mouth of its east fork.[29] On 14 August, Day ran into the camp of William Burgess, George Hill, and Joseph Parry who had ventured to the junction of the rivers the day before allegedly to get "some fish." The officer and his company, including twenty-four-year-old interpreter Johnny Grant and an unnamed topographical engineer, accompanied the Mormon trio to Fort Limhi, where they arrived just after the men with horses had pulled out.[30]

Lieutenant Day and his men were following the trail of "some Indians who had killed some emigrants while on the way to Oregon in 1854," David Moore said.[31] That the Mormons had already met these Indians was indicated by Charles Dalton who noted that day, "four O'clock forty Oregon soldiers come to our fort hunting for the Indians that murdered the emigrants, friendly to us."[32] Friendly they may have been, for the moment, but the sheer barbarity of their alleged deed the year before hardly held the assurance of peaceful relations and security in the future. The atrocity, one of the most savage ever committed on America's overland trails, had inspired Lieutenant Day and his command to show no mercy to the Western Shoshone, or Snake Digger, perpetrators.

R. H. Thompson: Their Most Brutal Violence

In reporting this butchery, U.S. Indian agent R. H. Thompson penned a graphic picture of what rescuers witnessed in 1854 when they reached the Ward massacre site on Boise River, near the junction of the Oregon Trail and its Jeffrey/Goodale Cutoff, twenty-five miles east of Fort Boise.[33]

[29]A native of Virginia, 1st Lt. Edward Henry Day entered the U.S. Military Academy from Tennessee and was graduated in 1847. The Report of the Secretary of War for 1859 lists him absent from duty from "ill health." He died the following year.

[30]Noted mountaineer John Francis "Johnny" Grant was the son of retired Hudson's Bay chief trader Richard Grant who directed the company's Snake River operations and managed Fort Hall from 1842 to 1851 after the firm acquired the trading post in 1837.

[31]Salmon River Mission Journal, 14 August 1855.

[32]Charles Dalton Journal, 14 August 1855–58.

[33]The Jeffrey/Goodale Cutoff of the Oregon Trail generally followed the line of today's U.S. Highways 26 and 20 from Fort Hall to rejoin the main route some thirty miles east of present Boise, Idaho.

THOMPSON TO PALMER, 3 SEPTEMBER 1854,
ANNUAL REPORT OF THE OFFICE OF INDIAN AFFAIRS,
HOUSE EXEC. DOC. 1, (33-2), 1854–55, VOL. 1, 486–88.

On arriving at the place where the attack was made, they found the bodies of Alexander Ward, his son Robert, Samuel Malugin, Charles Adams, Mr. Babcock, and a German, (name unknown;) about a quarter of a miles from this point the bodies of Dr. Adams, a German, and a Canadian Frenchman, names unknown. The latter was a packer, who had come up a short time before the attack. Following the trails about three hundred yards the body of young Amens was found; about one hundred yards further on, the body of Miss Ward (18 years of age) was found, having been shot through the head with a musket-ball; her person was much bruised. She had evidently fought with desperation in resisting the attacks of the savages to accomplish their hellish purpose upon her youthful person. A piece of hot iron had been thrust into her private parts, doubtless while alive. Some distance from here they found the body of Mrs. White, (said to be the wife of Mr. White, who lives in Looking Glass prairie, Umpqua valley.) She was stripped of her clothing, scalped, shot through the head, and the skull beaten in with clubs; her person showed signs of their most brutal violence. A quarter of a mile further on they discovered where the Indians had been encamped; it consisted of sixteen lodges. Here were found the bodies of Mrs. Ward and her three children, her body stripped of its covering and much cut and scarred; a wound on the face inflicted by a tomahawk, probably caused her death. The children were found lying on the fire, having been burnt to death, and the mother no doubt compelled to witness the horrid tragedy. What renders this case still more shocking, Mrs. Ward was pregnant and would soon have been confined.

Even before he reached Fort Limhi, Lieutenant Day had levied harsh retribution for the 1854 bloodbath that took the lives of nineteen men, women, and children. On his return to Fort Boise, the officer reported that he had "fallen in with six of the murderers on Salmon river; that in attempting to secure them three of them were shot dead, and one badly wounded; that one made his escape without being hurt, (the wounded man also escaped,) and one was taken and hung, making four killed out of the six found."[34] There was "a party of Mormons on Salmon river, who were making preparations to commence a settlement on that

[34]Olney to Palmer, 31 August 1855, House Exec. Doc. 93 (34-1), 1856, 96, 97. Charles Dalton gave the Indian version of this action: "In the evening two of the Shoshone Indians came to the fort and said that the Oregon soldiers ravished their squaws, shot four Indians, hung one, and stole thirty of their horses and then left for the Dall[e]s. This horrible deed was committed at or near Carmash Prairie." See Charles Dalton Journal, 12 September 1855.

stream," he added.[35] But he might have been surprised to hear that soon after his visit they knowingly baptized the one of the natives who escaped from his command.

Before that ritual took place, on 15 August Lieutenant Day "invited Col. Smith and a number of others to dine with him and his officers which was complied with." The following day he "took a part of his troops" and marched south up today's Lemhi River in search of his quarry, who had likely crossed the great divide to the Missouri River headwaters, while the rest of Day's men took care of the horses. The officer returned on 17 August and "after congratulating Col. Smith and Mission in general on the improvements already made by them on Salmon River, marched north down the river with his company for Fort Boise."[36]

Meanwhile, the five men who took off early with eight horses, possibly acquired from the Indians the lieutenant was pursuing, arrived at Snake River where David Moore and Everet Lish broke away from the party to look for a shorter route to Salt Lake Valley. Following a mountaineer's advice, they rode some thirty-five miles up the right bank of Portneuf River on the line of today's I-15 between Pocatello and Salt Lake City. They discovered that the river was "one continual beaver pond from the numerous dams made in some ages past" and impossible for wagons to cross.[37] Where the Portneuf came from the east at present McCammon, Idaho, they gave up the search. Backtracking some ten miles to a ford, they crossed over and joined a party of emigrants on Hudspeth's Cutoff between Soda Springs and Malta, Idaho, which took them to the Fort Hall Road to Malad Valley and their destination at Ogden.

They arrived three days after the mail carrier, B. F. Cummings, who covered the distance in eight days at an average of nearly fifty miles a day to reach his twenty-year-old wife, Catharine, before she had a baby. He barely made it. Cummings arrived home late on 20 November and the following night "she was taken with labour pains." He went next door for help, he said, "but before it arrived she was delivered of a son."[38]

---

[35]Ibid.

[36]Quotes in this paragraph are from Salmon River Mission Journal, 15–17 August 1855. For Johnny Grant's imaginative account of Lieutenant Day's expedition, see Meikle, ed., *Very Close to Trouble: The Johnny Grant Memoir*, 51–59.

[37]Ibid., 20 August 1855.

[38]Biography and Journals of Benjamin Franklin Cummings, 21 August 1855.

Thomas S. Smith: All Want to Learn to be Mormons

Cummings stayed with his wife for a full day before riding south with John Galliher to deliver Thomas S. Smith's letter to Brigham Young at Great Salt Lake City. The mission president's epistle was detailed, but it was most notable for the information it did not contain, which was instead delivered in person by the two couriers.

Smith to Young, 10 August 1855, Brigham Young Papers.

August 10th. 1855
Origon Salmon River Fort Limhi

Beloved Brother Brigham I imbrace this opportunity of writing to you to inform you of my health and whare I am and what I am a doing in conexon with the bretheren that was sent with me on the northen mission we are all well except Brother Ezra Barnard he has ben sick ever since the 15 of july but his health is improveing now in his boddy but he has got a very bad foot I do not know but it will be a feaver Sore if it is not cured soon I have Sent him home to have it docterd we had good luck on our journey we started from farmington on the 15 of May and arived at this place on the 18 of june a distence of 400 miles according to our judgemens the Mountaineers call it two hundred miles from fort hall we found a great deal better road than I expected to find. We found a great deal of sage to traivel thru which made it hard on our teams I will omit the discription of the country betwean here and Salt lake but will try to discribe this country as far as we have explored we are on the east fork of Salmon river about 15 miles from the junction it is a nice stream of as good water as I have seen in the mountains, about the size of provo[39] and runs very swift and runs throu[gh] some as good land as I have seen any whare the bottoms are from a half mile to a mile wide with excelent cottonwood timber along the river thare is 7 creeks emties into the river within 8 miles of our fort this vally is some five miles wide with low mountains on eather side thare is plenty of pine timber in the mountains and is very easy to be got at thare is plenty of timber to sustain a large Settlement within four miles of this place we have found Stone Coal within one mile we do not know how extencive the mine may be for we have not opened it yet but have found it in two places and thare is no doubt thare is plenty thare is a great deal of wild frout [fruit] here sarvesberreys and currents and read rosburyes [raspberries] and goos and straw buryes and the greatest place for fish that I ever saw

[a page appears missing]

[39] The Provo River, a substantial stream that ran from Heber Valley to Utah Lake.

expect them here to winter we came on and when we got within about fifty miles of this place we met the bannock Chief he had herd that we ware a comeing and he came to meet us and to invite us to Stop somewhare in his country he told us that we ware welcom to go any whare or locate just whare pleased and he would go and show us his country and he appeard to be afraid that we would not stop and we camped about 25 miles up the river and he came and showed us this place and we told him that we would stop here and he said if we would he would go and get his famely and come and live here to[o] and he moved up here and since that time we have had the [w]hole tribe to visit us and a great many Shoshonees and the nepersions [Nez Percés] have ben here and the chief expressed a great deal of friendship and thare has ben some flatheads to see us and all appear very friendly and all want to learn to be mormons I think that thare is a good Spirit prevaling among all the indians throu[gh]out this hole country they are very anctious [anxious] for us to bring our famelyes here for they say that if we do not we will go away and leave them some time and will not come back any more the nepersions [Nez Percés] are all roman cathelics and are very strict but they do not like thare priests for they say that they talk crooked and they do not like them the indiens are now gon[e] on thare hunt and will not come back until fall we have not had much chance to learn thare tong[u]e as yet but the bretheren have learned well for the chance that they have had thare is some that can talk Shoshonee tolarble well and brother hill has got severel hondred words of flathead wrote down and can talk some we shal[l] have a good chance to learn this winter for thare will be several tribes here this winter and we calculate to improve the time the flathead tong[ue] will be very dificult to learn and it will require considerable patients [patience] and time to learn it I have sent some of the bretheren back for supplys and seed grane and have sent two back with the mail Brother Commens [Cummings] and Galliher I expect will bring the mail back and I want you to write to me and give me all the instruction and council that you think will be for my benafit or fore the benafit of the mission for i feel my weakness and i want all the instruction that i can get thare is 12 a comeing back for supplyes Brother Francillo Derfy is the captain of the company and i expect that he will come and see you and if you want any information concerning this country or any thing concerning the mission here you can get it from him if you think it best for us to build a mill i wish you would give brother derfy what you think best thare is one thing that I forgot conserning our location I think it is the best and most Senteral [central] one that we could of found fore we are on the main thurerfare [thoroughfare] for several tribes to pas[s] to the buffalow country and we can have as many here as we can tend to and be here to rais[e] grain at the same time I want you to excuse me for being so tedious and for the mistakes I will close by asking your blessings to rest uppon me and all that pertains to this mission and ask god my hevenly father to bless all the exertions that is made for the building up of the Kingdom of god in the name of jesus amen

From T S Smith
To Brigham Young

B. F. Cummings: To Be Put in to One Bag and Sent to President Young

Cummings said the Mormon leader was "well pleased" with what he learned, and for a reason Smith had chosen not to put in writing. When Cummings "saw the president again," three weeks later, Young said that he had "concluded to send Lot Smith and John Clawson out to Salmon River with me to ascertain the truth about some reports relative to there being gold in that region, as they were acquainted with digging gold."[40] Both Smith and Clawson as teenagers had served with the Mormon Battalion in California during the Mexican War in 1847 and prospected along the Sierra Nevada following the discovery of gold at Sutter's Mill on 24 January 1848.

Now in their mid-twenties, Smith and Clawson rode back to Fort Limhi with Cummings on a covert mission to determine whether the shining mineral in the water at the forks of the river was the precious metal.[41] But this secret could hardly be kept from the Mormons on Salmon River. On 30 September, a Sunday, Cummings reported to his fellow missionaries on his visit to Utah settlements and delivered "some general remarks on the present prospects of the Church and the Mission, the situation of the gentiles &c, followed by L. Smith and J. Clawson." Then the meeting got down to the more important business.

Biography and Journals of Benjamin Franklin Cummings, 1855.

The President then arose and made some remarks in relation to the prospects of there being gold in the country, and wished to know of the brethern if they were willing to do as he wanted them to in case it was found

[40]Ibid., 13 September 1855.

[41]While Young warned followers against the temptation to seek gold in California, he and other Mormon leaders secretly sent adopted sons and others on "gold missions" to harvest the precious metal on shares. For more on this, see Davies, *Mormon Gold: The Story of California's Mormon Argonauts,* and Bishop, *Henry William Bigler: Soldier, Gold Miner, Missionary, Chronicler, 1815–1900.*

and they could have the privilege of digging when they all to a man said they were. He then proposed going tomorrow to prospect and in case gold was found, for a few to dig and the balance to carry on the other business as usual and for the gold all to be put in to one bag and sent to President Young which was agreed to.

October

Mon 1st. President Smith, L. Smith, J. Clawson, Geo. W. Hill, B. H. Watts and myself. Started down the river to prospect. We continued on down about 40 miles without finding much sign of gold. However we did find a few very small particles on a gravel bar on the river down about the lowest point where we went but nothing that would begin to pay for workin[g]. From the appearance of the country I think the gold we found must have washed down the river from some place up on the west fork, for we saw no place that it could have washed from.

After Satisfying our Selves that there was nothing in that part of the country of what we were hunting we returned to the fort again whare we arrived on the 5th.

Sat 6th. I remained about the fort [while] brothers Smith and Clawson and the president prospected some on a small creek north east of the fort.

Sun 7th. Prest. Smith J Clawson and L. Smith went down to the forks of the river again to se[a]rch still farther to ascertain the truth of a story told by an Indian about finding gold there.

Mon 8th. Wrote a letter to my wife one to brother James one to B. W. Nowlin my brother-in-law and one to N. Mallory

Tues 9th. Brethern return from below discovered a bed of coal but no gold.

Wed 10th J Clawson and L Smith start for home

Not far behind the disappointed pair came a new visitor who would also potentially play a role in the mission's destiny. Frederick H. Burr from Bitterroot Valley, over a hundred miles to the north, was on his way to Great Salt Lake to see his father, David H. Burr, the newly appointed surveyor general of Utah, and his brother David A. Burr, a member of the elder Burr's staff. An engineer himself, Frederick Burr arrived in Bitterroot Valley in 1853 with the Stevens Expedition to survey a northern route for the transcontinental railroad. He stayed in the great valley, then a part of Washington Territory, to raise livestock and trade with overland emigrants and Indians. Burr's departure from the Flathead Trail and detour across the Continental Divide to visit the Salmon River mission on 19 October before riding on to Utah perhaps reflected only the interest the Mormon fort had already aroused in the region. But he may have come less from curiosity than to provide an eyewitness report on the settlement to his noted father.[42]

First Women

As he neared Great Salt Lake City, Burr met returning missionaries with wagonloads of supplies donated by the people of Utah's Box Elder, Weber, and Davis counties.[43] The party also included the first white females to come to settle at Fort Limhi. They were Cynthia and Emma Durfee, Francillo Durfee's wife and ten-year-old daughter by a former wife, respectively; Elizabeth Clark, first of Israel Clark's three wives; Mrs. Everet Lish; Charles McGary's wife, Charlotte; Susan Moore, first wife of David Moore, and Louisa Catherine Smith, their adopted daughter, age thirteen.[44] Other first-timers to Salmon River included Jonathan and Joseph Bowen, ages twenty-one and eighteen, respectively, sons of Cynthia Durfee by a former marriage; Israel Justus Clark's three sons, Jesse, the oldest at fifteen, James, and Cyrus; Washington Barber, an overland emigrant hired by George R. Grant; and twenty-year-old Lewis Warren Shurtliff, whose affair with a Shoshone chief's daughter would provide an unusual perspective on the early Mormon practice of polygamy.

David Moore: We Here Found One Henry Miller

In the meantime the supply train on 1 November reached abandoned Cantonment Loring on Snake River east of Fort Hall where David Moore described the condition of the station.[45] The clerk also reported an encounter that day with twenty-year-old Henry Miller, who had mar-

[42]David H. Burr was a nationally-renowned cartographer who had served as geographer to the U.S. House of Representatives. His maps in the 1830s were among the first to show the explorations of Jedediah Smith. His reports to the General Land Office in 1855–1857 were included in the documents President Buchanan sent to Congress in 1858 to justify his ordering a U.S. Army expedition to Utah in 1857 to impose federal law in the territory. See House Exec. Doc. 71 (35-1), 115–24.

[43]A list of contributors can be found in the original Salmon River Mission Journal.

[44]Louisa Catherine Smith, the youngest of Addison Smith's four children, was just over a year old when the Moores adopted her in 1844 after the death of her mother, Laura Bentley, at Nauvoo, Illinois. Mormon families adopted Smith's other three children.

[45]U.S. Army Col. William W. Loring established Cantonment Loring in 1849 as a base for two companies of mounted riflemen. The post was soon after replaced by a fortification at the Dalles on Columbia River.

ried Francillo Durfee's daughter and later fled from Utah Territory for undisclosed reasons. Durfee himself may have delivered the young woman, named Marian or Maria, to her husband.

SALMON RIVER MISSION JOURNAL.

> After making a short stay at Fort Hall the Company passed on to old Fort Lorin. This old station was built in 1849 by some U.S. troops that endeavoured to winter their stock in Cache valley the winter following and there lost (according to report) some 900 head out of 1,300. The fort is 7 miles from Fort Hall up Snake River. There is only 3 or 4 rooms standing at present & they are occupied by Capt. [Richard] Grant as a kind of trading post. We here found one Henry Miller a refugee from Salt Lake valley, he is in Capt Grants employ, at the present. At night the said Miller made himself very fresh about Fr. Durfey's wagons, which made some of the Camp much provoked at F. Durfey for allowing him in camp.[46]

DAVID MOORE: LEAVING HIS BUFFALO ROBE ON THE GROUND

The following day Francillo Durfee, captain of the company, ordered Jonathan Bowen and Everet Lish back to Utah "on account of the apparent approach of winter and the scarcity of provisions" at Fort Limhi.[47] On arriving there 17 November, the supply train members found that their companions had made many changes. As the natives

[46]Moore does not say what the wagon dispute was about, but Henry Miller was born in Addison County, Vermont, also the birthplace in 1839 of Durfee's daughter, Marian or Mariah Braidfoot Durfee. In 1856, R. H. Lansdale, U.S. Indian agent for the Flathead tribe, hired Miller and his wife, named Maria or Marian, at Fort Hall. Over the next two years they worked at the Jocko Flathead agency, some twenty miles north of present Missoula, Montana, and at the Dalles on Columbia River. Mountaineer Louis R. Maillet recalled: "In [spring 1856] a man named Henry Miller brought his wife, a young Mormon girl, to Fort Hall. He had married her two years before at Ogden, and in some way had incurred the enmity of her people, so that he was obliged to flee from the land of Saints. During his absence his wife's relations had brought every influence to bear upon her to become the spiritual wife of an old Mormon who already had three wives. The young wife resisted, although she was told that she should never see her husband again and that he would be killed if he ever dared appear in Mormondom again. Through the assistance of friends, Miller managed to correspond with his wife, and in time she was enabled to effect her escape and join her husband. At this time Dr. Lansdale, Indian agent for the Flatheads and Pend d'Oreilles, was in Salt Lake on business, and returning to the Jocko by way of Fort Hall, was persuaded by Maillett to engage Miller and his wife to go to the Jocko and keep house for him." According to Montana pioneer Frank H. Woody, the Millers returned to western Montana in 1860 and settled the following year in Utah. See R. H. Lansdale Journal, 1856–58, 30 May 1856; Maillet, "Historical Sketch of Louis R. Maillet," 4:205, 206; Woody, "A Sketch of the Early History of Western Montana, 2:94; and Dunbar and Phillips, eds., *The Journals and Letters of Major John Owen: Pioneer of the Northwest, 1850–1871*, 1:132.

[47]Salmon River Mission Journal, 2 November 1855. For unspecified reasons, Everet Lish and his wife remained with the party.

looked on, they had enlarged their common field, plowed and sowed virgin land, and cut and piled stacks of hay for the winter. Moreover, they had also begun a rich harvest of Israel's remnants in Oregon Territory, the natives they had come to redeem. On 21 October, George Hill had preached in the Shoshone tongue to a gathering of Indians at the fort and so captivated his listeners that fifty-five volunteered for baptism.

Some of his native conquests were entered in the mission record that day by their Indian names and others were shown by the names "given to them at the time they were baptized by Br. G. W. Hill."[48]

SALMON RIVER MISSION JOURNAL.

Males, Sho.Sho.nees and Bannacks
Abraham
Te-go-cho
I-vish-e-ma
Par-hu-ro
Sam
Chu-me
Chee-hu-e
Pap-par-he
Cuh-hu-ah
Pad-ed-zo
John
Co-ud-it-sey
Sam
Saw-nee
Isaac
John
Jacob
Tome
James
Tosh-e-quit-som-be
Pu-ro
Poo-e-wats
William
Can-o-we
Ah-nav-ve
Pam-e-cot-ile
Do-de-ah
Harvey
Ah-ho-wo

So-ses
Tosh-e-wash-up
Par-gow-e-ah
Yo-e-nip-pet
    Samuel
    In-near-nack-et
John
Thomas
Spi-get
Sam
    James
    Mo-heo
    Tin-go-sho
Females
    Martier
    Nab-be-a
    Mary
    Sar-har-gats
    Too-roots
Martha
    Mary
Pat-se-gope
    Yap-pa
Martha
Nap-pam
    Pah-be-ze
Kat-too

[48]Salmon River Indian Mission, 21 October 1855.

Three weeks later, the productive Indian missionary ran up his score with a haul of the gospel net that included the warrior who had escaped punishment by Lieutenant Day for his alleged part in the Ward massacre.

SALMON RIVER MISSION JOURNAL, 11 NOVEMBER 1855.

> The brethren at Fort Limhi held meeting as usual. G. W. Hill preached to the Indians who were present after which the following were baptized by President T. S. Smith. Ti-o-von-du-ah, generally known by the name of Snag; Richard, Horace, Jacob, Par-sho-up, Wash-up, Pe-get-seif. This last named Indian was taken prisoner by the soldiers in the course of last summer and tied, both hands and feet, to a stick and that passed under his legs, but as soon as it was dark and the soldiers had all retired to rest, except the guard, he managed to loose the cords from his wrists and legs and as the guards passed from him, he made a spring and cleared himself and made his escape, leaving his buffalo robe on the ground where he was tied.[49]

Even before they won their first converts, individual missionaries had broken the rule against bartering with the Indians, a policy established to avoid misunderstanding and conflict. In June Nathaniel Leavitt had given "a gun and some other articles" to some Bannocks on Birch Creek for a horse. Not long after, Thomas Smith had censured Everet Lish "for trading a gun to an Indian contrary to his order."[50] The rule became even harder to obey as ice began to form on the river and log houses became crowded with Indians "coming in with their deer and antelope skins to trade and to get some Tosh-a-te-cup."[51] The temptation to deal with them became virtually irresistible.

Finally, in late November, Thomas Smith acted to strengthen the policy that was intended to enhance Mormon influence over the Indians, not enrich the missionaries or invite trouble. He told his followers "it was necessary that some one person should be elected to do all the trading for the Mission, that one system of action might be carried out and thereby general satisfaction rendered among the Indians." It was then "duly voted that President Smith be the only person to trade with the Indians at this Fort." The stricter course was timely as the natives were

[49]Johnny Grant said this Indian's name was Pigate and that he was peaceable and good. "He said to me, 'you know I never killed anyone or stole horses,'" Grant said. "I told him I knew it, but that I could not do anything for him." See Meikle, ed., *Very Close to Trouble: The Johnny Grant Memoir,* 52, 53.

[50]Salmon River Mission Journal, 10 June and 15 July 1855.

[51]A phonetic rendering of the word for bread in the Shoshone language. See Huntington, *Vocabulary of the Utah and Sho-sho-ne or Snake Dialects.*

"anxious to trade for ammunition" before crossing the Continental Divide to hunt buffalo along Horse Prairie Creek on the Missouri side.[52]

In the meantime, wives and children gave the little colony the look of a permanent settlement. In early December, native neighbors saw new signs of expansion when Smith, Cummings, Taylor, and others surveyed twenty-six lots, each of five acres, between the first and second creek south of the fort. The missionaries then drew lots for these future homesteads for themselves and "for those who were absent."[53]

The white newcomers had plowed and planted, preached, and traded in the ancient fishing and hunting grounds on Salmon River's east fork—a scenic valley long possessed by others. And as Eagle from the Light had warned, they were sowing seeds that would one day produce an unwanted harvest.

---

[52]Salmon River Mission Journal, entries on 19 and 27 November 1855.

[53]Ibid., 7 December 1855.

Chapter 4

Of Grasshoppers and Reformation

We tried to head them off the crops with a water ditch. We caught them morning and evening in sacks, [dug] holes in the grain 3 to 8 rods apart and drove them into the holes with brush 3 to ten men forming a circle to drive them into the hole and bury them sometimes a peck of them in a hole. —*Jacob Miller*

Even Bannock Chief Shou-woo-koo, also known as Le Grand Coquin or Rocky Kay, was astonished to see so much snow that winter in the valley of Salmon River's east fork. As temperatures plunged in December 1855, a worried Thomas Smith inventoried food supplies and realized that stores on hand would fail to feed all who expected a place at his table during what promised to be an unusually hard winter. Adding to the looming shortage were the new families that had arrived with the supply train and the Indians who came daily "complaining about being very hungry and unable to get any game on account of the snow being so deep and the weather so cold."[1] He could not ignore their suffering.

With the snow ten inches deep and weather so cold the men could not cut timber, it was the worst of times to travel in the mountains. But Thomas Smith had no choice but to reduce the number depending on the mission's food supply by sending some on a 380-mile winter journey to Utah settlements. He gave those who had worked at the fort during the summer the option to return home for the winter. Those who decided to go, Ira Ames, William Batchelor, William Burch, Thomas Butterfield, George Hill, Joseph Parry, Isaac Shepard, Baldwin Watts, and Abraham Zundel, left on 4 December. They took four horses, three wagons, six yoke of oxen, and not enough food to cover the distance.

---

[1]Salmon River Mission Journal, 29 December 1855.

RICHARD GRANT
When a party from Fort Limhi came out of the snow and stomped into his isolated cabin on Snake River, the former Hudson's Bay trader at Fort Hall sat up in bed and threw up his hands. "My God," he cried, "and where did you come from?" *Courtesy, Jean Schurman.*

A WINTER JOURNEY

Reaching the low divide between Salmon River and Birch Creek, the hard-pressed travelers saw a sure portent of severe winter. Hundreds of elk, driven from the mountains by heavy snow, had come down to the valley to look for food. By 16 December, when they reached Fort Hall, their own supply was gone. At Cantonment Loring, an alarmed Richard Grant sat up in bed when they stomped into his cabin. "My God," he cried, throwing up his hands, "and where do you come from?"[2] The former Hudson's Bay trader was astounded that anyone could travel in such weather and with such an outfit. From his own limited stores he gave them some beef, a little bacon, and moccasins.

Indian footwear provided little protection on the divide between the Columbia River drainage and Great Basin where the snow was so deep the men had to break a trail for their animals. Travel slowed that day to only three miles. On the rim of the Basin they camped in a whiteout snowstorm without food or water or a fire to keep warm. More than three weeks after starting, they limped into the northern Utah settle-

[2]This story is told from the recollections of one of the missionaries in Bluth, "The Salmon River Mission," 3:11, September 1900, 810.

ments frostbitten and "mighty hungry," but otherwise in good shape. At Ogden, Joseph Parry found his wife and three children actually better off than when he had left them in a tiny log cabin seven months before, for then "their condition was deplorable."[3] But when William Batchelor reached home, he learned that the woman he had married just before leaving was dead.

While Batchelor mourned at home in Great Salt Lake, the little colony of thirty-two men, women, and children on Salmon River partook of "as good a Christmas dinner as the circumstances would permit," and afterward held a dance. This favorite Mormon recreation was greatly enhanced by the participation of five wives. For the men, drills in "the broad sword exercises" also brightened the dull winter days. "I was called upon to act as teacher," said B. F. Cummings. "Had quite a past time with our wooden Swords again today," said Moore, with tongue in cheek.[4]

Ever watchful for "signs of the times," the millennial-minded religionists shortly before New Year beheld "a very singular" manifestation in the heavens and wondered what it portended. Carefully the mission clerk described the phenomenon: "When about an hour high above the top of the west mountain, there were two semi-circles somewhat resembling rain bows above the sun with no less than three bright sundogs in the first and three more in the second in a direct line with the three first and the sun, but not so bright as the first or inside three."[5]

David Moore: Bringing Several Decks of Cards Here

For some, the omen from above meant punishment. On 9 January Thomas Smith and three others marched over to "old" Manuel's lodge outside the fort "to inquire into some reports about Br I. Shepherd laying with a squaw in November last," Moore said.[6] "Manuel firmly stated

[3]Bluth, "The Salmon River Mission," 3:11, September 1900, 811.

[4]Paragraph quotes are from the Salmon River Mission Journal, 25 December 1855 and 1 February 1856, and Autobiography and Journals of Benjamin Franklin Cummings, 26 January 1856.

[5]Salmon River Mission Journal, 28 December, 1855.

[6]Ibid., 9 January 1856. Manuel may have been a Mexican trader who came to Bitterroot Valley as early as 1852 when John Owen hired him to make adobes for his fort. Burr purchased ammunition and tobacco from him in 1857. Frank Woody spoke of "an old Mexican trapper named Emanuel Martin, generally known as and called 'Old Manwell, the Spaniard.'" See Dunbar and Phillips, *The Journals and Letters of Major John Owen*, I:45, 46; Journal of Frederick H. Burr, 1857–58; and Woody, "How An Earlier Pioneer Came to Montana," 161.

that the said Shepherd did actually lay with a Sho-sho-ne Squaw two nights while he (Manuel) was living in Shepherd's house." Charles Dalton had noted such wayward behavior as early as June 1855, when he reported that "Shepard has been trying to get a squaw to live with ever since we have been on Salmon River." The alleged offender, having returned to Utah, was beyond the arm of mission discipline. Nor was he the only wrongdoer.[7]

SALMON RIVER MISSION JOURNAL, 9 FEBRUARY 1856.

> At evening Pres. Smith requested all the Brethren to come together at his house which was done. The meeting was opened by prayer by Pres. Smith after which Br Everett Lish was called in question about trading or allowing his wife to trade for two small deer skins & then telling the Indian that the trade was made with, to keep it secret. This with several other circumstances such as bringing several decks of cards here on the mission for trade & making use of them, thereby giving the lie to the President & others which had told the Indians that no such things was used or kept by the Mormons for trade. After much talk & Councelling [*sic*] on the subject before the mission & no spirit of Repentance evident on the part of Br Lish, it was motioned & duly carried by the unanimous vote of the mission that Br Lish is hereby suspended from this mission and the fellowship of the Brethren thereof until such time as he the said Lish brings forth fruit meet for repentance.

B. F. CUMMINGS: SUFFERING AMONG THE PEOPLE

For starving Indians, Fort Limhi's rapidly shrinking food supply held a far greater appeal than repentance or celestial wonders. Shou-woo-koo, the unpredictable Bannock chief, rode in with his band from Horse Prairie and "wanted to get some flour." He and other Indians kept coming back "to beg a little bread and flour."[8] Mountaineers also saw the fort as a handy market. Like the natives, they came for food during the day, then spent the night gambling a short distance away. Before the end of February, the mission's flour had almost vanished. Facing the specter of famine, Thomas Smith led a seven-man party on a winter journey to Utah to remove some of the plates at his table and obtain supplies.[9] The

[7] Charles Dalton Journal, 24 June 1855.

[8] Biography and Journals of Benjamin Franklin Cummings, 21 February, 4 March 1856.

[9] Members of this party were Thomas Smith, B. F. Cummings, William Burgess, Charles Dalton, David H. Stephens, Israel Clark's sixteen-year old son, Jesse, and Washington Barber, a non-Mormon emigrant hired by George Grant.

snow was too deep for wagons so they went by horses and packs. This disappointed Cummings, who had crafted a crude wheel-mounted odometer to measure the distance to Ogden. "They took fifteen head of horses with them," Moore said.[10]

In northern Utah they were to find conditions almost as bad as the place they had left. An invasion of the black-shelled grasshoppers, the infamous Mormon crickets, had virtually wiped out the 1855 wheat crop, forcing many to live on bran and the carcasses of dead animals. In the intense cold of the 1855–1856 winter, later known as "the hard winter," more than two thousand Mormon cattle had frozen to death in Cache Valley.[11] Cummings described their journey from the mission to Utah.

BIOGRAPHY AND JOURNALS OF
BENJAMIN FRANKLIN CUMMINGS, MARCH 1856.

Wed. 12th. Started about 9 A.M. Continued on up the Valley to the forks of the river. Crossed the east fork and bore to the south leaving the waggon road to the east. Camped about sunset in a thicket of willows on a small creek cold and windy, feed very scarce. Snow about 14 to 20 inches. Shortly after we camped Shah-o-co[12] came in to camp. He had seen us pass his camp at a distance and knowing where we were going he packed up and started to go with us. He had one of his wives and her sister a young girl and two children with him and also a brother in law who went on ahead to find Thos. Pambrin's [*sic*] camp which he said was not far off.[13]

Thurs. 13th. Start 10-1/2 A.M. Travel about 3 miles and found Pamrins camp. He had with him a half breed by the name of Meshall an old mountaineer and several Indians. Having learned from them that they were going to start on toward Fort Hall the next morning and being acquainted with the best rout for the winter we concluded to stop and go with them. Feed was poor and wood scarce. We stop[p]ed on a spring branch south side of a point of the mountain that extended out from the east.

Fri. 14th. Start 11-1/2 A.M. travel nearly a south course up the creek six miles not much snow then turned to the left over a high ridge about 4 miles through deep snow, to the dry Quaking Asp grove on the wagon road six

---

[10]Salmon River Mission Journal, 9 March 1856.

[11]Bluth, "The Salmon River Mission," 3:11, September 1900, 812.

[12]Shou-woo-koo, the Bannock chief.

[13]Mountaineer Thomas Pambrun was born in 1814 in British Columbia, as was his younger brother, Alexander Pambrun. Both are mentioned often in journals and memoirs of early Montana pioneers. For examples, see Meikle, ed., *Very Near to Trouble: The Johnny Grant Memoir.* John B. Pambrun, Thomas Pambrun's son by an Indian mother, served at Fort Shaw as a U.S. Army scout and claimed that as a child he lived in Utah with his father from 1855–1860.

miles to the north of the divide and camped. Night very cold. Horses get tolerable good feed on a side hill that was here.

Sat. 15th. Pambrins Company started about 10 A.M. We waited until about 11-1/2 A.M. Crossed the divide near the wagon road and then bore to the left and traveled about three miles and camp at a quaking asp grove on the head of Bear creek. The snow today was deep and drifted. Feed good.

Sun. 16th. Pambrin and Meshall concluded to stop a few days. We started 9-1/2 A.M. Shah-o-co also stoped for us to break the road for him. We found the snow bad in places but got along very well. Camped about three miles below the big springs near the head of Spring Creek.[14] The snow was mostly gone below the springs,—feed good.

Mon. 17th. Start 9-1/2 A.M. Went to the point of the mountain east of the mouth east of Spring Creek Valley and camped. Not much snow today. Feed good. Saw several flocks of Antelope.

Tues 18th. Start 8-1/2 A.M. Travel an easterly course. Soon came in to the snow again which continued to increase to 12 to 18 inches. Crossed Muddy Lake on the south of the mouth of Kammosh Creek.[15] Camped about 5 miles from the Lake in the sage brush. No feed worth naming. Snow one foot deep.

Wed 19th. Start 8-1/2 A.M. and arrived at the Big Slough or Snake river about 5-1/2 P.M. Here we found an Indian by the name of Mattigan who had left Salmon River with his family in the winter for Fort Hall. We had followed his trail about 20 miles. He arrived about 2 hours before us. We found him destitute of provisions and living on dried raw hide envelopes used for packing their baggage, but our circumstances would not admit of our lending him any assistance as we were short of provisions ourselves, having to feed Washington Barber through G. R. Grants neglecting to furnish him the necessary amount. He being out before we left Spring Creek Valley. The sky has been cloudy for two days and strong indications of a thaw misting some this evening. Snow today about two feet.

Thurs. 20th. Start 9-1/2, thawing considerable. Snow very bad. Traveled about 13 miles and camped. Very little feed. The ground beneath the snow covered with water.

Fri. 21st. Thawed all night. Start 8-1/2. Found the traveling much better than yesterday. Wind continues from the south and thaws fast. Camp at Wind Point. No feed. Travel about 14 miles.

Sat 22nd. Clear last night and froze some which made very bad traveling. Start 9-1/4. Travel about 2 miles and found a patch of good feed and stoped till 2 P.M. then went on down the river 6 or 8 miles and crossed over on the ice, went on down about 2 miles and camped. Food tolerable good.

---

[14]Now Birch Creek.

[15]Camas Creek.

Shah-o-co overtook us the day we arrived at Snake River and has continued with us.

Sun 23rd. Shah-o-co left us this morning and went ahead in order to reach Capt. Grants, at old Fort Lorain.[16]

We started 9-1/4 A.M. Traveled about 15 miles and camped on the south side of Blackfoot But[t]e, had considerable snow. Shah-o-co's family continued with us. Feed good.

Mon 24th. Start 8-1/4 A.M. Went down on Grants and stoped a short time. C. Dalton got some flour, tobacco and dried antelope meat of John Grant for a debt that was due him. As they expected to send some men over to Salmon River in a few days by request of Brother Smith I wrote a line to Brother Taylor.[17] Brother Smith got some flour for Barber. Having completed all our business here we went down to Fort Hall. Called a halt for a few minutes and then continued on across the bottom to the fort on Portniff and camped. We found a large wagon tire which we carried about four miles in order to cache it where we could get it in the summer when we returned.[18]

Mar. Tues. 25th. Start 8-1/2 A.M. Cross the Portniff. Buried the iron by the side of the road and went on. Found no snow. Camped about 6 miles above the forks of the Bannac Creek on the main branch. Feed good.

Wed. 26th. Start 8 A.M. Travel up Bannac Creek Valley about 10 miles and crossed over into the Malad at the Malad Springs. Found the Malad country enveloped in snow. Camped near grindstone point.[19]

Thurs. 27th. Start 7-1/4 A.M. Arrived at Barnards about noon.[20] Found the few inhabitance [*sic*] in rather destitute situation for provisions.[21] Here we first learned the distressing account of the hard winter that had passed. That on account of the deep snows and severe cold that a large portion of the stock in northern settlements had died, and that there was a great deal of suffering among the people for the want of food. We were also told that Bear River was to[o] high to ford and that the ferry was not in operation

---

[16]Cantonment Loring.

[17]Smith probably asked for assistance in deciding where and how to build a gristmill, a necessary addition in making the settlement on Salmon River permanent. The original company had picked up a grindstone in Malad Valley on its way north. It was a common practice during this period to employ wintering emigrants to Oregon or California, usually millwrights, to perform this function.

[18]Iron in any form was a valuable commodity at this time.

[19]Probably a mountain spur where they had found the grindstone the year before.

[20]John Porter Barnard established Barnard's Fort in 1855 some five miles north of present Plymouth, Utah. To reach the site, leave I-15 at Plymouth Exit 394, turn west to the old highway that parallels I-15 and go five miles to the marker on the west side of the road erected in 1931 by LDS Vanguard Scouts of Malad Stake. The fort was abandoned in 1858.

[21]Charles Dalton said the settlers at Barnard's Fort "had nothing but bread and water to eat." See Charles Dalton Journal, 28 March 1856.

> yet.[22] We went on about 2 miles and stoped and baited our animals and then went on to Bear River. Found the river had raised considerable but had no difficult in fording. Camped on the opposite side. Here we found John Barnard who was herding sheep for his father.[23] He gave us considerable information relative to times in the valley during the winter.

Cummings found his family at Ogden living with his sister, Mary, and husband, Bryan Nowlin,[24] "in more prosperous condition than I expected after first hearing of the circumstances of the times." He went to work to better their condition before returning to Salmon River, but labored under a serious handicap. Thousands of horses and cattle had died during the winter "and those that were lef[t] were so poor and weak that they were not fit to use, so that it was almost out of the question to hire a team." But he made time to take a second wife, eighteen-year-old Mary Jane Yearsley from Pennsylvania, who at last accepted his proposal "after some little demur[r]ing." He had his reluctant new bride and first wife, Catharine, "sealed to me over the Altar" in the Endowment House at Great Salt Lake City.[25]

Indian Baptisms

While the new polygamist got ready to return, a reduced colony of fourteen men, five women, and six children at Fort Limhi saw increasing native traffic as spring touched the upper reaches of Salmon River. On 19 March Snag came to report that the Bannocks and Nez Percés had gambled all winter and, while so occupied, had stolen each other's horses. The Nez Percés wanted to go to war against their old enemies, but the Shoshone chief had "preached to them the words that Brigham Young had told him, that it was not good to fight, that the Lord was not pleased with those that wanted to fight, and he (Snag) felt that it was good talk."[26] True or not, Snag's talk was good for a meal at the fort. Next Snag's brother, Te-ah-to-wah, and nephew, Ten-toi, also known as

---

[22]Emigrants to California and Oregon on the heavily traveled Hensley's Salt Lake Cutoff would not begin to arrive at the Bear River crossings between Honeyville and Collinston for another three months.

[23]Twenty-seven-year-old John Porter Barnard, Jr., was a brother of Fort Limhi missionaries Lachonias and Ezra Barnard.

[24]Bryan Ward Nowlin, age thirty-nine, was a farmer from Tennessee. The couple then had four children.

[25]Biography and Journals of Benjamin Franklin Cummings, entries on 30 March and 12 April 1856.

[26]Salmon River Mission Journal, 19 March 1856.

"young Bonapart" after his father, arrived with their families from the upper valley.[27] Some eight lodges of Nez Percé also rode up from Horse Prairie and camped nearby.

Over the next six weeks, the missionaries baptized and gave English names to nearly thirty natives, all Bannocks and Shoshones. On the first Sunday in April, George Grant preached in the Shoshone language, which produced four for "washing," Te-ah-to-wah, Snag's brother, renamed Lehi;[28] Mopeah, "Horn of hair in the forehead," and Eas-e-to-roat, both Bannocks, who received the names Joseph and Thomas, respectively;[29] and Am-a-ri-ko ("Buffalo meat under the shoulder") of mixed Bannock-Shoshone parentage, also known as Napirce, Arrow, Arrow-mo, and Aramon.[30] Nez Percé visitors watched the proceedings respectfully, but made no move to join in, having been won to Catholicism years before by Jesuit missionaries. Especially gratifying to their new Mormon brethren, Thomas and Joseph soon after commenced to farm with them.

The following Sunday saw fourteen more, also Bannocks and Shoshones, buried briefly beneath the frigid waters of Salmon River's east fork under the hands of Pleasant Green Taylor. Mission records reported the male natives were Con-e-bone-e-ah, renamed Cyrus; Pan-tag-e-wick-up, Henry; Mormon, no native name given; Pe-e-ge-tah, William; Zeame, another of Snag's brothers, David; and O-haw-wag-e-ah, George. Among native women baptized were Te-ah-to-wah's wife, Jane; Yam-pe-ah, Mopeah's wife, Mary; Po-e-chah, Te-ah-to-wah's mother, Esther; Up-se-man-na, Te-ah to-wah's wife, Elizabeth; Cu-e-bah, another of Te-ah-to-wah's wives, Louisa; Eas-e-to-roat's wife, Jane; his sister, Sarah; and his mother.[31]

---

[27]Fur traders gave the name Bonapart to Ten-toi's father, a noted Bannock chief, because of his courage and commanding appearance. Ten-toi's mother belonged to the Shoshones, known as Sheepeaters, who lived in the mountains along the upper waters of Salmon River. After the death in 1863 of Snag, his uncle, Ten-toi took his place and became a noted native leader in his own right. See Crowder, *Tendoy: Chief of the Lemhis.*

[28]Possibly the same Lehi who was killed by Col. Patrick E. Connor's command in the Battle of Bear River in 1863.

[29]Mopeah in 1860 was described as a friend of the Mormons and chief of some forty-five lodges or about three hundred natives. For more on him and the eastern Shoshones and Bannocks, including Grand Coquin, Snag, and Ten-toi, during this period, see Madsen, *The Bannock of Idaho;* and "The massacre at Mountain Meadows, and other massacres in Utah Territory," Sen. Exec. Doc. 42 (36-1), 1860, 121–39.

[30]In 1873, Aramon signed an agreement with the U.S. modifying the 1868 treaty that created the Fort Hall Reservation. See Madsen, *The Bannock of Idaho*, 335.

[31]The Indian names of these women were not recorded.

A week later, 20 April, four Bannocks requested baptism, Pie-o-wits, renamed Ralph; Eas-e-to-roat, Thomas; Ho-at-see, Mark; and Mo-to-win-ne, Pie-o-wits's son, James. And the next day, Taylor performed the ceremony for three more natives who wanted to be baptized before leaving for Snake River. They were Pas-tim-mah, labeled Levi, a Shoshone, and Pan-sook-mud-zu-eve and Nabi-gye-yah, Bannocks, christened Louis-Joseph and Eli, respectively.

On Sunday, 25 May, natives crowded the fort to hear the recently returned George Hill, their favorite preacher, hold forth in the Shoshone tongue. So well had Hill honed his native language skills while away for the winter that Yo-ko-ap, (Israel); Tis-sea-da-make (Alfred); Cots-se-qua-me-at (John); Taw-haw-i-be (William), and Mopeah and his wife, Yampeah (Joseph and Mary), requested baptism, the latter pair apparently for the second time.

While they gathered natives on Sunday, Zion's workmen labored on other days with urgency born of survival to lay in an earthly harvest. Frost in the earth still reached to a depth of four feet when they began to dig irrigation ditches and prepare the land for planting. Before the end of March native inhabitants saw a strange sight in their mountain valley as three plows and harrows went into full operation. On 15 April the missionaries reported with satisfaction that they had "sowed some 80 bushels of wheat, five bushels of barley, two bushels of oats, and about two bushels of peas, making in all about 90 bushels of seed grain sowed since the 28th of March, seventeen days' labor." And they did all this "with teams which were weak from the severity of the winter."[32]

Nor were the animals the only ones suffering from the lack of food. On 20 April Gilbert Belnap rose to preach that Sunday when he fainted and fell backward. "From the twentieth of March my mode of living had been very poor," he said. "My food consisted of milk and roots and but very little meat." He had performed his share of work, he said, "yet it came very near costing me my life." After this "public ex[h]ibition of suffering," he went on, "the situation of the Fort was inquired into and those who had no bread were supplied with a scanty allowance."[33]

To prepare a hoped-for harvest for the oven, Belnap joined P. G. Tay-

[32]Salmon River Mission Journal, 16 April 1856.

[33]Autobiography of Gilbert Belnap, 20 April 1856.

lor, Moore, and Galliher in exploring nearby canyons for timber suitable to build a gristmill. On 29 April 1856 men and teams began hauling logs from the south canyon for the new mill as others worked to fence newly planted fields. In June new arrival Joseph Harker was hard at work "digging a mill seat."[34] To divert the river into the mill, he and Abraham Zundel dug the millrace. In early July the frame went up for "a building 20 feet square by about 13 feet high" to house the mill.[35] Cummings arrived that month "to work on the mill with Bro. Moore who was the Mill write." By 16 August the pair had "got the mill so far completed as to turn the water on the wheel, which performed very well."[36] Three days later cheers went up as "the mill did its first grinding."[37]

By then, however, there was little wheat for the facility to crush and even more mouths for it to serve, not counting the always-hungry natives begging for bread. On 15 May Joseph Parry had arrived with twenty-seven men, eleven wagons, twenty yoke of oxen, and seventeen cows to strengthen the Mormon expansion into Oregon Territory. The party numbered twenty new missionaries to the northern tribes, called at the church's April general conference.[38] Most of the newcomers were untested members of the faith averaging in age just over thirty, several years younger than the first company. But like their predecessors, they were a reflection of the millennial religion's rapid spread in the United States and Europe.

Eight were foreign-born, while the remainder hailed from the same number of states. Six, the most from any one place, came from England: Sylvanus Collett, admired for his heroic physique, age nineteen; Thomas Corless, twenty-three; Thomas Day, Jr., forty-one; the aforementioned Joseph Henry Harker, the bishop of West Jordan, thirty-eight; John Preece, forty-five; and James John Walker, twenty-three. They also numbered Alexander Hill, forty-five, from Scotland, and Canadian William

[34]Joseph Harker Journal, 20 June 1856. The term "mill seat" originally referred to the best location for a water-driven mill, usually a place where the river fell sharply over a short distance. Over time, it came to mean the foundation for a mill.

[35]Ibid., 2 July 1856.

[36]Biography and Journals of Benjamin Franklin Cummings, 14 July and 16 August 1856.

[37]Salmon River Mission Journal, 19 August 1856. The exact location of the mill is unknown, but it was apparently on Lemhi River south of the fort.

[38]Returnees from 1855 parties were Parry, Ezra Barnard, Nathaniel Leavitt, George W. Hill, B. H. Watts, William Batchelor, and Joseph Bowen.

Bailey Lake, thirty. Of the rest, six came from New York or New England and the rest came from Pennsylvania, Ohio, Tennessee, Illinois, and Missouri.

Twelve were married, eight of them with dependent children, and at least two had more than one wife.[39] Henry Alanson Cleveland, the oldest at age forty-six, was joined by his son, Henry Rogers Cleveland, twenty-one. Francis Marion Molen, a substitute for John R. Murdock from Lehi, was youngest at nineteen. The party also included Thomas Marsh Abbott, twenty-four; Clifton Smith Browning, thirty-five; Hathron Chauncy Hadlock, thirty-one; George McBride, twenty-nine; Wallace Marshall McIntire, twenty; Jacob Miller, twenty; William J. Perkins, forty; and William Montgomery Shaw, twenty-nine. Thomas Bingham, a thirty-one-year-old Mormon Battalion veteran, would later leave his name on Bingham Canyon in Salt Lake Valley. The party also included hired hand William Bard, about whom little is known. Two of the twenty would be killed by Indians.

Jacob Miller: We Tried to Head Them Off

These arrivals more than tripled the number of laborers and gave an immediate boost in output in various enterprises, "such as irrigating grain, hauling timber, ploughing and various other work."[40] But the reinforcements could do little to stretch the growing season for land that stood over 4,400 feet above sea level. "The wheat grows very slowly," Moore wrote on 13 May. "Some of the brethren are out of bread-stuff, and the harvest seems distant, yet all seem to enjoy themselves well and look forward to a day of plenty," he added hopefully. Thirteen days later, his optimism turned to despair. "The grasshoppers have commenced to devour the wheat on the bottom lands," he said.[41]

Journal of Jacob Miller.

June 2, 1856, we commenced fighting grasshoppers, which continued to the 23rd. Grasshoppers were very thick. We tried to head them off the crops with water ditches. We caught them morning and evening in sacks. We dug holes in the grain fields five to eight rods apart and drove them into the

[39]Joseph Harker and William Bailey Lake.

[40]Salmon River Mission Journal, 25 May 1856.

[41]Ibid., 13 and 26 May 1856.

holes with brush, five to ten men forming a circle to drive them in and then bury them, sometimes a peck of them in one hole. Two such sets were working part of the time. The grasshoppers destroyed most of the crop.

For three weeks from dawn to sundown all hands defended their young grain against the ugly invaders, but even as they fought, a capricious natural environment dealt them a second late spring surprise. "There was quite a severe frost last night," Moore said on 11 June, "which destroyed much of the vegetables."[42] By the end of that disheartening month, their garden was gone and the grasshoppers had all but finished their destruction of the wheat crop. From living on boiled corn for weeks at a time, Joseph Harker became weak and "spit blood for some days."[43] Suffering from overwork and malnutrition, some of the first missionaries now became discouraged.

Thomas Smith: Onely One Thing They Are Good Fore

Without permission, the rebellious Belnap and eight others, two of them with their families, took off on the last day of June for Salt Lake Valley.[44] At Mud Lake, however, the backsliders ran into Mission President Thomas Smith heading back with nine others to assert his authority at the Salmon River colony. In his party were three tardy members of the year's missionary call-up: Pardon Knapp Webb, thirty-seven, and Henry Nebeker, thirty-eight, both from Payson, Utah; and blacksmith Richard B. Margetts, thirty-three, the seventh Englishman to join the northern Indian mission that year.[45] On arrival at Fort Limhi, Smith promptly reported the dissenters to Brigham Young in a letter carried by Pleasant Green Taylor and Lewis Shurtliff, who took off on horseback, one day ahead of a party that left the fort on 28 July to obtain supplies and return in the fall.[46]

---

[42]Ibid., 11 June 1856.

[43]Joseph Harker Journal, 16 July 1856.

[44]The make-up of this party: Belnap, captain, John W. Browning, Israel Clark and family, John Galliher, George R. Grant, Everet Lish, Charles McGary and family, William Perkins and William Shaw. It also included seven wagons, eleven yoke of oxen, all of the cows but one, and a half dozen horses.

[45]Other members of Smith's party were B. F. Cummings, Charles Dalton, William Burgess, David Stephens, Thomas Butterfield and Ira Ames.

[46]Members of the supply party were Francillo Durfee, William Brundage, George McBride, Ezra Barnard, H. C. Hadlock, Clifton S Browning, Charles Dalton, Henry Cleveland, Alexander Hill, Thomas Corless, Thomas Day, Henry Nebeker, and F. M. Molen.

SMITH TO YOUNG, 27 JULY 1856, BRIGHAM YOUNG PAPERS.

Salmon River Fort Limhi
July 27th. 1856

President Young

As thare will a company start tomorrow morning for Salt lake I thought I would drop a few lines to you to inform you of our healths [*sic*] and prospects of our mission I started from home the 16 of june in company with 9 others of the Bretheren for this place and arived here on the 9 of july in good health and had a prosperous journey before I got within 150 miles of this place I met some nine of the members of the mission on thare return home they had got fri[gh]tened because the grasshoppers had eat and distroyed a part of the grain and they thought they was certainly a going to starve if they stayed any longer thare names I will mention J W Browning G R Grant I J Clark J Galaher C MCGara G Bellknap Everett Lish W Perkins W Shaw that is some of these that we can get along without very well if you can think of any thing that they are good for any whare els for thare is onely one thing they are good fore here and that is to grumble and find fa[u]lt with every thing that is done Everet Lish has had the hand of fellow ship withdrawn from him on the account of repetadely [repeatedly] disobeying council and George R Grant and Wesly Browning is in the same fix as far as the bretheres feelings are conserned tho they have not had a tryel but thare is non[e] that I have herd express thare feelings but what say they never want to see them come back on the mission again I will not say any thing mor[e] at presant concerning them but if you want to know more about it [you can do so by] inquiring of Green Taylor who was left in charge while I was gon[e] and will present this to you every thing is write with the indiens and a good Spirit prevails thare has be[en] 100 baptised and thare is several that want to go to farming another season we have had bad luck with our farming opperitions [operations] this Seosen the grasshoppers has used up every thing except our wheat and the most of that but I think by being car[e]ful in harvesting we can save from 100 to a 150 bushels and I do not know but may raise some potatoes as the grasshoppers have mostly left and the potatoes have come up again I beleave this to be a good country for every thing that we have put in has don[e] first rate for the chance that it has had This company is in want of three more hands to assist them in getting back with thare loads and I will prepos [propose] the naims if it is agreeable to your mind I would like to have Milton D Hammond Ebenezar Robinson and James R Alred Reddins brother[47] thare is one thing that the bretheren wants to know very mutch and that is whether it is your intention to make a settlement here or not for if every thing is wright with your

[47]Milton D. Hammond, Ebenezer Robinson, and James Riley Allred, younger brother of Redden Alexander Allred.

> feelings thare is some that think that they can take care of thare famely better here than they can thare and if it should be according to your feelings to have some small famelyes come this fall give brother Taylor the nessessary instruction as he has the charge of the company I wish you to rite to me if conveneint by the company
>
> Thomas S Smith

As they awaited Young's reply and the return of the supply train, the colonists drew in their belts and salvaged, almost kernel by kernel, all they could of their ravaged crop. "We began gleaning the smutty wheat the grasshoppers had left," Jacob Miller said. "We cut it with a butcher knife, threshed it with a stock, washed the smut off in a tub, dried the wheat in an oven, ground it in a coffee mill, baked it, bran included, and had some bread once more," he went on. "Oh! What a treat!"[48] On being irrigated, their fields "again shot up new stalks and promised yet to afford some grain," Cummings reported. To stop raids on their horse herd, allegedly by Blackfeet, they also built a "commodious" corral out of adobe, or mud, "on the south side of the fort."[49]

Offsetting such hopeful developments was a decline in the spiritual harvest. Moreover the approach of fall saw other indications of native estrangement and potential sources of future trouble. On 8 September Lewis Shurtliff and John Leavitt arrived with a wagonload of twenty-seven bushels of salt with which to pickle fish, while others constructed a trap on the river to haul them in more efficiently. Soon after, B. H. Watts and Abraham Zundel left to deliver more horses to Salt Lake Valley. Nor was the flow of horses the only sign of an active and spreading trade with the Indians.

"Three Indians arrived for Horse Praire asking for Council for all the Indians to keep away from Capt Grant & his son John & to come here for their trade, and desired a writing to that effect to show the Indians so that they would be believed by them," B. F. Cummings said on 21 September. Acting as temporary clerk, Cummings went on, "Pres. Smith would only give them a certificate of membership & a Recommendation which seemed to satisfy them."[50] The request seemed to seek verification

[48]Journal of Jacob Miller, 11 August 1856.

[49]Biography and Journals of Benjamin Franklin Cummings, 14 July 1856. The remains of the corral walls can still be seen at the site, now owned by Ross and Sue Goddard.

[50]Salmon River Mission Journal, 21 September 1855. Mission clerk David Moore left on 11 September for Salt Lake Valley with John Leavitt and Pardon Webb.

of rumors among the natives that the mission sought to create a monopoly position in trade. Since reading was not a common Indian skill, Richard and Johnny Grant probably originated the stories. The papers Smith gave the converts only verified church membership and commended the holders as emissaries of the faith. But the question itself hardly signified improvement in already unfavorable relations with the region's white denizens, who wielded great influence over the tribes. It did point up the issue of trade as a source of misunderstanding and resentment.

Brigham Young: To Be Filled with the Holy Ghost

Meanwhile as some sowed the wind on Salmon River, Mormon leaders far to the south in Utah did the same on a regional scale, vowing "to become a sovereign State in the Union, or an independent nation by ourselves."[51] After Congress refused to consider their bid for entry into the Union as the State of Deseret,[52] that September they launched a great reformation to cleanse Israel and merit divine intercession. The theocratic territory moved toward a potential confrontation with its parent republic. Led by firebrand Jedediah M. Grant, Brigham Young's second counselor, the spiritual conflagration spread confessions, rebaptisms, and an intrusive inquisition, called "the catechism," to probe the obedience of the faithful.[53] "Green" Taylor brought notice of the flaming revival when he returned on 4 November with the supply train.

Young to Smith, 7 October 1856, Brigham Young Papers.

President's Office
G. S. L. City Octr 7th 1856

Col Thomas S. Smith.

Dear Brother,

As Bro Green Taylor is about to return to his mission at Fort Limhi, I considered that I would write you a few lines to let you know concerning our welfare, and make such suggestions for your benefit as shall occur to me.

---

[51]Brigham Young, *Deseret News,* 17 September 1856, 220.

[52]A synonym for the theocratic Kingdom of God.

[53]For more on the 1856 Reformation, see Sessions, *Mormon Thunder: A Documentary History of Jedediah Morgan Grant,* 203–63; and Bigler, *Forgotten Kingdom: The Mormon Theocracy in the American West, 1847–1896,* 121–39.

Our conference closed this evening, there was an immense congregation, variedly estimated from 10 to 12,000. An excellent spirit prevailed, and we think that much good has been done: a general spirit of reformation rested upon the people; this caused our hearts to rejoice, and inspired us with renewed encouragement in behalf of the people, and of receiving the blessings of our God.

We have finished a baptismal font near the endowment house, which has been dedicated, and is now used for baptisms. Many are going forward renewing their covenants before the Lord. We trust that the spirit of reformation may prevail over the entire community. There is need enough for it; for truly the people were falling asleep; becoming covetous, and the spirit of apostacy appeared to be prevalent to considerable extent.

It is necessary that the saints should examine themselves, and know that they are inspired by the right spirit in order to help themselves on the right track, and continue to (it is their duty as well as privilege to do) be filled with the Holy Ghost, which will guide them in the way they should go.

In regard to your affairs, I do not deem it wisdom for any more persons to remain at that place, than are sufficient to maintain the post, until another harvest; neither for any more families to go; but if another company comes back this fall, that as many of the women as can return, and especially those who have children.

We do not know but Indian hostilities might extend to your neighborhood, in which case you are aware that all such persons had better be in some safe place. We have no impression, or information of this import, but feel it much the best policy to be on the safe side. We want you to keep all the men you have provision for, and not unnecessarily weaken the post. Indians you know are uncertain, and your safety requires vigilance, and the necessary precaution.

Three companies of the hand Carts have arrived, and two more consisting of near a thousand souls are yet on the plains, besides 100 ox wagons.

A Call has been made upon the people to go out to meet them with extra teams, clothing, provisions &c, which has been very liberally responded to, and we think of starting on Monday next with a small company on the same errand, they are quite late which requires this extra exertion on their behalf.[54]

We feel gratified bro Thomas with the exertions which that mission have made, and the good, and salutary influence which it has exercised over the

[54]Young did not accompany any of the relief parties. Two days before he dictated this letter, Young launched the rescue of the Willie and Martin handcart companies, mainly of emigrants from England and the Scandinavian countries, who had left the Mormon emigrating base at Iowa City too late in the season, depending on the Almighty to hold back the oncoming winter. In the greatest tragedy in America's move west, more than two hundred men, women, and children perished in the blizzards of an early winter.

Lamanites in that region. We hope, and pray that it may continue, and increase, and that you may be instrumental in accomplishing a good and a great work in behalf of the poor & forlorn descendants of faithful Abraham. That you may be enabled through the blessing of the Lord to save a portion of fallen Israel back to the knowledge of the Lord God of their fathers, that they may become a people in whom we can again take delight as in days of old.

Praying that you may be blessed with all those who are faithful on your mission, and that the Lord will preserve you, and give you wisdom commensurate with every duty devolved upon you, and finally grant you all that you in righteousness can desire.

I Remain Your Brother in the Gospel Covenant
Brigham Young

Besides news of the Reformation, Taylor brought eighteen missionaries, including five new ones and four reformed backsliders, plus supply wagons loaded with over six tons of flour and nearly 140 bushels of wheat.[55] The first-timers numbered two of the three men Thomas Smith had asked Young to send: twenty-five-year-old Milton D. Hammond and Ebenezer Robinson, Jr., age twenty-one, both natives of New York. The others were Mormon Lachonias Barnard, Ezra Barnard's brother, age eighteen; Owen T. Dix, twenty-nine; and Haskell V. Shurtliff, twenty-five. In keeping with Young's instructions to keep no more men than needed "to maintain the post," Smith gave ten missionaries permission to go home for the winter.[56]

Taylor's supply train also brought 1,445 pounds of salt, an amount that exceeded mission needs either for its own use or for trading. The size of the load pointed instead to the labors of six-foot-two Jacob Miller, known to the Indians as "Covhera Avonan" or "Tall Standing." A handy man with tools, Miller had almost as many other names as the skills he possessed. Natives who needed him to stock, resight or fix their guns came and asked for "Ida Naup" or "Gun Maker." And as curious Indians watched him work that summer at the main task to which Smith

[55]Reformed dissenters were Israel Clark, Gilbert Belnap, Charles McGary, and William Perkins. Besides Taylor, other returning missionaries included Francillo Durfee, Thomas Corless, George McBride, William Brundage, H. C. Hadlock, Francis Molen, and Thomas Day. John Galliher, John W. Browning, Everet Lish, and George R. Grant never returned to Fort Limhi.

[56]Thomas Bingham, William Burch, Thomas Butterfield, Henry A. Cleveland, Sylvanus Collett, George W. Hill, William Bailey Lake, Richard B. Margetts, Jacob Miller, and John Preece left on 10 November.

had assigned him, they called Miller "Owee Naup" or "Dish Maker." They probably did not understand that the vessels the tall missionary was turning out were "fish barrels in which to pickle salmon for our future use, here at the fort and to take home."[57]

In Utah Territory, white settlers were using advanced methods to harvest fish from Utah Lake, some thirty miles south of Great Salt Lake City. The fish were then cured and stored in barrels to be shipped to Mormon tables elsewhere. This had already become a major source of conflict with the natives of that region. For centuries the Utah tribe had depended on the freshwater body in Utah Valley, then one of the most productive fisheries in western America, for its main food source. The Bannocks and Shoshones of southeastern Oregon, whose survival depended on salmon, could hardly be expected to accept aggressive fishing by their new neighbors peacefully.

In the meantime, while Taylor's wagons carried "the spirit of the J. M. Grant reformation" to Salmon River,[58] Thomas Smith soon discovered that success in lighting the emotional fires of revival was usually gauged in inverse relation to the distance from Great Salt Lake—and few places were as removed as Fort Limhi. The day after Young's letter arrived, the mission president tried "to arrouse the brethern but the meeting passed off rather dull," Cummings observed. After fasting all day, "a better spirit was manifest" at candlelight when they met again, he continued. "The brothers seemed more lively and generally expressed a renewed determination and interest to do all in their power to build up the Kingdom of God."[59] In keeping with the Reformation ordeal, the missionaries were rebaptised and reconfirmed as members of the faith the next day.

Closely tied to the purpose of the Reformation was the commission that Pleasant Green Taylor carried in his head as he returned to Fort Limhi, an assignment too secret to be committed to writing. As the Great Basin theocracy prepared for independence and a potential showdown with the American republic, Brigham Young ordered him to contact the Hudson's Bay agent in charge and enter a bid to buy Fort Hall. While the

[57]Miller and Miller, eds., *Journal of Jacob Miller,* 33.

[58]Ibid., 34.

[59]Biography and Journals of Benjamin Franklin Cummings, 5 November 1856.

decline of the fur trade had forced abandonment of the trading post, the rise of a new political power in the Rocky Mountains gave the Snake River location new strategic importance. For not only did it overlook the northernmost immigration and communication routes to the West Coast, it was also the key to a move north in case the Kingdom of God failed to prevail in an expected confrontation with the United States.

Chapter 5

A Gathering Place for Israel

The above information when considered with Mormonism was very interesting to us as we could not help thinking that some day Bitter-Root valley as well as other portions of the country over east of the mountains would become the abode of the saints. — *Benjamin Franklin Cummings*

In 1834 an enterprising New England icemaker and member of the American Society for Encouraging the Settlement of the Oregon Territory built Fort Hall as a trading post on the left bank of Snake River, near present Pocatello, Idaho. Nathaniel Jarvis Wyeth unfurled the Stars and Stripes that year over his unfinished stockade, and named it honor of his oldest business partner, Henry Hall. Stung by this threat, Hudson's Bay Company immediately founded Fort Boise, also on Snake River, some three hundred miles farther west, and raised its crimson HBC banner which, some wags said, stood for "Here Before Christ." Three years later Wyeth sold out to the powerful British firm at a loss of $30,000 and went back to the ice business.

As the fur trade declined and a rising tide of overland emigration swept west, the post became "the trade center of a hungry land."[1] Hudson's Bay chief trader Richard Grant, a tall British veteran of the War of 1812, directed operations at Fort Hall assisted by two sons, Richard and John, during a period of dramatic change. The 1846 boundary settlement with Great Britain placed the Oregon border along the 49th parallel and introduced the rapid transition from the fur trade to commerce with emigrants on the Oregon and California trails. Debilitated by rheumatism, Grant took a medical discharge from the company in 1851 and hired Neil McLean McArthur, another Hudson's Bay representative, to carry on the daily work of trading with Indians and emigrants.

[1]Minto, "Reminiscences of Experiences on the Oregon Trail in 1844," 215.

McArthur in turn hired seventeen-year-old Louis Maillet, whom the Mormon Indian missionaries met in May 1855 at the Portneuf Bridge.[2]

Emigrant travel via Fort Hall peaked in 1849, the first year of the Gold Rush, when as many as ten thousand wagons rolled past the Snake River trading post. But that year Hudspeth's Cutoff opened a more direct route west from Soda Spring to Raft River, near present Malta, Idaho, bypassing Fort Hall. The same period saw a sudden drop in the London market for beaver fur. These changing fortunes led Hudson's Bay to abandon Fort Hall in 1855 as a center of trade and, in 1856, to the consternation of its native patrons, to shut down the post for good.

Brigham Young Bids for Fort Hall

While closure ended Fort Hall's short commercial life span, its strategic location on the Snake River Plain attracted the interest of a rising theocracy in the American West with a standing military tradition and a defensive attitude toward the American republic. The fort, or a similar post east of it, controlled the northernmost lines of communication and travel to the West Coast, especially since emigrant traffic had begun to by-pass Fort Bridger, purchased by the Mormons in 1853. Fort Hall overlooked the wagon road from the Oregon Trail on the north into Salt Lake Valley. And it commanded the natural lines of expansion north to the region Brigham Young coveted as "the key to this continent," the headwaters of the Missouri River and the transportation opportunities the waterway offered.[3]

B. F. Cummings: Visit to Bitter Root Valley

Reflecting Young's strategic vision was his decision in 1856 to acquire the Snake River trading post. The opportunity came that fall when Neil

[2]A fearless and romantic French-Canadian, Maillet once bared his breast and dared a drunken Nez Percé chief to shoot him. A friendly native struck the gun at the last moment to save his life. As a trail guide, Maillet on another occasion ordered the men of an emigrant party to charge hostile Indians who threatened the cattle. A sixteen-year-old girl from Philadelphia, the new bride of a young emigrant to California, went forward in the attack alongside her husband, determined to share his fate. They both survived. Years later, in recalling the episode, Maillet said: "Every man in the outfit instantly fell in love with her. As for myself . . . I love her still." See Maillet, "Historical Sketch of Louis R. Maillet," 4:197–228.

[3]Report of meeting with Brigham Young 6 September 1857, Wilford Woodruff Collection, MS 5506.

This view from the crest of Lemhi Pass, looking west, shows the trail up from Fort Limhi to the Continental Divide. Cummings and his party passed here in November 1856 on the way to Bitterroot Valley. Lewis and Clark crossed in 1805, going the other way. *Photo by Will Rusho.*

McArthur, Hudson's Bay's former agent at Fort Hall, told Pleasant Green Taylor at Great Salt Lake City that he hoped to sell the abandoned fort for the fur company. The missionary carried this word to Young who gave him a secret assignment to investigate the possible purchase of the property. On his return to Salmon River, Taylor and two Fort Limhi companions, Ebenezer Robinson and B. F. Cummings, rode north in November to the Bitterroot Valley, then a part of Washington Territory, to locate McArthur, who had taken up a new career as a rancher. They were directed to find out if the price was right for the church to complete the transaction. Cummings kept a record and made a map of their journey.

BIOGRAPHY AND JOURNALS OF BENJAMIN FRANKLIN CUMMINGS.

Nov. [1856] Brother P. G. Taylor, previous to leaving Salt Lake this fall, had some conversation with Mr. Mc Arthur, formerly of Fort Hall relative to the purchase of that place, as he (McArthur) was anxious to sell it for the

Hudson['s] Bay Fur Company to whom it belonged. Brother Taylor afterwards being advised by Pres. Young to make the purchase in as much as it could be done on reasonable terms concluded so to do and for the accomplishment of that purpose to make Mc Arther a visit in Bitter Root Valley whither he had gone.

Accordingly on the 13th inst he set out from Limhi accompanied by Brother Ebenezer Robinson and myself.

Nov. 13th. Left Limhi 11 A.M. Travelled east up Limhi creek kanyon 8 miles which brought us on to the divide between it and 2 creek kanyon. 3 miles further over several ridges and up and down several bad hills and we found ourselves on the summit of the Rocky Mountain range between the head of 2nd creek and Horse Prairie.[4] One mile down the east side of the Mountain which was tolerable steep brought us to the first waters of the Missouri a small creek emptying into Jefferson ~~creek~~ Fork of that river running east through the little valley called Horse Prairie. We continued on down the creek 6 miles and camped. We were accompanied over here by a young Indian who said he was going down the country below, to where there was some Indians camped for winter quarters, in search of a wife. We here also overtook an Indian family who was moving from Salmon River to the same place.

We found plenty of dry grass for our horses, but fuel was scarce, nothing but small willows. The evening was cold and clear. The creek mostly frozen over.

Fri. 14th. Cold and frosty last night. Start 8-1/2 A.M. Continue [on] an easterly course down the valley. 6 miles and passed the To-he-rone Butt[e], the head of a ridge that makes out across the valley from the north and resembles in appearance an Indian lodge although the name in Sho-shone signifies a California or Mountain Lion. Five miles further down we intersected the Flat head trail, now traveled by traders with wagons, communicating with Snake River Valley and Flathead Country. Which we took turning to the left, bearing a north west by north course.[5]

Horse Prairie is a small valley varying in width from 1 to 4 miles and I should judge from appearance that it must be 30 or 40 miles long. It is situated on one of the head branches of the Jeffersons Fork.[6] It is high and has the appearance of being very cold. The soil however is good and the grass abundant. It is bordered on either side by low hills, affording abundance of

[4]This is Lemhi Pass, crossed by Lewis and Clark in 1805, on the Continental Divide between the waters of the Pacific and Atlantic Oceans.

[5]Later called the Salt Lake Road, the Flathead Trail is followed today by a graveled road from Grant to Bannack City, Montana, then Route 278 to Wisdom. Lt. John Mullan first surveyed the trail for a wagon road in 1853.

[6]Horse Prairie Creek is a headwater of the Jefferson River, which joins the Madison and Gallatin rivers at Three Forks, Montana, to form the Missouri River.

To-he-rone, or "Mountain Lion" in the Shoshoni tongue, the distinctive butte on Horse Prairie Creek, a headwater of the Missouri River, where the trail from Fort Limhi meets the Flathead Trail. The Mormon party camped here in November 1856. *Photo by author.*

rich grazing for the numerous antelope and Mountain Sheep that frequent these regions. We followed the Flat head trail about 12 miles crossing a low hilly divide and came on to another creek run[n]ing South East which we followed up in a North North Westerly course and camped.[7]

The country round about seemed to consist of high bench land and low hills apparently surrounded by low Mountains, those on the west seemed covered with pine timber.

Sat. 15th. Froze hard last night. Morning cold and clear. Start 8-1.2 A.M. followed the wagon track which generally kept with the trail, bearing a northwest course 5 miles, crossing 3 small branches, then taking a westerly course, 2 miles brought us on to another divide. The ascent was very gradual. We now descended a hill, in some parts quite steep 1-1/2 miles in to Big Hole or Flat Spring Valley—About 1-1/2 miles further we came on to a small creek which we followed 4 miles in a northerly direction, then ascended on to a high point of bench keeping the same course—3 miles further and came on to a creek again—10 miles further down the valley in the same direction and camped.

[7]The Mormon party this day passed Grasshopper Creek, a tributary of the Beaverhead and future site of Bannack City, the first capital of Montana Territory, where prospectors six years later would make the region's first major gold discovery.

Big Hole is a valley from 5 to 10 miles wide east and west and 50 or 60 long. The Mountains on the south and west are covered with pine timber which in many places extends down to the valley. The mountains on the North and east are partially covered with timber.

Sun. 16th. The soil is good and grass abundant where it was not burnt. But the valley had the appearance of being high, bleak and cold. The ground was so full of Badger Holes that it was dangerous riding fast.

Last night clear and cold. Slept but little. Start 8-1/2 A.M. Continue down the valley 3 miles, then bore to the North west—Crossed the Main Creek of the valley which was from two to three rods wide and from 8 to 14 inches keep, with a smart current.[8] Mostly frozen over. We continued on 6 miles crossing several small branches on the ice, then ascended on to a bench keeping the same course 4 miles and descended onto another large creek running northeast which we crossed and immediately entered a large kanyon which at the mouth presented a forest of white mountain pine. The timber was small though very tall. As we ascended the timber began to disappear in the bottom of the kanyon, which soon became entirely clear except of small willows along the creek. The mountains and sides of the kanyon however were entirely covered with timber.

The ascent was very gradual and but little in the way to obstruct the passage of wagons.

We continued on up the kanyon 10 miles and camped. Found considerable snow in the kanyon from 4 to 10 inches.

Nov. Mon. 17th. Start 8 A.M. Commenced snowing about the same time. Traveled up the kanyon about 7 miles. The mountains appearing very low on each side. Here we left the kanyon and turned to the west up a very gradual ascent—1 mile to the summit of the Rocky Mountain range through a dense forest of the before mentioned timber.[9] The storm had now ceased and the sun shone out very pleasant. The snow here was about 14 inches deep but as Mc Arthur had passed along a few days before with three wagons and about a hundred head of cattle, we found the road pretty well broken. We now descended from the divide down a point of the Mountain about three miles, which in many parts was very steep and dangerous for our teams, into a large kanyon—abounding with Yellow or Norway pine of great size and heidth [height]. We followed down the canyon N.N.W. 6 miles to its mouth and entered a small valley called Rosses Hole.[10] Soon after leaving the mouth of the kanyon we crossed the main branch of Bitter-

---

[8]They forded Big Hole River, a tributary of Jefferson River, near present Wisdom, Montana.

[9]The trio crossed the Continental Divide at 6,941-foot Gibbons Pass to return to the Columbia River drainage.

[10]Ross' Hole is named after Hudson's Bay trader Alexander Ross, who was snowed in at that location more than a quarter century before and lost most of his livestock. An earlier historic event happened in 1805 when the Lewis and Clark Expedition met the Flathead Indians in this small upper valley of the Bitterroot River.

Root River which runs west thru this valley near its south border and enters a deep kanyon where it passes through the mountains to Bitter-Root Valley. The stream here was about 2-1/2 or 3 rods wide.

We continued a northerly course about 8 miles up an open hilly valley with low mountains on each side when we again entered a forest of yellow pine and commenced the ascent of a very steep hill. One mile brought us on to the summit of a very narrow ridge. Here we turned to the west, traversing the ridge winding in various directions crossing several notches or low places and ascending considerable for about 5 miles which brought us on to the highest point of the ridge. From here we had a partial view of the point of Bitter Root Valley, which lay to the west of, and far below us.

We now descended a very steep hill about a half a mile and proceeded along the ridge about a half mile further when night overtook us and we camped. The mountain was thinly covered with yellow pine. The kanyon below appeared a dense forest. The ground was partially covered with snow—Plenty of grass where it was bare. Considerable of the grass not green, no water.

Tues. 18th. Last night was quite mild until near morning when the wind commenced blowing and the snow began to fall. Se[e]ing it was going to storm we concluded that the sooner we got off from the mountain the bett[e]r. So we packed up and started about an hour before day.

We groped our way along the ridge in a northerly course through the darkness as well as we could for about 3-1.2 miles, descending considerable in places. When the light of a stormy morning succeeded in dispelling the thick darkness with which we were enshrouded, enabling us to see surrounding objects and to form some conclusion relative to our position. We now turned to the left (west) down a point of the Mountains about 2-1.2 miles. Very steep in places, and found our Selves in Bitter-Root Valley, probably about 10 miles from its head.—Our Snow storm by this time having turned to rain. The valley here is about two miles wide. As we descended the mountain we passed a large band of Indian horses in charge of a young Indian who was herding them. We spoke to him about it but could not make ourselves understood.

Homeland of the Flatheads

Brigham Young's emissaries from the arid Great Basin marveled at the grandeur of the homeland of the Flathead Indians as they rode north down the valley of Bitterroot River, where "for many generations" a proud people had been "born, raised, lived, died, and been buried."[11]

[11]Lansdale to Nesmith, 22 September 1857, Sen. Exec. Doc. 11 (35-1), 1858, 666. The name Flathead set the tribe apart from the Northwest Indians who practiced ornamental skull deformation. In contrast, the Flatheads preferred to leave their domes as nature had formed them. They never used this name, but called themselves "Salish," or "the people."

From the south, near present Conner, Montana, the valley extended more than ninety miles to the river's mouth at today's Missoula and reached widths of up to twenty miles or more. Girdled on three sides by high mountains and open only on the north, Bitterroot Valley was a fortress, designed by nature and fiercely defended by fewer than five hundred Flatheads against their more numerous enemies, the Blackfeet.[12]

Cummings, Taylor, and Robinson were neither the first of their kind nor the first of their faith to see the northern stronghold of the Flatheads. At the request of the natives, Belgian Jesuit Father Pierre Jean de Smet came with two priests and four lay brothers in 1841 to found St. Mary's Mission at present Stevensville. He planted the region's first crops and with Father Anthony Ravalli, after whom the county is named, built a gristmill there in 1845. Five years later, John Owen, then age thirty-one, a sutler with the Mounted Rifle regiment at Cantonment Loring, purchased the abandoned mission, built a stockade, and named his new trading post Fort Owen. The earliest Mormons to visit the valley were stock traders who acquired worn-out cattle from emigrants on the overland trails and took them to the valley for fattening and resale.[13]

B. F. Cummings: The Most Picturesque and Romantic Scenery

The agents for Brigham Young who rode down the Bitterroot in November 1856 took particular note of the valley's agricultural potential. Before them they saw fertile land that lay a thousand feet below the elevation of Great Salt Lake Valley and promised a longer growing season with abundant water and timber. They may have foreseen that the valley would become a center for the production of grain, hay, sugar beets, fruit, and dairy products as it is today. In the meantime, Cum-

[12]Indian Agent Richard Lansdale in 1857 estimated that the Flatheads in Bitterroot Valley numbered about four hundred natives with some four thousand horses and one thousand cattle. He said that the other Salish tribes on the west and north, the Pend d'Oreilles and Kootenais, added up to about 1,300.

[13]They included George and Frank Knowlton, brothers-in-law of William H. Hooper, future Utah delegate to Congress; Arch and Alma Williams, brothers of Thomas S. Williams, Hooper's controversial business partner; and E. V. Van Etten, livestock agent for Brigham Young.

mings labored for words to do it justice as he continued his account of their journey.

BIOGRAPHY AND JOURNALS OF
BENJAMIN FRANKLIN CUMMINGS, NOVEMBER 1856.

We turned to the right down the valley about a mile and a half and crossed a creek which runs out of the mountains from the east. Here we halted and turned out our horses to graze while brother Taylor and myself went in search of the Indian camp to see if we could find out anything relative to the whereabouts of McArthur. We followed up the river about 1-1/2 miles and found a lodge belonging to a Ponderay, the owner of the horses we had seen.[14] We learned from a squaw who spoke Shoshone also some little English that McArthur was about a days ride down the Valley. So we returned to our horses which we had left in charge of brother Robinson; it having stoped raining we again mounted and pursued our way down the valley about a due north course. We traveled about a mile and crossed the river which was 5 to 6 rods wid[e] and 18 inches of water in the deepest place, with quite a rappied [rapid] current. The river here runs close to the bluffs on the east side of the valley.

We now entered a beautiful bottom, interspersed with large groves of beautiful yellow pine and openings of prairie. The groves being entirely free from underbrush or fallen timbir [*sic*] and the ground which was even and smoothe covered with a luxuriant growth of grass though now dry and white. The Soil generally in this part of the valley appeared to be tolerable good though in some places hard and gravelly.

We traversed this bottom about ten miles. Crossing several beautiful creeks, when our road again led us back on to the east side of the river, which was much larger here on account of the numerous creeks emtying [*sic*] in above.

We now traveled about 5 miles mostly on the bluffs keeping the Indian trail and leaving the wagon road which crossed the river several times; the river running near the bluffs on the east side of the valley.

We now descended from the bluffs on to a beautiful prairie where the valley widens out several miles to the east. Here we were overtaken by a furious snow storm, which completely obscured our view of surrounding objects. We groped our way along the trail amid the driving storm, for about half an hour, when as if by magic, the snow ceased falling, the clouds burst asunder and the sun shone out in all its splendor, displaying to our astonished vision, the most picturesque and romantic scenery, I had

[14]A common rendering of Pend d'Oreille, which means "ear pendant." The Pend d'Oreilles are closely related to the Flatheads, Kalispels, and Kootenais. These tribes comprise the Salishan language family.

ever beheld. We found ourselves in the midst of a praireis [*sic*] several miles in extent, smoothe and even as if it were the production of art, carpeted with rich growth of bunch grass and gently inclining toward the river.

At a short distance from the road to the right was a short ascent to a low bench, extending several miles to the east, equally as smoothe as the bottom and laden with an abundant covering of the same, while beyond were low hills also presenting a smoothe grassey surface. Succeeded by those of greater dimensions. Whose smoothe verdant surfaces were interspersed with occasional groves of pine. These in turn being succeeded by low mountains, backed by those of higher order and covered with a dark mantle of the same kind of timber. While beyond, far in the distance and rising high above could be seen the dark summit ridge of the mighty Rocky Mountain Range enveloped in one continuous covering of the same never fading pine.

To our left at the distance of from one to two miles could be seen Bitter-Root River wending its devious course to the north, through a skirt of cottonwood and other small timber, dotted now and then with a high crest of yellow pine. Succeeded beyond by groves of pine interspersed with bountiful prairies and threaded across with numerous streams of pure water. Which came leaping joyously from a stupenduous [*sic*] chain of mountains rising abruptly from the western border of the valley to a gigantic heidth and covered with the same saple garments as those on the east. Still beyond these could be seen the lofty summits of other mountains peering ov[e]r the heads of their front rank, in to the valley, like so many spies intent upon watching the movements going on in the world below.[15]

The scenery was grand and sublime in the highest degree. The variety displayed in the surrounding mountains. The arrangements of timber and prairie in the valley, together with the river and its tributaries presents nature in a manner inimitable by the hand of art and calculated to gratify the most romantic imagination.

About three miles further we crossed another small creek and camped.

Wed. 19th. Started 8-1/2 A.M. Traveled over a prairie of rich soil about 4-1/2 miles and came to Mc Arthurs place—consisting of several log cabbins, sheds caraals [corrals] etc.[16]

---

[15]Bitterroot Valley is guarded on the east by the Sapphire Mountains and on the west by the Bitterroot Range, which rises some 9,000 feet.

[16]McArthur's residence, some twelve miles south of Fort Owen, was the abandoned Cantonment Stevens, built in 1853 by Lt. John Mullan as a base camp for northern railroad explorations. John Owen had returned home the day before from a trip to Fort Benton. The Mormon party did not visit his trading post and Owen does not mention their coming to Bitterroot Valley. See Dunbar and Phillips, eds., *The Journals and Letters of Major John Owen, Pioneer of the Northwest, 1850–1871,* 1:151.

Here we found Mr. Mc Arthur, Mr. Addams formerly Indian agent here and 8 or 10 other whites mostly in the employ of Mc Arthur.[17]

We were hospitably received by Mr. McArthur who entertained us as well as his circumstances would admit. After some conversation between him and brother Taylor concerning Fort Hall he concluded that he was not prepared to make the sale of that place in a manner that would be safe to the purchaser and wishes a postponement of the business until he could get further instructions from the company, which he would endeavor to do in the course of the winter and as he was going to Salt Lake in the spring he would pass by Limhi and let brother Taylor know what he could do.

Nov. [date not entered] The valley here was about 10 miles wide, the soil appeared rich but we were informed that the land on the opposite side of the river was the best. We also were informed that the valley extended about 40 miles further down to the junction of Bitter-Root and Hells Gate river.[18]

That the country below was similar in appearance to what we had seen with the exception of richer soil and more timber. That the country down about Hells Gate was open for settlement by virtue of a treaty made with the Indians by the Government that the upper part of the valley was talked of for an Indian Reservation, but not yet decided upon.[19]

We also learned that the northern railroad survey passed over the divide of the Rocky Mountains from Fort Benton on the Missouri down Hells Gate river across the north end of the valley west. That it was only 200 miles from the mouth of Hells Gate river across to Fort Benton, and 270 from there to Fort Union the present head of navigation on the Missouri and from Surveyors reports which I saw, that the Missouri could be navigated 30 miles from Fort Benton by steam boatts [*sic*] of the lightest

---

[17]Thomas Adams came to Bitterroot Valley with Lt. John Mullan in 1853 as an artist for the Northern Pacific Railroad Survey. Governor Stevens named him special Indian agent to the Flathead Indians in 1854, a position he held only a year. Later as a miner and trader he became one of Montana Territory's prominent citizens.

[18]The location of today's Missoula, Montana. Earlier known as the Hell Gate, this river is now Clark Fork of the Columbia River.

[19]While the Flatheads did not then realize it, the treaty that Gov. Isaac Stevens negotiated on 16 July 1855 opened the entire Bitterroot Valley, including its upper reaches, to white settlement and relocated the Flatheads and the two other Salishan tribes well to the north along the Jocko and Flathead rivers. Upon conclusion of the negotiations at Council Grove, some nine miles west of present Missoula, the great Flathead chief, Victor, only signed the pact on the condition that the "Great Father," the U.S. president, would come himself and decide that the above location would be a better place for his tribe than its preferred Bitterroot Valley homeland. After appearing to accept this condition, Stevens, in effect, ignored it and took advantage of Flathead friendship for the U.S. He shoved through a treaty that established the combined reservation in its present location south of Flathead Lake. Chief Alexander of the Pend d'Oreilles, or Kalispels, and Michelle of the Kootenais also signed the treaty, which the U.S. Senate ratified on 8 March 1859. See Kappler, comp., *Indian Affairs: Laws and Treaties*, 2:722–25. Stevens was killed during the Civil War at the Battle of Chantilly in 1862. His name lives on at Stevensville in Bitterroot Valley, where historic St. Mary's Mission, founded in 1841, and Fort Owen, established in 1850, are located.

B. F. Cummings's maps of the route from Fort Limhi to Bitterroot Valley submitted to Brigham Young with his report of the venture to investigate the purchase of Fort Hall.
Courtesy of the Church Archives, The Church of Jesus Christ of Latter-day Saints.

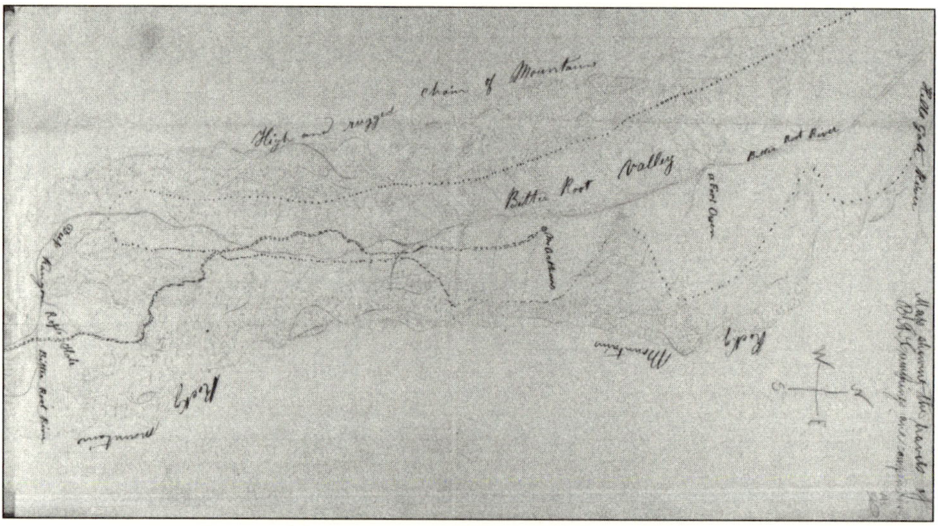

draught, and that there was a good rout for a waggon road from Fort Benton to the Mouth of Hells Gate River. That the present cost of transportation from St. Louis to Fort Union was 5 cents per pound and from that place to Fort Benton by flat boats was 7 cents, which of course would be much reduced by the increase of business and having the transportation made all the way up by steam boats.

The above information when considered with Mormonism was very interesting to us as we could not help thinking that some day Bitter Root valley as well as other portions of the country over east of the mountains would become the abode of the saints.[20]

Nov. Thur. 20th. 10-1/2 A.M. took leave of our host and started on our return, feeling that it would not be safe to stay to explore the country any further notwithstanding we felt very much inclined to do so, as the snow was gathering in the mountains and one nights storm might shut us in for the winter.

We traveled up the Valley about 23 miles and camped.

Fri. 21st. Start 8 A.M. passed over the first mountains and camped at the foot of the next. Several inches of snow had fallen on the mountains since we crossed the first time. The weather was cold and squally.

Sat. 22nd. Light snow falling most of the night. Start 7-1/2 A.M. Crossed over the 2d mountain and camped about 4 miles from the mouth of long kanyon, in Big Hole Valley.

Sun 23d. Snowed part of the night. Morning very cold. Start 7-1/2 A.M. Stormy most of the day. Cross the next divide and camp on a small creek about 3-1/2 miles from the summit by a small grove of dry Quaking Asp.

Mon. 24th. Start 7-1/2 A.M. Morning cold and clear. About 4 inches of snow on the ground. Kept the wagon road about 6 miles, then turned to the right a little across the hills to Horse Pairie which we struck about 4 or 5 miles above the road. Found the country very broken and bad traveling. Although we gained several miles in the distance, it was overbalanced by the loss of time ocasioned by the roughness of the rout.

We camped a little below To-he-rone bute 2 P.M. We met here some Indians from Salmon River. Two lodges camped by us.

Tues 25th. Morning extremely cold. Start 9 A.M. Cross the mountain pass down 2 Creek Kanyon into Salmon River Valley and arrive at the Fort about 5 P.M.

Found the brethern all well.

---

[20]That this information was also certain to interest Brigham Young is shown by his open letter in 1855 "To Those Who Are Engaged in Freighting on The Western Waters." Pointing out that "steamboats of heavy burden and deep draft have made annual trips for the fur companies far up the Missouri," Young called for "a new field of enterprise" to transport goods by the waterway to the nearest possible point from Mormon settlements "by boats of the lightest available draft." He proposed to build a fort at the head of navigation to receive such shipments and move them the rest of the way by wagon. See *Deseret News*, 21 November 1855, 5:37.

An Express to Young

By mid-January 1857, mail riders Baldwin Watts and Abraham Zundel still had not come to make the fall delivery and carry a report on Taylor's mission back to Utah.[21] Unwilling to wait longer, Thomas Smith "proposed that a company should start for Utah to inform President Brigham Young of brother Taylor's and company's doing in regard to Fort Hall and the prospects of the Flat Head country."[22] On 20 January, "horses were traded for and it was decided that Prest. Smith, P. G. Taylor, L. W. Shirtliff and Lachonias Barnard should be the persons to go." They left at noon two days later "with some ten or twelve head of horses. L. Barnard having traded for several head from the Indians."[23] A January thaw had melted the snow, but all knew that it was a dangerous season for travel in the mountains.

Milton Hammond: Belnap Traded for a Cow

Left in charge at Fort Limhi, B. F. Cummings quickly discovered that the mission president's authority, received by the "laying on of hands," was not easily delegated. At the 29 January prayer meeting, the independent-minded Israel Clark came out against the faith's intrinsic doctrine of "obedience to counsel" and advocated instead the radical idea "of every person judging for themselves whether the counsel was right," Cummings said. "Feeling it my duty I arose and reproved him for his seditious teaching which made him very angry." Before long, Gilbert Belnap joined Clark in defying the acting mission head. "It seems as though the powers of hell were let loose on us," Cummings said.[24] The issue soon came to a head.

Salmon River Mission Journal.

Sunday Feby 22. G. Belnap traded for a cow with Ben Simonds a Delaware Indian in presence of another Indian which was a direct transgression of the Rules of the Mission.[25] Pres. Cummings called him in question for it. He Belnap showed a willful and stubbourn Spirrit. I. J. Clark also took up in behalf of Belnap. This state of affairs seems to have continued until the

[21]The first mail of the year to Fort Limhi did not arrive until 25 March when Zundel and Charles Dalton delivered it.

[22]Salmon River Mission Journal, 18 January 1857.

[23]Ibid., 20 and 21 January 1857.

[24]Biography and Journals of Benjamin Franklin Cummings, 29 January and 8 February 1858.

[25]A Delaware, Ben Simonds was chief of a mixed band of Bannocks and Shoshones, who adroitly played both sides in conflicts between Mormons and their enemies to the benefit of his followers.

11th of March when the parties i e Belnap & Clark was brought before the mission and the hand of fellowship was withdrawn from them. They then arose & made a full confession when it was voted that they be rebaptised & received again into fellowship upon the Mission. This is the substance of the minutes kept of the affair by M. D. Hammond. D. Moore Clk.

Lewis Shurtliff: The Blood from Our Horses Legs

While Cummings struggled with disobedient spirits, the party of four men and a dozen horses waged a desperate fight of their own to overcome a wilderness environment and carry his report and maps on Bitterroot Valley to Brigham Young. Lewis Shurtliff described the midwinter journey.

Life and Travels of Lewis Warren Shurtliff.

On the twenty second of January Eighteen hundred fifty seven I started in Company with Thomas S. Smith, P. G. Taylor, and Lachoneam [Lachonias] Barnard for Salt Lake. The weather was fine and the snow nearly all of[f] the ground, but as we neared the divide the snow became deep and it was with great difficulty that we could cross the Divide.[26] And to add to our difficulties a dence [*sic*] fog settled over us which prevented us from following the course that we wished to follow, this almost discouraged Mr. Barnard but we continued our journey until we arrived at Muddy Lake. Here I rode a wild horse and got thrown of[f]. When we arrived at Medicine Lodge Crick the snow was three feet deep and here for the first time I saw that all were discouraged and we fully made up our minds to live on horse flesh a good portion of our journey; after wading through the snow for some days we reached the ten mile stre[t]ch. Here it cleared up and the fog disappeared. The snow began to soften and when we reached Snake river it began to rain and in the morning the water was an inch deep in our bed. Crossed Snake River on the Ice. Continued our journy without interruption. Crossing the Portneuf and rass fork [Ross Fork] I was much displeased with one of our party and expressed myself accordingly.[27] The President rebuked me and I took the same very ill indeed.

In crossing the divide it was extremely cold and the snow was drifted fearfully.[28] And as we passed down Malad Valley the snow [was] four feet deep and our trail could be followed by the blood from our horses legs but after travel day after day at the slow rate of three or four miles per day we

[26]The divide between the waters of Lemhi River and Birch Creek.

[27]An obvious reference to Lachonias Barnard.

[28]The northern rim of the Great Basin, which divides the waters of the interior drainage and Snake River.

> ar[r]ived at Bro Barnards on the ninth of Feby. when we heard of the death of Jedadiah M. Grant.[29] On the tenth inst. we arrived at Calls fort[30] tired and hungry but we could not get to stop with them and were under the necessity of traveling four miles farther to Bro John Gibbs[31] where we found plenty to eat and a kind reception. On the Eleventh we rode to Willow Creek; the snow all of[f] the ground. Took dinner at Bro Zondels.[32] After dinner we rode home. Found all well.

Soon after reaching his father's home at Ogden, Shurtliff "attended fast meeting," as he had often done before going to Salmon River, and ran into the emotional firestorm called the Reformation. Suddenly he was put off by "the most vulgar preaching . . . that I ever heard." Nor was the slender Indian missionary alone in his repugnance. "Many were disgusted," he went on, "and left the house." Disgusted or not, there was no escape from the fires of reform. Along with others of the faith at that time he was "catechised" to lay bare his offenses.[33] Then he "went to the Baptising," where he "saw many rebaptised" for the remission of their sins and restoration of church membership.[34]

Brigham Young Looks North

Even as a guilty people was purified in the fires of the Reformation, their leader kept his options open in the event they failed to measure up to the higher standards necessary to merit divine favor for his bid to win

---

[29]The firebrand of the 1856 Reformation, Jedediah M. Grant, second counselor to Brigham Young, died at age forty on 1 December 1856 of typhoid and pneumonia after exhorting and baptizing in cold mountain waters as winter came on.

[30]Next to Barnard's Fort, the northernmost outpost of early Utah Territory, Call's Fort was located some seven miles north of Brigham City, just south of today's Honeyville. Constructed by Anson Call in 1855, the original fort was an adobe house surrounded by a stone wall three feet thick, six feet high, and 120 feet square.

[31]Englishman John Gibbs was the first to settle in the vicinity of Call's Fort. At age forty, he and George Foster located their families there in 1852.

[32]Sixty-year-old Jacob Zundel, a native of Germany, and his wife, Sarah, lived at Willow Creek, now named Willard, just south of Brigham City, Utah. They were the parents of Salmon River missionary Abraham Zundel, the express rider.

[33]The so-called catechism that was administered by the "teachers" included such questions as: Have you ever committed adultery? Have you ever spoken evil of Authorities or anointed of the Lord? Have you ever betrayed your brethren? Have you ever stolen or taken anything that was not your own? Have you ever took [*sic*] the name of God in Vain? For one version, see Ekins, *Defending Zion: George Q. Cannon and the California Mormon Newspaper Wars of 1856–1857*, 216–18. For more on this interrogation see Sessions, *Mormon Thunder: A Documentary History of Jedediah Morgan Grant*, 220–21.

[34]Life and Travels of Lewis Warren Shurtliff, February 1857.

independence from the United States. At the start of the great revival in 1856 Brigham Young had instructed Pleasant Green Taylor to investigate purchasing Fort Hall. As early as 13 January 1857 he had told Utah Chief Arapeen that he was "going North with a company of my brethren next spring, and if You can leave and go we would like to have you with us."[35] And just before reading Cummings's report on Bitterroot Valley, he wrote Thomas Smith that he was "going to the North country this spring & purpose paying you a visit."[36] As most federal officials took flight to report that the territory was in a state of rebellion, Young's interest in the north country as a sanctuary in the event that Israel failed to gain a sovereign position only seemed to grow.

Less than a week after receiving the Flathead country report, on 22 February Young announced before the congregation in the Tabernacle at Great Salt Lake that he would travel north as soon as the weather allowed to Fort Limhi. Named that Sunday was a "large number" of Utah's top religious, military, and settlement leaders "to accompany prest B. Young to Salmon River in Oregon."[37] Unlike his journeys south each year, this trip would not include the customary stopovers at most settlements along the way. At a meeting of Mormon leaders later that day, Apostle Wilford Woodruff said:

> The Journal & travels of Benjamin F Cummings to Bitter Root Valley was read which was interesting. President Young said I would abandon the road that we have contemplated taking & cross at the south pass or wind River Chain. We will find a good pass there. The price of freight will come down when settelments are made in that Land. There is a good place there to make a settelment of the saints. I can tell you that we intend to fill many places yet if they will let us alone. Brother Cummings says that the mountains are much higher than here. That shows that the vallies are lower than here. Those Places are filled with streams & the streams with fish & the fish with eggs.[38]

---

[35]Young to Arrapeen, Chief of the Utahs, 13 January 1857, Brigham Young Papers. Also see Young to Cannon, 31 January 1857, Box 21, Folder 2, Moorman Collection.

[36]Young to Smith, 3 February 1857, Brigham Young Papers. While Smith and Taylor reportedly reached Salt Lake Valley about 12 February, one or both may have ridden ahead to deliver their report, prompting Young's decision to visit Fort Limhi. The first mail riders from Utah that year reached the fort on 25 March. They said they had been on the trail thirty-one days, having left "some eight days" after Smith and companions had reached Mormon settlements. The date of Young's letter indicates it was dictated before he received the report on the Fort Hall purchase and exploration of Bitterroot Valley.

[37]Brooks, ed., *On the Mormon Frontier: The Diary of Hosea Stout,* 2:623; Journal History, 22 February 1857.

[38]Kenney, ed., *Wilford Woodruff's Journal,* 5:26

But Bitterroot Valley offered more than fish eggs, Young told Apostle George A. Smith, then in Washington, D.C., the day after he announced his northern trip. It was also "very favorable for pasture, fish, soil, timber & climate."[39] The more he thought about the north country the more his interest appeared to grow. Writing to Apostle John Taylor in New York, he reported that the president of the Salmon River mission "speaks favorably of the Flat head valley 100 miles no. of them; and from all we can learn, many portions of the British possessions about 500 miles NO of this, and west of Lake Superior, are very good for climate, soil, water, game, fish Wood & furs, and there is, or may be, direct Water communication from this Lake to England."[40]

"Utah": To Join the Mormons in a War Against the Government Forces

From its early days, the millennial movement commonly known as Mormonism had attracted such intense outside interest and found it so difficult to keep its plans secret that it had adopted the creed: "Mind Your Own Business." But its opponents never paid much attention to this advice. So it was that less than two weeks after Young announced his trip north, a *New York Times* correspondent in Great Salt Lake City, identified only by the pseudonym "Utah," wrote on 5 March a surprisingly complete report on the journey, including much speculation as well as new information. While the writer's identity cannot be determined for certain, there can be little doubt he was a federal officer in Utah, possibly U.S. Indian Agent Garland Hurt or David A. Burr, the brother of mountaineer Frederick H. Burr, who worked for their father David H. Burr, surveyor general of Utah. Government officials by this time had come to distrust the security of their mail at the Great Salt Lake Post Office so his report was probably sent with a traveler or courier via the southern trail to Los Angeles.

New York Times, Great Salt Lake City, 5 March 1857.

Arapeen, the Chief of the Pah-Utah Indians, has been in the City recently. While here he was very assiduous in endeavors to ascertain what the Mormons were going to fight the Americans for. He said they had been urging

[39]Young to Smith, 23 February, 1857, Brigham Young Papers.

[40]Young to Taylor, 1 March 1857, Brigham Young Papers.

him to join them in such a war, but declared that he had refused absolutely to have anything to do with it. There is much food for meditation and conjecture in these statements of the friendly chief, taken in connection with movements known to be contemplated by the Mormons who seek his alliance.

Brigham Young, Heber Kimball, and other heads of the Church propose to leave here in April for a trip to the North. They take with them between two and three hundred men, the names of a large list of whom were read off publicly in the Tabernacle on Sunday, the 21st ult. Where they are going or with what design is a profound mystery. Some say they are about to leave the country entirely, and settle in the British possessions; but I can see no reason to put any faith in so improbable a rumor. The British Possessions present no such eligible location as that the Mormons now occupy, and their removal would involve an immense expenditure and loss of property such as they can ill afford to sustain. Besides, they could not hope for the toleration and indifference at the hands of the British Government which they have enjoyed under the flag of the Union. Another rumor is that they go to Bitter Root Valley, in Washington territory, to establish there a new "stake." Still another suggestion is, that Brigham is going on a tour among the Northern Indians, to excite them against the Gentile whites, and induce them to join the Mormons in a war against the Government forces, should any be sent out against them. My own impressions favor the latter view, although it is not improbable that a founding of a colony in Bitter Root Valley is a part of the programme. The only clue we have to their proposed route is a letter from Brigham shown by Arapeen, in which the former invites the Chief to accompany him on his tour, stating that he will pass through the country of the Bonnacks, the Nez Perces, and the Flatheads.

Garland Hurt Lays a Snare

Preparations for the northern trip caught the eye of U.S. Indian Agent Garland Hurt, one of the few federal officials who stuck to their post during this stormy period. Soon after coming to Utah in 1855, Hurt had alerted Washington to the call of Indian missionaries, which included the northern outreach to the tribes. The Virginian had become convinced that Young's followers were encouraging the natives to make "a distinction between the Mormons and Americans."[41] In early 1857 he feared his superior, Governor and Superintendent of Indian Affairs Brigham Young, intended to spend most of the federal appropriation

[41]Hurt to Young, 31 October 1856, House Exec. Doc. 71 (35-1), 182.

that year and throw the burden of squaring the agency's expenditures on him. The announcement of Young's Oregon trip gave Hurt the opening he was looking for. Loudly he blew the whistle on his superior.

In a "private" letter, posted at Fort Bridger, Hurt told the commissioner of Indian Affairs at Washington, D.C., that Young planned to visit the Indians outside of Utah, his legal jurisdiction. "His Excellency is now arranging an outfit of goods to be expended by him on an exploring expedition through the Territories of Oregon, Washington," he said, "and perhaps British Columbia."[42] Later that year, Commissioner J. W. Denver treated Brigham Young to an unaccustomed reprimand. Among other things, he said, "you fitted out an expedition yourself, and conducted it northward, out of your superintendency, to give presents to Indians not under your control."[43] Carefully Hurt had laid a snare, but in so doing, he underestimated his old adversary.

In the meantime, even before Young left that spring for Salmon River, all of Utah's non-Mormon officials, but one, had fled eastward. Once safe in the nation's capital, they would report that an American territory had declared its independence. It would be another four years before Confederate cannons opened fire on Fort Sumter in Charleston Harbor. The last official to leave was Agent Hurt, who moved to the Indian farm on Spanish Fork to seek protection from the Utah tribe he had served. At the same time, top Mormon commander Lt. Gen. Daniel Wells announced on 1 April 1857 the reorganization of the territorial militia, better known as the Nauvoo Legion. All able-bodied white males in Utah between ages eighteen and forty-five were ordered to enroll for military training in units patterned after "the good old Bible rule of Captains of 10's 100's &c."[44]

Events elsewhere were acting together to transform Fort Limhi from an obscure mission to the remnants of Jacob in Oregon Territory into a strategic location of primary importance in the Mormon kingdom's prophesied destiny.[45]

---

[42]Hurt to Manypenny, 30 March 1857, OIA, Utah Superintendency.

[43]Denver to Young, 11 November 1857, House Exec. Doc. 71 (35-1), 186–88.

[44]Brooks, *On The Mormon Frontier*, 2:623.

[45]Mormons at this time believed that God had inspired the framers of the U.S. Constitution to create a land of religious freedom where His Kingdom would be restored and supersede, as it prevailed to universal dominion, the American republic and all other earthly realms. To them the nation's charter was a stepping stone to a higher, millennial form of government, conducted in the church's early years through the ultra-secret Council of Fifty.

Chapter 6

GOV. BRIGHAM . . . COMING ON

I will settle in the north all the time in preference to the South, for health, strength and beauty I would rather go 500 miles north than 100 miles south.
— *Brigham Young*

Happiness to the self-ruled sovereign of God's Kingdom in the American West was to travel at the head of a great parade of his followers to some far-off settlement, like King Solomon on an excursion. An observer in 1854 described the colorful procession of carriages, wagons, and horsemen. It "lengthened out over a mile, winding leisurely along the side of a mountain, or trotting blithely in the hollow," he said, with everyone "taking the word of command from the leading wagon." As it passed, the valleys resounded with "musical choruses from the whole party . . . to the tune of 'bonny breastknots.'"[1]

A Mormon father likes to see his Mormon family agree,
The prattling baby at his knee cries: Daddy, I'm a Mormon!
Eh! the merry, oh! the merry, eh! the merry Mormons!
I never knew what joy was till I became a Mormon!

BRIGHAM YOUNG'S LONGEST JOURNEY

The longest of Brigham Young's annual travels in the Rocky Mountains began before daylight on Friday, 24 April 1857, when the customary parade of people, animals, and vehicles formed at Great Salt Lake City. Promptly at the appointed hour of 7 A.M. it rolled north for Fort Limhi. On Saturday its members camped at Box Elder (later Brigham City), where they held Sunday morning service and welcomed Apostle Lorenzo Snow and some others from the Ogden area to the company,

[1]Carvalho, *Incidents of Travel and Adventures in The Far West,* 188, 189.

DANIEL H. WELLS
Recently promoted to lieutenant general, Nauvoo Legion, Brigham Young's second counselor and member of the ruling Mormon triumvirate was among the top religious and military leaders who accompanied Young to Fort Limhi.
Courtesy of the Church Archives, The Church of Jesus Christ of Latter-Day Saints.

before moving that afternoon up the east bank of Bear River to the ferry at present Honeyville. By the time the operator had deposited all safely on the other shore it was after dark. But before anyone turned in for the night, Young organized the company.

Elected unanimously were Young and his two counselors, Heber C. Kimball and Daniel Wells, presidents; apostles Orson Hyde, Franklin D. Richards, and Lorenzo Snow, chaplains; Robert T. Burton, captain; Jesse C. Little, marshal; Warren S. Snow, sergeant of the guard; Albert Carrington, Jesse W. Fox, and Thomas D. Brown, engineers; James W. Cummings and T. D. Brown, clerks. In keeping with Mormon custom, the expedition was also formed into five companies of ten, each with a captain, like the hosts of Israel.[2] Young headed the first; Nauvoo Legion Col. Robert T. Burton, the second; Chauncey W. West from Ogden, the third; George Peacock from Manti, the fourth; and John Nebeker from Great Salt Lake, the fifth. The company added up to "115 men, 22

[2]Each of the five companies actually numbered more than ten members.

women and 5 boys, with 168 horses and mules, 54 wagons and carriages, and 2 light boats with decking planks for ferrying."[3]

Except for the boats, the cavalcade appeared much like the others that had trailed Israel's chief on his earlier travels in the Great Basin. As usual, there were a number of family members in the company. Young himself took three of his wives on the excursion, Lucy Ann Decker Young, age thirty-four, his first plural spouse; Clarissa, twenty-eight; and Zina Diantha Huntington Jacobs Smith Young, thirty-five, whose many names told a history in polygamy that included a first husband and two Mormon prophets. Three different wives gave Young the five sons who went with the company.[4] It was customary, too, for Heber C. Kimball, Young's first counselor and loyal associate, to bring family members on such outings. This time they included two wives, Sarah Ann Whitney Kimball, thirty-two, and Lucy Walker Kimball, thirty-one, and two sons.[5]

Other women in the company were Margaret Ann Boyce Andrus, age seventeen, ninth wife of Milo Andrus, forty-three; Wispit, wife of Arapeen, Utah Indian chief, ages unknown; Lucinda Bingham, thirty-one, sister of Thomas Bingham, thirty-two; Sarah Texana East Blair, sixteen, sixth wife of Seth M. Blair, thirty-eight; Elizabeth Hardman Burch, forty-seven, wife of Frances Burch, forty-eight; Louisa Chase, twenty-three, who went with her father, Isaac Chase, sixty-five; Jeanette Thomas Dives, twenty-one, wife of twenty-two-year-old Verulam Dives; Charlotte Campbell Dunn, seventeen, third wife of Thomas Dunn, thirty-five; Barbara Ann Ewell Evans, thirty-seven, second wife of David Evans, fifty-two; Nicoline Erickson Farr, eighteen, fifth wife of Lorin F. Farr, thirty-six; Mary Bell Heywood, eighteen, the fourth wife of Joseph L. Heywood, forty-one; Emily Hoagland Little, nineteen, second wife of Jesse C. Little, forty-one; Mary Jane Walker Pack, twenty-two, fifth wife of John Pack, forty-seven; Sarah Elizabeth Whiting Snow, seventeen, latest by four days of thirty-eight-year-old Warren Snow's four wives; Mary Hoagland West, age

[3]"Excursion to Fort Limhi," *Deseret News,* 10 June 1857, 7:14, 108, 109. Appendix C contains the complete text of this article.

[4]Young's sons on the journey were Joseph A., twenty-two, Brigham, Jr., twenty, and John W., twelve, all by Mary Ann Angel; Brigham Heber, eleven, by Lucy Ann Decker; and Oscar Brigham Young, eleven, son of Harriet Cook.

[5]Lucy Walker Kimball and Sarah Ann Whitney Kimball were both former wives of the faith's first prophet, Joseph Smith. The sons were William H., thirty-one, and Charles S., fourteen.

twenty-eight, Emily Little's sister, first of thirty-year-old Chauncey W. West's three wives; Olive Foss Woolley, wife of Franklin B. Woolley, both twenty-two; and Sarah McCleve Young, twenty-two, Irish third wife of Brigham Young's older brother, John Young. He was sixty-five.

A closer look at members of the 1857 expedition revealed there was more to this journey than the usual outing with favorite wives or Young's known fondness for travel. Since 1851, when Hudson's Bay agent Alexander C. Anderson at Fort Colville reported there was "no room to doubt that in [the] course of the summer the Flathead Country will be largely colonized by Mormons,"[6] there had been repeated reports the Mormons would move north, even as far as Alaska.[7] The makeup of Young's company to Oregon seemed at last to add substance to these rumors. It was an unusual collection of the Rocky Mountain theocracy's top religious, military, and settlement leaders.

At the head of the cavalcade were all three members of the ruling triumvirate, or First Presidency, Young, Heber C. Kimball, first counselor, and the new Second Counselor Daniel H. Wells, who also served as commander of the Nauvoo Legion, newly promoted to the lofty title of lieutenant general and elevated to the First Presidency to replace Jedediah Grant. The company numbered three of the four Quorum of Twelve apostles who were at home at the time, Orson Hyde, Lorenzo Snow, and Franklin D. Richards. Only Wilford Woodruff was left at Great Salt Lake City to pilot the ship of Zion through gathering storm clouds.

Generals George D. Grant, Franklin D. Richards, William H. Kimball, Warren S. Snow, and James Ferguson led a line-up of young military officers who would win fame later that year during the Utah War. They included Lot Smith, Robert T. Burton, John D. T. McAllister, Stephen Taylor, Howard Egan, Chauncey W. West, Nathaniel V. Jones, James M. Barlow, and Warren Snow. The company also counted eleven veterans of the Mormon Battalion, the unique military command that marched two thousand miles from Council Bluffs, Iowa, to San Diego and Los Angeles during the Mexican War to claim California for the United States.[8]

---

[6]Anderson to Simpson, 21 April 1851. Sir George Simpson, Incoming Correspondence, Hudson's Bay Co.

[7]See Sessions and Stathis, "The Mormon Invasion of Russian America: Dynamics of a Potent Myth," 22–35.

[8]They were Elisha Averett, Thomas Bingham, Thomas Dunn, James Ferguson, Phillip Garner, Arza E. Hinckley, John G. Holman, Dimick B. Huntington, Nathaniel V. Jones, William W. Rust, and Lot Smith.

To make the round trip, many military and settlement leaders were forced to travel long distances because they hailed from places south of Great Salt Lake. Those from Manti faced a journey both ways of more than a thousand miles. And Col. William H. Dame, commander of the Iron Military District from Parowan, had to cover roughly the distance from the former Mormon city-state of Nauvoo on the Mississippi River to Salt Lake Valley. Offsetting this hardship, however, was the chance to see firsthand the topography and trails to the Salmon River outpost. Reflecting this interest, too, was the task of three party members, Albert Carrington, the Nauvoo Legion's chief topographical engineer; former schoolteacher Jesse W. Fox; and Thomas D. Brown, the territorial road commissioner, who brought the "instruments for taking observations in the mountains."[9] They mapped and measured the route to Fort Limhi and the Lewis and Clark Pass to an accuracy of one-thousandth of a mile. Published in the *Deseret News* on Young's return, the waybill for travelers was the equivalent of a modern road map.[10]

Finally, traveling with the company to meet with tribesmen in Oregon Territory, outside Governor Young's jurisdiction as superintendent of Indian Affairs in Utah, were two prominent native leaders. Arapeen was chief of the Northern Wasatch Utahs and a half-brother of the famed War Chief Walkara, who had led his warriors against Mormon settlements in 1853. After Walkara's sudden death in 1855, Arapeen had decided to stop fighting his white cousins and join them. One benefit of such cooperation was that he and his wife, Wispit, enjoyed their own wagon, provided by Dimick B. Huntington, Young's personal interpreter and emissary to the tribes. Escorting the Utah chief were a "number of his braves."[11] Possibly also in the party, but not listed on its roster, was Kanosh, the Mormon chief of the Pahvant Utahs, who lived on Corn Creek, near present Fillmore.[12]

On Monday, 27 April, a chilling wind and flurries of snow reminded

---

[9]"Excursion to Fort Limhi," *Deseret News*, 10 June 1857, 7:14, 108, 109.

[10]Ibid. Jesse W. Fox in 1862 published an expanded version for travelers to the Montana gold mines, *General Courses and Distance from G. S. L. City to Fort Limhi and Gold Diggings on Salmon River.*

[11]Roberts, *A Comprehensive History of The Church of Jesus Christ of Latter-day Saints*, 4:8.

[12]Appendix B presents for the first time a correct list of Brigham Young's company to Fort Limhi, prepared by James W. Cummings, clerk of the camp.

the camp on Bear River's right bank that it was rushing the season as members packed their wagons and headed north at 8:30 A.M. to begin a 308-mile journey to Fort Limhi.[13] Brigham Young led the parade of mule- and horse-drawn wagons that stretched for more than a mile on the old wagon road up the Malad River. Scouts on horseback ranged the valley and foothills ahead to look out for troublesome Indians. Several miles in advance a work party toiled to make smooth the highway for wagons through the wilderness. If unwelcome, such labor was not without compensation. For the disposition of the man who led the parade was only as kindly as the ruts in the road were free of rocks and holes.

Far behind the last wagon, one of the seven returning Salmon River missionaries in the column rode by himself, "alone and lonesome."[14] The usually high spirit of Lewis Shurtliff, just turned twenty-one, had been cast down by the rebuff of the girl he loved at Ogden. The slender youth was grateful for the solitude of his post as rear guard to nurse "a sad heart" as he returned to his "northern home."[15] But Shurtliff's taste for adventure and strong spiritual leanings made it difficult to feel sorry for himself for very long.

His recovery began two days later when the company camped at the headspring of Little Malad River, where Hudspeth's Cutoff of the California Trail crosses Dairy Creek, near the divide between the Great Basin and Snake River. There, some seven thousand feet above sea level, young Shurtliff was struck with awe as Brigham Young, like an Old Testament patriarch in the wilderness, offered up a "soul inspiring" prayer that seemed to the young man "to cause the ground to shake."[16] Several days later at the Snake River crossing he would see another side of his strong-minded leader.

On its way to that point, the company traveled the existing route to the Oregon Trail on Snake River, except for the six-mile stretch from the Fort Hall Road's junction with Hudspeth's Cutoff to the rim of the

---

[13]Elias Blackburn from Provo faithfully records starting times and mileages, but regrettably little else. See Elias H. Blackburn Journals and Papers, 27 April 1857.

[14]The Fort Limhi missionaries in Brigham Young's party were Thomas S. Smith, Pleasant Green Taylor, Thomas Bingham, Lewis W. Shurtliff, Henry Smith, John Preece, and future missionary Amos R. Wright.

[15]Life and Travels of Lewis Warren Shurtliff, April 1857.

[16]Ibid.

Great Basin, when it followed the more gradual ascent made by the first missionary party two years before. On meeting the Oregon Trail, it took a segment of that great emigrant highway that bypassed Fort Hall on the south. Crossing Ross Fork on a bridge in today's Fort Hall Indian Reservation, the party turned left to reach Snake River near Ferry Butte, where the first missionaries had crossed, because it was too early in the season to use the fords of Blackfoot and Snake rivers on the Flathead Trail, near present Blackfoot, Idaho.

THE SNAKE RIVER CROSSING

"The ford on Snake River is 13.5 miles above the ferry, at a point where three islands divide the river into four channels, but the water, though low for the season, was too high for crossing with wagons, as was also the Blackfoot Fork," explained one of the recorders, probably Thomas D. Brown, for the information of future travelers. "Should travel ever warrant the alteration, the ferrying point should be near the ford and a bridge be made across Blackfoot, thus shortening and otherwise bettering the route," he said in conveying information provided by Thomas Smith.[17] At the swollen Snake River, where they arrived at 2 P.M. on the first of May, they built a wharf to make the dangerous operation safer. John Brown described the crossing:

AUTOBIOGRAPHY OF PIONEER JOHN BROWN, 1 MAY 1857.

> The President had two new boats which he had brought along for the purpose, taken from the wagons, on which they had been used for boxes, and launched them. They were lashed together and we commenced ferrying our wagons across, and by 10 P.M. all of our wagons and carriages were on the north side. We had fifty-three wagons and carriages. Early next morning we drove our animals into the river and they all swam over in safety. The river was high with a very swift current. The boats were cached as we would not need them any further.

Hardly had this procedure begun when "the brethern got in a hurry and came near losing a woman in the river," Lewis Shurtliff said. He now saw an angry Brigham Young abruptly order his followers to "tie up

[17]For a description of these routes and crossings, see "Excursion to Fort Limhi," *Deseret News*, 10 June 1857, 7:14, 108, 109.

the boats until their heads got settled."[18] Shurtliff's broken heart virtually mended with pride later that day when the Mormon leader himself called on him and Pleasant Green Taylor to ride in advance and "car[r]y the news to Fort Limhi" of his company's approach. To cover the remaining 172 miles to the outpost, the honored pair spurred their horses "day and night."[19]

The following day, as they rode up the north bank of Snake River, they met other travelers on the Flathead Trail headed the opposite direction toward Fort Hall. Frederick Burr, the cattle trader from Bitterroot Valley, was driving a small herd, which he intended to sell before going on to California. Burr recorded the meeting that day: "Two Mormons passed on an Express to Salmon River, they report Gov Brigham with 115 men coming on behind." On 3 May, when he met Governor Young's main company, the mountaineer received alarming news. "Heard Father had gone to the states," he said, adding, "Howard Egan made me an offer for my cattle."[20]

Frederick Burr's father, the former cartographer to Congress, had proved himself one burr too many under the Mormon saddle after his appointment by President Franklin Pierce in 1854 as Utah surveyor general. The duty to divide the Mormon homeland into townships and sections before it was put on the market for sale to all comers, as provided by federal law, placed David H. Burr in a continuing confrontation with religious leaders who had other ideas about ownership of the Kingdom's domain. On 13 February 1857, he and Indian Agent Garland Hurt had come before district Judge George Stiles and demanded to know "whether he held the laws of Utah to have the preference to the laws of U. S."[21] The federal pair "went out of the house in the form of a sled, using the seat of their honor for runners," according to Apostle Wilford Woodruff.[22]

On 28 March that year, Burr reported to U.S. General Land Office Commissioner Thomas Hendricks that "these people *repudiate the author-*

[18]Life and Travels of Lewis Warren Shurtliff, May 1857. The ford on Snake River was located on the Flathead Trail, near present Blackfoot, Idaho.

[19]Ibid.

[20]Frederick H. Burr Journal, 1857–58, 2, 3 May 1857, Beinecke Library.

[21]Brooks, *On the Mormon Frontier: The Diary of Hosea Stout*, 13 February 1857, 2:622.

[22]Woodruff to Smith, Journal History, 1 April 1857.

ity of the United States in this country, and are in open rebellion against the general government."[23] Ten days before Brigham Young's departure to visit Fort Limhi, the surveyor general and "nearly all the gentile and apostate Scurf in this community left for the States," reported Hosea Stout, speaker of Utah's House of Representatives.[24]

On hearing this news, Frederick Burr gave up his plan to go to California. Instead he sold his herd to Egan for later delivery and went to Great Salt Lake City to see his brother, David A. Burr, a surveyor on the elder Burr's staff. What they talked about is not known, but David A. Burr soon after followed his father, taking flight from Utah, while Frederick Burr went back to Bear River where on 4 June he met his partner, John W. Powell, and turned his herd over to Howard Egan. The pair now moved up Bear River, via Soda Springs, to Thomas Fork, near present Border Junction, a dozen miles north of Cokeville, Wyoming, to trade with emigrants on the Oregon Trail. Here on 24 June, a full month before it was announced in Utah, Burr heard "News of troops coming to Salt Lake."[25] During Brigham Young's trip to Fort Limhi, President James Buchanan had unseated him as governor and launched a U.S. Army expedition intended to escort a new governor and uphold federal authority in an allegedly rebellious territory.

Young's Arrival at Fort Limhi

In the meantime, news of Young's approach, carried by Shurtliff and Taylor on 5 May, found the missionaries, their number nearly doubled by recent returnees, already at work to make a good impression on their leader.[26] Some fixed fences; Abraham Zundel "helped clean up the fort;"[27] others worked "hauling rubbish from about the Fort."[28] To

[23]House Exec. Doc. 71 (35-1), 1858, 118–20. Italics in the original.

[24]Juanita Brooks, *On the Mormon Frontier*, 15 April 1857, 2:625.

[25]Frederick H. Burr Journal, 24 June 1857, Beinecke Library.

[26]Returnees included William Bailey Lake, Richard B. Margetts, David Moore, and William Shaw, who came on 17 April. Ezra Barnard, William Burch, Thomas Butterfield, Henry R. Cleveland, Sylvanus Collett, Thomas Corless, Hathron C. Hadlock, Joseph Harker, George W. Hill, Jacob Miller, Henry Nebeker, Haskill V. Shurtliff, David H. Stephens, and possibly others, arrived with six wagons loaded with supplies on 22 April.

[27]Abraham Zundel Diary, 2 May 1857.

[28]Milton D. Hammond Journal, 2 May 1857.

Joseph Harker, the unfavored bishop from West Jordan, fell the assignment of "making a backhouse."[29] Milton D. Hammond, George McBride, and "Eben" Robinson found a new route and "fixed a road to save coming down the rocky slope 2 miles south of Fort."[30] They camped out that night under a four-inch fall of wet snow and worked all the next day, but the undermanned road crew won no thanks for its efforts.

The day of Young's arrival, Friday, 8 May, was "squally snowing very fast at times which made it disagreeable traveling." When the Mormon leader at last pulled up at 5 P.M., he was tired, cold, and distempered after an unpleasant journey in a heavy spring storm over a muddy mountain road that was disrespectfully primitive. He retired at once, hurtfully delegating to his counselor, Heber C. Kimball, the important ritual of dedicating the northern mission. That night Jesse C. Little, marshal of the visiting company, called the whole camp together and the apostle left no stone unprayed for. Kimball "Dedicated the Fort, farms, timber, watter, the valley & everything pertaining thereunto to the Lord God of Israel, which was sanctioned by a hearty Amen."[31]

At least, "Some of the brethern seemed well satisfied," Mission Clerk David Moore, said resentfully, "while others did not like the place or the Road to it." Prudently failing to name the most ill-humored critic, he continued: "Query. What would have been their feelings if they had been required to leave their homes & families & Break their own roads for such a distance over sage, sand, & rocks without the aid of an Indian trail ~~it self~~, as did the first Mission to this place & that too without a whine or murmer with little or no exception."[32]

The answer came next morning under clearing skies. A rested Brigham Young told Jesse Little to assemble the camp again and moved to restore the pride he had injured the night before. After all had gathered, the Mormon chieftain himself delivered another dedication prayer, the second in less than twenty-four hours. Not to be outdone, he "felt to dedicate the Mission & the whole Country in General to the God of

[29]Joseph Harker Journal, 6 May 1857. Harker once took down the names of ten missionaries for playing ball, "which had been forbidden yesterday in the meeting," and reported them.

[30]Milton D. Hammond Journal, 6 May 1857.

[31]Salmon River Mission Journal, 8 May 1857.

[32]Ibid.

Heaven & Earth which was also heartily responded to by Amen from all present after which he gave the Brethren who had come in with him some council in regard to trade. [He] did not wish them to interfere with the established system of trade." In return, "The Brethren gave the free use and possession of their houses to the Presidency the 12 Apostles present and others of the Authorities so far as there was any room," said a mollified Moore, "feeling at the same time thankful that they had the priveledge [*sic*] of so doing."[33]

James W. Cummings: The Appearance of Industry and Frugality

Just the same, Young ordered work parties out to clear away the rocks and fill in the steep places over six miles of road through the river narrows before he headed back. Nor did he spare the men of his own company, most of them leaders in their own right. As the high and the humble labored together, he told the missionaries to obey the system of trade at the colony, which meant that only Thomas Smith was authorized to deal with the natives.[34] And he closely inspected the outpost on Salmon River, described by James W. Cummings, the clerk of Young's camp.

James W. Cummings, Travel of President Brigham Young to Oregon, 1857.

We found the Brethren at the fort all well. The men numbered forty two; there was also one woman Bro Durpheys wife.

Fort Limhi is situated on a small creek in Oregon Territory called Limhi Creek which empties into Salmon River which passed the Fort on the west about a quarter of a mile distant.

The Fort consists of an area of 16 rods square enclosed with cottonwood polings sat in the ground so they touch each other and stand nine feet above the ground. Within this enclosure are thirteen log cabbins that were finished and four not yet completed. Those cabbins were occupied by the Brethren of the Mission.

In addition to the Fort they have a Corral or inclosure for their Stock enclosed with a Spanish wall seven feet high and divided into different com-

[33] Ibid.

[34] Salmon River Mission Journal, 9 May 1857.

> partments by good substantial pole fences. A portion of the west side of the enclosure is fixed with posts and timbers on the top to make a place for stacking hay at the same time affording sheds to shelter their stock in the inclement season of the year.
>
> They also have about three hundred acres of land enclosed with a good pole fence and about one hundred and fifty acres of that under cultivation; the most of which is sown to wheat.
>
> Every thing about the Fort boar the appearance of industry and frugality; every thing was neat and clean and in its place which spoke volumes for the Brethren of the Mission, and proved that they were men that understood their calling and were preparing themselves by their practice and experience to assist in building up and beautifying Zion.
>
> The Spirit of union prevailed in their midst which could be felt by every one that visited them
>
> Pres. Young and the brethren with him expressed themselves highly gratified with the work of the Brethren of the Mission and said that it was the neatest and cleanest place they had seen in any of the settlements of the Saints in the Valeys of the mountains out side of Great Salt Lake City. The work done credit to those that had been engaged in it.

As night fell on the first full day of Young's visit, a Saturday, the missionaries and visitors gathered around a great bonfire to renew old friendships, hear spontaneous speeches, and enjoy an evening of fellowship. For just such an occasion the renowned Mormon favorite, Scotsman William C. Dunbar, had traveled north with the visiting party. The thirty-four-year-old actor, vocalist, and bagpiper now thrilled the assembly of nearly two hundred with "songs of Zion" as embers from the fire rose in the darkness and enhanced the sense of oneness all felt.

On 10 May Marshal Little convened the camp around another "good fire in the center of the fort" for Sunday services. In his opening remarks, Brigham Young said for support and protection he wished the fort was "a little nearer our settlement." He called on the missionaries "to sustain their dignity" among the Indians, known as Lamanites, a remnant of Jacob in the New World, and avoid gambling with them. Said he:

> We have one of them along with us (Aropene) one of the most intelligent Indians there is in the mountains. He has been contrary cross and complaining all the time because I can ride in a carriage and he has to ride in a wagon as though I was riding in his carriage . . . If Aropene had any under-

> standing I would take him and cuff his ears or have some one to do it. But we must have patience with them and try and teach them the gospel of salvation. They are of the house of Israel.[35]

Marrying a Chief's Daughter

Apostle Franklin D. Richards spoke next, followed by Apostle Lorenzo Snow who introduced a subject of some interest to the missionaries, giving them "much good instruction in relation to forming an allyance with the Lamonites here in the Mountains." Heber C. Kimball further developed this theme. "We have got to become one and connect ourselves with the House of Israel," he explained. "We have got to unite together, and our interests must become one." Lest anyone still wonder what this meant, Daniel H. Wells, Young's new second counselor, put it even more plainly. "In relation to our connections with the Lamonites I would say that the marriage tie is the strongest tie that can be found, and said Tis your duty Bror Franklin & Bro [Orson] Hyde to enter into these things."[36]

Finally, the outspoken first counselor in the Mormon First Presidency drew a picture on the subject that no one could misunderstand.

> "Bror H. C. Kimball spoke again and brought up the figure of grafting, and said Are the Indians any worse than we are no they are not. They are of the seed of Abraham. Is it a disgrace to connect our selves with them? No it is not it is an honor. They have got to be grafted in and those cursed Scoundrals in the Mountains destroyed.[37] When a man marries a Chief's daughter he marries the whole family! Yes the whole nation."[38]

Lewis Shurtliff listened to these words, but did not appear to take them seriously. "Bro. Heber C. Kimball gave us some stray doctrine concerning the marrying of squaws," he said.[39] Before many weeks passed, however, "stray doctrine" about marrying a chief's daughter would have surprising consequences for his hopes to marry the girl he loved and had left behind at Ogden.

---

[35]Cummings, Travel of President Brigham Young to Oregon 1857, 10 May 1857.

[36]Ibid.

[37]A clear reference to the mountaineers who married Indian women and challenged Mormon efforts to win the loyalty of the tribes.

[38]Cummings, Travel of President Brigham Young to Oregon 1857, 10 May 1857.

[39]Life and Travels of Lewis Warren Shurtliff, May 1856.

Brigham Young: I Do Not Urge It upon You

At the Sunday meeting, Brigham Young rose to clarify what previous speakers had said and provide information on the future prospects of Fort Limhi. First he signaled that the Oregon settlement was the beginning of an overall shift to the north in the direction of Mormon colonization. "I will settle in the north all the time in preference to the South, for health, strength and beauty I would rather go 500 miles north than 100 miles south," Young said. "The nations of the north are far superior to those of the South in point of intellect and bodily strength."[40] To William Dame from Parowan, more than two hundred miles south of Great Salt Lake on the southern trail to California, the message was clear: "[The presidency] felt well toward the brethren in this place and said the settlements must go north instead of south . . ."[41] Then the Mormon president came to the topic of marriage with the natives.

James W. Cummings, Travel of President Brigham Young to Oregon, 1857.

With regard to the Elders becoming connected with the Lamonites—when this Mission was called there were several others called at the same time,[42] and they were all instructed to become identified with the natives by marriage at least there were sufficient instructions given for them to understand, that had the Spirit of it. It has been urged upon you this morning but I do not urge it upon you. If you do not feel the Spirit of it do not enter into it. When this is to take place the Spirit will dictate and urge it upon them . . . In relation to the Brethren connecting them selves with the Indians here, I do not feel to urge it upon the Brethren because I believe there is not a squaw here that if she was married to any of the Brethren would prove true to them.

Salmon River Mission Journal, 10 May 1857.

Pres. H. C. Kimball & Wells addressed the Missionaries as well as the Brn. Present, on the importance of the missionaries being faithful in the discharge of their duties and for them to marry the native women, that the marrige [*sic*] tie was the strongest tie of friendship that existed &c &c. after which Pres B. Young said, he did not wish the Brethren to feel in a hurry about any thing but live their Religion and when the Lord opened the way

---

[40]Cummings, Travel of President Brigham Young to Oregon, 1857, 10 May 1857.

[41]William H. Dame Journal, 18 May 1857.

[42]An apparent reference to the Elk Mountain and Las Vegas Springs missions, and possibly other settlements, such as Fort Supply.

> before them so that they could marry Girls, they would be very likely to be enabled to keep them. But if the Brn were to marry those old ranegadoes [*sic*] they would be off with the first mountaineer that came along.

Jacob Miller grasped that Young "gave more leniency" than other leaders, when it came to marrying native women.[43] Yet some missionaries still seemed not to understand that Young had held out the opportunity to avoid a religious obligation, made possible by the practice of polygamy. "Brothers Brigham and the twelve Spoke to us and told us that we had to marry Squaws and ware well pleased with us and said if we would continue to do wright that we would be blessed with heavens choisest blessings," Abraham Zundel said.[44] Zundel and others may have thought that the Holy Spirit's failure to dictate such a course would be looked upon as a lack of faith.

JAMES W. CUMMINGS: SEEING THE BIG MORMON CHIEF

Apart from marriage, Brigham Young moved to create closer ties with the natives of Oregon later that day when Shoshone Chief Ti-o-von-du-ah, "with his band numbering sixteen lodges," moved up from their camp at the forks of the river. In 1855 "Old Snag" had been among the first Indians baptized at Fort Limhi. The following year he had been joined by many of his family members, including his mother, Po-e-chah, given the name Esther, and three brothers, Te-ah-to-wah, Zeeme, and To-buds, renamed Lehi, David, and Two-Bits, respectively, by the missionaries. The clerk of Young's company described the meeting.

JAMES W. CUMMINGS, TRAVEL OF PRESIDENT BRIGHAM YOUNG TO OREGON, 1857.

> [Snag] came for the purpose of seeing the Big Mormon Chief and get some presents which he had been told he would get by visiting the Fort.
>
> The Chief and his men came into the Fort and sat around the fire when we had held our meeting and smoked and talked with Canosh the Chief of the Utah's who had accompanied us from Great Salt Lake City on our Tripp to this Place.[45]

---

[43]Miller and Miller, eds., Journal of Jacob Miller, 10 May 1857.

[44]Abraham Zundel Diary, 10 May 1857.

[45]Since Cummings did not include Pahvant Chief Kanosh on the company roster, he may have confused him here with Utah Chief Arapeen who did take part in this pow-wow.

> D B Huntington the interpreter distributed some tobacco among them. They were very friendly and appeared to feel well and pleased that we had made them a visit.
>
> This band of Sho-Shonies number several hundred and are much scattered over the country and are very seldom together.
>
> The Chief was wounded in the thigh by an accidental discharging of a pistol which causes a running sore out of which several pieces of bone have worked. He is compelled to walk on crutches this lameness makes him very peevish and fretful.

The following day, Governor Young "distributed many presents of blankets, &c., on the 11th of May, which were very gladly received,"[46] but not everyone was allowed to participate in meetings with the Indians. Most of the male members of Young's traveling party had to prepare for their leader's departure on Wednesday. Topographical Engineer Albert Carrington said "60 men from our camp and several from the Fort were detailed to grade some spurs on [the] right bank of Salmon [River] above the Fort in order to avoid the 2 crossings of Salmon [River]," adding "presents given to the Inds. by Gov. Young."[47]

If most white visitors failed to attend, even more conspicuously absent from these talks were the Bannocks, led by their six-foot-four chief, Shou-woo-koo, known as Le Grand Coquin, "The Great Rogue," the most unpredictable and warlike of southeastern Oregon's native inhabitants. For the Mormon settlement, the friendship of Snag and his Shoshones was well enough, but the goodwill of the Bannocks, who claimed the Salmon River fishery as their homeland, was a condition of survival. Yet during Young's visit only a few members of the tribe "pitched their lodges adjacent to the fort" from whom "red sided salmon were purchased." They were a "fine flavored fish" that averaged "about two and a half feet in length."[48]

Over the next two days, David Moore said, "The Presidency and others travelled over the surrounding country to examine it."[49] With a customary eye for defense, Young saw that the stockade stood in the shadow of a bench, "a good many feet higher than the place selected for the fort," which commanded the east wall and virtually invited attack.[50]

---

[46]"Excursion to Fort Limhi," *Deseret News,* 10 June 1857, 7:14, 108, 109.

[47]Albert Carrington Diary, 11 May 1857.

[48]"Excursion to Fort Limhi," *Deseret News,* 10 June 1857, 7:14, 108, 109.

[49]Salmon River Mission Journal, 11 May 1857. [50]Ibid., 18 June 1855.

The "high bench" above the fort, he told Thomas Smith, without dwelling on the obvious, was a "good place for a fortification." He advised the missionaries to "dig for water" on the inside of the fort rather than depend on the nearby creek or the river a quarter-mile away. He also ordered the construction of log blockhouses, or bastions, at two corners of the stockade.

Lt. Gen. Daniel Wells took the final steps necessary to strengthen the location's defensive posture "about 7 oclock P M" on 12 May when "the Bretheren of this Mission were called together in the Fort and organized into a Military Company."[51] The Nauvoo Legion commander appointed David Moore adjutant. The other officers he named were Benjamin F. Cummings, captain, 1st Ten; Francillo Durfee, captain, 2nd Ten; Pleasant Green Taylor, captain, 3rd Ten; and Gilbert Belnap, captain 4th Ten. Afterward Mormon leaders stopped by Chief Snag's lodge, where John D. T. McAllister "Sung him and his braves Some Songs of Zion which was interpreted by Bro George Hill who preached to them the principles of the Gospel."[52]

As these measures indicate, Young had learned from personal inspection that the mission's location at the far end of a ninety-mile approach between high mountain ranges left Fort Limhi dangerously exposed. In the event of Indian trouble, it could be easily cut off and would be difficult to support from the outside. Companies sent to its relief would face a potential ambush at almost every turn of the primitive wagon road that ran between today's Beaverhead Mountains and the Lemhi Range. If the fort were attacked, it must be strong enough to withstand a siege until a large military expedition could be organized and sent to its relief.

On the other hand, the very conditions that left the outpost dangerously exposed also made Fort Limhi appear almost divinely placed as a midway point of resupply and rest on a trail from Salt Lake Valley to the Missouri River headwaters and Bitterroot Valley. In the event the Great Basin theocracy failed to prevail in its coming confrontation with the United States, the mission offered a haven of refuge and renewal on a long avenue guarded for most of the distance from Snake River to the

[51] Cummings, Travel of President Brigham Young to Oregon 1857, 12 May 1857.

[52] J. D. T. McAllister Diary, 12 May 1857.

Lewis and Clark Pass over the Continental Divide by impassable mountain ranges. Young had seen for himself the route "from the fort to Horse Prairie and the waters of the Missouri River." He was aware that it was precipitous and narrow, but extended only "some 10 or 15 miles."[53] Carrington also noted that "the Horse Prairie has the Missouri water nearest to Limhi and some say 10 and some say 15 ms. to that Prairie, the Beaver Head Creek comes next and is the stream on which old Grant wintered his animals cattle & horses last winter and they looked very well when we passed them on Snake river."[54]

Having guarded against the danger, Brigham Young accepted the risk and seized the opportunity. On 12 May he and other leaders "walked out a mile or two this morning to examine the surrounding country . . . and learn some of its facilities for settlement."[55] They selected a location for a second settlement about two miles down the river from the first fort. Young next gave the missionaries permission to bring their wives and children to the northernmost colony of the faith. Ten men left for home the following morning, a few hours ahead of Young's returning company.[56] Young further promised to send new settlers, men, women and children, to expand and strengthen the colony. By these moves he converted Fort Limhi from a mission outreach to the Indians to a permanent settlement of strategic importance to the destiny of his Rocky Mountain kingdom.

In keeping with their new status, the missionaries soon afterward made plans for "laying off their farms," Moore said. "It was agreed that the farms should begin south of the Fort and be laid off down the river or north as the bottoms would admit, and each of the brethern to have what land they could cultivate." After finding there was not enough fertile land near the fort for an enlarged settlement, they decided that "about one half of the mission should built another fort some two miles down the river," the location chosen by Brigham Young. "Consequently

---

[53]"Excursion to Fort Limhi," *Deseret News,* 10 June 1857, 7:14, 108, 109.

[54]Albert Carrington Diary, 8 May 1857. "Old Grant" was trader and rancher Richard Grant. The condition of the cattle showed that the Missouri River headwater offered good grazing for animals, even out of season.

[55]Cummings, Travel of President Brigham Young to Oregon 1857, 12 May 1857.

[56]Owen Dix, Thomas Abbott, Wallace McIntire, William Perkins, Ira Ames, William Bachelor, Joseph Bowen, and Henry A. Cleveland traveled by ox team. William Shaw accompanied B. F. Cummings and his brother, James W. Cummings, Young's company clerk, on horseback.

a Fort was laid off 26 rods east and west, by 16 north and south, containing 28 lots 1 rod by 2 with a space of 2 rods wide between the houses and wall," the mission clerk said.[57]

The Redemption of the Sons of the Forest: Amos Wright's Blessing

In the meantime, before Young's company left on 13 May 1857, "Thomas Smith and members of Quorum of the Twelve present," apostles Orson Hyde, Lorenzo Snow, and Franklin D. Richards, "set apart" seven new missionaries "who had not been blessed and set apart before."[58] They were Joseph L. Bowen, Sylvanus Collett, Owen T. Dix, Henry Nebeker, Haskell V. Shurtliff, Lewis W. Shurtliff, and newcomer Amos R. Wright, age seventeen, who had arrived as a teamster with Young's company and asked to stay on as a missionary. Typical of all was the blessing Apostle Hyde pronounced on Wright.

ANDERSEN, *MY GRANDFATHER SAID . . . A STORY OF THE LIFE OF AMOS R. WRIGHT*, 39–40.

> Brother Wright, in the name of Jesus Christ, we lay our hands on thy head and set thee apart to this mission and calling. Thy name shall stand upon the records of the Church and Kingdom of God amongst thy brethren. Thou shalt be a comfort to them, being a part of this mission and bearing a portion of the labor in strengthening this fort, and laboring among the remnants of Israel. Seek for the Holy Spirit to lighten thee and them in darkness. We pray the Lord to aid thee in keeping the commandments of God. Gird on the armor of truth and righteousness and keep it bright. Thy heart shall yearn for the salvation and redemption of the sons of the forest. You pray in faith and the angels of God shall guard and comfort you, and the Lamanites that behold in thee truth and light shall apply unto thee for instruction. We dedicate and consecrate thee to this mission that the blessings of them which are over you may rest upon thee. These blessings and all pertaining to this mission shall rest on thee, in the name of Jesus Christ, Amen.
>
> Thomas D. Brown, scribe.

On the company's return home, it stopped at the crossing of Ross Fork,

[57]Salmon River Mission Journal, 23 and 31 May 1857.

[58]Cummings, Travel of President Brigham Young to Oregon 1857, 12 May 1857.

"where Captain [Richard] Grant, agent of the Hudson's Bay Company, and a few Indians had their buffalo robe lodges," said Leonard E. Harrington. He went on: "President Young and several of the brethren, myself among them, called on the captain at his lodge—he was very sociable and generous in his treatment. His wife was a squaw, though of fine stature and nicely dressed in her Indian costume. The captain had several children (half breeds of course) two or three of whom were daughters nearly grown."[59] The entourage arrived back in Great Salt Lake City on 26 May.

BRIGHAM YOUNG: THE FARTHER WE WENT NORTH . . .

"In my travels with the Saints, up to this day, I can truly say that I never had the pleasure of journeying with so peaceful and orderly a company as the one with which I traveled to Salmon river," a renewed Brigham Young told a gathering of his followers in the bowery at Great Salt Lake on the first Sunday after returning from the most important journey of his career in the Rocky Mountains.[60] "If any body was out of humor, or cross, or irritated, it must have been myself," he said, although he had tried "to keep my own temper as cool as possible." Otherwise, he had little good to say in public about the northern country he had seen. "I begged [the brethren] not to take all the rock out of the road, for if they did there would be nothing to travel on," he said. At the start of their trip, the Malad Valley, north of Bear River, had seemed "pretty desolate, cold, hard, sterile," he went on.[61]

REMARKS BY BRIGHAM YOUNG ON 31 MAY 1857, *DESERET NEWS*, 10 JUNE 1857, 7:14, 107/1–3.

But after we had traveled over the Basin rim into Bannack Valley, descending a mountain beside which the one we call the Big Mountain is a mole hill,[62]

[59]Harrington, "Journal of Leonard E. Harrington," 24. After the death of his first wife, Johnny Grant's mother, Richard Grant married Helene Kittson McDonald, the daughter of trader Finan McDonald and a Pend d'Oreille woman. The couple had three daughters, Adeline, Julia Priscilla, and Helene Wilhelmina, then ages six, eight, and eleven, respectively. See Meikle, ed., *Very Close to Trouble: The Johnny Grant Memoir*, 12.

[60]Though Young found great pleasure in this journey, it is seldom mentioned by most of his biographers. Young's company arrived at Great Salt Lake at 6:30 P.M. on Tuesday, 26 May, after an absence of thirty-three days.

[61]*Deseret News*, 10 June 1857, 7:14, 107/1–3.

[62]The steepest climb on the Mormon Trail between the Missouri River and Salt Lake Valley, located east of Salt Lake City on Utah Route 65.

> down through the Little Bannack Valley on to Shanghi Plain and traveled northeasterly and northwesterly almost in a semicircle to Spring Creek, then up Spring Creek over to Salmon River and wended our way down that stream through swamps and willows, and climbed over points of bluffs to keep from being mired, and had paid our brethren a visit and returned again to Malad Valley, it looked to us like one of the most beautiful valleys that any person had ever beheld, while before this experience we thought that nobody could live there; and I expect that if we had gone a few hundred miles [farther] north it would have looked still better to us, for the farther north we went the further we found ourselves in the northern country. And if the Malad is a good valley, we can go further north to those not quite so good, and the further we go north, the less good characteristics are connected with the valleys, except in the articles of fish, water and, in some instances, timber, and when people are obliged to live in the north country, that will be high time for them to go there.

Privately, however, Young told a different story. Three days after his return, he wrote Apostle Orson Pratt in England that "we saw much land some little of it good soil, much good grazing land, but the best soil we are told 'lies still ahead' in the Bitter root valley and in the vallies still further east on the head waters of the Mo. R. [Missouri River]." He continued: "We saw enough to satisfy us, had we hitherto been ignorant of the fact, that the world is not yet over peopled, and, there are thousands of acres of good arable and pasture land where thousands of the honest and industrious poor now immured in factories and other civilized prisons could sustain themselves and thrive as industrious bees of Deseret's hive breathing a pure and wholesome air, free to do all the good they can to the human family and to themselves."[63]

Brigham Young: The North Is the Place for Us

Later that year, as an American army and a new governor approached Utah, the northern country appeared even better. On 6 September, Young called the attention of trusted inner circle leaders to Fort Limhi. "Now do we not want a station about half way from here say near fort Hall?" he asked them. "Should we not send men say 20 to make a station there?" Others at the closed meeting, including John Bernhisel, Utah's delegate to Congress, and apostles George A. Smith and Wilford

[63]Young to Pratt, 29 May 1857, Box 21, Folder 1–6, Moorman Collection, Weber State University.

Woodruff, agreed that they should. "[Young] said that the north is the place for us & not the South," according to Woodruff. "No one but the Saints would want the Cold North Country." The Mormon leader went on: "This is the [key] of this Continent & I think we had better keep near the lock & keep the [key] in our own hand." If we send a company, he said, "We want to send them this fall so that we can put in grain there this season."[64]

Garland Hurt's Snare Misfires

When the trap that Agent Garland Hurt set for Brigham Young four years before finally snapped shut in 1861, such grandiose plans to move north had been long forgotten. At the direction of Congress, the new superintendent of Indian Affairs for Utah that year investigated Brigham Young's expenditures in from 1856 to 1857 when he served as head of Indian Affairs for the territory. Benjamin Davis examined dozens of witnesses under oath and afterward marveled that he had never seen "in a practice of many years at the Bar" a time when so many witnesses "concurred with such precision and exactitude." Such "perfect recollection," the newcomer to Utah went on, "could not have failed to convince the most skeptical of the truthfulness of their statements."[65]

Perhaps so, but Davis's report listed a bill for $1,044.50 from Mormon merchant Levi Stewart on April 24, the day that Young left for Salmon River, for "Indian goods furnished Brigham Young, superintendent, for the Indians in Weber, Cache, and Malade valleys," but made no mention of Oregon. It also showed a total payment of nearly $400 to four members of Young's party to Fort Limhi, plus two who did not make the trip, for services rendered "on a visit to the Indians on Weber, Cache, and Malade Valleys," all in northern Utah.[66] The eyewitness records of Superintendent Young's trip to Fort Limhi in spring 1857 make no mention of any such visits, but based on the "perfect recollection" of these witnesses, Davis cleared Young of any wrongdoing.

[64]Kenney, ed., *Wilford Woodruff's Journal,* 6 September 1857, 5:90.

[65]See "Accounts of Brigham Young, Superintendent of Indian Affairs in Utah Territory," House Exec. Doc. 29 (37-2), 1862.

[66]Ibid., 60–65. This remarkable document has never received the careful study it deserves.

This absolution, however, did not result in the immediate payment of the accounts by a Congress that was struggling to finance a war, nor did it entirely disentangle Brigham Young from Garland Hurt's snare. "It is a very difficult thing to get a money claim through Congress now from what it was before the bombardment of Fort Sumpter, and it may be more difficult hereafter," congressional delegate John Bernhisel warned Young in March 1862. "I greatly fear that your claim cannot be got through Congress at the present session, and perhaps not until the war is at an end if it ever comes to an end, without employing the machinery (the men & means) frequently resorted to here in prosecuting private claims," he continued. Young agreed to hire Simpson P. Moses to lobby for the claim in exchange for twenty percent of the final settlement.[67]

The need to settle the case grew more pressing when former Utah federal judge John Cradlebaugh, acting as Nevada's territorial delegate, denounced the claim before the U.S. House of Representatives in February 1863:

> There is now pending in this house a claim for thirty or forty thousand dollars, which includes about four thousand dollars for goods distributed by John D. Lee to the Indians about the Mountain Meadows, within twenty days after the massacre; and also includes pay to Lee while he was engaged in the commission of the massacre. Whether Brigham will get it or not, I do not know.[68]

As Bernhisel predicted, Young's claim remained unpaid until the end of the Civil War, but not for lack of trying. Bernhisel's successors William Hooper and John F. Kinney both struggled to have the claim settled. Without notifying Simpson Moses, about December 1864 Kinney engaged J. T. Stevens's "assistance in the prosecution of this just demand against the U.S." in exchange for fifteen percent of the settlement.[69]

Ultimately, "in the face of all Cradlebaugh's venomous conduct," Stevens persuaded Congress to approve payment of $38,487.53 to

---

[67]Bernhisel to Young, 24 March 1862; and Moses to Bernhisel, 24 March 1862, Brigham Young Collection, LDS Archives.

[68]Cradlebaugh, *Utah and the Mormons,* 21. Historian Juanita Brooks concluded Cradlebaugh's charge was true. See Brooks, *Mountain Meadows Massacre,* 153–54.

[69]Stevens to Young, 30 March 1866, Brigham Young Collection.

Brigham Young in 1866. Judge Kinney wrote to Young saying he had "assured Mr Stevens that you would deal justly by him," but Simpson Moses blamed Kinney's "ridiculous gladiatorial encounters on the floor of the House" for the delay. Upon learning he would not be paid for his services, Moses complained to the Mormon leader that he had "actually disbursed" five hundred dollars "in the early stages of the case" and was "in honor bound to distribute among gentlemen whose relations to public affairs are such as cannot be disregarded" another five hundred dollars. Brigham Young apparently ignored Moses's pleadings.[70]

Yet the government payment did not end lingering suspicions about Young's 1857 Indian claims. After a former U.S. deputy marshal charged in April 1877 that U.S. Attorney Sumner Howard had suppressed "vital portions" of John D. Lee's confession implicating Brigham Young in the Mountain Meadows massacre, Howard looked for a way to fend off this and other charges that he had protected Mormon interests in the Lee trial at the expense of justice. He wrote to U.S. Attorney General Charles Devens and proposed reexamining Young's Indian accounts. Howard claimed he "had very good evidence" that the Mormon leader "had the benefit of the property of the murdered Emigrants and defrauded the United States." Devens sent Howard copies of the claims, but a lack of funds hampered the subsequent investigation, which ended with the death of Brigham Young.[71]

Trouble on the Frontier

All this lay in the future, but in the spring of 1857, a wave of rumors touched off by the Mormon leader's journey to Oregon rolled across the Northwest. Accounts of Young's pow-wows with the Indians circulated swiftly among the tribes. They alarmed white settlements and the thin blue line of U.S. Army posts that picked them up on the eve of Indian uprisings in Washington and Oregon territories.

"A very curious statement was recently made me by some of the Indians near Steilacoom," said George Gibbs in Washington on 29 November that year. "They said that the Klikatats had told them that

[70]Kinney to Young, 2 April 1866; Moses to Young, 30 April 1866; and Moses to Young, 8 September 1866, Brigham Young Collection.

[71]Dwyer, *The Gentile Comes to Utah,* 105–06.

Choosuklee, (Jesus Christ,) had recently appeared on the other side of the country, and all would be well for themselves," he said. Concluded Gibbs: "It needed only a little reflection to connect this second advent with the visit of Brigham Young to the Flathead and Nez Perces country."[72]

In repeating this story to U.S. Army headquarters, Gen. Newman S. Clarke at San Francisco, the commander, Department of the Pacific, included frightening words from a "private" letter on 1 December from Capt. Ralph W. Kirkham at Fort Walla Walla. "The Snakes tell our Indians that they are well supplied with ammunition, and that they can get from the Mormons any quantity that they wish," the officer reported. He continued, "and they further tell our Indians that the Mormons are anxious to supply them, to wit: the Nez Perces, the Cayuses, and Walla-Wallas, with everything they wish."[73]

Similar stories prompted James W. Nesmith, the superintendent of Indian Affairs for Oregon and Washington, to notify his superior, James W. Denver, U.S. Commissioner of Indian Affairs, on 1 September 1857 that he had "taken steps" to investigate the "large colony of Mormons" on Salmon River. Nesmith sent Dr. Richard H. Lansdale, forty-six-year-old Flathead agent, to look into reports that Mormons at Fort Limhi were "supplying the Indians with arms and ammunition and inciting them to hostilities."[74]

In August 1857 Lansdale visited Bitterroot Valley, but not Fort Limhi, and later reported these stories were "unsustained by sufficient proof, if not altogether groundless." At the same time, "the leading Flathead chiefs have serious fears lest the Mormons, being driven from their present settlements by the government, should overrun and occupy their lands in force," he continued.[75] "They expressed their fears in the formal talks I had with them." While the Bible-reading agent "used every possi-

---

[72]Clarke to Thomas, 1 January 1858, Sen. Exec. Doc. 1, v. 2, pt. 2 (35-2), 1858, 335, 336.

[73]There is enough evidence of Mormon trade in arms and ammunition, mainly by individual missionaries, to initiate such stories among the tribes. For example, the unedited Salmon River Mission Journal in LDS Archives and Utah State University, reports on 24 July 1857: "The Indians are now catching a great many fish a portion of which they trade for ammunition and sundry other Indian trade and some for flower [*sic*]." At the same time, the author has found no evidence of a widespread campaign to arm the Northwest tribes as this report alleges. The shortage of gunpowder in Utah Territory in 1857 indicates the Mormons simply did not have ammunition available to distribute to the Indians.

[74]Nesmith to Denver, 1 September 1857, Sen. Exec. Doc. 11, v. 2, (35-1), 1858, 612.

[75]Ibid., Lansdale to Nesmith, 22 September 1857, 663–69.

ble effort to allay" Flathead fears of the Mormons,[76] such rumors only persisted as the months passed until General Clarke on 12 January 1858 alerted U.S. Army units at Fort Walla Walla:

> Information from various sources and points on the frontier leads to the conclusion that through the Mormons the Indians are being inclined to hostility, and that a conflict in Utah may be the signal for trouble on the frontier, and it is not improbable that the Mormons may move north.[77]

---

[76] R. H. Lansdale Journal, 8 August 1857.

[77] Mackall to Steptoe, 12 January 1858, Sen. Exec. Doc. 1 (35-2), 1858, 336.

Chapter 7

One of Nature's Ladies

I told them of the lovely fair creatur[e] whom I loved and that I wished not to shrink from any duty but I would like to marry a white girl first.
— *Lewis W. Shurtliff*[1]

When the Mormons first came to Salmon River in June 1855, the natives "received their company with the best of feelings, yet they were not asleep for they had already undertaken to prove the chastity of the men by offering them their females," said Clerk David Moore, "but in this they failed to bring any into transgression."[2] As Thomas Smith later admitted to Brigham Young, the missionaries had not realized at the time that one of their responsibilities, as emissaries to the "remnants of the House of Jacob," was to marry Indian wives, a policy made possible by the practice of polygamy. After Young's visit, they attempted to correct this misunderstanding. Recalled Pleasant Green Taylor:

> President Young had told us to go and identify ourselves with the Indians or Lamanites. The following day after our arrival at [Salmon River] some 500 Lamanites came to our camp and were very friendly. Many fathers among them brought their daughters and desired us to marry them but not understanding the meaning of the term identify as used by President Young, he knowing that if we should take this course it would have the effect of uniting us and causing them to remain our friends. When they found that we would not take their daughters they departed.[3]

Invitation to Marry

As the mountain men understood, the invitation to marry their daughters was an expression of tribal acceptance and friendship, but the

---

[1]All quotes in this chapter, not otherwise indicated, are from Life and Travels of Lewis Warren Shurtliff. [2]Salmon River Mission Journal, 23 June 1855.

[3]Pleasant Green Taylor Autobiography and Family Record.

Mormon newcomers mistook it as a test of their morality. By rejecting the offer they set themselves apart from their native cousins to the benefit of their mountaineer adversaries, as later events would point up. In the meantime, the oldest of the missionaries wasted little time in showing that there was at least one member of the company who welcomed the opportunity to form an alliance with their new neighbors.

Forty-eight-year-old Isaac Shepard from Farmington "has been trying to get a squaw to live with ever since we have been on Salmon River," reported Charles Dalton on 24 June 1855. Later that year, Shepard "took one into his house to keep unbenouns [unbeknown] to the President or to any one else of the mission until in the afternoon he then told of it and on the 25th the president made him turn her away," Dalton said. The wayward missionary further "had a Spaniard and his family living in his house with him at the same time the squaw went away and stayed two days, returned, and lived with the spaniard until the 17th of November when the Brethern returned from Salt Lake," Dalton went on. "Manuel also said that Shepard is sleep[ing] with his squaw."[4]

With only this known exception, prior to Brigham Young's visit in May 1857 the missionaries maintained a deliberate distance from native women. At that time, Young asked the mission president "why we had not identified ourselves with Israel," according to Pleasant Green Taylor, and a puzzled Thomas Smith answered, "he did not understand what he meant by that term." So Young's first counselor spelled out what it meant for the seed of Abraham "to be grafted in."[5] President Kimball "told us to go now and take their daughters to wife," Taylor said, "to which President Young replied that Brother Kimball says for you to 'go and get wives from among the daughters of the Lamanites,' but I do not say for you to marry them but I say for you to go and try for I think the time is past, it is now too late."[6]

Having been told to "go and try," Taylor that same day "took eight of my brethern with me and went out among the Indians and we tried hard to get them to marry us but they said no."[7] As Young had predicted, the

[4]Charles Dalton Journal, entries in June, October, and November 1855. For Manuel's probable identify, see Chapter 4, note 6.

[5]Cummings, Travel of President Brigham Young to Oregon 1857, 10 May 1857.

[6]Pleasant Green Taylor Autobiography and Family Record.

[7]Ibid. Eventually at least three missionaries did marry Indian women. Englishman Thomas Day, Jr., at age forty-three married a Bannock woman on 22 December 1857; twenty-seven-year-old Ezra Barnard took

natives rebuffed their overtures, which may have been a blessing for the thirty-year-old Kentuckian. For "Green" Taylor already had three wives in Utah, including two sisters of Lewis Shurtliff, plus seven children, five by his first wife and two, plus one on the way, by the second. Just before leaving Ogden with Brigham Young's company to Fort Limhi, he had married Shurtliff's younger sister, Jane Narcissus, age sixteen.

Acting mission head Thomas Bingham on 19 July advised the missionaries to go slow when it came to marriage with the local inhabitants.[8] "Pres Bingham gave us some advice as to trying to get wives from among the Natives," said Jacob Miller, acting as the mission recorder in place of the absent David Moore. "They have refused to let thier [*sic*] daughters go or at least seem not willing and said the Pres [Bingham] it is enough for the present let it rest say nothing more about it."[9]

At the same time, there were two schools of thought on this question. Forty-year-old New Yorker Crandall Dunn from Ogden brought it up before the Sunday meeting on 30 August. "Br. Dunn in his remarks seemed to be very pointed upon the subject of our not having done any thing for which we were sent out here referring to remarks of Pres. Kimbal[l] when he was here," Miller recorded.[10]

Most of the missionaries, however, shared the feelings of twenty-three-year-old Charles Franklin Middleton about the duty to forge marital ties with the natives. "As far as us marr[y]ing squaws is concerned I can say that if that is [the] only way of bring[ing] them about to what the Lord wants of them I am afraid the thing will be prolonged some time yet from the fact that the natives are not that way inclined at all, neather do I believe that there are but few of the Mormon boys in this place that are very keen to perform that part of their religion," he wrote his wife, Martha Browning. "I can say for one that if it should be made known to me that it was the only way for me to secure my salvation I mite go forward in the performense of that duty though with a degree [of] reluctence."[11] When Middleton went to Fort Limhi in October

a native wife on 28 December 1857; and Richard Bishop Margetts, also from England, at age forty-three married an Indian woman. All three had other wives in Utah. As far as it is known, these unions produced no offspring. See Journals of Charles F. Middleton and Charles Dalton, December and January, 1857–1858.

[8]On 18 June Thomas Smith left with a party of fifteen to bring their families in Utah to the settlement.

[9]Salmon River Mission Journal, 19 July 1857. [10]Ibid., 30 August 1857.

[11]C. F. Middleton to Martha Middleton, 27 November 1857, Charles F. Middleton Journal.

1857, he left his wife and their two sons, the youngest less than three months old, at Ogden.

Of all the missionaries, perhaps the one least interested in the idea of "grafting" with the seed of Abraham in the wilderness, formally or otherwise, was twenty-one-year-old Lewis Warren Shurtliff. Being the only male out of eight children born to his father, Luman A. Shurtliff, and Eunice Gaylord, the first of his five wives, the young missionary had already learned much about the opposite sex from his seven sisters. But he still found it difficult to establish a lasting relationship with one of its members.

In Iowa he had "formed an acquaintance with a young Lady whose name was Eliza Hadden." They became "intimate friends and passed many happy hours together," he said. But after his family left for Utah in 1851, "we never met but once; and that was on the plains in Eighteen Sixty three." By then "she had been twice married and was then a widow," he later remembered.

His family moved into Bingham's Fort in 1854, established three years earlier by Vermont native Erastus Bingham and guarded by a redoubt of mud and adobe within the present limits of today's Ogden City. Boasting a population that year of more than seven hundred, the settlement offered ample opportunities for a young man to form "acquaintance with many fine young men and women or girls." The first young woman Shurtliff "kept company with" was a "girl of no learning, or refinement, and this I could not endure," he said. "I could tolerate, and even associate with men who were uncouth, but could (not) endure such rudeness in the op[p]osite sec [*sic*]."

"To the fair daughters of Eve" Lewis Shurtliff had little to say over the following year. He built a house and "kept company" with several young women. "The last of this number was Jane Fay," he said, but then added, "We fell out." Discouraged and unhappy, he hired himself out to Nathaniel Leavitt as a proxy to go to Salmon River in his place for six months at twenty-five dollars a month. It was then that his fortune changed. As he left Ogden on 19 October with a party bound for Fort Limhi, "I first saw She [*sic*] who after ward became my wife, and made the remark that such would be the case," he said. "She like myself was on her way to Salmon River." Among this company were the first white females to settle in present Idaho, including the subject of Shurtliff's attention, a young woman who turned thirteen on the day they arrived at the mission, 17 November 1855.

Louisa Catherine Smith was the daughter of Addison and Laura Bentley Smith of Vermont, who adopted Mormonism and gathered in 1843 with latter-day Israel to its new city-state of Nauvoo on the Mississippi River. Soon after their arrival, her mother became ill and died, leaving four children, ranging in age from eight to the youngest, Louisa, less than one year old. Because her father "was also sick and destitute of means," the children were "scattered to different places." Asked to "take a little girl," David and Susan Moore, a childless couple, went to see Smith about "taking Louisa" and he "gave me the child as my own," the Canadian said. She was a "little over a year old when we took her."[12]

Lewis Shurtliff: A Butifull Vision

For Lewis Shurtliff the winter of 1855–1856 at Fort Limhi "wore away almost impreceiptibly [*sic*]." He broke the boredom by hunting and "put myself assiduously to the task of learning the Indian Language or Dielect" [*sic*], both with success. He spent holidays "in dancing and social entertainments where I formed an acqua[i]ntance with Miss Louisa C. Smith, an adopted child of David and Susan Moore." Otherwise, "the winter wore on and we were constantly studying and attending to our daily avocations." Finally spring came and "put on her richest foliage and the wildnes[s] of the Mountain scenery delighted and pleased me."

Life and Travels of Lewis Warren Shurtliff.

Our Summer labours now began to bear heavily upon our men, and it seemed a treat when Sunday came. July fifteenth I attended meeting, or services after Worship. Feeling somewhat lonely I sauntered out for a walk bending my steps towards the River. After crossing a fine streach [stretch] of butiful meadows covered with fine wild flowers, as I wandered alone, along the River I saw a butifull vision near the stream. She was warbling some little song.

I stood fixed to the spot, not knowing whether to approach her or not, fearing the fair creature should leave me and all become an illusion.

I approached and said fair Maiden, you have wandered far from your cot-

[12]Compiled Writings and Life History of David Moore, 19.

tage? Are you not fearfull that some young Bannock Chief will become Enchanted or enamored with one so young and butifull and spirit you away to his rude Lodge there to bask in the light of thy smile.

Oh, no kind Sir. I have no fear of those red men, there is a power that binds them in my presence.

I am not alone as you suppose, there is one near who is ever watchfull for my saf[e]ty and will protect the Lonely Wanderer.

We sat down together on the green sward in order to arrange a boquet of wild flowers which we had gathered from the Meadows. I was no longer my own master. I was enslaved by this young Maiden. She had won my heart.

After a pleasant walk we returned to our home which stood a short distance from the River. Surrounded in the distance by Mountains covered with perpetual snow.

Soon after this idyllic interlude, Shurtliff took off on horseback with Nathaniel Leavitt, riding fifty miles a day, to obtain a load of salt from Mormon settlements so that the mission could begin to ship pickled fish to Utah. Before leaving, he saw Louisa again and apparently allowed his religious zeal to gather Israel's remnants in the wilderness to overwhelm the desires of his heart. It was a mistake he would quickly regret.

LIFE AND TRAVELS OF LEWIS WARREN SHURTLIFF.

I one evening took a walk and met Louisa Moore on the road to the field. We sat down together on the hillside and chatted. I knew she loved me and I told her (although contrary to my feelings) that we never could be else but Brother and Sister. This was like a dagger to her heart, the color left her butiful cheeks, and she seemed perfectly lost. After a short time in silence she arose. Standing there in all the dignity of her sec [sex]. She stooped down and imprinted a kiss upon my cheek, and was gone before I could rally. When I did come to, I was alone. Long I sat in meditation and wished that I could recall those bitter words that I had spoken. But alas it was to[o] late.

Shurtliff soon became "a lonely wanderer" while Louisa Moore "found the society of others that seemed to suit her." The two did not meet again before the young woman left Salmon River later that year "to finish her education" in Utah. Shurtliff rode alongside her party for a few miles, but "did not converse privitly [*sic*] with Miss Louisa Moore." As winter came on, Shurtliff devoted himself to "improvements of the mind" and kept himself busy at the mission where he was "installed Chief Cook," which "took most of my time. To overcome his loneliness, he "determined to make a good use of my present advantages by apropriating all of my time to useful study."

Then there came in late January an unexpected, if dangerous, opportunity to see Louisa again. Thomas Smith named Shurtliff as one of a four-man party, including P. G. Taylor, Lachonias Barnard and himself, to make a perilous midwinter ride to Great Salt Lake and to deliver to Brigham Young the report and map by Benjamin F. Cummings on Bitterroot Valley. To better their chances for survival, they took three horses each, but still often covered only three or four miles a day as they fought their way through heavy snow along the divides.[13]

Reaching his father's home at Ogden in mid-February, Shurtliff greeted his family and enjoyed his full first meal in nearly a month before hurrying to David Moore's house "to see Miss Louisa." To his regret, he found that "her affections were weened from me," he said, admitting, "I had no one to blame but my own dear self." The meeting was "cool and formal; each seemed ill at ease." He left "much depressed in spirit." He tried to forget his sorrow as he prepared to return to Fort Limhi, but Louisa Moore seemed always to be on his mind. He once saw her at a public gathering and that night "dreamed that we were married." Shurtliff thought this fantasy would never come to pass, he said, "but little did I understand the providences [*sic*] of my Heavenly Father." Without seeking such outside help, however, he put down his stubborn spirit and humbly begged the young woman to forgive him.

LIFE AND TRAVELS OF LEWIS WARREN SHURTLIFF.

Ogden City
March 6th 1857

Miss Louisa
It is with pleasure, I write a few lines to you, To inform you of my present feelings, I feel verry lonesome at present but I hope for better days. Do not be offended with me for this letter. But remember our friendship while at Fort Limhi; which I look upon as happy days, often have I been to places, where we have sat together, and talked of different subjects, Alas, those happy hours are past, and now am left alone, I want you to forgive me, if you can, for it seems as if I was deprived of my best friend, if you cannot forgive as I shall be verry unhappy, write to me the first chance, I remain, your friend, and lover.
Lewis W. Shurtliff

[13]For the story of this undertaking, see Chapter 5.

His letter brought no response and the young missionary's hopes seemed blasted. On 31 March he "went to see my girl," and discovered "another man there." Leaving her suitor in the house, he took Louisa Moore outside and "went out on the well curb" where he poured out his heart. "She was much affected with my confession and she wept," he said. "We parted the best of friends." Soon afterward, however, he "went to see Louisa" again. "All was now over," he said. "She treated me with the utmost coldness." Four days later he went to see her again, he said, and "she treated [me] scornfully." The day before he left to return to Fort Limhi as a member of Brigham Young's company, he addressed a final note to the young woman he loved and had seemingly lost.

> Ogden City April 24th 1857
>
> Miss Louisa, It is with a sorrowful heart, that I take my pen in hand to write a few lines to you, not to make you unhappy (because that would make my own heart bleed) but to ask of you one small favor, to remember you by, when Sorrow and gloom shall surround me, and I shall rover over the mountains, to drive away those unhappy feelings that now fill my breast. I feel that I am despised and hated and I know not the cause. I have tried to think wherein I have hurt your feelings, but I cannot, I done as I agreed by comeing to see you, what more could I do [?] we met at Farmington you treated me coolly. I saw you at Conference [when] you still treated me the same, I went to your house your treatment was severe. Prehaps [*sic*] you never want to see my face again, if so your wish shall be granted although it would be hard for me if I have to stay in the mountains for years, Oh that I could call back those happy days that we have spent together, but no, they are past and gone forever, yet you have denied me the comfort of seeing you, or conversing with you whitch was my only joy. Oh my dear girl I am almost led to wish that we had never met, but it is wicked to make such a wish, when an overruling power has caused it to be so. I wish I could tell you my feelings. I am alone and am lonesome, permit me to enjoy your parting hand before I go, let me see you one moment before I go, I wish to know why you have forsaken me. I cannot write any more at present.
>
> I remain as ever your friend, and lover
> Lewis W. Shurtliff

Receiving no answer, the young missionary started the next day, 25 April 1857 "for my northern home, with a sad heart, in the Company of the President and Company," he said. "I rode as rear guard." Later, at Fort Limhi, he heard Apostle Heber C. Kimball enlighten the missionaries on their responsibility to "connect ourselves with the house of Israel," hopefully with a chief's daughter, for "when a man marries a chief's daughter," Kimball said, "he marries the whole family! Yes the whole nation."[14] That Shurtliff had a mind of his own he had already demonstrated during the great Mormon revival, known as the Reformation, when he called one church leader's sermon "the most vulgar preaching" he had ever heard. And he dismissed Kimball's instruction to marry Indian women as just "stray doctrine."

Accordingly, the young missionary did not join "Green" Taylor and the others who went out to the Indian camps over the next month to investigate the availability of Indian women they might marry. Instead he spent his time "in herding cattle and horses" and "continued to cook during the month."

The Chief's Daughter

Then came the fateful day. "Friday twenty fourth of July George Hill asked Snagg the Snake Chief, for Catherine his daughter." The Ohioan "returned to the Fort in high spirits telling all that he would soon marry the Chiefs daughter." Although tribal interest in forming marriage ties with their Mormon cousins had cooled, it did appear that there was one native maiden who seemed anxious to take this step.

She was Catherine, the daughter of Shoshone Chief Ti-o-von-du-ah, better known as Old Snag, who had been baptized with other members of his large family at Fort Limhi in November 1855. Before becoming available for marriage she had been the live-in wife of Bitterroot Valley trader Frederick H. Burr, who had started for California earlier that year, encountering Brigham Young's company to Fort Limhi on the Flathead Trail along Snake River. This was apparently unknown to the missionaries. That the Shoshone woman was comely, and that her former husband had been smitten by her, is suggested at the end of Burr's 1857 journal. Over a page listing trade goods he scrawled in large letters the name "Catharine" as if daydreaming.[15] But his departure had left her alone and ready to establish a new relationship.

---

[14]Cummings, Travel of President Brigham Young to Oregon 1857, 10 May 1857.

[15]Frederick H. Burr Journal, December 1857, Beinecke Library.

LEWIS SHURTLIFF: IT WAS ME SHE WANTED

When George Hill rejoiced that he had obeyed Apostle Kimball's instruction and won the hand of the chief's daughter, "Some one told him not to be two [*sic*] sanguine of success," Shurtliff said. "At this remark there was a thrill ran over my whole frame. What could it mean[?]" He soon answered his own question.

LIFE AND TRAVELS OF LEWIS WARREN SHURTLIFF.

The next day this fair daughter of the Rocky Mountains came to see me, returned the following day and told me plainly that it was me she wanted, this announcement was astounding, and had it not been for an open window near at hand I should have fell. I finally rallied and said I am to[o] young to marry; this she contradicted. I done all that I possibly could to dissuade her from such a rash (and I thought an imprudent) step; but all to no purpose. She said she did not want Mr. Hill that he was two [*sic*] old and that if she did not get me she would have no one.

When this dark Damsel left me I sat down and wept. My thoughts were of Louisa. She to whom I was devoted both soul and body, [and] here I was, either must disobey the President's wish or marry this woman. I saw the sacrifice that I was now called upon to make. I must forever abandon the thoughts of marrying the girl of my choice.

No sleep came to my eyelids nor food passed my lips. Often would this thought come to my mind. Shall I shrink from a duty imposed on some one, by the President of the Church to marry this particular [woman] or should I do whatever they told me and trust the event with God.

Before the dawn of day my mind was made up to confer with our President,[16] over the question in regard to the matter.

Morning came at last and breakfast being ready I told the President of my situation. He sympathised with me; but shook his head in silence, he called the Brethern of the Mission together and after the matter was fully put before them they desided [*sic*] I should take her. This I felt was my death knel[l] sounding in my ear.

I told them of a lovely fair creatur[e] whom I loved and that I wished not to shrink from any duty but I would like to marry a white girl first.

This request being denied me I saut [sought] the solitude of the grove; where I oft had wandered, here I asked the Lord to strengthen me for the task.

The following Evening this dusky maid came to see me and asked me to go home with her, this wish I complied with; We had a long talk together and I can assure you it pertook of the romantic.

[16]Mission President Thomas Smith.

This brought to pass a dream that I had some time previous. I had an interpreter who went with me to see the girl's father and he said that she could not marry without sertain papers from the former husband. Catherine told me that Geo. W. Hill had not acted fairely with me but that he had been disseatfull and asked her father for himself instead of asking for me. All this I was prepared to endure. It mattered but little what should be my fate for all was now lost.

A few days passed by and the Old Chief moved away down the River Catherine staying untill after dark then out of galentry [gallantry] I saddled my horse and went with her and her Brother to take a ride of twelve miles in the butifull moonlight with one of Nature's Ladies. Reminds me of wandering in Berlin Museum among the statuary.[17]

Her Brother was sent ahead and we rode alone. She confessed her passion for me and at our parting said she would see me again. We parted, I to a twelve mile ride she no doubt to dreamland. But it is doubtfull whether those dreams were pure and free from sensual desires, for she was an uneducated unsafistakated [unsophisticated] Squaw—

A few days brought her back to our house. She stayed there for some days and like Patipher's she saut [sought] to ceduce [seduce] a boy.[18] I soon got clear of her and then I began to feel free again.

Lewis Shurtliff: Two Rose Trees Had Grown and Twined

As if in answer to the young man's prayers, events worked together to "clear" him of Chief Snag's daughter. While there was no escape from his companions' judgment that obedience to counsel required him to marry her, the obligation rested on her desire to do so. On 16 September Thomas Harris, Dr. Atkinson, and David Pattee came from Fort Owen to "get some mill irons made" by the mission blacksmith. When they left two days later they "took with them Indian Snags d[a]ughter her Husband having sent for her."[19] Catherine's "husband" was Frederick Burr. He had left that spring for California, but after meeting Brigham Young's party on Snake River and visiting his brother, David A.

[17]Shurtliff's offhand comment refers to a visit to Germany after he was called to the LDS British Mission in 1867.

[18]Potiphar was one of the pharaoh's officers who purchased Joseph from the Midianites after his brothers had sold him into slavery. For the story of his wife's attempt to seduce the young son of Jacob, see Genesis 39:1–20.

[19]Salmon River Mission Journal, 16, 18 September 1857.

Burr, in Great Salt Lake City, he had decided to return to Bitterroot Valley instead. He then sent for her, and she dutifully went back to him.

At the same time, the evidence also points to the intercession of Thomas Smith, who engineered Shurtliff's release from the religious duty and opened the way for him to realize his heart's desire. In keeping with Brigham Young's promise to expand the colony in Oregon, Smith returned to Utah that July to collect a new company of settlers and lead them back to Salmon River. Events indicate that while in Utah he discussed the problem with Young and won approval to release Shurtliff from this duty. Moreover, the outcome suggests that he talked with David Moore and even Louisa herself, who appears to have concluded that she had made the young missionary suffer enough for his earlier rejection. For while Catherine left, she came of her own will.

To carry the good news, Smith left his main settlement company at Market Lake on Snake River and rode ahead with Milton Hammond and William Marler to arrive on 22 October at Fort Limhi. "I listened to the reports with anxiety, in their report I should hear my destiny," Shurtliff said. "I stood in a retired corner of the house [and] at last the President said Where is Lewis I have news for him." He went on, "Miss Moore is coming in this Company, but I think she is looking in another direction." Shurtliff did not believe that. "I saddled up my horse," he said, "and rode out to meet the company."

LIFE AND TRAVELS OF LEWIS WARREN SHURTLIFF.

I met Miss Louisa. The meeting was not like some of our former associations—Spent the Evening with the Company [and] great was our joy to once again see each others faces.

And now after an estrangement of years our meeting in the same place of our first acquaintance was all that our hearts could desire, we now revisited the butifull spot where we had met and there we found two rose trees had grown and twined their slender branches together. This thenomenon [*sic*] we looked upon as a token of our own futur[e] happiness, and here beneath the azure sky just as the sun had sank behind the lofty mountains casting its dim last rays of light upon our peacefull and butifull little Valley; It was here just as the stars shed their glimering light upon the scene, here we plighted our future; to love each other. There was one thing concerning this meeting that caused us to look forward to the future with some anxiety.

Those two rose bushes after they had come to perfection one of them faded and died. Not being superstitious, we tried to treat this Bad omen of our future with indifference.[20] Still there was something which would whisper your future may not allways be that perfect happiness and joy. We returned to our homes after our Stroll.

Soon after winning back Louisa's affection, Lewis Shurtliff asked David Moore for his daughter's hand, Shurtliff said, and "he gave his consent and a fathers blessing upon us." Moore's wife, Susan, who had come with the latest settlement party to Salmon River, "also gave her heartfelt blessing upon her only adopted child." The couple's "joy was now full and we only wanted the bond of Matrimony to make our happiness complete."

The fourth of January 1858 was the "Eventful Day" for twenty-two-year-old Lewis Warren Shurtliff. As the threat of Indian trouble grew around the isolated colony in Oregon, nearly four hundred miles north of main Mormon settlements, Thomas Smith married the young missionary—but not to the daughter of a Shoshone chief, as instructed by the leaders of his faith. Instead he married him to the girl of his choice. His new wife, Louisa Smith Moore Shurtliff, whose middle name was also Catherine, was fifteen.[21]

---

[20]This "bad omen" unfortunately proved true in October 1866 when Louisa Shurtliff died at Ogden, Utah, five months after the birth of their fourth child.

[21]The other Catherine, Shoshone Chief Snag's daughter, apparently had other husbands besides Frederick Burr in later years. See Epilogue.

Chapter 8

The Mormon Rebellion

In the evening Bro. [Thomas] Smith come in from Salt Lake. He brought the news that Pres. Young had declared our Independence. — *Joseph Harker*

"We started from here to rest the mind and weary the body," Brigham Young said on returning from Oregon in May 1857, "and so far as the body is concerned I believe all parties will agree with me in saying that we have done that most effectually." His journey to Fort Limhi "rested my mind," he told his followers, adding, "I feel that I have renewed my strength, renewed the vigor of my body and mind; and I believe that I am as ready to act in any capacity now as ever I have been in my life."[1] If so, Young's trip to Salmon River had prepared him for the greatest crisis of his career—a military confrontation with the United States. The emergency would also elevate Fort Limhi to a position of primary strategic importance in the Mormon leader's design to establish God's Kingdom as an independent state in the American West.

James Buchanan Sends in the Troops

While Young was in Oregon, Pres. James Buchanan sacked him as governor of Utah, an office he had held since 1850, and ordered the U.S. Army to enforce federal authority in a territory the president considered to be in a state of rebellion.[2] On 28 May 1857, Brevet Lt. Gen. Winfield Scott ordered "not less than 2,500 men," to march west to Utah.[3] He told the expedition's commander, Brevet Brig. Gen. William

[1] *The Deseret News,* 10 June 1857, 7:14, 107, 1/3.

[2] President Millard Fillmore appointed Brigham Young to a four-year term as governor of Utah in 1850. He had continued in office after his term expired under a provision of the territorial organic act, which said that the governor was to serve four years, "and until his successor shall be appointed and qualified."

[3] Scott to Adjutant General, et al, 28 May 1857, House Exec. Doc. 71 (35-1), 4.

Harney, that his command was to serve as a *posse comitatus* in aiding a new governor and other federal officers to keep the peace and enforce the law.[4] The commander in chief further ordered that U.S. soldiers were not to attack any "body of citizens," except in self-defense.[5]

To justify his action, Buchanan later gave Congress some sixty reports by federal officials from 1851 to 1857 charging Mormon leaders with disloyalty and other offenses.[6] Pointing up the importance of early Mormon-Indian relations, more than forty came from the Office of Indian Affairs, most written by U.S. Indian agents in the field. Not counted in Buchanan's filing were a number of other accusations during this period that may have influenced his decision. They included the protests of the emigrants who wintered in Salt Lake Valley in 1850 and 1851;[7] the allegations of Utah's first non-Mormon office holders, who took flight in 1851;[8] Maj. Edward J. Steptoe's 1854 charges of Mormon tampering with the Indians;[9] Justice John F. Kinney's assertions of Mormon manipulation of the courts;[10] and many reports of disloyalty and persecution by emigrants to California and Oregon.

Brigham Young's reply demonstrated why he was known as "the Lion of the Lord" to his followers. "As for any nation's coming to destroy this people," he roared, "God Almighty being my helper, they cannot come here."[11] So it came to pass four years before the South opened fire on Fort Sumter that an appointed governor of an American territory, whose four-year term in office had run out, threw down the gauntlet to a president of the United States. "CITIZENS OF UTAH," he proclaimed on 15 September, "We are invaded by a hostile force." He branded the

---

[4]A *posse comitatus* is a force representative of all citizens called to enforce the law by the legitimate authority of a political jurisdiction.

[5]Lay to Harney, 29 June 1857, House Exec. Doc. 71 (35-1), 7–9.

[6]These reports are compiled in "The Utah Expedition," House Exec. Doc. 71.

[7]See Slater, comp., *Fruits of Mormonism, or A Fair and Candid Statement of Facts Illustrative of Mormon Principles, Mormon Policy, and Mormon Character, by More than Forty Eye-Witnesses*; Bigler, ed., *A Winter with the Mormons: The 1852 Letters of Jotham Goodell*; and *The Daily Union*, Sacramento, 28 June 1851, 2/2–4.

[8]See "Information in reference to the condition of affairs in the Territory of Utah," House Exec. Doc. 25 (32-1), 1852.

[9]See Selected Letters from Col. E. J. Steptoe, 1854–55, DNA, and Miller, "The Impact of the Gunnison Massacre on Mormon-Federal Relations: Colonel Edward Jenner Steptoe's Command in Utah Territory, 1854–1855," M.A. thesis, 1968.

[10]See Records relating to the appointment of Federal judges, attorneys, and marshals for the Territory and State of Utah, 1853–1901, 1855–1856, DNA, UHi.

[11]Remarks by Brigham Young, 13 September, 1857, *Journal of Discourses*, 4:226.

U.S. Army expedition "an armed mercenary mob," declared martial law, and mobilized up to seven thousand men of the territorial militia, better known as the Nauvoo Legion, to repel the "threatened invasion."[12] According to some, he went even beyond this.

Two days before Young's proclamation, Oliver Lee Robinson from Bountiful went to the Sunday meeting in the bowery at Great Salt Lake. There "Prest. B. Young Declared our independence," the twenty-three-year-old New Yorker wrote. "He said if we would live our religion god Would fight Our Battles."[13] An edited version of Young's talk in the church-owned *Deseret News* included such seditious-sounding sentiments as, "This people are free, they are not in bondage to any Government on God's footstool," and the national government would "go by the board through its own corruptions, and no power can save it," but no mention of a declaration of independence as such.[14] Even so, on 12 September Young wrote Apostle Orson Pratt in England that he had sent word to the approaching U.S. Army that "we shall not permit troops to enter our settlements," whether there was an armed confrontation or not. "We are now free," he said, "and we have determined to remain so."[15]

This pronouncement and other actions appeared to confirm Buchanan's opinion that Utah had thrown off the federal yoke. On Young's order, a territory of fewer than forty thousand people defied, almost to a man, a nation of more than thirty million and took comfort from their leader's vow that if it came to an armed test, "one would chase a thousand, and two will put ten thousand to flight."[16] The time would come, Young said, when "a man will go out and say to an army of a hundred thousand men, 'do thus and so or we are upon you', and they will hear the rumbling of chariots and the rushing of troops as in the days of Elijah."[17]

---

[12]"Proclamation by the Governor," 15 September 1857, House Exec. Doc. 71 (35-1), 34, 35. Copies of the proclamation are located in Marriott Library, Univ. of Utah. Variant copies of this document dated 5 August 1857 survive, but Brigham Young's diary reveals that Daniel Wells did not compose the proclamation until late August. See Cooley, ed., *Diary of Brigham Young 1857*, 29 August 1857.

[13]Oliver Lee Robinson Diary, 13 September 1857. For other reports that Young at this time declared Mormon independence from the U.S., see Joseph Harker Journal, 21 October 1857; Milton D. Hammond Journal, 13 September 1857; Brooks, ed., *Not by Bread Alone: The Journal of Martha Spence Heywood, 1850–1856;* Brooks, ed., *On the Mormon Frontier: The Diary of Hosea Stout*, 2:636; and "Letter from a Mormon on the Great Desert, to a Friend in Sacramento," *Sacramento Daily Union*, 19 February 1858.

[14]Remarks by Brigham Young, *The Deseret News*, 23 September 1857, 7:29, 228, 229.

[15]Young to Pratt, 12 September 1857, Moorman Collection. [16]Deut. 32:30.

[17]Remarks by Brigham Young, *The Deseret News*, 23 September 1857, 7:29, 228.

The Mormon leader's defiance apparently rested on the hope that the federal government would become so involved in civil warfare over slavery in Kansas and Missouri that it would ignore the challenge to its authority in the Mountain West.[18] "If we can avert the blow for another season, it is probable that our enemies will have enough to at tend to at home," he said.[19] His strategy aimed to block the federal expedition from entering Salt Lake Valley that fall and allow Divine Providence time to work its will on events elsewhere. Nauvoo Legion soldiers fortified Echo Canyon on the Mormon Trail, the defensible passage through the Wasatch Mountains west of Fort Bridger, while small mounted companies used guerilla tactics to slow the advance of widely scattered and disorganized U.S. forces. Only if American soldiers tried to move past Fort Bridger that fall would their blood be spilled.

Consistent with this strategy were Mormon moves to forge an alliance with their Biblical relatives in the Rocky Mountains. From the first days of the controversial faith, *The Book of Mormon* prophecies that identified the Indians as "a remnant of Israel" and an instrument of divine retribution had aroused fear and opposition among settlers on the American frontier.[20] Such forecasts now seemed to come close to fulfillment as Mormon emissaries told the natives "that our enemies are also their enemies . . . that they must be our friends and stick to us, for if our enemies kill us off, they will surely be cut off by the same parties."[21] To the Gentile nation Brigham Young on 13 September issued a veiled threat. "The people do not realize what they have done by driving us into the midst of the Lamanites," he said. "They prevented Joseph [Smith] from associating with the Indians, but they, through their igno-

[18]According to a teamster who reached California that fall, "the first question the Mormons ask a stranger is, 'How is the Kansas matter?' They have been persuaded by their leaders that this question is to involve the nation in such a furious civil war that it will have no time to attend to the case of the Mormons." See *Sacramento Daily Union*, 13 February 1858, 14:2148, 3/2.

[19]Remarks by Brigham Young, *Journal of Discourses*, 13 September 1857, 4:229.

[20]*The Book of Mormon*, 3 Nephi 20:15–16: "And I say unto you, that if the Gentiles do not repent after the blessing that they shall receive, after they have scattered my people then shall ye, who are a remnant of the house of Jacob, go forth among them; and ye shall be in the midst of them who shall be many; and ye shall be among them as a lion among the beasts of the forest, and as a young lion among the flocks of sheep, who, if he goeth through both treadeth down and teareth in pieces, and none shall deliver." Also see Mic. 5:8.

[21]Wells to Evans, 13 August 1857, David Evans Papers. Also see Adjutant General to Pace, 13 August 1857, Utah Militia Records; Dimick Huntington Journal, September, October 1857; and Brooks, ed., *The Mountain Meadows Massacre*, 34, 35.

rance . . . have driven us into the midst of the Lamanites."[22] Even as he spoke, the coyotes fed on the remains of some 120 emigrants to California who had been murdered two days before by Nauvoo Legion soldiers and their Indian allies on the Spanish Trail in southwestern Utah, at a scenic resting place known as Mountain Meadows.[23]

As mounted companies of Mormons burned grass on the Oregon-California Trail, rustled U.S. Army herds, and torched federal supply trains on the high plains of western Wyoming, Young took action on other fronts to uphold the Mormon theocracy's bid for sovereignty. To prepare for a possible confrontation with the United States, the call to come home and "stand by the kingdom" had gone out as early as December 1856 to settlements at San Bernardino and Carson Valley in present western Nevada.[24] Now these outlying colonies were told to hurry up their return. For no longer would the Kingdom of God compromise or coexist with the Gentile nation. If all else failed, its people would pull up their roots in the Great Basin and move in the only direction they were instructed to go that fall.

Brigham Young: On the North Side of Lake Superior

On 12 September Young ordered Apostle Orson Pratt in England to redirect the Kingdom's life-giving flow of immigrants from Europe away from the Oregon-Mormon Trail, now filled with American troops marching west from Fort Leavenworth. Instead he instructed that new converts to the young millennial faith from England and the Continent should be sent to the north.

Young to Pratt, 12 September 1857, Moorman Collection.

I mentioned in my last, that you had better turn our emigration to the Canadas. You will bear in mind in so doing that good able men should

---

[22]Remarks by Brigham Young, *The Deseret News*, 23 September 1857, 7:29, 229. Joseph Smith was Mormonism's founding prophet.

[23]For more on the 1857 Mountain Meadows Massacre, see Bagley, *Blood of the Prophets: Brigham Young and the Massacre at Mountain Meadows*; Brooks, *The Mountain Meadows Massacre*; and Bigler, *Forgotten Kingdom: The Mormon Theocracy in the American West, 1847–1896*, 159–80.

[24]Remarks by Brigham Young, *The Deseret News*, 23 September 1857, 7:29, 228. For the call to return as early as December 1856, see Bigler to Presidents of Seventies Quorums, 22, 24 December 1856, Nephi Mass Quorum of Seventies Journal. Young finally sent direct orders in August 1857 to evacuate Carson Valley and San Bernardino and return to Utah.

> attend each ship load of passengers, who can calculate for the people, and who are capable to selecting locations suitable for the Saints to Colonize. By referring to the map you will perceive that on the north side of Lake Superior, and along the chain of small Lakes dividing the United States and British possessions there is abundance of space for settlements as that country has none at present. I have been informed by mountaineers, acquainted with that Northern country, that the soil is exceedingly fertile—vegetation rank, and the seasons sufficiently lengthy for raising grain. Those Lakes abound in trout and other fish, game is plentiful, and there is also abundant supplies of useful woods and timber. Should we get a foothold there, I think, the climate will be found sufficiently cold to protect us from the rapacity of those too lazy and villainous to work for a living.

At the same time, Young directed veteran Nauvoo Legion officer Col. Andrew Cunningham to lead a company of fifty colonists north to Snake River and build a new settlement on the trail to Fort Limhi. On Blackfoot River, near present Blackfoot, Idaho, the forty-year-old Virginian and his men erected cabins, planted grain, and cached food near the Snake River ford on the Flathead Trail. The new supply station was roughly halfway between Salt Lake Valley and the Salmon River mission. Under this design, Fort Limhi was viewed as a settlement of pivotal importance. For if all else failed, it would be a sanctuary of rest and supply in a Mormon move to Bitterroot Valley and the headwaters of the Missouri River.

Fort Limhi Strengthened

To prepare Fort Limhi for its lofty new role, Mormon leaders moved to raise the Indian mission on Salmon River to the level of a permanent settlement and strengthen it with reinforcements. As the faithful returned to Zion from San Bernardino and Carson Valley, they called out new settlers and encouraged the existing missionaries to move their families north. While Nauvoo Legion troops mobilized like the hosts of Israel in tens, hundreds, and thousands and marched east to meet the U.S. Army that September, Thomas Smith collected most members of a northbound company at Ogden. The new colonizers added up to about seventy men, women, and children, including six men who left after the main group.[25]

[25]Those who left later were Ezra Barnard and Willliam Perkins, who arrived at Fort Limhi on 5 November 1857; James McBride, Andrew Quigley, and Fountain Welch, who came on 9 November; and George McBride, who rode in on 22 December with the mail carrier, John Barnard.

Charles F. Middleton from Ogden, then twenty-three, was one of some seventy settlers sent in October 1857 to strengthen the Salmon River colony even as outlying settlements elsewhere were called back to Utah to defend Zion against an American army. *Used by permission, Utah State Historical Society, all rights reserved.*

Of the twenty-two veteran missionaries moving north that fall, eight were relocating their families to new homes in the expanding settlement.

Those returning to Fort Limhi, including family members, were Ezra J. Barnard; William Batchelor; Jonathan S. Bowen and wife, Adeline Zerilda Rice; Joseph L. Bowen; Clifton S. Browning; Israel J. Clark, wife, Emily Jane Pearson, and son, Jesse, fifteen; Thomas Corless; Charles Dalton, wife, Eunice Daniels, and son, John Luther, fourteen; Thomas Day, Jr.; Francillo Durfee, wife, Cynthia Harrington Bowen, and daughter, Emma, ten; Hathron Chauncy Hadlock, wife, Eliza Jane Bowen, and daughters, Sally Louisa, three, and Eliza Maranda, two; Milton D. Hammond; Richard B. Margetts; George McBride; David Moore, wife, Susan Mariah Vorce, and adopted daughter, Louisa; William J. Perkins; Haskell Vincent Shurtliff, wife, Elsemina Emergene Shurtliff (Lewis Shurtliff's oldest sister), and children, Mary Ann, five, Haskell Albert, two, and Hascaline, nine months; Thomas S. Smith; Pleasant Green Taylor, wife, Jane Narcissus Shurtliff (Lewis Shurtliff's youngest sister); Baldwin H. Watts; James John Walker; and Amos R. Wright.

Of the twenty-one men moving to Oregon for the first time, eighteen hailed from the northern Utah settlements of Ogden, Kaysville, or

Farmington and ranged in age from eighteen to thirty. All except Reuben Collett, born in England, and Andrew Quigley, Jr., from Ireland, were native Americans. Eighteen were married and brought their wives and children with them or left family members at home. Like many of those returning to Fort Limhi, at least three had more than one wife. William H. Perry had wed two sisters and fathered two children by each. Eighteen-year-old William R. Taylor married two young women on the same day, 27 September, four days before leaving for Fort Limhi.

Bound for Oregon for the first time were new settlers: Mormon Battalion veteran James Riley Allred from Spring City, age thirty; Reuben Collett, brother of missionary Sylvanus Collett, from Lehi, eighteen; Stephen Harris Gheen, twenty-two, and his wife, Mary Adelia Hardy; Henry Martin Harmon, thirty-five, and wife, Susan Marler, who was expecting her first child; Martin Henderson Harris, thirty-seven; William Norton Marler, age unknown; James McBride, brother of George McBride, twenty-six; Charles Franklin Middleton, twenty-three; Frederick Andrus Miller, nineteen; James Thadeas Miller, nineteen; William Howard Perry, thirty-four, wife, Alice Stowell, and children, William Stephen, age four, and Cynthia Earnestine, two; Andrew Quigley, age twenty-six; Oliver Lee Robinson, twenty-five; Orson Hyde Rose, twenty; William Smith, forty-four, wife, Ann, and daughter, Elizabeth, thirteen; Levi Taylor, twenty-seven; William Riley Taylor, eighteen; Fountain Welch from Great Salt Lake City, twenty-three; and James David Wilcox, thirty. Two brothers of Thomas S. Smith were among the newcomers: Henry Smith, twenty-three, and wife, Helen Maria Fox, expecting their first child; and Jesse W. Smith, twenty-one, wife, Catherine Van Velsor, and son, Jesse William, age eighteen months.

Acting Clerk Jacob Miller: The Imps of Hell

As the new company prepared to leave, the missionaries at Fort Limhi watched events unfolding around them with a growing sense of loneliness and fear. On 22 August Ezra Barnard and his brother Lachonias arrived with mail from home and word that the expected company of new settlers and returning missionaries and family members would not leave for Salmon River until the fall after the mail carriers had returned to Utah. They also broke the news at the mission of the impending military showdown between the Mormon theocracy and the United States.

SALMON RIVER MISSION JOURNAL, 22 AUGUST 1857.

News from the United States and other parts of the world were interesting and joyfully perused. This is our only way of obtaining intelligence from any part of the world except the incredable [*sic*] reports of Natives of these mountains. News from the valley all is right. Brigham Young still reigns in the peaceful vales of Ephriam [*sic*]. The imps of Hell according to the news of the day very busy serving thier father the Devil and thereby unconsciously Bringing about the purposes and predictions of the almighty. 2500 Soldiers with 700 baggage waggons 1500 tea[m]sters and assistants are now come to Salt Lake for the purpose as we are told of escorting a new Governor to fill the place of Br. Brigham and establish peace among the Saints.

The "news of soldiers coming" and Mormon troops "going to prevent them" spread rapidly among the Indians. They "don't know which is going to eat the other up," said a worried Jacob Miller. Contrary to the hopes of Brigham Young, Miller saw them "becoming more impertinant [*sic*] and aggressive."[26] The mission clerk and others watched anxiously for relief from Utah, but hopes seemed dashed when the usually friendly Bannock, Mattigan, came from Salt Lake with bad news.

SALMON RIVER MISSION JOURNAL, 14 OCTOBER 1857.

An Indian named Madigen also came ~~this~~ this evening. [He] had came [*sic*] the road from as far back as the Portnif. [He] Saw nothing of a Co. [He] had been in the Valley about 2 moons ago then at Soda Springs [and] from there to here. Says Soldiers are at Green river and Soda Springs and in one moon will be at Fort Hall. There are Mormon Spies watching thier movements. The mountaineers have left that District of Country. There will none of those whom we have been expecting from the Lake ~~will~~ come unless 2 or 3 as mail to come and return. [Mattigan says] When the snow is gone he will return to the Lake and see which party are killed etc. Indian news is not at all times to be relied upon and how much of this is true we know not but hope for the best knowing there is a God who will over rule all things for the good of his Saints and his Kingdom.

Thursday the 15th. The Brethren did but little work. There seems to be some little concern about whether the Co. will come or not. Madagin's wife says (or at least so we are informed by Indians) that he Madigen Started from Salt Lake with letters and gave them to the Soldiers and that he is not

[26]Quotes from Jacob Miller Journal, September–October 1857.

> the Mormon friend. It is suspected that the Soldiers or mountaineers have sent him here as a spy. His stories are various and do not in all respects agree. It is thought best for two of the Brethren to start Back toward Salt Lake and either travel until they get there or meet with some one or more come from there.
>
> Friday the 16th. This morning Bros. A. Zondle and Sylvenus Collett with four horses started toward the Lake.

The two men chosen to ride south toward Salt Lake were Englishman Sylvanus Collett from Lehi, age twenty, and mail rider Abraham Zundel from Willow Creek, now Willard, twenty-one. With a spare horse each, the pair covered more than forty miles a day. Three days later at Market Lake, the riders met Thomas S. Smith's northbound company, which had left Ogden for Fort Limhi on 5 October 1857. Milton D. Hammond, one of the returning company, reported on 18 October, "S. Collett and A. Zanndel come into camp about 10 o'clock at night having been 3 days enroute from Ft. Limhi." Another member, Charles F. Middleton, said, "In the night. A. Zondel & S. Colet came into camp from Salmon River on their way home."[27] Collett and Zundel alerted Thomas Smith to the increasingly hostile mood of the natives on Salmon River and "went on to the [Salt] Lake with lief [leave] from Pres. Smith."[28] As shown below, these entries indicate that Smith and other Salmon River missionaries testified falsely during the trial of Collett for murder twenty-one years later.

JAMES MILLER: A FEELING HE WOULD NEVER RETURN ALIVE

As Smith left the train and rushed ahead to tell the fourteen men and one woman at Fort Limhi that help was coming, James T. Miller, a new missionary in the northbound party, described the march to his new post. Called to go to Salmon River, the nineteen-year-old younger brother of Fort Limhi veteran Jacob Miller left with "a feeling he would never return alive." But he shook off the premonition and got ready to fulfill his religious obligation. Before leaving home, however, he asked his sister,

[27]See Journals of Milton Datus Hammond, Charles Franklin Middleton, and Oliver Lee Robinson, 18 October 1857.

[28]Salmon River Mission Journal, 22 October 1857.

Lovisa Hammond, wife of Milton D. Hammond, also a missionary, "to name her expected child for him if she had a boy."[29] Miller then joined his brother-in-law in Thomas Smith's company. According to his sister, the child was born two months after her husband and brother left for Fort Limhi and was christened James Thadeus. The young missionary from whom the child took his name related his journey to Salmon River.

PRIVATE JOURNAL OF JAMES T. MILLER.

Thursday, October 1, 1857. Having been called upon the Salmon River Mission to labor under the direction of Pres. Thomas S. Smith, I started today for that place with two yoke of oxen, a wagon and one cow, in company with several others for the same place. We stopped all night on the Sand Ridge [now Syracuse], five miles from Kay's Creek [now Kaysville]. We had to stand guard to keep our cattle from running back.

Friday 2nd. We traveled to Five Mile Creek north of Ogden City. Saturday 3rd, our cattle went back last night and it took us all day to hunt them. I stood guard tonight.

Sunday 4th. We traveled to Box Elder. Monday 5th to Bear River. Tuesday 6th. We traveled to Spring Creek, three miles south of J. P. Barnard's.

Wednesday 7th. It rained considerably last night. Pres. Smith and some others came to the camp in the night. We traveled to Henderson Creek at which place the Company, consisting of 34 men, 14 women, 26 wagons, 7 horses and about 150 head of cattle, was organized by electing P. G. Taylor Captain, Milton D. Hammond Sergeant of Guard, D. Moore Clerk and I. J. Clark, C. Dalton and R. Margetts Chaplains and J. Walker Chorister.

Thursday 8th. The Company commenced standing guard. We drove to the Muddy. Friday 9th. We drove to the head of the Malad and stayed all night at the spring. Saturday 10th. We went over the Fort Hall Divide and camped from Divide on the Bannock. Sunday 11th. It rained until about noon. We traveled to within one mile of the Fork of the Bannock.

Monday 12th. We drove to the Portneuf. Tuesday 13th. We crossed the Portneuf and drove to Old Fort Lorin [Cantonment Loring]. Somebody set fire to the buildings and most of them burned down in the night.[30] Wednesday 14th. We stayed at Ft. Lorin all day and hunted for iron.[31]

---

[29]"Notes from the record of Lovisa Miller Hammond," Miller and Miller, eds, *Journal of Jacob Miller*, 48.

[30]Colonel Smith may have had orders to burn the former army post to prevent its use by the Utah Expedition.

[31]The marginal quality of ore deposits in southwestern Utah defied early Mormon attempts to make iron near Cedar City and made it almost as valuable in the territory as gold. Mormon parties scoured the trails for hundreds of miles looking for iron scraps. According to Dr. Thomas Flint in 1853, a Missourian on the southern trail to California "burned 25 wagons the year before and threw the iron into the deepest holes to keep it from the Mormons who had robbed or killed the mule teams." Flint, "Diary of Dr. Thomas Flint," 116.

Thursday 15th. We drove to the ford of the Snake River and met C. McGary and C. Dunn who stayed all night with us.[32] We passed a location selected by Pres. Cunningham known as the Blackfoot Mission.[33]

Friday 16th. We crossed the Snake River. C. Dalton broke his wagon tire. We camped twelve miles above the ford. Saturday 17th. We camped at the upper end of the Ten Mile Stretch and had a violent snow storm at night.

Sunday 18th. We drove to the slough two miles north of Snake River.[34] S. Collett and A. Zundell came into camp and reported all well at Salmon River and considerable excitement amongst the Indians.

Monday 19th. T. S. Smith, M. D. Hammond and W. Morley [Marler] started on with horses for Ft. Limhi. We drove to Camas Creek.

Tuesday 20th. We drove to Muddy Lake and camped four miles north of Muddy Lake. Wednesday 21st. We started before daylight and drove to Spring Creek and camped. Tuesday 22nd. We traveled twelve miles up Spring Creek and camped. Friday 23rd. Camped on Chicken Creek.

Saturday 24th. We traveled across the Salmon River Divide and camped on the head of the Salmon River one mile north of Quaking Asp Grove.

Sunday 25th. We traveled to the Rocky Slough. Monday 26th. We traveled to the crossing of the river six miles above Ft. Limhi. Tuesday 27th. We got into Ft. Limhi about noon and found all well and in good spirits.

Fort Limhi is the name of the place where the Salmon River Mission is located, which is about fifty miles north of the divide and about forty miles down from the head of the river. The bottom land on the river bottom is for the most part narrow. There is considerable timber and underbrush interspersed with patches of the wild gooseberry, some currants, etc. The origin of the name Salmon River is from the fact that large numbers of salmon fish come up this stream from the Pacific every summer. We have here also the herring, speckled and other trout, spring salmon, suckers, etc.

The river bottom affords narrow strips of good arable land with some few good meadows and a very extensive range for stock on both sides of the stream.

Ft. Limhi is built of cottonwood pickets nine feet above ground accompanied with an outer fort, the walls of which are built of mud seven feet high in which are stackyards, cattleyards, etc., so that grain and stock may be guarded from the wild Indians. A band of Shoshones inhabit the nearer surrounding country, although it is claimed by the Bannocks, who with other

[32]Charles McGary and Crandall Dunn, a forty-year-old New Yorker from Ogden, left Fort Limhi on 6 October for home "against the protest" of acting mission president Thomas Bingham. See Jacob Miller Journal, 6 October 1857.

[33]Three weeks later Jacob Miller on his return home said that Andrew Cunningham and his company "did some plowing, stacked some hay, built some log houses and then had gone home for the winter, leaving the location vacant." See Jacob Miller Journal, 6 November 1857.

[34]Market Lake at the big bend of Snake River, north of present Idaho Falls, Idaho.

Shoshones resort here in the summer for their supplies of fish and sometimes for gambling and other amusements, after their hunting seasons are over. In these amusements passing bands of Nez Perces Indians occasionally join.

The surrounding country for hundreds of miles, is inhabited only by the different bands and tribes of the wild natives of the forest, with now and then a hardy mountaineer or trapper who identifies himself by marriage with the roving Indian and lives almost similar, living in a wigwam of skins or canvas and roaming about as convenience may demand or occasion require.

The aspect of the surrounding country is quite picturesque in the sublime grandeur of nature, though the outlines are mostly rugged mountains and vales with their numerous streamlets and canyons with their steep, rugged and rocky sides, which together with the mountain sides, are checkered off with conifers and other evergreens among which the lofty pine is conspicuous. A few of the falling trees of the river bottom, which follow the streamlet sides up the rugged canyons are also found on the lofty sides of the mountains and the mountain grass has not failed to climb to their very summits.

To describe the habits and customs of the natives here would be almost useless. They accord well with the sketches of the venturesome explorers and even the novelist, who delights to paint so highly, everything he brings before his readers, has not failed to describe the Indian in his right character, from the stern notions of the haughty chief down to the lowest and meanest tricks of his subjects.

The mountaineers and traders have supplied the Indians to a considerable extent with guns and ammunition, which supersedes greatly the necessity of the bow and arrow. They generally dress well in their skins and robes and delight to view with the glass, their faces which they attempt to beautify with paint.

Brigham Young: The Saints Shall Be Free

Five days before James Miller and the main company rolled through the outpost's gate, Thomas Smith, Milton D. Hammond, and William Marler reached Fort Limhi on 22 October, "which filled the hearts of the Brethren here with joy as we had for some time been rather in suspence not knowing whether any of the Brethren were comeing or not," said Jacob Miller. "They had left the company a few miles this side of Snake river (where the two boys from here met them) and came ahead with a wagon and 4 horses, hearing the news we had concerning them," he wrote. "The two boys from here [Collett and Zundel] went on to the

Lake with Lief [leave] from Pres. Smith."[35] The arrivals carried exciting news from home as the Mormon Kingdom and the United States moved closer to bloodshed on the battlefield.

> SALMON RIVER MISSION JOURNAL, 22 OCTOBER 1857.
>
> News from the Lake and from the world and the United States in particular, cheering as they inform us of the speedy rolling forth of Christs Kingdom and the fulfilling of ancient Prophecy. There was a considerable sickness in the Valley when the company left. Uncle Sam's Soldiers or a portion of them about 2000 or there about in No have came as far as Green River for the purpose of relieving the women of U.T., Thinking it seems that they are in bondage. Pres Brigham Young has declared in the name of Isreals [*sic*] God that the Saints shall be free from all gentile Government has also said the Soldiers shall not come to the valley. Different companies have ~~not~~ gone to meet them and if they (the Soldiers) turn not back blood has been shed ere this. News in this Isolated place is always some time behind.
>
> Friday the 23rd. Brethren at sundries. Some of them converseing upon the news Brought by our brethren. All feel glad to hear that the time is at hand when the Saints will defend ~~their~~ rights and cause by the force of arms.

The arriving company on 27 October turned its livestock into the new mud corral and Jacob Miller greeted his younger brother James. The long procession under Captain Pleasant Green Taylor added up to "25 wagons, 32 men, 14 women, 3 boys some fifteen years old and 12 young children, 92 oxen, 27 cows, besides some yearlings and young calves."[36] Bringing up the rear were latecomers Ezra Barnard and William Perkins on 5 November; Andrew Quigley, Fountain Welch, and James McBride four days later; and George McBride on 22 December.

For the next forty-eight hours the Miller brothers were inseparable as Jacob, the oldest, packed his belongings and prepared to leave with the party making a delivery to Utah that was not likely to please the Bannocks. Miller's carpentry skills were manifest in many heavy barrels packed with pickled salmon, for centuries the primary food source of the region's native peoples. On 28 October, he and nine others "left the Fort for their homes in Salt Lake, taking with them eight wagons and ten or twelve yoke of oxen, having each wagon well loaded with fish."[37] According to the mission journal, the party's members were Joseph

[35]Salmon River Mission Journal, 22 October 1857.

[36]Ibid., 27 October 1857.

[37]Ibid., 28 October 1857.

Harker, Thomas Bingham, William Burch, Henry R. Cleveland, James Hill, William Bailey Lake, Miller, Henry Nebeker, John Preece, and David Stephens. A final member, Ebenezer Robinson, the eleventh, waited until next day before leaving with the mail to overtake the wagons.[38]

The Trial of Sylvanus Collett

Twenty-one years later the make up of the eleven-man company that left Fort Limhi in late October would be disputed in the sensational murder trial of Fort Limhi missionary Sylvanus Collett. Collett was arrested for the homicide on about 25 November 1857 of John Aiken, one of a group of six men from California known as the Aiken Party, who rode into Utah that October and were arrested by mobilized Mormon soldiers. Aiken and four others of his party were killed following the arrest. The trial of Collett in October 1878 for his murder followed the 1874 passage of the federal Poland Act, which stripped Utah's probate courts of the extraordinary powers bestowed by Mormon lawmakers and restored original criminal and civil jurisdiction to the territory's district courts under judges appointed by the U.S. president.

According to the late historian Harold Schindler, four of the six, including John Aiken and his brother, Thomas, Tuck Wright, and Colonel Eichard, were killed near Nephi, Utah, by the four-member Mormon escort supposedly convoying them safely through the settlements to California. William A. Hickman later confessed that he killed a fifth party member, A. J. "Honesty" Jones, north of Great Salt Lake. At the trial witnesses identified the escort as Orrin Porter Rockwell, John R. Murdock, John S. Lott, and Sylvanus Collett, all except Rockwell from Lehi, Utah. The tall Englishman from Salmon River was the only one arrested and brought to trial for the twenty-one-year-old murders.[39]

---

[38]Ibid.

[39]The author is indebted to the late Harold Schindler for a copy of his unpublished manuscript, "The Aiken Massacre Reconstructed," and reports of the trial from 10 to 17 October 1878 in *The Daily Tribune* at Salt Lake City. For more on this episode, see Schindler, *Orrin Porter Rockwell: Man of God, Son of Thunder*, 268–81, and Bigler, *Forgotten Kingdom: The Mormon Theocracy in the American West, 1847–1896*, 309–12. For reports on the Aiken Party in California, see articles in the *San Francisco Bulletin*, 18 January and 16 February 1858, which copy earlier stories in the *Argus* and *Index* newspapers at Placerville, Calif.

Sylvanus Collett, as he appeared some years after his 1878 trial for his alleged role in the Aiken party murders in 1857 as an accomplice of Orrin Porter Rockwell. A jury freed the Englishman on the false testimony of former Salmon River missionary companions. *Used by permission, Utah State Historical Society, all rights reserved.*

Collett, then forty-one, testified that he had remained at Fort Limhi until "the last of October or 1st of November" 1857 when he left with an ox team party of "some eleven or twelve men" under Joseph Harker to deliver wagon loads of pickled salmon to Utah. He had reached Salt Lake "about the last of November" and gone home. His attorney argued that Collett could not have killed John Aiken because he was "hundreds of miles away" at the time of the murders. In support of Collett's testimony, former mission president Thomas Smith "produced his diary to show that on the 28th of October, 1857, Collett left Salmon river with the ox teams and was about twenty-seven or thirty days making the journey." It was "physically impossible for the prisoner to have been present in Nephi when the Aikens were there," the defense attorney said.[40]

Smith's testimony that when he reached Fort Limhi that October he found Collett there not only contradicts the journal entries of other party members that have come to light in recent years, but his own jour-

[40]See trial testimony, *The Salt Lake Tribune,* 10–17 October 1878. An entry in Smith's journal indeed lists Collett as one of the eleven men who left Fort Limhi with the fish delivery, but this document appears to have been rewritten and does not square with the Salmon River Mission Journal, which does not include Collett as a member of this party. See Thomas S. Smith Journal, 28 October 1857.

nal as well.[41] Smith was not likely to forget that it was the news of "considerable excitement among the Indians," delivered by Collett and Zundel at Market Lake, that had motivated him to ride ahead with Milton Hammond and William Marler and tell the mission that help was coming. Nor would he have forgotten, even at age sixty, that he himself had given "lief" for Collett and Zundel to go on to Salt Lake Valley from Market Lake as reported 22 October in the unedited mission journal.[42] Even so, Smith at the trial "read from a written memorandum" the names of those who left Fort Limhi with the fish on 28 October, most of which were correct, if misspelled.[43]

Other Fort Limhi missionaries stricken with faulty memories at the trial included Richard B. Margetts, who returned to the mission with Smith's company of new settlers. His claim that when he arrived on 27 October 1857 he found Collett there and "saw him leave" the next day" did not square with the reports of others at the time in his company. And in rambling testimony, Joseph Harker, the captain of the fish-hauling party, said that he thought "they reached Salt Lake the latter end of December."[44] His journal, which was available to him at the time, now shows that the fish party arrived on 17 November, even then in time for Collett to escort the Aiken Party when it began its last journey three days later.[45]

In fact, at the rate Collett and Zundel traveled on horseback from Fort Limhi to Market Lake, about forty-two miles a day, they would have reached Salt Lake in time for the Englishman to spend several weeks at home before joining Rockwell's escort. Even so, his own false testimony at the trial and that of the others who served with him at Fort Limhi does not by itself prove beyond doubt that he shot-gunned John Aiken to death as one accuser alleged. But it does reflect a pattern of

---

[41]On 18 October 1857, Smith wrote, "[We] travilled up to the Slew near Market lake and Silvenes Collet and Abraham Zondle came to the camp from Salmon river."

[42]Salmon River Mission Journal, 22 October 1857.

[43]See *The Salt Lake Tribune*, 15 October 1878. According to the Salmon River Mission Journal, Smith erroneously added Collett and George W. Hill and failed to include Jacob Miller and Henry Nebeker. Nor do the names he gave at the trial entirely square with his own journal.

[44]See *The Daily Tribune*, 15 October 1857.

[45]See Joseph Harker Journal, 17 November 1857. Jacob Miller left Harker's party at the head of Malad River and walked the rest of the way to his home in Ogden, arriving 13 November. Jacob Miller Journal, 13 November 1857.

obstructing justice that non-Mormons in Utah often complained about during this period. So it was that the jury freed the former Salmon River missionary to return to his ranch in southwestern Wyoming.

Though Collett did not accompany him, a true member of the fish-hauling party on 28 October 1858 "loaded for Salt Lake" and later that day "made an evening drive," Jacob Miller said. The two Miller brothers found it almost impossible to say goodbye. "My brother James went with me and slept with me and continued our visiting," he said. Next day the little train of eleven men, eight wagons, and thirteen yoke of oxen covered fifteen miles, but "to visit further with James," Jacob Miller dropped behind. "It seemed that we could hardly part and we little thought that we would not meet again on earth." At last he hurried on and overtook the ox train "just as they were starting after the noon rest," while the younger brother returned to the mission.[46]

On 6 November Jacob Miller's salmon-hauling party "reached the location made by Andrew Cunningham and a company who had located on Blackfoot Fork," but found the cabins they had built at today's Blackfoot, Idaho, vacant.[47] A month before, Brigham Young had warned Cunningham that U.S. soldiers might head his way and alerted him to "be wide awake" and avoid being trapped. "And if you deem it proper," Young had said, "you are at liberty to return home with your company at any time," which the Virginian prudently did.[48] Jacob Miller arrived at Farmington on 13 November. The captain of the party, Joseph Harker, contrary to the testimony he gave at the Collett trial, arrived home in West Jordan only four days later.

The Second Fort

Meanwhile, back at Fort Limhi, Thomas Smith on 29 October assigned the eighteen new arrivals and their families to go to the planned second fort, two miles north of the existing stockade, and make their future homes there. Marked off after Brigham Young's visit the May before, the new redoubt was to be nearly one-third larger than the origi-

[46]Jacob Miller Journal, 28, 29 October 1857.

[47]Ibid., 6 November 1857.

[48]Young to Cunningham, 9 October 1857, Brigham Young Collection, Ms 566, Reel 1.

nal fort, in keeping with the mission's elevated status as a settlement. The projected stockade was rectangular in form with its north-south sides 264 feet in length and walls on the east and west 403 feet long. To provide more living space for families, its twenty-eight inner lots allowed the construction of cabins of 533 square feet as opposed to the largest house in the first fort of only 288 square feet. A space of thirty-three feet was planned between the houses and wall.

Those sent to the new location were James Allred; Clifton S. Browning; Stephen Gheen and wife, Mary; Hathron Chauncy Hadlock, wife Eliza, and two children; Milton D. Hammond; Henry M. Harmon and wife, Susan; Martin H. Harris; William N. Marler; Charles F. Middleton; Frederick A. Miller; James Miller; William H. Perry; Oliver Lee Robinson; Orson Rose; Haskell Vincent Shurtliff, his wife, Elsemina, and three children; Levi Taylor; William Taylor; and James D. Wilcox. Placed in charge of the little colony was Milton Hammond. For those who went there the promise of more future space was offset by the lack of current accommodations. Despite the colony's ambitious plans, that fall the so-called "fort" was little more than a scattering of hastily erected cabins.

Military Moves on the High Plains

While the location's residents hurried to build new shelters before winter set in, far to the south the commander of the U.S. Army's expedition to Utah was finding himself outgeneraled by an opponent who boasted a lofty title but little schooling in the science of warfare. As senior officer, Col. Edmund Alexander of the Tenth Infantry had become the commander of the scattered Army of Utah after the reassignment of Gen. William Harney, its first commanding officer, to duty in Kansas. But the scorched-earth tactics of his Mormon opponent, Lt. Gen. Daniel Wells, whose Nauvoo Legion companies rustled Army cattle and burned its supply trains, left the elderly Alexander befuddled and indecisive. While he dithered on Hams Fork, near present Granger, Wyoming, water froze overnight in the soldiers' canteens and the signs of an early winter warned the hastily-called expedition of disaster if it remained on the open plains.

Fortunately for both sides, a forceful new commander was riding hard to take control of the endangered expedition. Named to replace Harney was Col. Albert Sidney Johnston, age fifty-four, commanding officer of the crack Second U.S. Cavalry, then in Texas. Athletic in build and grave in manner, Johnston was a native of Kentucky, a West Point graduate, and former secretary of war for the Republic of Texas, his adopted state. Leaving his regiment in the hands of its capable second in command, Lt. Col. Robert E. Lee, he hurried west from Fort Leavenworth to take command of U.S. forces and shape them into an efficient instrument of national authority. Ironically this gifted soldier would fall five years later while leading a Confederate army against the government whose laws he now sought to uphold.[49]

As temperatures plummeted below zero and blizzards of an early winter swept across the high plains in 1857, Johnston ordered his widely scattered forces to concentrate at Fort Bridger. Against an enemy they were unprepared to face, American soldiers fought their way through the weather and gained the shelter of Bridger's trading post on Blacks Fork, now in southwestern Wyoming, by the closest of margins. Their march from Hams Fork, near present Granger, covered only thirty-five miles but took fifteen days to accomplish and claimed the lives of some three thousand cattle, horses, and mules. Johnston later said that his command "took the last possible step forward at Bridger in the condition of the animals then alive."[50]

Believing the Mormons "have placed themselves in rebellion," Johnston ordered that they be "treated as enemies," a policy that would have unforeseen consequences.[51] Meanwhile, axes rang at Fort Limhi and Fort Bridger in November 1857 as the denizens of both places prepared to fight a common enemy—winter. Settlers on Salmon River worked to build housing for themselves and their families while their imagined enemies on Blacks Fork, four hundred miles to the south, thwarted in their efforts to reach the safety of Salt Lake Valley settlements, labored to

[49]Johnston sent his surgeon to care for other soldiers and died himself of an untended wound on the second day of the Battle of Shiloh in 1862. Some in Utah took his death on 6 April, the anniversary of the founding of the LDS church, as a sign of divine retribution.

[50]Johnston, *The Life of Albert Sidney Johnston, Embracing His Services in the Armies of the United States, the Republic of Texas, and the Confederate States,* 214.

[51]Johnston to McDowell, 5 November 1857, House Exec. Doc. 71 (35-1), 46.

construct primitive shelters. Johnston named his winter post Camp Scott in honor of the nation's top general, Winfield Scott, and planned a frontal assault on Echo Canyon as soon as spring opened the mountain passes. A more immediate concern was to replace animals and supplies lost to Mormon marauders.

The colonel ordered Capt. Randolph B. Marcy to lead a hazardous midwinter expedition across the backbone of the continent to obtain horses, mules, and cattle at Fort Union, near Las Vegas, New Mexico. In a heroic feat, the captain, along with his forty enlisted volunteers and twenty-four civilian guides, ate their mules and broke trail through heavy snow in the Rocky Mountains on their hands and knees, but accomplished their mission, returning in the spring after losing only one man.[52]

Two weeks later, Johnston dispatched a pack party northward to purchase the animals his command needed from mountaineers wintering along the Beaverhead and Big Hole rivers and in the Bitterroot Valley of present Montana. Leading these hired civilian scouts was one of the West's most colorful, if largely unsung, adventurers, who would play, unwittingly or otherwise, a large role in the destiny of Fort Limhi.

---

[52]For the story of this remarkable exploit, see Marcy, *Thirty Years of Army Life on the Border.*

Chapter 9

The Devil Is At Work Among the Lamanites

The Indians came up to us and demanded our powder riding in their war Circles. But they were told plainly that they would get no powder only through our rifles. This they did not like and verry sullenly left us.

— *Lewis W. Shurtliff*

That the Bannock, the region's most powerful tribe, patently ignored Brigham Young's visit to the mission in May 1857 was a troublesome sign, although few seemed to see it as such at the time. Possibly threatened by the ostentatious display of interest in their homeland, Bannock leaders signaled by their absence a lack of interest in expanding relations with the religious newcomers. However, growing unrest that fall among Fort Limhi's Indian neighbors had less to do with Young's visit than it did with earlier causes of strife between Mormon settlers and indigenous peoples elsewhere.

To Beg for Their Subsistence: Causes of Indian Unrest

In Utah Territory, the southward push of colonization from Salt Lake Valley that began in 1849 had displaced native inhabitants from their fishing and hunting grounds and provoked two Indian wars and many skirmishes by 1857. For centuries the western branch of the dominant Utah tribe had lived close to its main food source in Utah Valley, the fresh waters of Utah Lake, then one of the most productive fisheries in the Mountain West. The tribe resented the newcomers' use of modern fishing methods to net hauls of trout, suckers, chubs, and whitefish for pickling and shipment to places outside its homeland. And the rapid spread of fortified towns and fenced fields drove the game from the tribe's traditional hunting areas. By 1855 a once-proud people had become "exceedingly destitute . . . and turned upon the white settlers to beg for their subsistence," reported U.S. Indian agent Garland Hurt.[1] And ready to fight.

Giving rise to conflict, too, was the notion, common among whites, that American Indians were essentially alike and cultural differences between tribes were superficial and bridgeable. This idea was imbedded in the Mormon belief that the Indians were one people, known as Lamanites, who descended from ancient Israel's tribe of Manasseh. Yet the natives knew in their bones that the tribal ethnic group to which they belonged was a unique people, as distinctive to them in language, custom, and appearance from other Indian nations as the Irish were different from Hindus. Mountaineers understood that acceptance by one tribe required them to adopt its friendships and hatreds toward other peoples. But missionaries often became entangled in old intertribal feuds with unintended consequences.

Intensifying prior causes of discontent in fall 1857 was the word that flew swiftly among denizens of the wilderness, natives and mountaineers alike. "The Indians have the news of soldiers coming to Utah, and of [Mormon General] D. H. Wells going to prevent them; and don't know which is going to eat the other up," Jacob Miller said. "They are becoming more impertinant [*sic*] and aggressive." That October, Bannock Chief Mattigan virtually gave the fort an advance notice of Indian trouble. "[He] Said the soldiers are at Green River and Soda Springs and in one moon would be at ft Hall," Miller said. "Said when the snow is deep Soldiers and Mormons would fight."[2]

Quick to perceive conflicts among white interlopers on tribal homelands, whether settlers, soldiers, or missionaries, the natives were equally ready to exploit them. In this, some old enemies of the Mormons would no doubt give them plenty of encouragement. The "mountain men" were the loners and misfits of civilized society who lived in the wilderness by their own choice and saw that the communal-minded religionists, who moved in all things as one, posed as great a threat to a cherished way of life

[1]Hurt to Young, March 1855, Letters received by the Office of Indian Affairs, Utah Superintendency, 1849–1890.

[2]Jacob Miller Journal, entries in September and on 14 October 1857.

as any Indian ever did. The mountaineers did not want any true believers, whose communal symbol was the beehive, swarming in their backyard.

Jacob Miller: A Signal from Black Feet Indians

To some sporadic invaders from present northern Montana, however, differences in tribe, skin color, or way of life meant little or nothing. The Blackfeet treated all others exactly the same. Anyone not of their kind was an enemy to be robbed, exploited, or exterminated as opportunity offered. That the Blackfeet were peerless thieves, as well as pitiless killers, the missionaries learned in September 1857 after they turned their horses into the fenced field and foolishly saw no need to guard them. "This was a great mistake," David Moore confessed after the marauders made off with every animal.[3] Lewis Shurtliff and "Eben" Robinson mounted the last two horses, which had been kept within the mud corral, and pursued the raiders over the Continental Divide. Shurtliff and Robinson rode fifty miles only to come to "where they had killed those that gave out."[4] They were fortunate not to overtake the thieves. Earlier that month fear of the Blackfeet prompted a practical joke that broke up an Indian wake and embarrassed a chief.

Salmon River Mission Journal, September 1857.

Sunday the 6th. This Morning about two AM voices of Mourning were heard at the Indian camp accompanied with reports of guns which was found to be the connections and friends of the sick Indian before referred to. He had just died and they were mourning his departure. Tho a very degraded people yet thier feelings seem to be very tender on an occasion of this kind. This morning some of the Brethren Dug a grave and interred the body in the silent earth. Scarce was this done when the Indians Discovered what they took to be a signal from black feet Indians either for a chalange or a desire to communicate which was hoisted on a little mountain about 1 1/2 miles east ~~south~~ north east from the fort. Nine Indians on horseback Striped painted and besmeared with white clay with thier bows arrows and some few guns (this being thier preparation for fight) went to see what it was. It was found to be some willows put there by one of thier own tribe most likely to fool them but for the Chief this fooling was not much fun as he was thrown from his horse and kicked and considerable hurt.

---

[3]Salmon River Mission Journal, 25 September 1857.

[4]Life and Travels of Lewis Warren Shurtliff, September 1857.

First Signs of Trouble

While the Blackfeet brought frequent excitement and occasional danger to both whites and Indians along Lemhi River, these intruders could be guarded against and did not represent a mortal threat. On the other hand, the goodwill of native inhabitants in the mission's backyard was a condition of survival. For this reason, the signs of growing hostility among local tribesmen that began to appear in 1857 were much more troublesome.

The first portent of danger was hardly a straw in the wind with no apparent relation to the mission. Two Bannocks arrived at the fort on 10 June 1857 from Horse Prairie on the Missouri headwaters with the word that twenty-two members of their tribe were on their way to the Flathead country to steal horses "from the Ponderays [Pend d'Oreilles] as they had stolen several head from them last spring," acting Clerk Jacob Miller said.[5] As natives collected on the river to catch salmon, five Nez Percés rode in five days later looking for "some 60 head of horses stolen from them (including the Co or lodges with which they belonged) night before last," Miller said. "They had hunted for them without success until to day," he went on. "About noon some Bannacks past that way a few days ago for the purpose of stealing horses, some ponderays having taken thiers a few days ago and it is expected they have got them." The Nez Percé warriors from the Clearwater River region, perhaps suspecting the Shoshones, "had quite a talk with Chief Snag" who shifted the blame and "told them about the 22 Bannocks."[6]

Just before leaving for Utah on 17 June to bring back family members, Thomas Smith sent a letter to John Owen "agent of the Flat Head Nation desiring him to use his influence to have the Bannock horses restored saying we would use ours to have the Nez Perces returned to them again," Miller said.[7] The Fort Owen owner seemed unaware of the latter tribe's loss. His only comment on receiving Smith's note was that the Bannocks wanted "satisfaction from the Pondesreilles for the loss they have Met with in horses last winter in the Vicinity of Beaver Head a

[5]As noted, the Pend d'Oreilles or Kalispels were related by language and culture to the Flatheads and inhabited the same regions in Flathead and Bitterroot Valleys.

[6]Salmon River Mission Journal, entries on 10 June and 15 June 1857.

[7]Ibid., 16 June 1857.

favorite Wintering ground."[8] On 23 June he sent "his willingness to unite with us in settleing the difficulty Should opportunity offer but the Indians in that vicinity were absent at this time hunting and digging roots," according to Miller. Owen said "he would consider it his duty to warn us of any thing that threatens our mission from his vicinity and that he would cheerfully carry it out."[9] Not until 1 July did Owen find out "about the Nez Perce camp in the Big Hole having lost a great many horses by the Bannacks."[10] But by then it was too late to act on Smith's request.

The failure to settle the dispute came at a time of deteriorating relations between the mission and its native neighbors, even before the expansion of the settlement that fall and the shipment of pickled fish to Utah. Milton Hammond noted the difference on his return that October. "The Indians did not seem to be possessed of a very good spirit," he said.[11] The mission head saw it, too, but seemed unaware of the reasons for the unfriendly mood. "Pres. Smith made some remarks in respect to his views of the Cause why the natives had acted as they had while he had been gone," the mission clerk wrote. "He said that some had not filled thier Calling as they should & had given away to a spirit of lightness and folly [and] had been guilty of several things unbecoming elders of Israel such as pitching quotes [*sic*] & gambling for supplies &c &c."[12] The increasingly hostile attitude toward the mission intensified the potential of the fight over horses to involve Zion's northern settlement and to spin out of control.

A Harmful Rumor

Adding to this likelihood was a report that the Mormons planned to kill Richard Grant, former Hudson's Bay agent at Fort Hall, as well as

[8]Dunbar and Phillips, eds., *The Journals and Letters of Major John Owen*, 18 June 1857, I:167. The Beaverhead region takes its name from Beaverhead Rock, a three-hundred-foot landmark on Beaverhead River, so named by the Shoshone Indians because it so strikingly resembles the head of a beaver. Sacagawea recognized it in 1805 and told Lewis and Clark they would soon find her people. It is located on State Route 41, near Twin Bridges, Montana, about fifteen miles north of Dillon.

[9]Salmon River Mission Journal, 23 June 1857.

[10]Dunbar and Phillips, eds., *The Journals and Letters of Major John Owen*, 1 July 1857, I:169.

[11]Milton D. Hammond Journal, 22 October 1857.

[12]Salmon River Mission Journal, 1 November 1857. The tossing game "quoits" is similar to horseshoes.

his son John Francis, known as "Johnny," Frederick Burr, and John W. Powell. Who started the rumor is not known. But it was apparently spread by one or more of the four mountaineers, who came in mid-November from Bitterroot Valley, via today's Lost Trail Pass, down Salmon River's North Fork on the line of U.S. Highway 93. Guided by Louis Maillet, this party included Hugh O'Neil; the eccentric physician, Dr. Monroe Atkinson; and a man named Ramsey, who were going to Fort Bridger to meet the U.S. Army.[13] Aware of the animosity between Mormons and mountaineers, Maillet rode ahead to "find out if the Mormons were hostile" while the rest hid in the willows a few miles north of the fort. He reached the fort on 14 November just as the main gate was being opened and received "the best meal the place afforded."[14]

Instead of continuing south to its professed destination, the party for unexplained reasons traveled east on 17 November over the Continental Divide toward the Beaverhead region. At the mouth of Blacktail Deer Creek, near present Dillon, Montana, Maillet said they met mountaineer John Jacobs, who "gave such a terrible account of Mormon scouting parties" that O'Neil and his companions stayed with Jacobs during the winter. Maillet continued down the Beaverhead to the cabin of Richard Grant, who owned one of the largest herds in the valley. He found Grant crippled by rheumatism and alarmed by the warning given by the French-Canadian or someone else "that the Mormons hated him" and "intended to rob him."[15]

The frightened Grant hired Maillet to move the Grant family and livestock north to the Flathead country, but the transfer looked more like flight than a move. Grant's young son James and Antoine Poirier drove the wagons, while "Mrs. Grant and her daughters drove the band of horses of about one hundred head, the band of cattle, numbering

---

[13]Maillet, "Historical Sketch of Louis R. Maillet," 208–09. John Owen said that Dr. Atkinson was "an old Miner from California who intends prospecting the country thoroughly." He has been called "a queer man" who prospected on horseback with field glasses and did no digging. Hugh O'Neil, then twenty-six, was a native of Ireland who was noted for his "feats of strength, heroism and endurance." Before he died in 1895 he served as miner, farmer, U.S. marshal, and member of the 1864 vigilante movement. See "Death of An Old Timer," *Missoulian,* 22 February 1895, 4/5. Little is known about Ramsey except he and O'Neil came from the Colville mines on the upper Columbia River.

[14]Maillet, "A Historical Sketch of Louis R. Maillet," 208–09; Salmon River Mission Journal, 14 November 1858.

[15]Ibid.

JOHN W. POWELL
Known to be selfish and reckless, the mountaineer escaped from Fort Limhi during the December 1857 quarrel over horses between the Bannocks and Nez Percés. Eyewitnesses afterward accused the Virginian of inciting the Indian attack that forced abandonment of the mission.
Courtesy of the Montana Historical Society.

two hundred head, being driven by Indians."[16] The old Hudson's Bay trader "used up his animals very badly," said Frederick Burr. "He is scared very much on account of the Mormons."[17] For the same reason, Johnny Grant drove his herd of some two hundred cattle and a number of horses north from the Beaverhead to Deerlodge Valley at the confluence of the Hell Gate, now Clark Fork, and the Little Blackfoot rivers, east of Missoula near present Garrison, Montana.

Other mountaineers with less to lose remained along the Beaverhead and Big Hole rivers as the rumor of Mormon militancy spread. On 6 January 1858 word reached Bitterroot Valley "that the mormons have sworn to kill, Old Grant, Johny Grant, Powell & myself and that they are about to build a fort on Beaver Head," Frederick Burr wrote, "and will make a descent here in the spring." Possibly sent by Powell, this report was an incentive for action against the settlement on Salmon River.

[16]Ibid. As mentioned, Grant married Helene McDonald Kittson at Fort Vancouver in 1845, following the death of his first wife. Their three daughters were: Helene Wilhelmina, eleven, Julia Priscilla, nine, and Adeline, seven. See Warner and Munnick, *Catholic Church Records of the Pacific Northwest, Vancouver,* 1:57, 80, 104, 119. James Grant was an illegitimate son by an Indian woman.

[17]Frederick H. Burr Journal, 14 January 1858.

LEWIS SHURTLIFF: WE WOULD CAST LOTS

In November, Thomas Smith evaluated the settlement's exposed position and weighed his responsibility for the welfare of so many women and children. He had ample grounds for concern. The increasing hostility of local natives was enough in itself to stir alarm. Added to this were new rumors of conflict between Mormon and American forces passed on by the four mountaineer visitors. Later that month he called for a volunteer to accompany him on a midwinter ride to carry the mail to Utah and consult with leaders of his church. Predictably stepping forward was young Shurtliff, who recalled the dangerous journey.

LIFE AND TRAVELS OF LEWIS WARREN SHURTLIFF.

Saturday twenty seventh of November I started in Company with Thomas S. Smith, bidding all adieu. This was quite a trial for Louisa. She would not see me start from the fort. Many of the people predicted our return without making the through trip. The first night stayed at our herd which lay a few miles up the River. Spent the evening very agreeably with the Brethern who were taking care of the cattle and horses. The next day we passed an Indian Camp, and after a hard days drive we camped on the last crossing of Salmon River. Next day crossed the Divide the snow three feet deep and the weather was extremely cold. Next day we traveled down Spring Crick [Birch Creek]. My best riding horse was lame, and two others were sick. I felt quite discouraged but kept the same to myself. We continued our journey, the snow increasing at every step, and the fog was so dence [*sic*] that it was almost imposible to follow the road. At the Crossing of Snake River the snow was one foot deep and very hard, but we persevered and went down to Steam Boat Rock.[18] Here the snow drifted untill we could not follow the road any farther. Our horses had not had water that day. I cut a hole in the ice, and the snow drifted so bad that our animals could not drink, we undertook to make a fire but failed our hands being too cold to strike a ma[t]ch.

We now could see that our time had come to return or perish in attempting to face this terrible storm of sleet. But rather than propose a retreat I would perish in the attempt to proceed.

At last Bro Smith said we would cast lots or draw cuts whether we went on or whether we returned. I made the lots and he drew. This was an important step. After the lots were in my hand the Spirit said to change them on the other side and that he would draw such a one. The lots were drawn and we were to return. Our hearts now seemed to lighten and after a hard and weary ride of three days we came to Spring Crick. Here as I was looking

[18]A possible reference to Eagle Rock at present Idaho Falls, which later became the main crossing point of the Snake River.

about I saw sign of Indians but did not think there was any danger. After we had traveled a few miles up the stream we made, what travelers call a dark camp, that is to say we did not kindle or make a fire, but took a few bites of cold frozen provisions, or Eatables, and after turning our horses some distance from our [camp] in order to get feed for them we retired to rest but not to sleep. The night was densly foggy and cold, and some time passed in low conversation, and our weary bodies were fast giving way to Morpheus when all at once I heard a footstep and in less time than it takes to note it our pieces were brought to bear upon two or three redskins, and at the click of our firearms, those murderous Savages took to the brush and were out of sight in an instant. Here we lay all night not knowing whether they would return and murder us or try to get our horses then they would have us completely in their power. No doubt the latter was their intention, for as the day dawned upon us I started to find our horses and there saw the footprints of the Indians trying to follow the horses but could not find them. I followed our horses trail for seven miles and was pleased [to] once more feel the back of my favorite animal and right well pleased was Bro Smith to see me return with all our animals safe. After a hearty breakfast we set out upon our journy passing up the Valley stopping before night to cook our suppers then traveling untill after night and tying up two of our best horses beside our bed.

Tuesday 8th [December] the Indians came up to us and demanded our powder riding in their war Circles. But they were told plainly that they would get no powder only through our rifles. This they did not like and verry sullenly left us. We passed over the Divide into Salmon River Valley. Now the snow began to disappear and our camp was made in the brush near the river—next day we arived at Fort Limhi [and] found all well.

The December Confrontation

Less than a week after Smith's return from his failed attempt to carry the mail to Utah, the quarrel over stolen horses almost flared into open warfare between the Nez Percés on one side and the Bannocks and Shoshones on the other—with Fort Limhi squarely in the middle. On 17 December "the old Nezperce chief," identified above as Eagle from the Light, and his interpreter, Alexsey, arrived at the mission "from a chase after the Bannocks who had stolen their horses." The chieftain asked permission "to stay at the Fort while Alexsey continued his search after the horses" and Thomas Smith granted his request.[19] But this act of friendship was certain to offend local tribesmen.

[19]Salmon River Mission Journal, 17 December 1857.

Tension between warring tribes escalated further on 20 December when a not-so-welcome visitor from the mountaineers' wintering ground on the Beaverhead arrived with "several of the Shoshones."[20] Twenty-three-year-old John W. Powell was a Virginian who came west in 1853 "as one of the young men of the Stevens expeditions" and, like his occasional partner, Frederick Burr, adopted the life of a trader. He had an Indian wife, who was either a Bannock or Shoshone, and he exercised great influence on both tribes. A friend, John J. Healy, described him as "an educated gentleman but chose the wild life to civilization at his old home in Virginia."[21] But Burr expressed a different opinion. Powell "never had any [pity] to waste on anyone," he said. "He was selfish, reckless, and able to despoil his best friend if he could."[22]

Forty lodges of Shoshones followed Powell the next day from the Beaverhead country and set up their tepees on the field near the fort. On 26 December Thomas Smith, David Moore, and Israel Clark went to the native encampment and asked the Virginian to use his influence "to have the Indians stop burning the fence," which he professed he had done.[23] About noon Powell started for the upper river valley, but about two miles south of the mission he was surprised by fifty or sixty Nez Percé warriors. This was the same war party, "looking for stolen horses," that Milton Hammond had encountered earlier that day while moving livestock to the upper herd ground. To the missionary, the Indians "seemed to be perfectly friendly."[24] They were not so to Powell, whom they apparently knew. They "took him prisoner and marched him down to the fort again, singing their war songs and yelling in a frightful manner."[25]

John J. Healy: He Went up the Travois Like a Cat

Fearing the Bannocks had killed Eagle from the Light, the Nez Per-

[20]Ibid., 20 December 1857.

[21]Healy, "J. W. Powell and Fort Lemhi Told by Johnny Healy." Before assuming his duties as Washington's territorial governor, Maj. Isaac I. Stevens gave his name to the railroad survey expedition he led from St. Paul, Minnesota, to Puget Sound in 1853.

[22]Burr to Stuart, 12 October 1868, Frederick H. Burr Journal. For more on Powell, see Helming, *John W. Powell: An Historical Biography of a Notable Western Montana Mountain Man*, and Thrapp, *Encyclopedia of Frontier Biography*, 2:1168–69.

[23]Salmon River Mission Journal, 26 December 1857.

[24]Milton D. Hammond Journal, 26 December 1857.

[25]Salmon River Mission Journal, 26 December 1857.

cés rejoiced to discover him within the stockade. They kept Powell under guard inside the Mormon fort and "in a particular manner paid great respect to their old chief." Moreover they "showed much friendship towards us," David Moore said, supposedly for treating their chief as an honored guest. To keep the goodwill of their Nez Percé visitors, the missionaries made no effort to free Powell who tried to get away without their help, "but was soon followed and brought back and a strict watch placed over him."[26] John J. Healy, Powell's friend, later recounted the mountaineer's yarn of how he made his escape. Vouching for Healy's veracity, if not for Powell's, the *Helena Independent* in 1878 said: "Mr. Heely does not need to varnish his sketches for his adventures in these mountains are as full of romance as the most brilliant of imaginative writers could desire . . . and they are full of facts."[27]

JOHNNY HEALY, "J. W. POWELL AND FORT LIMHI."

> At one time Powell was with a band of Bannocks at Fort Lemhi, a Mormon post, when the Pend d'Oreilles [Nez Percé] who were at war with the Bannocks caught Powell, the Bannocks escaping into the willows which lined the banks of Salmon river. Powell pleaded with the Mormons to save him. Instead the Mormons left him to his fate. Lemhi had an adobe stockade fourteen or sixteen feet high, the gates were closed and the Indians thought their prisoner safe in the yard with Indians walking about in the yard. There happened to be a travois leaning against the stockade. Powell was light and young and active and he went up the travois like a cat and was over the stockade and into the willows among his friends before the Pend d'Oreilles could head him off. After that Powell and the Bannocks made war upon the Mormons and actually forced them to leave or abandon Lemhi.[28]

Lewis Shurtliff called this episode "the start of our trouble" and gave a different version of it. Said he: "A mountaineer came to our fort and hung around with the Indians. His name was Powel. He told us that he came from the flathead country, but the Nepirzes came about 500 of them and he got away. They followed him two miles and brought him back. He was afraid they would kill him and while they were watching

[26]Ibid.

[27]Healy, "An Adventure in the Idaho Mines," ed. Clyde McLemore, *Frontier and Midland: A Magazine of the West*, reprinted in *Sources of Midwest History No. 26*. Born in Ireland, Healy at age eighteen joined the U.S. Army and served in the Second Dragoons during the Utah War of 1857–1858. He left the Army in 1860 to take up an adventurous life in present Montana and Alaska as fur trader, gold miner, journalist, educator, hotel operator, and sheriff. The "daring, restless, lovable Irish immigrant" died at San Francisco in 1908.

[28]Healy, "J. W. Powell and Fort Lemhi Told by Johnny Healy."

him he made a break for the brush on the river and gained them after a few shots being fired after him but I believe without effect. The Indians tried to hunt him out but to no purpose."[29]

Seeing how well their chief had fared at the Mormon table for more than a week reminded the fifty Nez Percé warriors that that they had gone without food for three days. Their hunger put an unexpected demand on limited supplies, but after "some consultation," Thomas Smith "called on the Mission to help feed them." The newcomers took bread and other food "very gladly," but when the Shoshones learned about the mission's generosity to their enemies, "quite a number of them came to the Fort much excited." Pretending not to notice them, the Nez Percés "ate their suppers and then had a war dance" that went on until long after nightfall. "One of them would go out at a time and dance around the fire, holding his tomahawk before his bre[a]st until he got done," Moore said. "He would then raise it over his head and give a yell which was repeated by all present, the dancer would then leave his place for another."[30]

If the mission's hospitality to the Nez Percé angered its neighbors, Smith's call for a parley the next day to make peace fared even worse. Eagle from the Light and his leading warriors "with some of the Shoshones were prevailed upon to come to the meeting when there was an effort made to try to get them to make friends of each other." But the Nez Percé refused "to be friends until the Bannocks and Shoshones would return all the horses that they had stolen from them." The latter denied the theft, but during the talks Alexsey rode up with ten Nez Percé horses "he had re-taken from the Bannocks, by stealing them at night." A scuffle broke out when Powell's father-in-law, identified only as "an old Shoshone," refused to surrender a horse claimed by the Nez Percés, who took it from him by force. At this, the Shoshones "showed fight" and the Nez Percés left the meeting, "dressed themselves up and came out, formed in line, while the old chief made quite a long speech to them." After much posturing by both sides, the Shoshones "backed out" and the Nez Percé "discharged their guns and returned to their quarters again."[31]

[29]Life and Travels of Lewis Warren Shurtliff, December 1857.

[30]Salmon River Mission Journal, 26 December 1857.

[31]Ibid., 27 December 1857.

Oliver Robinson: "The Indians About Us Do Not Feel Just Right Toward Us"

Peace appeared to prevail the next day when the Nez Percés "left for their camp again." Before leaving, the visitors begged for "some food to take them home," a practice "very customary with most of the northern tribes." But mission food was the least of the prizes the northern tribesmen made off with. First they "took two of Powel's ponies away with them," then they came back that night and dealt their adversaries a punishing blow that would have far reaching consequences.[32] Their retaliation was not aimed at the mission that fed them, but it would irreparably harm Fort Limhi's standing with local natives and undermine the influence of the chief who had cooperated with the Mormons. The mission recorder described what happened.

Salmon River Mission Journal.

Tuesday 29th. [December 1857] This morning the Shoshones came to our forts en mass all painted up and much excited. The Nezperces, it appears, returned during the night and stole some 60 or 70 head of their horses by way of retaliation. Powel was also along and painted up like the natives. They demanded Snag's fish and his cattle, and in fact all the fish that had been left in care of the brethern at the Fort. President Smith tried to reason with them but all to no purpose. The fish and cattle they were bound to have. Powel in the meanwhile kept on his horse and near the gate, thereby showing a guilty conscience. His conversation also betrayed his feelings in prompting the Indians against us, for he stated in a sort of threatening manner that we would find it to our advantage to give up the fish to the Indians. After consulting with several of the brethern, President Smith considered it a matter of policy to give up the fish. The squaws took it and after having several rows over it getting it divided, left, the Indians stating that they would go the next day and get the cattle. This they said was because Snag had turned traitor to them and joined the Nezperces.

The Shoshones were "very much inraged [*sic*] at Snag," Thomas Smith reported. "They said that Snag had told the Nezpercias to steal thare horses and they ware a going [to] have his fish and cattle to pay fore them."[33] To restore the friendship of neighboring tribes, the fort next day prepared a feast of bread and boiled wheat and invited all of

[32]Ibid., 28 December 1857.

[33]Thomas S. Smith Journal, 26 December 1857.

the Indians along the river to come and eat as much as they wanted. Most came, but "some would not eat, saying that they were not dogs, nor even hungry enough to set down and eat off the ground," Moore said. "They accordingly stood off and looked on acting quite mumfey."[34] "The indians about us do not feel just right toward us because we fed the Nepersias when they were here," said Oliver Robinson.[35]

The native mood appeared so hostile that Smith sent Lewis Shurtliff ten miles to the mission herd to get their horses. "There I found my old friend Ezra Barnard with his squaw and there had come an Indian and squaw to take Ezras Wife away," Shurtliff said. "I plainly told them they could not do it but they persisted and succeeded in getting her out of the camp when I told Ezra that if he would keep the Indians of[f] I would take her back which I did by carrying her in my arms."[36] But the freeze in marital relations revealed the rejection of neighboring tribes, and Shurtliff's use of force could only widen the breech, especially since Shoshone custom allowed a wife to leave her mate any time she chose.

On the eve of 1858, the Mormon families at both settlements on Salmon River's upper waters put aside their fears for a few hours to celebrate the coming of what they hoped would be a better year. Thomas Smith, Lewis Shurtliff, Louisa Moore, and a few others rode through the snow to the settlement downstream and joined couples there in a dance. At the main stockade the choir about midnight "passed around the Fort singing a few verses of a hymn at each door in honor of the New Year," which indeed appeared to open with promise. On 4 January President Smith married Shurtliff and Louisa Moore and three days later the mission welcomed its newest member when Helen Smith, wife of Thomas Smith's brother Henry, "gave birth to a daughter."[37]

Meanwhile news of Nez Percé horse theft spread far beyond the habitation of the Shoshones to cause strife across a wide area. In Bitterroot Valley Frederick H. Burr on 23 January 1858 "received a letter from Powell saying the Nex Perces had put him afoot as well as the 'sheep eaters' on Salmon River."[38] The next day he added, "the Nex

[34]Salmon River Mission Journal, 29 December 1857.

[35]Oliver Lee Robinson Diary, 29 December 1857.

[36]Life and Travels of Lewis Warren Shurtliff, 30 December 1857.

[37]Salmon River Mission Journal, 31 December, 1857, and 4 and 7 January 1858.

[38]A common name for the Shoshone Indians, now known as Lemhis, who inhabited the upper branches of Salmon River.

perces & Flatheads [are] about to quarrel because those horses were stolen from the Snakes some of whom are related to the Flatheads."[39]

At Fort Limhi, growing signs of unrest followed the raid. On 11 January David Moore said, "The Indians are passing to and fro making preparations to go and fight the Nezperces." More ominously, he added, passing natives from the southwest warned that Mattigan, the Bannock chief, "recommends them to fight us before they go to fight the Nezperces."[40] As the Indians had also "talked of taking some cattle," Thomas Smith next day ordered eight men to go to the herd "as early as possible the next morning and if they found that they had taken any of the Cattle off with them to follow after and get the pay for it, if possible."[41] They reached the herd too late, however, to stop Ezra Barnard's wife who "left & took some things."[42] Nor did they arrive in time to keep three Indians from making off with an ox belonging to Jonathan Bowen. Leaving two men to guard the herd, the other six went after the cattle thieves. David Moore described the pursuit.[43]

SALMON RIVER MISSION JOURNAL, 13 JANUARY 1858.

They took up the large creek on west side of Salmon River and after following up for some 4 or 5 miles found that the natives had taken off to the right following up a small Branch of said Creek some 3 miles farther found where the Indians had killed the ox & packed the meat on their horses. Continuing on after them the company came in sight of them in about 5 miles from west fork of Salmon River.[44] As soon as Pete & Wad zeece discovered the Company after them they put out as fast as thier horses could travel. The Company was at this time on the Summit or near it of the big mountain which lies between the two Branches of Salmon River[45] & had some 3 miles to decend before they could get where horses could travel fast but this was soon done & then the Chase became more swift & after arriving at the River edge, the trail turned suddenly to the left.[46] They followed on up some a mile or more where they come up with Tin gosho Son & wife & another squaw having with them four ponies all more or less laden with Beef. The

[39]Frederick H. Burr Journal, 23–24 January 1858.

[40]Salmon River Mission Journal, 11 January 1858.

[41]Ibid., 12 January 1858. The eight men were P. G. Taylor, David Moore, B. H. Watts, George McBride, Clifton S. Browning, Lewis Shurtliff, Ezra Barnard, and Reuben Collett.

[42]Charles F. Middleton Journal, 12 January 1858.

[43]The six pursuers were Taylor, Moore, Watts, McBride, Barnard, and Shurtliff.

[44]Not Salmon River's west fork, but the main channel, which flows north to present Salmon, Idaho.

[45]The towering Lemhi Range separates Salmon River from its east fork, Lemhi River.

[46]They are now on Salmon River followed by today's U.S. Highway 93, just south of Salmon, Idaho.

> company surrounded them & told them to stop which they did. B. H. Watts & L. W. Shirtliff then talked to them for acting so mean with us, & told them that our Captain wanted pay for the ox. This the Indians was not very willing to do at first, but wanted us to follow up Pete & Wad Zeese. This the company did not wish to do. He then said he would give one of his ponies. The company then returned to the foot of the big mountain keeping up a strict guard during the night while in camp. A very cold night.

They returned the next day and turned over the Indian pony to Thomas Smith. While Bowen received payment for his ox, the increase in theft was an unusual and worrisome indication that the valley's inhabitants no longer accepted the mission. Even so, Clifton Browning ignored this ominous sign and bravely "went down the river about 7 miles to see a Shoshone woman."[47]

On 20 January two mountaineers came on an alleged trading junket. David Pattee had left Fort Owen eighteen days before. At the Beaverhead he had enlisted John Jacobs, who had visited the fort in November and afterward spread alarming stories of Mormon militancy, as guide. The pair stayed for a week with the Durfees "where they were well treated by all the mission."[48] "Considerable trading going on with our gentile Breathern," Hammond said. "I guess they will get about all the skins on the river from both Mormons & Indians."[49] Pattee bought the horse seized from the Indians a week before as forced payment for the stolen ox. With a horse of problematical ownership, he took from his visit some yarns about his Mormon hosts that he spun three weeks later at Fort Owen.

The mountaineer described the settlement on 19 February as being "in fine spirits having no Fears of Brigham being routed from Salt Lake by the U. S. troops," John Owen said. According to Pattee, the mission had plenty of wheat on hand but was very short of other items, particularly ammunition. "They say they will have to flee to the Mts to carry

---

[47]Charles F. Middleton Journal, 30 January 1858.

[48]Salmon River Mission Journal, 27 January 1858. David Pattee came to Fort Owen in 1856 from Fort Colville, an early Hudson's Bay Company trading post on the upper Columbia River, now in northwestern Washington, and built the first gristmill for John Owen. Mountaineer John M. Jacobs, "one of the last of the true mountain men," is often mentioned in the writings of Frederick H. Burr and Granville Stuart. He reportedly brought cattle and horses to Montana in 1856 and later guided emigrant parties over the Bozeman Trail, which he helped discover, to the gold mines in Alder Gulch. See Weisel, ed., *Men and Trade on the Northwest Frontier as Shown by the Fort Owen Ledger*, 7–8.

[49]Charles F. Middleton Journal, 21 January 1858.

out the prophecy of Jos Smith the founder of the Society," Owen wrote. "They say there is Seven years provision cached in the Mts.," he added. "They say that Brigham Young is to save the republic & that he will be president of the U.S." Be that as it may, the doubting owner of Fort Owen said, "it is going to cost Uncle Sam More than he first anticipated."[50]

David Moore: The Young Indians Held a War Dance

If they were short of ammunition, as Pattee said, the missionaries could hardly desire their increasingly restless Indian neighbors to discover the weakness. Perhaps that was why some of them held a shooting match at the upper fort on the first of February. "About a doz[en] of the boys shot their guns at a mark two hundred & fifty yards to four hundred," Charles Middleton said. "My gun [k]nocked the boards down (250 y[ards]) & it was the only gun that struck the board," he proudly added. But if their hope was to intimidate the natives by showing them they had powder to burn and lead to waste on shooting contests, it failed as events soon after confirmed.

Salmon River Mission Journal, 1858.

> Wednesday [February] 3rd. The whole band of the Sho-sho-nes that are camped on this river came to the Fort all painted up in quite a fancy style, with their guns, bows and arrows and other weapons of war. The young Indians held a war dance in the Fort and were very saucy, acting as if they wanted to commence a fight with us. President Smith got some of the old men together and talked to them, they said they wanted flour and many other things. This the mission had not any to spare, but President Smith told them that he and the brethern would give them three sacks full of wheat provided they would not come again in the shape of war as they had done this time. This they agreed to and the mission gave them about six and a half bushels of wheat, and they all returned to their lodges about sunset.[51]

During the day some of the Indians reported that the mountaineers had been telling them that the "Mormons are going to kill them all off and take their lands," David Moore said. "From other statements it must

[50]Dunbar and Phillips, eds., *The Journals and Letters of Major John Owen,* 19 February 1858, I:192.

[51]The mission could not produce meal or flour due to mechanical problems and the lack of spare parts at its recently completely gristmill.

have been Powell and John Jacobs who told them this falsehood, for they were the only mountaineers who had been down amongst them."[52]

For a few days relations with the local natives seemed to improve. On 7 February some two dozen Shoshone warriors rode up to the fort seeking shelter from a cold winter storm with blowing snow from the east. The war party "put their ponies into the corral and stayed all night." The following day more Indians arrived, including some Bannocks, bringing their number at the fort up to about forty. "We gave them a hearty breakfast and bread and boiled wheat to take with them," Moore said, "and they appeared very friendly toward us and some were on their way after the Nezperces which band was somewhere near the Flathead country."[53] Middleton "bought a sheep skin from boryavat," a Bannock, better known as Boo-e-wat and renamed Harvey after his baptism.[54]

But the appearance of friendship was an illusion. The hope of peaceful relations between the fort and its Lamanite kin virtually died on 9 February when an Indian came from the east with alarming news. Ten soldiers were camped on the Beaverhead, he said, and "they had two Mormon prisoners." According to this native, the captives had "their hands tied together" and "they wanted to get away very much."[55] That the messenger intended only trouble became clear after he reached an agreement with Richard Margetts, a blacksmith, to exchange his horse for a spear blade. Margetts finished the blade after dark, when the Indian "took it and privately went to the corral, stole one of the Presidents Smiths [*sic*] horses and fled with it, leaving his own in one of the yards."[56]

After an all-night search, Smith named six men to go after the Indian who had made off with his best horse. They discovered that he had apparently tried to steal all the horses in the Mormon herd, but failing that had taken the finest animal he could find and headed east again over the Continental Divide to the Missouri River headwaters. Smith selected four more men to bring the company up to ten and sent them after the

[52]Salmon River Mission Journal, 3 February 1858.

[53]Ibid., 7 and 8 February 1858.

[54]Charles F. Middleton Journal, 8 February 1858.

[55]Ibid., Salmon River Mission Journal, 9 February 1858. There were indeed agents of the U.S. Army from Fort Bridger in the Beaverhead area at this time trying to buy cattle for the Utah Expedition, but they were not soldiers, nor did they have any Mormon prisoners. The latter story was apparently intended to provoke a clash between the missionaries and Col. A. S. Johnston's emissaries from Camp Scott.

[56]Ibid.

miscreant. As they rode out, "Pres. Smith thought it the safest & best plan for us to live in one fort," Oliver Robinson said. "Those that had families [at the lower settlement] moved Thursday & we expect to move in the Spring." The remaining men also drove their livestock closer to the fort and strengthened the corral. "The Devil is at work among the Lamanites," said Robinson.[57]

David Moore: He Was Going to Tell the Soldiers

Those who undertook the dangerous assignment of recovering Smith's horse and checking out reports of U.S. soldiers with Mormon prisoners made up a Nauvoo Legion company of ten, as organized in May 1857 by Lt. Gen. Daniel Wells. Its captain, thirty-one-year-old Pleasant Green Taylor, had earlier been warned in a "dream by inspiration" of trouble with the Indians. The Kentuckian related his vision to those at the unfortified second settlement and insisted "upon them going at once and bringing their families and cattle."[58] His command included David Moore, Milton Hammond, Ezra Barnard, George McBride, Lewis Shurtliff, William Marler, Thomas Corless, Jesse Smith, and Baldwin Watts. Tracking the Shoshone horse thief, they headed east toward the Beaverhead River and then northwest to the lower valley of the Big Hole. Recorder David Moore described their hazardous midwinter expedition.

Salmon River Mission Journal.

Thursday 11th. [February 1858] The company left the Fort about 10 A.M. and camped at To-e-rone at night, some 30 miles from the Fort.[59]

Friday 12th. The company left early this morning and camped on a large creek some 35 miles further east, passed over two mountains and up and down canyons. Snow on mountains deep, none of us were ever in these parts before. We had no guide but to follow the trail made by the war party already mentioned. We named this creek on which we camped McBride Creek.[60]

---

[57]Oliver Lee Robinson Diary, 10 February 1858.

[58]Carter, ed., *Our Pioneer Heritage*, 7:177.

[59]The company left the main stockade and rode over today's Lemhi Pass on the 1805 Lewis and Clark Trail and camped at the distinctive landmark on Horse Prairie Creek that B. F. Cummings said resembled "an Indian lodge although the name in Shoshone signifies a California or Mountain Lion." See Biography and Journals of Benjamin Franklin Cummings, 14 November 1856.

[60]The company crossed the Flathead Trail near present Grant, Montana, and continued almost due east to camp on Red Rock River, a tributary of the Beaverhead River, which the party followed northward toward present Dillon.

Englishman Thomas Corless was age twenty-six when he rode with a picked company of ten missionaries over Lewis and Clark pass on a dangerous winter journey to recover a stolen horse from Indian and mountaineer camps along Beaverhead and Big Hole rivers.
Courtesy of the Church Archives, The Church of Jesus Christ of Latter-day Saints.

Saturday 13th. Snow falling fast this morning and continued to fall most of the day. The company had much difficulty in finding and following the trail on account of the snow and wind. We at last came to a level prairie where no more trail was to be seen and we had to find our way as best as we could to some timber that was faintly seen through the cold storm. As we approached the creek (on which the trees stood) some of the company discovered a smoke in the distance, and up the creek about half a mile above us. We all were soon on the spot and there found some four or five lodges of Sho-sho-nees. Part of the company stopped at their lodges while the rest, with an Indian with them, went in search of their horses. The boys soon returned with Col. Smith's horse and then commenced hunting for the Indian who stole it, and soon found him covered up with a number of buffalo and other skins in the first lodge we had come to, although the Indians denied his being anywhere about. B. H. Watts scolded him for being so mean, but he paid no attention to anything that was said. He got up, put on his war cap, took his spear mounted a small pony and put off saying he was going to tell the soldiers.

The party had now reached the favorite mountaineer wintering ground on the Big Hole and Beaverhead rivers at a point just north of present Dillon, Montana. They found the Indian lodges on a creek a few miles upstream from the winter camp of trader Robert Dempsey and his family.[61] Within less than a day's ride were the camps of Granville and

[61]Johnny Grant said that Dempsey was an Irishman, "who did not forget his own brogue when he learned Indian." The mountaineer's wife was related to the noted Sheepeater Chief Tendoy, also known as "young Bonapart." See Meikle, ed., *Very Close to Trouble: The Johnny Grant Memoir,* 65, 189.

James Stuart, John M. Jacobs, Robert Hereford, Delaware Indians Jim and Ben Simonds, and other early Montana mountaineers, including one already well known at Fort Limhi, John W. Powell.[62] Here several men stayed with Ezra Barnard, who had been injured the day before when his horse fell with him, while the rest followed an Indian boy down the stream to look for the stolen horse. They discovered it some "3 miles above Dempse[y's] camp and about 12 miles from Beaver Head Valley," Hammond reported.[63] Shurtliff also related the episode.

LIFE AND TRAVELS OF LEWIS WARREN SHURTLIFF.

The weather was so verry severe that some had already frozen their ears and fingers and we held a council to know what to do and the Spirit directed that we should go North, which we did and was soon in sight of a small river and on looking up the stream saw a smoke proceeding from Indian lodges which we has[t]ened to come to and there enquired for the horse and Indian. One said he knew nothing about him [but] another young boy said to another where is the man that came last night with the Esharobah horse.[64] The lad was made to mount one of our horses and lead the way to the band there we caught the animal and returned, then searched the camp [where we] found the Indian. He made of[f] for the soldiers camp saying he would bring them on us, which after[ward] we found was the case.

As the Indian's threat indicated, the Mormon pursuers were now dangerously near the volunteer party that came from Fort Bridger to the Beaverhead country to buy horses and cattle from wintering mountaineers for the U.S. Army. Not knowing who the soldiers were or their number, the Fort Limhi party prudently retreated from the unfamiliar region as described by David Moore, who appraised the valley's potential for settlement.

SALMON RIVER MISSION JOURNAL.

[13 February 1858] We turned our course towards home and camped on McBride Creek again. We tied our horses up close by our camp to prevent a stampede in case the Indians should make an attack on us during the night.

Sunday 14. Made an early start and travelled to To-e-rone on the north bank of the head waters of the Missouri River. It is a kind of sugar loaf

[62]See Phillips, ed., *Forty Years on the Frontier as seen in the Journals and Reminiscences of Granville Stuart,* I:125–26; and Stuart, "A Memoir of the Life of James Stuart," 38–39.

[63]Milton D. Hammond Journal, 13 February 1858.

[64]A Shoshone word that means "pinto" and is properly spelled aishadabá. For this information, the author is indebted to Drufilla Gould, who teaches in the American Indian Studies Program at Idaho State University, Pocatello.

> mountain or hill of a brown color, some 200 feet high with tolerably level table lands for some distance around. This entire country over which we have passed cannot well be surpassed for grazing. Plenty of creeks but not much timber on them. Plenty of pine on the high mountains.
>
> We found our trail as we approached the main divide completely filled with snow, had a hard time to get over the mountain. We arrived at the Fort about 4 o'clock P.M. We found all well and all the families had moved up from the lower fort, and the rest of the men are soon to move up on account of the apparent spirit of war and thieving in the natives.

The returning company found the cabins at the main fort crowded with women and children from the lower settlement as Thomas Smith prepared the mission for Indian trouble. Two days behind them came Le Grand Coquin, the giant, unpredictable native whose mood on this visit was anything but friendly. "The old Bannock Chief, Shou-woo-koo, generally known by the name of Rock-e-ka, came to the Fort and wanted flour, but as that was scarce, Col. Smith gave him some wheat," David Moore said. "He went into the corral and examined it all around," which the missionaries "thought queer as he had been there and seen it before."[65]

What the six-foot-plus Indian was looking for was unknown. But what Taylor's company had discovered during their midwinter journey to the Beaverhead country was clear and alarming. They found out, said Oliver Robinson, "that there was Soldiers over there."[66]

---

[65]Salmon River Mission Journal, 16 February 1858.

[66]Oliver Lee Robinson Diary, 15 February 1858.

Chapter 10

THE HILLS WERE BLACK WITH INDIANS

As we were decending the bench the Indians fired on us hiting my suspender & the bullett lodging in my horses jaw. My horse jumped & throwed me. Br Barnard caught my horse. As I fell my revolver fell out of my hand. While I was looking for it they fired with a revolver, Br. McBrides I suppose, and hit the leaf of my hat. I then took down for my horse and as I got on they fired again at me the bullet passing through the upper part of my arm.

— *Thomas S. Smith*

Seven days after Pleasant Green Taylor's party returned from the Beaverhead with Thomas Smith's horse, an unwelcome visitor from that region arrived at Fort Limhi. "Powel come back," Milton Hammond said.[1] On 22 February 1858, the mountaineer "passed down by the Fort from Beaverhead" to the large spread of Indian lodges five miles north of the lower settlement. On his way, Powell "met Joseph Bowen [and] told him that he would not stop at the fort, for some of the boys there were down on him."[2] Uneasy at the growing assembly of Bannocks and Shoshones so close to the new colony, Smith that day told the remaining men there to move up and join their families within the stockade walls. He did so as a precaution, not because he really expected trouble. Otherwise the mission went about its work as usual. Herders Orson Rose, Andrew Quigley, and Fountain Welch prepared to drive the livestock out of the corral and herd them during the spring. Not so trusting were some others.

William Perry two days later "went down to the Indian lodges" below the vacated cabins at the lower settlement to see Powell. The moun-

[1]Milton D. Hammond Journal, 22 February 1858.
[2]Salmon River Mission Journal, 22 February 1858.

taineer advised him to "to tell the Col. to keep a good wa[t]ch for the Indians had been talking of burning our stacks & take our cattle & horses," Charles Middleton said.[3] Powell told Perry "he had been up all night talking to the Bannocks to keep them from coming to burn our hay & straw & that we had better be careful of our horses & cattle, for they talked of leaving on Thursday," the next day.[4]

When David Moore heard this, he and several others stayed up long after dark to keep watch at the fort, which was usually unguarded at night. Early on 25 February he went to the mission president and asked "to know his feelings about Powel's statement." Smith shrugged off the mountaineer's warning, saying that "he thought it was some of Powel's lies." Unconvinced, Moore ran to the corral to claim his own animals before the herders drove the livestock out to feed on the foothills, "but the herd was at this time being driven out and I could not stop my stock without stopping the whole herd."[5]

Although forewarned, the mission that day almost seemed to invite attack by its unready posture as its members took off in every direction on widely scattered tasks some distance from the fort. David Moore went with Charles Dalton to the gristmill on the river to repair the millrace and grind wheat. Thomas Smith, P. G. Taylor, Lewis Shurtliff, Jesse Smith, and Amos R. Wright headed up the river to harvest timber, while Haskell Shurtliff, Milton D. Hammond, James Wilcox, Oliver L. Robinson, James Miller, Ezra Barnard, and Reuben Collett drove the wagons two or three miles downstream to recover hay and other property from their abandoned cabins. Francillo Durfee and his wife's sons, Jonathan and Joseph Bowen, went into the field to plow. The three herders, Rose, Quigley, and Welch, moved the stock toward the foothills on the east while the rest worked at the fort.

Milton Hammond: We Could Hear the Indians Whooping

About midmorning Moore looked to the northeast. He saw Indians on the bench riding upstream toward the herd. The Canadian ran to the

[3]Charles F. Middleton Journal, 1855–1858, typed copy made and indexed by the author.

[4]Salmon River Mission Journal, 24 February 1858.

[5]Ibid., 25 February 1858.

fort to give the alarm. Finding eight or nine men already preparing to go out on foot, he told William Taylor to take charge and save the livestock. Just after Taylor left, George McBride brought his horse in, hurriedly threw on the saddle and swung aboard. As the adjutant of the local Nauvoo Legion company, Moore ordered McBride to join Taylor's party and help the herdsmen. It was already too late. About this time Ezra Barnard rode up from the lower settlement. He had spotted the Indians, too, and warned his companions there to take off, but they had continued to load hay on their wagons as the Indians rode by on the bench. Milton Hammond told what happened to the little party.

JOURNAL OF MILTON D. HAMMOND, 25 FEBRUARY 1858.

While loading our loads we noticed that the Indians were traveling towards [the] upper fort in small bodies, yet there seems to be a great many of them. We began to fear that they did not mean any good by the coarse [*sic*] they were takeing. Yet they seemed to be friendly. Rocky Kay [Grand Coquin] sent Cartoos to us while they were passing to tell us they had heard that the Nezpersias were comeing on them and they was going to fight them. Yet from the course they were takeing we did not believe them. We all loaded up our loads and started with 2 loads of hay and 2 loads of wood, there being 5 of us, viz., J. D. Wilcox, O. L. Robinson, J. T. Miller, H. V. Shurtliff and myself. We left [the] lower fort about one o'clock P.M. Soon after we started we could see that the Indians had taken the herd and was guarding them on the bench that the trail crosses about half way between the 2 forts. We concluded to go up the bottom road and had not gone but a little ways before the Indians see us and commenced yelling and rushing towards us. Just before we got to the crossing of the creek they began to surround us and shot at O. L. Robinson and myself, we being close together. We drove on until some of the teams had crossed the creek and they kept fireing at us and riding in circles close to us. About this time Cartoos shot H. V. Shurtliff in the arm and the same ball hit O. L. Robinson in the hand. J. D. Wilcox tried to get his gun, it being on the hay. He could not find it but took my slide gun and we left our teams and started for the brush on the river. Before we got far a ball hit James T. Miller in the body but he continued to run with us. He spoke to J. D. Wilcox soon after he was shot and said that he was shot and could not do any more and told him to take his pistol. The Indians continued to rush on and shoot at us. I called on the boys (after we had got about half way to the brush) to stop and shoot at them. We stopped and turned on them but the Indians whirled their horses and run. We continued on and went into the brush and got seperated [*sic*]. James D. Wilcox and myself crossed the river and went down the river in the thickest brush we

Milton D. Hammond yelled "to stop and shoot them," when the Indians chased his hay-loading party into the brush along the river, killing James Miller and burning the wagons. The New Yorker found his way to the fort in the dark.
Courtesy of the Church Archives, The Church of Jesus Christ of Latter-day Saints.

could find. We could hear the Indians whooping and also heard 3 guns after we had got into the brush. We also could see that they had set our loads on fire. We did not have onely 2 colts Revolvers. The guns was not loaded. We went down the river nearly opposite the lower fort and laid in the brush until it began to be dark. We could hear the Indians drive the cattle as they were passing us. After it began to be dark we started up the river and kept in the brush until we had got to the place that they burnt our waggons.

Still Alive But Very Feeble: The Ordeal of the Herders

As Hammond's comrades ran for the brush along the river, the native raiders struck. Led by the Bannocks, they did not menace the stockade or the women and children inside, including two Indian wives. Their target was the herd, grazing on the hills about two miles east of the fort, and they took it. Only those who got in their way or tried to interfere suffered. In greatest danger were the three herders, caught in the open, hopelessly outnumbered, and cut off from support.

First to fall was twenty-three-year-old Fountain Welch. As he tried to

DAVID MOORE
On seeing the hills "black with Indians," Fort Limhi's militia adjutant ran to the fort and gave the alarm. An experienced military leader, the Canadian from Ogden, Utah, also served three years as clerk of the Salmon River Mission.
Used by permission, Utah State Historical Society, all rights reserved.

escape, the Indians shot him in the back, "struck him several times on the head with their guns," and left him for dead. Andrew Quigley was their next victim. They shot him in the shoulder and "beat him on the head with their guns, thereby injuring the skull as well as cutting several holes in his head; he was still alive but very feeble and still."[6] The Irishman was badly wounded, but he and Welch both escaped death by feigning it. Seeing the Indians chase Quigley behind the hill, directly east of the fort, the third herder, Orson Rose, rode for his life toward the mountains and got away.

By now, "the hills and both sides of the river were black with Indians," David Moore said.[7] When George McBride on horseback reached the footmen from the fort, Taylor told him to ride up to where he could see the cattle. If the Indians had them, he said, motion with his hat and they would try and get along a little faster. From the hill McBride saw the Indians had gathered most of the animals on the bench between the two settlements. He waved his hat and vanished from view as he spurred down the far side of the hill in a brave but reckless attempt to save two or three small bunches of strays. From three sides the Indians took him under fire. They shot him from his horse and seized his hat, shirt, and revolver.

[6]Ibid. [7]Ibid.

Soon after McBride fell, the party on foot discovered Fountain Welch, who had struggled to his feet and was trying to reach them. Some of the men supported him while the rest, including Taylor, Baldwin Watts, and Thomas Corless, acted as rearguard as they fell back toward the fort. Seeing the men retreat, the Indians followed and fired at them from a safe distance. One held up McBride's scalp and danced under it. When another riding McBride's horse pressed too close, Taylor ordered Watts to fire at the horse. This made the Indian "pull off," Moore said, yelling, "Sino mich Mormon Narient," which meant, "One Mormon is brave."[8]

THOMAS S. SMITH:
THEY WERE DRIVING THE BRETHREN BACK

As McBride had shown, courage could not balance the odds that day. Thomas Smith had seen the Indians riding toward the herd as he drove his team back with a load of logs. Hurriedly he unhitched the animals, mounted one, and headed with Ezra Barnard downstream toward the bench where the Indians had taken the stock. Seeing the animals completely under their control, the two men turned and tried to reach Taylor's retreating party. Smith described what happened then.

THOMAS S. SMITH JOURNAL, 25 FEBRUARY 1858.

The Indiens saw us and six of them took after us. We turned towards the Brethern and we saw that we could not make the point and we turned towards the fort and as we past down the bench they fire[d] on us the ball past throu[gh] my right suspender and lodged in my horses right gaw [jaw] a little below the joint. The horse jumped and my left sturip broke and throwd me off. I lost my pistol. The Indiens kept up fireing. Brother Barnerd cetched my horse and before I could [get] to him one ball passed throu the rim of my hat near my rite ear. As I was getting on to my horse another ball pas[s]ed throu the upper part of my right arm a little below the elbow. We reached the fort with out any more dificulty. In runing I had to hold my hand over the wound in my horse to keep him from bleading to death. Soon after I got to the fort the Brethren returned that went out on foot and brought in F Welch.[9]

[8]Ibid.

[9]Thomas S. Smith Journal, 25 February 1858.

Barnard's steadfast courage and a remarkable run of good luck rescued Thomas Smith from certain death, and the two men soon reached the safety of the fort's gate. The bullet that cut the colonel's suspender had struck his horse, and Smith's attempt to staunch the wound left him drenched in blood. He must have presented a terrifying specter to the shocked settlers who met him at the gate, and they immediately feared their steadfast leader was badly injured. Perhaps Smith shared their alarm, but a close examination revealed he had suffered only a flesh wound.[10]

Not until William Taylor's men came within twenty feet of the stockade did its pursuers finally break off and ride north to join the warriors driving the cattle and horses down river. The aggressors had what they came for, and by early afternoon, except for a few Indians watching the fort, the storm was spent. About this time, "Green" Taylor and Lewis Shurtliff, unaware of what had happened, drove their team in from the south with a load of timber. Attack survivors also began to arrive. Reuben Collett was the first from the lower settlement. Leaving the others and abandoning his wagon, he had whipped his oxen in a desperate race to save his team and himself. Haskell V. Shurtliff soon after arrived on foot with a gunshot wound in his left arm. He reported the natives had taken the cattle off the wagons, unyoked most or all of them, and set fire to the two hay loads. About 3 P.M. Oliver Robinson straggled in nursing a bloody hand, hurt by the same ball that passed through Shurtliff's arm. Neither of them knew any more about the fate of James Miller or their other two companions.

Thomas Smith now sent the Indian wives of Thomas Day and Richard Margetts out to talk with the warriors, who kept the fort under surveillance, to learn their grievances and try to recover the herd by conciliation.[11] But the women reported back that "the reason why they had taken our cattle was because we would not give them any clothing, food or ammunition, and if we would give them a good amount of ammunition they would give us our cattle back provided Col. Smith would go to their camp for them," Moore wrote.[12] At the same time, the natives said they did not want peace with the Mormons.

---

[10]Bluth, "The Salmon River Mission," 3:12, October 1900, 907.

[11]Charles F. Middleton Journal, 25 February 1858.

[12]Salmon River Mission Journal, 25 February 1858.

As night approached, Orson Rose straggled in unhurt. There were still five men missing, but the native women warned against going in search of them. Even so, Thomas Smith told Rose to guide a party of eight or ten under Pleasant Green Taylor out to where he had seen the Indians chase Andrew Quigley. Near that spot, about two miles from the fort, they found the Irishman still alive but weak and barely able to move. His attackers had taken his revolver and belt but not his scalp. Searchers then found George McBride. He had been shot through the chest. The ball had passed just under both arms, apparently killing him instantly. The search party carried them both in about sundown.

Two accounted for left three still missing. Shortly after Taylor's party returned, Smith and several others went in search but failed to find them. Well after dark Milton Hammond and James Wilcox called to the guard to open the west gate. They had worked their way up the river "and kept in the brush until we had got to place that they burnt our wagons," Hammond said, and waited until after dark to head in.[13] Then they followed the road to the stockade. "From the way he fell as he reached the brush," both believed James Miller was dead, and they did not think he could be found in the dark.[14]

Seventy-one occupants of a stockade, built to house a third that many, fought feelings of loneliness and fear as darkness fell, "not knowing what other disaster might come as most of the teams at the fort were taken with the herd."[15] Some cared for the wounded as best they could while others stood guard and organized the fort's defenses. "Our hearts almost sank within us when our condition was considered," Lewis Shurtliff said.[16]

Of the forty-three men present on the day of the attack, one was dead, one was missing and feared dead, while five others were wounded. None of the seventeen women, including the Indian wives, and thirteen children was hurt.[17] But the attackers had made off with nearly three hundred cat-

[13]Milton D. Hammond Journal, 25 February 1858.

[14]Salmon River Mission Journal, 25 February 1858.

[15]Jacob Miller Journal, 8 March 1858.

[16]Life and Travels of Lewis Warren Shurtliff, February 1858.

[17]Those present on 25 February 1858 were: James R. Allred, Ezra J. Barnard, William Batchelor, Jonathan S. Bowen, Adeline Bowen, Joseph L. Bowen, Clifton S. Browning, Israel J. Clark, Elizabeth Clark, Jesse Clark, Reuben Collett, Thomas Corless, Charles Dalton, Eunice Daniels Dalton, John L. Dalton, Thomas Day, Jr., Francillo Durfee, Cynthia Harrington Bowen Durfee, Emma Durfee, Stephen H. Gheen, Mary Adelia Hardy Gheen, Hathron Chauncy Hadlock, Elizabeth Jane Bowen Hadlock, Sally Louisa Had-

tle, almost all the teams, and nearly thirty horses. Unable to move, sixty-nine white settlers were "left over three hundred miles from our friends."[18] In a hopeful sign, seventeen cattle returned during the night.[19]

The Search for James Miller

At first light next day eleven men went to search for James Miller. They found him at the edge of the brush along the river, "about 20 rods from where the waggons was burnt, laying on his face, and from all appearances he had fell dead," said Hammond, who had been in Miller's hay party.[20] In a wound similar to McBride's, the ball that killed him had struck his left arm and passed through his chest. The Indians had stripped the twenty-year-old missionary, "torn out the bloody spots in his garment and left the pieces on the ground."[21] The searchers carried young Miller's body back and laid it alongside McBride. Bitterly Hammond said, "Some of the boys say that they see Powell the mountaineer in the fuss."[22]

Fort Limhi Buries Its Dead

The fearful settlers now prepared to bury their dead companions and leave the valley of Salmon River's east fork to its native inhabitants.

lock, Eliza Maranda Hadlock, Milton D. Hammond, Henry M. Harmon, Susan Marler Harmon, Martin H. Harris, Richard B. Margetts, William N. Marler, George McBride, James McBride, Charles F. Middleton, Frederick A. Miller, James T. Miller, David Moore, Susan Vorce Moore, William H. Perry, Alice Stowell Perry, William S. Perry, Cynthia Earnestine Perry, Andrew Quigley, Oliver L. Robinson, Orson H. Rose, Haskell V. Shurtliff, Elsemina Emergene Shurtliff, Mary Ann Shurtliff, Haskell A. Shurtliff, Hascaline Shurtliff, Lewis W. Shurtliff, Louisa Smith Moore Shurtliff, Henry Smith, Helen Maria Fox Smith, Baby Smith, Jesse "W" Smith, Catherine Van Velsor Smith, Jesse William Smith, Thomas S. Smith, William Smith, Ann Smith, Elizabeth Smith, Levi Taylor, Pleasant Green Taylor, Jane Narcissus Shurtliff Taylor, William R. Taylor, James John Walker, Baldwin H. Watts, Fountain Welch, James D. Wilcox, and Amos R. Wright. Names of the two Indian wives are not known.

[18]Salmon River Mission Journal, 25 February 1858.

[19]A later tally of losses came to seventy-one oxen, eighty-five cows, twenty-four two-year-olds, thirty-six yearlings, thirty-seven calves, and twenty-nine horses.

[20]Milton D. Hammond Journal, 26 February 1858.

[21]Salmon River Mission Journal, 26 February 1858. The attackers apparently tore out the bloody spots as a taunt. On completing temple rituals, Mormons received a cloth undergarment with symbolic markings to certify that they had been cleansed of the blood of that generation and were ready to receive the bridegroom. They believed (and no doubt told the natives) that the garment would protect the wearer from harm.

[22]Milton D. Hammond Journal, 26 February 1858.

Some dug holes in the frozen ground to cache the fruit of an abundant fall harvest, nearly two thousand bushels of wheat. Others worked to excavate a single grave large enough for two coffins. Skilled hands crafted simple wooden boxes for each of the men. "We buried George and James in the evening in the west end of the saw pit," Hammond said. "They were dressed in a full set of temple clothes and buried in separate coffins side by side."[23] Moore added that they were "interred after night in our corral near a saw pit, and the ground covered with hay, where the cattle soon blotted out all signs of the grave." He said, "This was done that the Indians might not find them after we left."[24]

After the burial, a wolf howled in the brush along the river. Every man rushed to his post as the guards sounded the alarm, "the Indians were upon us." James Wilcox said he saw shadows coming toward the fort, which kept everyone's nerves on edge for a long time, but no Indians appeared. The next day two warriors "came on the high bench north east a little out of gunshot and circled around in a daring manner."[25] Thomas Smith sent the two native wives out to talk to them, but nothing came of it. The intruders just wanted their female relatives back. The women refused to go.

Over the next forty-eight hours the mission president reconsidered his decision to leave in haste as no other Indians appeared or showed an interest in renewing their attack. On Sunday, 28 February, he called an outdoor meeting within the stockade and proposed to "stay until news could go and come from the valley."[26] Smith took "some considerable length of time" to give the reasons for his decision. They lacked the horses and animals required to move so many men, women and children, plus baggage and supplies, over a long distance in winter. With Indians on the warpath, he hardly needed to remind his followers that the ninety-mile passage between mountain ranges from the fort to Snake River Valley was a potential gauntlet from which none might emerge. Smith also knew the importance of the settlement in Brigham Young's strategic plans. And not least of these considerations was it that two wives of missionaries were due to deliver additions to the settlement roster.

[23]Ibid.

[24]Salmon River Mission Journal, 26 February 1858. To the best of the author's knowledge, no one has ever found the common grave where the remains of McBride and Miller lie undisturbed to this day.

[25]Ibid., 27 February 1858.

[26]Milton D. Hammond Journal, 28 February 1858.

Smith's new plan to stay and fight, if necessary, while swift riders carried news of their position to Great Salt Lake won the approval of all. They would swallow their fear and wait while two of the bravest among them made the 380-mile winter ride on the only horses "left us fit for the journey" and returned with word on what to do. Chosen for this daunting mission were Ezra Barnard, a knowledgeable mountaineer at age twenty-seven, and reliable Mississippian, Baldwin "Baldy" Watts, twenty-two, both founders of Fort Limhi and men of tested endurance and courage.

THOMAS SMITH: WE ARE PREPAIRING FOR A REGULLAR SIEGE

While Smith dictated a letter to Brigham Young, the remaining thirty-nine men, including the wounded, prepared to defend the fort. They formed four companies under Pleasant Green Taylor, William Hammond, Francillo Durfee, and William Taylor, captains. David Moore assumed overall command and assigned each company a location to rush to and defend in the event of attack. Hammond and Durfee took charge of parties to build bastions at the four corners of the stockade. Brigham Young had ordered this to be done in May 1857, but work had not started before the raid. On completion the elevated firing platforms commanded the bench and the four walls of the fort. As this work went forward, the mission president described their peril.

SMITH TO YOUNG, 28 FEBRUARY 1858, BRIGHAM YOUNG PAPERS.

Pres. Brigham Young — Fort Limhi, Salmon River
Dear Sir— — February 28th 1858

I take up the pen to inform you of the position of our affairs in this place. Since our last mail sent by Br Perkins & John Barnard which left here on the 5th of Jan,y last, the Natives both Sho.sho.nees & Bannacks have from time to time been gathering & dispersing during the winter. Quite a party of the Sho.sho.nees came to our Fort some where about 5 weeks past and was very bold and impudent. We got the Chiefs and some of their principle men togather, talked to them & gave them about 5 bushels of wheat besides a good amt of bread, upon which they agreed to not come to (the fort) any more. We have traded a little provisions and gave them a good deal. We have been able to pacify their anger which they have said all the time, was not against us but against the Nezpercies. We also strove to make friends between them & the Nezpercies while the Nezpercus were here but to no effect. Of late they have kept togather in camp some 8 miles down this river, hunted but little or none, and begged a good deal besides stealing about every thing they could get their hands on. About two weeks past the Bannacks from the direction of fort Boisy on Snake River have been gathering in to the Sho.sho.nee camp those same murderers that have killed the emigrants in years past.[27] Old Rock A Ka the Big Bannack also came in & one of his brothers with him, he complained of being angry with the Mormons for not giving him some white wives, he seemed in a very bad spirrit & went off so to the camp.[28] Although we talked to him kindly as usual he has stated that he had thrown you and all the Mormons Away because you nor them would give him any thing. After seeing the movements of the Natives we thought best to move the lower fort up to this, which was nearly done of the 25th three days past when the Indians in Mass to the No of 150 or over made a break on our herd which was under care of Andrew Quigly. Fountain Welch & Orson Rose, herders which had been engaged for the season. They fired on Fountain Welch who fell. They then beat him on the head with their guns & left him for dead. They also shot Andrew Quigley & beat him on the head with iron war picks till they left him for dead. Before this commenced I was up the river with my team. P. G. Taylor & L. W. Shurtliff was also up the river for timber. As I was returning I saw the Indians Making towards the herd. I drove down as fast as possible. They had discovered the Indians at their first move at the fort & Br. Moore had sent out Br Wm. Taylor with some 8 or 9 men before I arrived. Br. George McBride also had taken his horse & gone out. I took one of my horses & Took E. J. Barnard with his horse & put out for the Stock but soon found it of no use as the Indians had most all of the Cattle & all but 4 of our horses fully in their posession. Br. William Taylor & Co. being on foot could do nothing to stop the Cattle. They took Br Welch after seeing Br Geo. McBride shot from his horse, & commenced a retreat for the fort with him he having come to enough to walk by being helped. The Indians were following up the small party that had Br Welch & firing at them. I seeing this strove to get to them but was cut off by some half dozen of Indians. I then kept my course towards the fort. The Indians followed up, & as we were decending the bench the Indians fired on us hiting my suspender & the bullett lodging in my horses jaw. My horse jumped & throwed me. Br

[27]Smith referred to the Indians who committed the Ward Massacre.

[28]Instructing missionaries to marry Indian women raised a complicated question: would the Mormons provide Indian leaders with white wives? Both Kanosh and Walkara asked Brigham Young to do so without success, although Young arranged for Kanosh to marry "Sally," a Shoshone captive Young had adopted and raised. Indians killed Eunice Warner Snow's husband, John Warner, in October 1853, and shortly after the birth of their son six months later, "Chief Walker" visited and "said he intended, when I got around again, to have me for his wife. He told my father and mother his intentions. They did not let me known anything about it until he came several times to see me; when they told me it almost frightened me to death. I was obliged to keep in hidding [*sic*] from him for about six weeks, in fact until the good news came on morning that Walker was dead. He died very suddenly." See Gottfredson, *History of Indian Depredations in Utah,* 77–78.

Barnard caught my horse. As I fell my revolver fell out of my hand. While I was looking for it they fired with a revolver Br. McBrides I suppose and hit the leaf of my hat. I then took down for my horse and as I got on they fired again at me the bullet passing through the upper part of my arm. Just below my elbow. The Indians soon left and followed the herd which they had taken down the River. Five of the Brethren were on their way from the fort with 2 loads of hay & the remnant of the things left down there. They fell upon them killing Br Jas Miller of Farmington & wounding Brs. H. V. Shirtliff & Oliver Robinson the bullet passing through B. Shirtliffs left arm above the elbow & through br Robinsons right hand. The boys then ran into the brush and escaped to the fort. The indians then set fire to the hay burning up both wagons and loads. After the Indians had left I sent Br Taylor & a Company of men to bring in brs. G. McBride & Quigley. Br McBride was shot through the heart & then scalped. Br Quigley was shot in the shoulder. Br Jas. Miller through the heart. The Brethren was totally unaware of any design in the Indians of shooting & killing untill they fired on them & only one shot was fired back & that by order of Br Wm. Taylor to keep the Indians back while they could get Br Welch away. The wounded are fast recovering and we are prpairing [preparing] for a regullar siege should they attack us again. We have a good quantity of hay & feed on hand to keep our stock that is left & have commenced to hide up our wheat. We have on hand over 2 thousand bushels of wheat at the present. We have only 20 yoke of oxen left. 18 head of cows & yearlins came back & one colt from the Indians. They even took the oxen off the wagons after killing Br Miller & run[n]ing the boys into the brush.

We consider ourselves safe while we are in the fort but cant get out to farm any. The Indians are watching every movement we make & I don't consider it safe to leave the fort with the teams until some assistance can be rendered us, either to go or stay as you think best, but I think it is of no use to try to maintain this place with the forces we have here at the present.

Powel a Mountaineer was with the Indians and helped them to drive off the cattle & from every circumstance that we are acquainted with this whole affair has been concocted last summer at Soda Springs between the Mountaineers & Indians. In conclusion I feel to say that we have tried to carry out all the Councils that has been given us by you and have at all times when we have had a chance, talked to them and councilled them how to act and have tried all reasonable terms to get wives from amongst them & have tried to live as faithful as we could & to all appearance there has not been as much unity heretofore on the Mission as there has been during the winter Past.

I remain Your Brother
In the Gospel of Truth
T. S. Smith
Per D. Moore, Clk

Watts and Barnard prepared for their journey while one of the women stitched Smith's appeal into the latter's coat and Richard Margetts reshod their mounts. Normally each express rider would take two horses on a long distance run to rest one animal while riding the other and to have a spare in the event one became lame. This time there was no margin for such renewal or survival. Smith sent his favorite horse with Watts and Barnard rode his own, "the only ones left to us fit for the journey."[29] Just after dark, the two men slipped out the fort's east gate and kept to the eastern foothills to skirt the Indian camps along the river. Behind them prayers went up for their safety and fear seized every heart that any moment the darkness would torn by gunfire. But the dreaded sounds that would announce the discovery and death of the messengers never came.

Early next day a Bannock warrior appeared on the bench and called to the Indian women in the fort to come out, but this time Smith kept them under guard and refused to let them go. He feared that the native wives would inform their tribal kinsmen that Watts and Barnard had left the stockade during the night. That would endanger the lives of the express riders. Instead he told Amos Wright, an eighteen-year-old with a gift for Indian language, to converse with him. Wright called to the man to come down and talk, but he would not, saying "there were a great many Indians near by and they were going to kill us all off."[30] But the threat was more bluff than real because most of the Bannocks, who had instigated the attack, had already left with nearly the entire herd.

Unaware of this, Margetts, the English blacksmith, undertook that day to fashion a more visible form of intimidation. Helped by Moore, a millwright, he began to build "a houster [howitzer] gun," said Middleton. According to a later description, "It was made of iron staves bound together by wagon-tire bands." Mounted in a bastion, the imposing device attracted much curiosity among the Indians near the fort "as to its carrying power, and its destructiveness when fired." No adjective was spared to impress the natives with the awesome power of the homemade gun. "There is no doubt that the hostiles obtained some information of the 'big gun,' and what it would do, and that it had some weight in preventing an attack," one of its builders said in a further exaggeration.[31]

---

[29]Salmon River Mission Journal, 28 February 1858.

[30]Ibid., 1 March 1858.

[31]Bluth, "The Salmon River Mission," 3:12, October 1900, 910.

On the second day after the express riders left, an Indian occasionally employed at the fort as a herder and known as "Old Dad," turned up just after dark at the smaller gate on the west side and tried to open it. The guard almost shot the friendly follower of Chief Snag before he recognized him in the dark. The old Shoshone came from Horse Prairie Creek, east of the divide where the rest of his band was camped, and was unaware of what had happened. After eating a heavy meal of boiled wheat and learning about the attack, "'Old Dad' left us & said he would steel our cattle from the other Indians & drive them to us," Middleton said.[32] The old herder proved almost as good as his word.

David Moore: Cut Off from the Church

With the fort's immediate defense taken care of, the missionaries took up a more distant but no less pressing business—the eternal punishment of their attackers. On Fast Day, 4 March, they conducted a special meeting to "cut off from the church all those who had been baptized that were known to be in the band who engaged in robbing us, and killing and wounding the brethern on the 25th of February last."[33]

Salmon River Mission Journal.

Names are here given again intire & those guilty marked.

Te-to-wah	(Snags Brother)
*George	O-haw-wig-e-ah
Nah-pirce	(sometimes called A ro) a Bannack
Thomas	(killed by Ponderays 3 June/57)
*Joseph	(strove to kill Pres Smith)
Cyrus	Con-e-bon-e-vah
*Henry	Pan-tag-e-rick-up (Fish & root eater)
Mormon	
William	Pe-e-ge-tah
David	Zeeme (Snags Br)
*George	O-haw-wig-e-ah
*Ralph	Pick-o-mets (Bannock)
Thomas	Eas-e-to-roat (Bannock)
Mark	Ho-at-sey (Bannock)
James	Mo-to-win-ney (Ralphs son)
*Louis	

[32]Charles F. Middleton Journal, 3 March 1858.

[33]Salmon River Mission Journal, 4 March 1858.

Joseph	Pan-sook-mud-zu-we (fish, sucker)
Eli	Na-bi-gye-yah
Levi	Pas-tim-mah (Sho sho ne)
Joseph	Mo-pe-ah (Big Nose)
Israel	Yo-ko-ap
Alfred	Tis-sid-da-make
John	Cots-se-qui-mi-at
Jacob	Na-da-mo-tis-e-be
William	Taw-haw-i-be
Abraham	Te-go-cho-to-she-wash-up
	Par-go-e-ah
	To-e-nip-pit
Samuel	In-near-nocket
*John	Co-se-wat
Thomas	Spig-et
Sam	
James	Mo-hes
	*Tin-go-sho
	Saw-ne
Isaac	
*John	Tin-go-sho's Nephew
*Jacob	Tin-go-sho's Nephew
	*Tome or Pome Tin-go-sho's son
*James	Tin-go-sho son in law
	To-she-quit-som-be
	Pic-co
	*Poo-e-wats or Boo-e-wat
William	Con-o-we
	Ah-nab-be
	Pam-e-cot-ite
*Harvey	
	Ah-ha-wo
	Ti-vish-e-ma
	Sos-e-o
	I-vish-a-me
	Par-hu-ro
Sam	
	Che-me
	Che-hui
	Pap-par-he
	Cu-hoe-ah
	Pad-ed-zo

John	
	Oc-red-it-sey
Sam	
Snag	Ti-o-von-du-ah
Richard	
Horace	
	Par-sho-up
	Pe-get-sey
	Wash-up

Note. Those marked * thus were engaged more or less in the murder and Robbery 25 Feb 1858 and mostly were Indians who had been fed a great deal during our stay at Salmon River. There were some Squaws Baptised but it don't appear necessary to name them over as their names are in the former record.

The next day "Old Dad" came back bringing two other Indians, a Bannock and a Shoshone, who also planted themselves at the mission table. "They said that the Bannocks had left and taken all our stock with them but 30 head, which they would bring up to us the next day," Moore said. For three days the old herder and his friends failed to show up, but as word spread that expressions of remorse were good for a free meal, Indians began to appear from all directions, even some of the excommunicated ones.

Then Arrow-mo and other Bannocks came down from the low divide between Snake and Salmon rivers, but when they learned of the attack, "they were afraid to come into the fort."[34] Thomas Smith dispatched young Wright to invite him in. Arrow-mo came but kept his camp on the west side of the river. Not so distrustful was Old Dad, who brought Boo-e-wat, Mag-e-nup, Co-sa-wat, and a dozen or so other natives, who delivered twenty-eight head of cattle, all cows and yearlings, except five head of oxen. The old herder was "much elated with his success."[35]

On 11 March several more natives arrived bringing eight more cows and heifers. With them came one "Indian Jo," who turned himself in to be punished as Thomas Smith saw fit. The repentant native confessed that when the Bannocks first came, "they held a war dance and then wanted the Shoshones to help them or go with them and see them kill our cattle and fight us." But not all the Shoshones agreed to this, Jo said.

[34]Ibid., 8 March 1858. [35]Ibid.

"The Bannocks then held another war dance, and then told the Sho-sho-nes that if they would not go and help them steal our cattle," Jo said, "that they would fight the Sho-sho-nes." At this, "we came [and] took your cattle, killed some of the Mormons and shot some others, because we were bad Indians," he confessed, "for the Mormons have not hurt any of us, but they have always given us food when we were hungry."[36] But Smith was unimpressed by the feigned repentance and refused to see him.

"Old We-in-demps," also known as "Thick Lips," soon after returned Thomas Corless's horse. "This old scamp has killed two head of our cattle, after being fed by us every time he came to the Fort, since the first summer we came here," said David Moore resentfully. The Bannock Boo-e-wat, also called Harvey, and another native, identified only as Katallo's brother, passed the fort on 13 March heading south up the river. "They said they were going to Salt Lake," the mission clerk said, which seemed unlikely. "Old Boo-e-wat had two of our ponies and two head of cattle with him, but must have taken them by in the night as none of our stock was with theirs."[37] The treacherous Bannock slipped past with at least two Mormon horses in his possession, but he did not keep them for long.[38]

Finally, Chief Snag dispatched his two brothers, Te-to-wah, and To-buds, usually referred to as "Two-Bits," "to see if we were mad" before he dared to show up himself. On being assured that the Mormons were "not mad with any except those that had shot at us and stolen our cattle," the old Shoshone chief came from the Beaverhead country next day and started "begging for groceries of all kinds, of which we had none for ourselves." By 17 March the fort was "again filled with begging natives." For the missionaries to see some of the natives who had participated in the raid aroused feelings that "cannot well be described," Moore said.[39]

Snag had not taken part in the raid, but he did bring a report from the mountaineer camps on the Missouri River headwaters describing who was involved and why. The Shoshone chief said "a small detachment of soldiers or men from the camp of the soldiers at Bridger came to Beaver

[36]Ibid., 11 March 1858.

[37]Ibid., 12 March 1858.

[38]Ibid., 13 March 1858.

[39]Ibid., 17, 18 March 1858.

Head to buy stock." From the camp of this detachment a man named Powell came to the Bannock and Shoshone lodges on Salmon River two days before the raid, "inciting the Indians and giving them his aid and participation" in the attack. Afterward, the chief said, Powell arranged to meet the Bannocks at Soda Springs and "conduct them with their stolen stock to the camp of the troops, accompanied [by] the detachment to Bridger."[40]

The outrage caused by this report was overcome by the spontaneous celebration that erupted in the early morning darkness on Sunday, March 21, when B. F. Cummings and his advance company of ten men rode up on the east side of the fort and called to the guard to open the main gate. "Oh it was a happy time," said Lewis Shurtliff.[41]

To celebrate their deliverance, they decided a few days later to fire the howitzer that blacksmith Margetts and Moore had fashioned out of barrel staves and wagon-tire bands. "Last night we lo[a]ded the canon & tuck it out of the fort & shot it of[f]," Oliver Robinson said, "& bursted it all to piaces."[42] Not one piece the weight of a pound could be found, a witness said. "Fortunately no one was injured by the bursting of the gun."[43]

[40]Hooper to Cumming, 13 April 1858, Sen. Exec. Doc. 1, 1858, 74, 75.

[41]Life and Travels of Lewis Warren Shurtliff, March 1858.

[42]Oliver Lee Robinson Diary, 26 March 1858.

[43]Bluth, "The Salmon River Mission," 3:12, October 1900, 910.

BENJAMIN FRANKLIN FICKLIN
One of the West's most colorful figures, the adventuresome Virginian in 1857 led a party from Fort Bridger north to the Flathead country to buy cattle and horses for the U.S. Army, and probably touched off the Indian attack on Fort Limhi. *Courtesy of the Preston Library, Virginia Military Institute.*

Chapter II

Ten Men and Four Gallons of Whiskey

About January 1, 1858, there arrived ten men, under the command of B. F. Ficklin, who had been teamsters in the employ of Johnston's army. They were enlisted as volunteers, and sent out from the winter quarters at Fort Bridger to purchase beef cattle from the mountaineers. — *Granville Stuart*

Rumors that reached Fort Limhi of U.S. soldiers on the Beaverhead holding Mormon prisoners with their hands tied had been distortions, if not outright falsehoods, possibly intended to intimidate the settlers on Salmon River or provoke a confrontation with them.[1] But Chief Snag's report that ten men from the U.S. Army encampment on Blacks Fork had arrived on the Beaverhead that winter to purchase cattle and had incited the raid on Fort Limhi's herd carried a ring of truth. For camped on the tributaries of Jefferson River on the upper Missouri or in Deerlodge Valley at the time of the attack had indeed been a party of ten civilian volunteers from Camp Scott whose leader would be called "the first cattle buyer to come to Montana."[2] But the holder of this distinction was much more than that.

Bold, Imaginative, Restless: B. F. Ficklin

Benjamin Franklin Ficklin has been described as "a bold, imaginative, restless man, ruthless to outlaws and other evil-doers," and, even though this remarkable figure in western history has had few chroniclers, his

[1]The capture of Nauvoo Legion Major Joseph Taylor and his adjutant, William Stowell, by U.S. troops on 16 October 1857, near Fort Bridger, may have led to these unfounded reports.

[2]Fletcher, "The Day of the Cattlemen Dawned Early—In Montana," 27. Deerlodge Valley at the joining of Little Blackfoot River and Clark Fork, near Deer Lodge, Mont., is located on the Columbia River drainage.

reputation appears honestly won.[3] The beginning of the Utah War found the adventurous twenty-nine-year-old Virginian supervising a survey exploring party for Frederick W. Lander. Lander was chief engineer of the Fort Kearney, South Pass, and Honey Lake Wagon Road, a project to build a national highway to the Pacific.[4] On 6 October 1857, he told Lander he had counted seventy-two burned wagons on Green and Big Sandy rivers, where Nauvoo Legion Major Lot Smith two days before had torched three U.S. Army supply trains.[5] Such evidence of Mormon hostility moved the Virginian to oppose the alleged Utah rebellion actively.

On 4 November the territory's new chief justice, Delana R. Eckels, then with the Army, named Ficklin U.S. marshal *pro tem* and ordered him to take custody of Mormon Major Joseph Taylor, pending his trial for treason before the Green River County district court.[6] Three days later Ficklin won duty more to his liking. The Utah Expedition's new commander hired him and members of his wagon-road crew at the rate of $2.50 per day as civilian guides. His service to the Army during its struggle to reach the shelter of Fort Bridger proved so useful that Col. Albert S. Johnston doubled his pay retroactively.[7]

Once he had established his winter garrison near Jim Bridger's former trading post and christened it Camp Scott, Johnston took action to insure the survival of his command. To restore livestock lost to Mormon raiders and early blizzards, he sent Capt. Randolph Marcy and a company of enlisted and civilian volunteers on a winter journey across the

---

[3]Thrapp, *Encyclopedia of Frontier Biography*, 1:489. For more on Ficklin, see Epilogue, pp. 320, 321.

[4]Congress authorized the Pacific Wagon Road expedition in July 1856 and February and March 1857. Superintendent William Magraw received instructions on 1 May 1857 "to open a new road to avoid the detour *via* Salt Lake City." Frederick Lander replaced Magraw and in 1858 and 1859 opened the "Lander Cutoff" far to the north of Utah Territory, partly due to "the unsettled condition of affairs in the vicinity of Salt Lake City at the time." See "Report upon the Pacific Wagon Roads," House Exec. Doc. 108 (35-2), 3, 5, 7. The road's official name, the Fort Kearney, South Pass, and Honey Lake Wagon Road, misspelled the name of Gen. Stephen Watts Kearny and the fort named after him.

[5]Ecelbarger, *Frederick W. Lander: The Great Natural American Soldier*, 40. On Green River, near Seedskedee Wildlife Refuge, and at Simpson's Hollow on Big Sandy River, just west of Farson, both in present Wyoming, Smith burned enough supplies to feed the U.S. Army expedition at least two months.

[6]House Exec. Doc. 71 (35-1), 55–56. Since Ficklin had guarded Major Taylor, he may have started the rumor on the Beaverhead that the Army was holding Mormon prisoners with their hands tied. Holding incriminating orders from Nauvoo Legion Gen. Daniel H. Wells, Taylor and his adjutant William Stowell had blundered into a party of U.S. soldiers. Taylor later escaped.

[7]Porter to Dickerson, 19 November and 4 December 1857, "Army of Utah," letters sent 1857–1861.

Rocky Mountains to Fort Union in New Mexico.[8] At the same time, he named Ficklin to lead ten volunteers north and contract to purchase up to five hundred head of cattle from mountaineers on the headwaters of the Missouri and Columbia rivers in present Montana. Most of the men had served together under Ficklin before.[9]

While representing the U.S. Army, the northbound party was notably different from Captain Marcy's expedition. Not only smaller, it was made up entirely of civilians and lacked direct Army supervision. At its head was an impetuous man, prone to act first and worry about consequences later. For credentials, Ficklin bore written authorization from Johnston and letters of introduction from Utah's new governor, Alfred Cumming, to John Owen in Bitterroot Valley and Father Adrian Hoecken at St. Ignatius Mission on the Flathead Indian Reservation, some seventy miles north of Fort Owen. As superintendent of Indian Affairs at St. Louis, Cumming had participated in the Great Indian Council of 1855 at Fort Benton, also attended by Owen, when Washington Governor Isaac I. Stevens negotiated treaties with various tribes. Guiding Ficklin's party was F. W. Lander's former interpreter, Edward "Ned" Williamson, a twenty-nine-year-old Pennsylvanian, who gained his knowledge of the northern region and its inhabitants during the 1853 Northern Railroad Survey.[10] Finally, Ficklin carried greetings to Frederick Burr in Bitterroot Valley from his brother, David A. Burr, who had served as a surveyor for his father, David H. Burr, the runaway surveyor general of Utah Territory.

AN EXPEDITION TO THE FLATHEADS

Colonel Johnston directed his quartermaster on 4 December to give Ficklin six mules, four pack saddles, and enough rations for three months for "an expedition among the Flat Head Indians." The colonel also ordered the supply officer "to commute the rations not taken."[11] This

[8]Marcy told the story of this exploit in his *Thirty Years of Army Life on the Border*, 198–243.

[9]They were John Gabriel, John McDonald, John Brown, A. C. Ayers, John Hartly, Almangor Nolan, Charles R. Garis, William Justus, and William Hall.

[10]Williamson subsequently went to work for John Owen in 1859 and later served as an "expressman" for U.S. Army road-builder John Mullan and as a courier for Gen. John Gibbon's Sioux campaign of 1876. See Weisel, ed., *Men and Trade on the Northwest Frontier as Shown by the Fort Owen Ledger*, 202–03.

[11]Porter to Dickerson, 4 December 1857, U.S. War Dept., "Army of Utah," letters sent 1857–1861.

allowed the recipient to exchange food for other commodities deemed necessary for comfort or survival. Taking advantage of Johnston's indulgence, Ficklin on 9 December rode north with enough supplies for one month, plus four gallons of whiskey, apparently sufficient to fight off frostbite until he reached some wintering mountain men.

By now, the Virginian had seen the burned U.S. Army supply wagons on Green River and its tributary, Big Sandy, destroyed by Mormon Major Lot Smith. He had taken part in the Utah Expedition's winter march from the mouth of Hams Fork to Fort Bridger that had killed thousands of horses, mules, and cattle. He undoubtedly shared Johnston's belief that Mormon leaders showed "a mature and settled design" to occupy and hold Utah Territory "independent of, and irrespective of the authority of the United States." Brigham Young and his minions had, "with premeditation, placed themselves in rebellion against the Union, and entertain the insane design of establishing a form of government thoroughly despotic, and utterly repugnant to our institutions." Ficklin knew that Colonel Johnston had ordered "wherever they are met in arms, that they be treated as enemies."[12] On the day he left Camp Scott, he had every reason to believe a state of war existed between the U.S. and its theocratic Mormon territory. He understood that the welfare of the Army and its civilian dependents in large measure depended on the successful completion of his mission to acquire beef cattle and horses. Even without these considerations, Ficklin was a man who was mission-driven by nature.

All of these factors gave weight to Shoshone Chief Snag's charge that Ficklin or his party were responsible for the Indian raid on Fort Limhi's herd that had taken the lives of two Mormon missionaries and wounded five others. As far as is known, the cattle buyer kept no daily account of his journey. But the report he turned in afterward, supplemented by eyewitness accounts of mountaineers, missionaries, and Indian agents that have come to light since then make it possible to take a closer look at his movements in relation to this charge.

FICKLIN TO PORTER, "ANNUAL REPORT OF THE SECRETARY OF WAR," SEN. EXEC. DOC. 1 (35-2), 1858, 68–73.

Sir: I left this camp on December 9, 1857, with my party of ten men, twelve horses, six mules, and thirty days rations, for the Flathead country, with

[12]Johnston to McDowell, 5 November 1857, House Exec. Doc. 71 (35-1), 46, 47.

> instructions to contract for the delivery at this point of five hundred head of beef cattle by April 1, 1858; also to induce the mountaineers and Indians to bring in any horses they might wish to sell.

Ficklin took no funds to complete the purchase on the spot and drive the cattle back to Camp Scott by himself. His instructions were only to contract for delivery of the animals to the Army encampment, where the quartermaster would pay the seller the full amount due. To make up for losses the Army had suffered, Ficklin was also instructed to induce the mountaineers and Indians to bring horses to Camp Scott, which, intentionally or not, was virtually an invitation to steal them.

> The route to be travelled was left to my choice. In order to avoid collision with any party of Mormons I selected the route up Ham's Fork to the California emigrant route, followed that to the Soda Spring, on Bear river, thence due north across the mountains to Snake river, to a point twenty-five miles northeast of Fort Hall, arriving at Snake river on December 27, a distance estimated at above two hundred miles.

To evade Mormon patrols north of Fort Bridger, Ficklin doubled back over the Oregon Trail to Hams Fork, near present Granger, Wyoming, before going up this stream to Sublette's Cutoff north of present Kemmerer. He then took this short cut from Green River over the Bear River Divide to meet the Oregon Trail on Bear River at today's Cokeville, Wyoming. Near Soda Springs, where Bear River breaks through the Wasatch Mountains and turns south, the party left the emigrant road and headed due north over the mountains to reach Snake River at present Blackfoot, Idaho. Ficklin explained why it took his mounted pack party nineteen days to travel some 215 miles, an average of less than twelve miles a day.

> At the time of leaving this camp there was only about one inch of snow, but it gradually increased, until before arriving at the California emigrant route it was of an average depth of two feet, and in many places so much drifted that it was necessary for the men to open a trail for the horses to pass through. Travelling was very slow and laborious, both for animals and men.
>
> No incident worth mentioning occurred, except in descending the mountains to Snake river; I found it necessary to follow the side of a steep hill to avoid the snow drifts; a pack mule slipped and rolled to the bottom, (about two hundred feet,) and died a few days afterwards in consequence of its injuries.
>
> I was induced to seek a new route across the Snake River mountains,

> because it was more direct than the route by Fort Hall. Perhaps it was fortunate that I did so, as I afterwards learned that about fifty Mormons had, in October last, made a settlement on Snake river, at the mouth of Blackfoot creek, immediately on the Fort Hall trail; had, during the fall, built a fort, saw mill, &c., and had prepared grounds for this year's crop, but in the latter part of January the settlement had been broken up and the party returned to Salt Lake City.

Ficklin apparently did not see for himself the Mormon outpost constructed that fall by Andrew Cunningham on the Blackfoot River and gives no source for his report. While his description is fairly accurate, he misplaces it at the mouth of Blackfoot River, which is not on the Oregon Trail. Mormon sources locate it near the Flathead Trail ford of Blackfoot River between Ferry Butte and present Blackfoot, Idaho. On 15 October 1857 Thomas S. Smith said, "[We] traveled up to the [Snake River] ford. Stoped at the Black foot [and] visited a while with the Brethren from Salmon river."[13] James Miller, one of Smith's company, wrote, "We drove, to the ford of the Snake River and met C. McGary and C. Dunn who stayed all night with us. We passed a location selected by Pres. Cunningham known as the Blackfoot Mission."[14]

Ficklin continued:

> After getting into the valley of Snake river the snow was from nine to eighteen inches in depth. Believing it hardly possible that I could cross the mountains directly into the Flathead country, I concluded to go by the Beaver Head, on the Jefferson Fork of the Missouri, (the wintering ground of a number of mountaineers,) and the Hell's Gate pass. Following Snake river forty miles northeast, thence north fifty miles by an Indian trail, arrived at the foot of the mountains which divide the waters of Snake and Missouri rivers; was three days in crossing this mountain; on the third day was overtaken in a snow storm; had to make a forced march of thirty miles to get off the mountain; was compelled to abandon a horse and two mules. After the storm was over sent back for them, but only found one mule alive, the other having frozen to death.

A direct line over the mountains to the Flathead country was indeed impossible. Unless he went by way of Fort Limhi and today's Lemhi Pass, Ficklin in fact followed the only route to his destination that was open to him. From the Snake River ford at the islands just north of present Black-

[13]Thomas S. Smith Journal, 15 October 1857.

[14]James T. Miller Journal, 15 October 1857.

foot, Idaho, he took the Flathead Trail, now generally followed by I-15, to the Continental Divide at today's Monida Pass. As his party learned, the 6,870-foot passage from the waters of the Columbia drainage to those of the Missouri was dangerous in winter. In 1863–1864 one traveler who attempted to cross on the Montana freight trail was astonished to see "what I had never dreamed of before—several cattle in the moving train freeze to death in the yoke and go right down upon the ground."[15]

> After getting on the head waters of the Missouri the snow entirely disappeared. On the fourth our rations were exhausted, but I was not uneasy, as I expected to arrive soon at the Beaver Head, a point on the Jefferson Fork of the Missouri fifty miles above the Three Forks of the Missouri, and one hundred east of the Mormon settlement on Salmon river, a popular wintering ground of the mountaineers, on account of their stock.

At this point, Ficklin had reason to feel misgivings over his decision to carry whiskey instead of additional food supplies. On 4 January 1858 his party reached Red Rock River, a tributary of the Beaverhead, and found better conditions for travel down the stream. He was then little more than forty miles east of the Mormon mission, as the crow flies, on the opposite side of the Continental Divide. At Fort Limhi that same day, Thomas Smith married Lewis W. Shurtliff and Louisa Catherine Smith, the adopted daughter of David and Susan Moore. Only a week before, John Powell had escaped from the fort and Bannocks and Shoshones had blamed the mission and Chief Snag for the theft of their horses by visiting Nez Percé under Chief Eagle from the Light.[16] Ficklin learned these developments had not gone unobserved in the winter camps of the local ranchers and traders:

> To my surprise, on arriving at Beaver head, I found all the evidences of the mountaineers having left recently, and hastily, and taken the trail in the direction of Flathead valley. As I had no reasonable expectations of overtaking them soon, had to kill a broken down horse to eat.

The urge to take flight from the wintering grounds along the Beaverhead and Big Hole rivers and move north to the Deerlodge and Flathead valleys was hardly as general as Ficklin suggests. It had gripped mainly the mountaineers who owned large cattle herds and became alarmed at

---

[15]Madsen and Madsen, *North to Montana: Jehus, Bullwhackers and Mule Skinners on the Montana Trail,* 79–81.

[16]For the story of this confrontation between the tribes, see Chapter 9, pp. 205–11.

rumors the Mormons would come and seize them. Camped on the Big Hole at this time, within a twenty-five-mile radius of present Dillon, Montana, were Granville and James Stuart, Jacob Meeks, Robert Dempsey, Thomas Pambrun, John M. Jacobs, Robert Hereford, Jim Simonds, John Saunders, Rees Anderson, John W. Powell, and many others. According to Granville Stuart:

> About Christmas, 1857, they were joined by ten men under command of B. F. Ficklin, who had been teamsters in the employ of Johnston's army, and were enlisted as volunteers, and sent out from the winter-quarters at Ft. Bridger to purchase beef cattle from the Mountaineers. They were guided by Ned Williamson, and found very little snow on the route.
>
> They could not purchase cattle on terms to suit them, and fearing to return in midwinter, remained on the Big Hole until the general exodus in the spring, when they returned to Ft. Bridger, being compelled to eat some of their horses on the way, as, indeed, did also some of the mountaineers, game being unusually scarce, and the spring very stormy and bad, although the winter had been mild and pleasant.[17]

Ficklin continues his report:

> On the 10th overtook the camp of Mr. Herriford, where I obtained a supply of beef, and learned from him that about December first they had heard of the burning of the supply trains by the Mormons, and of threats uttered by the Mormons at Salmon River fork, against the mountaineers at Beaver Head. Fearing for the safety of their stock, they had started for the Flathead Valley, as a more distant and secure point.
>
> On account of the jaded condition of my animals, I left my party at Mr. Herriford's camp, and with one man started for Flathead valley.

Following the line of today's Montana Highway 41, Ficklin's party on 10 January reached the mountaineer camp, where he found stock-trader Robert Hereford and his family at the mouth of the Ruby River. There he heard the rumor that the Mormons were coming to kill John W. Powell, Richard Grant, the former Hudson's Bay trader at Fort Hall, his son, John Francis, widely known as "Johnny," and Frederick H. Burr, and build another Mormon fort on the Beaverhead. As mentioned, Louis Maillet, Dr. Atkinson, Hugh O'Neil, and Ramsey had visited Fort Limhi on their way to Fort Bridger the previous November. But when they learned about Lot Smith's raid on the Army's supply wagons and heard

[17]Stuart, "A Memoir of the Life of James Stuart," 38–41.

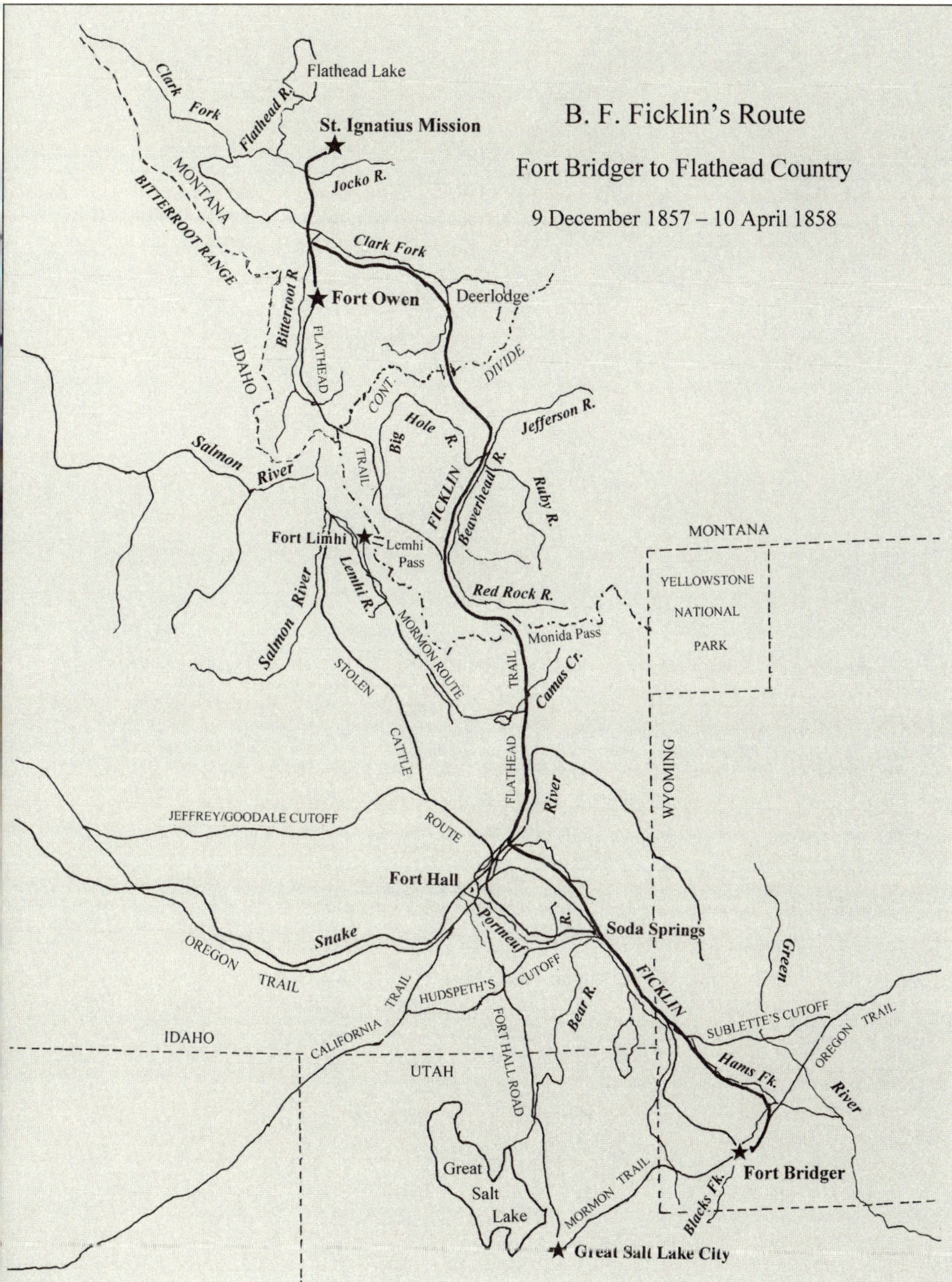

B. F. Ficklin's Route
Fort Bridger to Flathead Country
9 December 1857 – 10 April 1858
Flathead Lake
Clark Fork
Flathead R.
St. Ignatius Mission
Jocko R.
MONTANA
BITTERROOT RANGE
Clark Fork
Bitterroot R.
Fort Owen
Deerlodge
FLATHEAD
IDAHO
CONT.
DIVIDE
Big Hole R.
Jefferson R.
Salmon River
TRAIL
FICKLIN
Beaverhead R.
Ruby R.
Fort Limhi
Lemhi Pass
Lemhi R.
Salmon River
Red Rock R.
MORMON ROUTE
Monida Pass
TRAIL
Camas Cr.
MONTANA
YELLOWSTONE
NATIONAL
PARK
STOLEN
CATTLE
ROUTE
FLATHEAD
River
WYOMING
JEFFREY/GOODALE CUTOFF
Fort Hall
Portneuf
R.
Soda Springs
Snake
OREGON
TRAIL
Green
FICKLIN
CALIFORNIA TRAIL
HUDSPETH'S
CUTOFF
Bear R.
SUBLETTE'S CUTOFF
OREGON TRAIL
IDAHO
UTAH
FORT HALL ROAD
Hams Fk.
River
Great
Salt
Lake
MORMON TRAIL
Fort Bridger
Blacks Fk.
Great Salt Lake City

JOHN F. "JOHNNY" GRANT
Hudson's Bay factor Richard Grant's son guided a U.S. Army patrol to Fort Limhi in 1855 and two years later refused to drive his cattle to Fort Bridger out of fear of the Mormons.
Courtesy of the Montana Historical Society.

the Mormons were coming to the Beaverhead, they changed their plans and hurried instead to sound the alarm among the mountaineers, where their report threw some of these hardened frontiersmen into a panic.[18]

If the rumor was true, Richard Grant with two hundred cattle and a hundred horses on the Beaverhead had much to lose besides his life. Crippled by rheumatism, the old Hudson's Bay man had "grasped Maillet's hand and said he would not let it go" until the French-Canadian promised to take him and his family and animals to Flathead Valley, which he agreed to do.[19] Not far behind the elder Grant's dependent family, including his wife Helene, son James, and three daughters, ages eleven, nine, and seven, came his older son, Johnny, twenty-seven, who drove his own herd of some two hundred head only as far as Deerlodge Valley. A few others also moved north, but many of the mountaineers at the Upper Missouri wintering ground stayed put.

The man Ficklin took with him was Edward "Ned" Williamson. The rest of his party remained at Robert Hereford's camp at the confluence of the Beaverhead and Ruby rivers, not far from the place where Pleas-

[18]See "A Harmful Rumor," Chapter 9, pp. 201–03.
[19]Maillet, "Historical Sketch of Louis R. Maillet," 208–10.

ant Green Taylor's company from Fort Limhi a month later would recover Thomas Smith's horse. At that time, the Indian who had stolen it from the mission corral "put on his war cap, took his spear, mounted a small pony and put off saying that he was going to tell the soldiers."[20] The "soldiers" he was going to tell were the members of Ficklin's party.

> At the Deer's Lodge overtook another party of mountaineers, with whom I made a contract for the delivery of three hundred head of beef cattle, by April 16th, at ten dollars per hundred, also to bring down about one hundred head of horses. Afterwards proceeded to the Flathead valley, where I could have a contract for two hundred head of cattle, but their fear of the Mormons was so great that no price would induce them to undertake to deliver them here. Several were making preparations to move their stock to Fort Walla-Walla this spring, in order to be beyond the reach of the Mormons.
>
> Horses are very scarce, on account of the large number sold in the last few years, and a distemper which killed large numbers last summer.
>
> Great uneasiness was felt by the traders and Indians, on account of the Mormons.

In Deerlodge Valley at the confluence of Little Blackfoot River and Clark Fork, near present Deer Lodge, Mont., Ficklin found Johnny Grant, whose recollection of their earlier transaction differed somewhat from the Virginian's. Known more for survivability than courage, young Grant later said of himself that he often came "very close to trouble" but always managed to escape. In describing his meeting with Ficklin he showed that this occasion was no exception:

> Toward spring [1858] Mr. Thinkland [Ficklin] came to me to buy cattle for the troops. I sold him two hundred head. Then he went to Bitterroot to get some more, but he came back without any. He did not tell me the reason, but I imagined why he did not. He wanted me to take the cattle I was selling to him to Fort Bridger, at my own risk. I positively refused to do it; it was too much of a risk. I did not wish to give the Mormons a chance to give me any trouble, for I was certain to regret it if I attempted to take cattle to the troops, so I lost sale of those cattle.[21]

At Grant's camp, Dr. Monroe Atkinson joined Ficklin and the three men rode down Clark Fork, then named the Hell Gate, on the line of present I-90. The eccentric physician had spent four days at Fort Limhi

[20] Salmon River Mission Journal, 13 February 1858.

[21] Meikle, ed., *Very Close to Trouble. The Johnny Grant Memoir*, 67.

the November before and fled the Beaverhead with Grant and others who feared the Mormons. At the western end of the thirty-six-mile Hell Gate Canyon, the party on 17 January arrived at Neil McArthur's place at Hell Gate Ronde, near the mouth of Bitterroot River, where Ficklin rested while Ned Williamson rode up the valley to Fort Owen, some twenty-seven miles south of present Missoula.

"Late last Evening a Man reached here from the head quarters of the army Now cantoned at Fort Bridger." John Owen said on 19 January. "He is the advance of a party of ten Men under a Mr Ficlin Who was too tired to ride up here yesterday."[22] The trading-post proprietor, who also served as special agent to the Flatheads, had intended to leave for Fort Benton that day, but decided to put off the trip. Frederick Burr, his newly hired interpreter and trader at Fort Owen, also reported the news. "Ned Williamson came from Hells Gate, where he arrived yesterday in company with Mr Ficlin & Dr Atkinson," Burr said. "Mr F—, is from Fort Bridger with a party of men in search of beef & horses for the Army he reports them encamped at Fort Bridger, where they will winter & then in the Spring make a descent on Salt Lake." He added, "My brother [David A. Burr] is with the Army."[23]

Early next morning, 19 January, Burr rode out from Fort Owen to meet Ficklin at the mouth of the Bitterroot and deliver a note from Owen inviting him to visit the trading post. Accompanying him were Williamson and Henry Brooks.[24] The day was "clear and cold," and they found the road "very icy and the river crossings bad," but they arrived in good time at McArthur's ranch. There they found Ficklin and Dr. Atkinson. Also staying at McArthur's was Michael Ogden, the son of the noted Hudson's Bay trader Peter Skene Ogden, who "went with us to the Mission" in Flathead Valley.[25]

As they rode north the next day on the trail followed by present U.S. Highway 93, they overtook Richard Grant "camped on the top of the Mountain having broken both his wagons going up Coriacas's defile."[26]

---

[22]Dunbar and Phillips, eds., *The Journals and Letters of Major John Owen, Pioneer of the Northwest, 1850–1871*, 1:189. [23]Frederick H. Burr Journal, 18 January 1858.

[24]Henry Brooks was a rancher who came to Bitterroot Valley in 1855. He later became justice of the peace and performed the first marriage in Missoula County for which he became known as "Bishop" Brooks.

[25]Frederick H. Burr Journal, 19, 20 January 1858.

[26]Ibid. The narrow Coriacan Defile is the gateway between the Bitterroot and Flathead valleys. It was named after Koriaka, a Hawaiian trader, who was killed there by the Blackfeet.

Grant's animals were in "very bad condition" from his flight from the Beaverhead, but the old Hudson's Bay trader was not about to go back and face an imagined Mormon invasion. On 21 January Ficklin and Burr visited Ogden's spread on the Jocko River, where the trader also rejected an opportunity to supply the Army, no doubt for the same reason.

> I spent several days at St. Ignatius mission, (situated on one of the branches of Clark's Fork of Columbia, on forty-seventh parallell,) established by the Catholics, for the benefit of the Flatheads, Pen d'Oreilles and Hootenais.

Ogden accompanied Ficklin and others as they rode back that day to St. Ignatius Mission at present St. Ignatius on the Flathead Indian Reservation.[27] There the "Fathers seem very much pleased at the prospect of the Mormons getting a thrashing," Burr said.[28] Ficklin and his companions stayed two nights at the mission. The next morning, 22 January, they "passed old Grant going down the mountain" and returned to Brooks's ranch near the mouth of Bitterroot River. There they "partook largely of a fat beef to make up for fasting this morning at the Mission, it being Friday."[29]

While Ficklin and Burr visited Flathead Valley, John Owen sent detailed invoices of property belonging to himself and his employees to James Nesmith, superintendent of Indian Affairs for Oregon and Washington, totaling $36,000. He told Nesmith that the "astounding reports of the Mormon rebellion that daily reach me" had prompted him to "start my stock for the Walla Walla Valley as a place of greater security" just as soon the roads were open. He also thought "the only outlet the Mormons have to escape the strong arm of justice which they so deservedly merit" would be north—from the Great Basin to Bitterroot Valley.[30]

Meanwhile, Ficklin praised the local Indians:

> The Flatheads are undoubtedly the best Indians in the mountains. They often boast of never having shed the blood of a white man. Under the direc-

[27]Father Pierre Jean de Smet, the Belgian Jesuit, founded the first St. Ignatius Mission, the original Jesuit mission to the Kalispells, in 1844 on Pend Oreille River in present Washington. Ten years later Father Adrian Hoecken relocated St. Ignatius to Flathead Valley to escape flooding at the early site and establish a more central location among the Salish tribes.

[28]Frederick H. Burr Journal, 21 January 1858.

[29]Ibid., 22 January 1858.

[30]Owen to Nesmith, 20 January 1858, in Dunbar and Phillips, eds., *The Journals and Letters of Major John Owen*, 2:172, 173.

> tion of the priests they are improving rapidly in agriculture. This year they will sow about three hundred bushels of wheat; they raise large quantities of vegetables, especially potatoes, cabbage and beets.
>
> Their horses are superior to all other Indian horses, in size and power of endurance. The tribe, about sixty lodges, own about one thousand head of cattle.
>
> There were about fifty lodges of Nez Perces in the Flathead valley, returning from a buffalo hunt. They had caught the small pox from the Crows. Many had died, but the priests had succeeded in stopping it by vaccination.

Since he spent so little time in Flathead and Bitterroot valleys, Ficklin probably obtained most of this information about the tribe from Burr and Owen. Both reported the smallpox epidemic among the Nez Percés. Burr said the Catholic missionaries had only been able to vaccinate fourteen of fifty Nez Percé lodges because most members of the tribe preferred their own healer. "They have a medicine man among them who professes to cure them also that he can make Medicine to kill all the whites," he reported. "He calls himself Jesus Christ, and that he is the Son of God, that he can cure the Indians of all the ills that flesh is heir to." Moreover, "for a reasonable compensation he would agree to kill all the Mormons and save the Govt. that expense & trouble."[31]

> As it was impossible to buy stock in Flathead valley, on conditions contemplated in my instructions, on March 3d I started for Deer Lodge, expecting to start immediately on my arrival with what stock I had contracted for at that place.
>
> The contractors refused to deliver their beef at this place, but offered to deliver it there, as they were afraid of being robbed by the Mormons on the road.

At this point in his report Ficklin gives the misleading impression that he spent all of his time in Flathead Valley before heading back on 3 March to Deerlodge Valley, which was far from true. From 22 January, when the Virginian left St. Ignatius Mission with Burr, to 3 March, when he reportedly started back, his report offers nothing at all about his activities. In effect, it imposed a forty-day blackout on where he was and what he did during that time. But his movements can be traced to some extent from the accounts of others.

---

[31]Frederick H. Burr Journal, 23 February, 4 March 1858.

John Owen reported the arrival of Ficklin, Burr, and Atkinson at his fort in Bitterroot Valley on 23 January. "Mr F. is the accredited Qtr Master agent from Head qrts of the Army now at Bridger," trading post owner said. "He bears a letter of introduction to Me from Col Cumings the present Gov. of Utah. He also brought Me a Copy of Brigham Youngs proclamation of Martial Law."[32] The militant tone of Young's pronouncement only made Owen more anxious to send his herd to Walla Walla and less willing to make any deals with the agent from Camp Scott. Three days before, mountaineers John Jacobs and David Pattee had arrived at Fort Limhi on their alleged trading junket.[33]

For the next six days Ficklin tried in vain to purchase cattle in Bitterroot Valley. Finally, on 29 January, the resourceful Virginian "left to rejoin his camp leaving his Man, Williamson here Waiting the recovery of Dr. Atkinson who is to follow on Soon as he is able to ride," John Owen said. "Mr Ficlin failed in the object of his Visit Which Was for the purchase of Stock."[34] On 9 February, he wrote that Ned Williamson left Fort Owen "to join Mr Ficlin in Deers Lodge."[35] These accounts would place Ficklin at Deerlodge Valley with Johnny Grant by 1 February or in the Beaverhead region, where John W. Powell and other mountaineers were camped, by 6 February.

That he had gone as far as the Beaverhead was revealed on 23 February by John Owen, who was "much surprised" that day to see Mr Ficklin ride up after dark. "[Ficklin] left here the 29 ultimo to rejoin his camp in Deers Lodge & had been as far as Beaverhead," he said. He revisits this section for again trying to purchase Stock for the use of the U.S. Troops at Camp Scott. He tells Me [he] has already bought some 200 head of John Grant. He also gets some of Mr. Brooks the agent of Mr McArthur. He will now delay his return trip for some time until he thinks the route is free from Snow as he intends driving the stock with him."[36]

These accounts would easily place Ficklin at the Beaverhead on 9 February, when the Indian came to Fort Limhi and said that a company of ten soldiers were camped there with two Mormon prisoners, "who

---

[32]Dunbar and Phillips, eds., *The Journals and Letters of Major John Owen,* 1:189, 190.

[33]See Chapter 9, p. 212.

[34]Dunbar and Phillips, eds., *The Journals and Letters of Major John Owen,* 1:190. On the way to Fort Owen, Dr. Atkinson's mule slipped on the ice and injured the physician's ankle.

[35]Ibid., 190, 191. [36]Ibid., 193.

wanted to get away very much."[37] If that native's theft of Thomas Smith's horse had been staged to provoke a confrontation, Ficklin should have known about it. And when Pleasant Green Taylor's company caught the thief and recovered the horse four days later, not far from Robert Dempsey's camp, Ficklin could still have been on the Beaverhead that day and reached Fort Owen by 23 February, as Owen reported.[38]

At the same time, Owen places Ficklin in Bitterroot Valley the day of the attack on Fort Limhi, 25 February, which clears him of personal involvement in the raid. Yet the reason he gave Owen for making a round trip of well over four hundred miles and some twelve days to the trading post seems unconvincing. He knew by then that mountaineers with cattle were too afraid of the Mormons to deliver them themselves. Nor does it seem likely that they would let him to drive their stock to Camp Scott without first being paid, even if his orders permitted it. Whatever the answer, he and Henry Brooks went up the valley on 24 February to see Frederick Burr, John Powell's partner, whose only comment on their visit was "F[icklin] and I could not trade."[39] Burr did not specify what he had of value to trade since he had sold his own herd the year before. That day Robert Hereford, at whose camp Ficklin had left his party, "arrived from Beaver Head," Owen wrote.[40]

As Bannock and Shoshone warriors swept down on the herd at Fort Limhi on 25 February, Ficklin "left for Hells Gate rond," Owen said. While it is possible the agent returned to Flathead Valley and St. Ignatius Mission, there is no evidence that he made such a side trip and it is unlikely he did so.[41] Instead, as he told Owen, the cattle buyer would now be on the first leg of his return to Deerlodge Valley and points south, which does not square with his report that he started on 3 March, a full week later. Following Ficklin by two days from Fort Owen were Dr. Atkinson and Hereford, also going to Beaverhead, "from which point they intend proceeding to Camp Scott at Fort Bridger," according

[37]See Chapter 9, p. 214.

[38]To go from the Beaverhead to Fort Owen was about a six-day ride.

[39]Frederick H. Burr Journal, 24 February, 1858.

[40]Dunbar and Phillips, eds., *The Journals and Letters of Major John Owen*, 1:193.

[41]Archivist David A. Kingma, The Oregon Province of the Society of Jesus, Gonzaga University, Spokane, Wash., advised that "few records for that period are available" for St. Ignatius Mission. The extant diary of Mission founder Fr. Adrian Hoecken, S.J., covers only 1855–1856 and the mission's "house" diaries begin in 1874.

to John Owen.[42] Accompanied by mountaineer Jacob Meeks, the stock buyer tried to frighten Johnny Grant at Deerlodge Valley into driving his cattle to Camp Scott, but Grant feared the Mormons more than he did Ficklin. He recalled:

> He said to me in a commanding tone (thinking to frighten me), "If you go to the barracks and the officer asks you anything about the cattle, remember that I was not the party who went back on the bargain. You broke it. Now remember if you do not—I will make you sorry for it.
>
> His threats roused my temper, and I said to him, "Mr. Thinkland [Ficklin], you might have heard that I was a coward, because I never quarrel with anyone nor meddle with other people's affairs; but you are not able to make me own up to what I never said. You are the party who backed out of that bargain, and you cannot deny it. You say too that I will be sorry for this if I do not take the blame. I'm ready now. Come on; we will settle the matter here."
>
> He left me without saying another word. When I got to Fort Bridger, the officer commanding did not ask me anything about it.[43]

Ficklin's report continued:

> The Bannock Indians had, about March 1st, attacked the Salmon river fort, killed two Mormons and wounded three; had also killed and run off all their cattle (about three hundred), and most of their horses.
>
> The cause of this outbreak on the part of the Indians, is not known; but it is known that these Indians were extensively engaged in stealing stock from emigrants on the Mclisle [?] and Humboldt, and selling them to the Mormons. An express was sent from this fort to Salt Lake, and a party was sent to their relief. The settlement on Salmon river was broken up, and all returned to Salt Lake; one portion being two days ahead of me on my return, and the balance with three days' bread, behind me.
>
> Buying a few animals to replace those lost, started on March 12th to return, with thirty days' provisions, expecting to be able to make the trip in fifteen days.

News traveled fast in the mountains, but not so swiftly that Ficklin could have learned so much about the raid on Fort Limhi and its alleged causes before reaching Fort Bridger unless he heard it from someone who had come directly from the event while the pass east of the fort was still open. Although winter had been "mild and pleasant" on the upper Missouri, the spring of 1858 had turned "stormy and bad."[44] On 28

---

[42]Dunbar and Phillips, eds., *The Journals and Letters of Major John Owen,* 1:193.

[43]Meikle, ed., *Very Close to Trouble: The Johnny Grant Memoir,* 67.

[44]Phillips, ed., *Forty Years on the Frontier as seen in the Journals and Reminiscences of Granville Stuart,* 1:130.

March, when Granville and James Stuart with other mountaineers tried to cross the Continental Divide at present Monida, deep snow drove them back. It speaks for Ficklin's determination to complete his mission that his was one of the few known parties to cross to the Snake River side of the mountains before June—and it nearly met disaster. A mountaineer named Ross who had joined the party gave up and went back to report: "All hands snowed in & the devil to pay."[45] Ficklin described the ordeal:

> The new grass was beginning to grow finely before I started, on Jefferson fork; contrary to my expectation and information I had received from the oldest mountaineers, found the snow in the mountains, between Missouri and Snake river, from three to six feet deep for a distance of twelve miles; were three days in making eight miles. At the end of that time the horses were unable to go further; four of my men were helpless from being snow-blind; a heavy blow had filled up the trail, so as to make it as difficult to return as to go forward. For the next two days had a heavy snow storm; two Indian horses died from hunger and cold. On the third day the men were sufficiently recovered to be able to travel. Luckily for me, by two o'clock a warm sun had softened the snow, so that I was able to make two miles that day and two the next, which brought us out into the valley, when before reaching Snake river the snow had entirely disappeared.

It is noteworthy that Ficklin failed to include in his 15 April report that he had found the message that Cummings left on the trail to inform Colonel Cunningham of his recovery of the stolen horses from the Bannocks at Camas Creek. Only after he had been accused of causing the 25 February attack did he report this vital information. Nor did he mention the ambush of Cummings and his party on Bannock Creek on 31 March.[46] To do so would have revealed that he was in the vicinity and that the only source of such information would have been the Indians who made the attack.

> The animals were so reduced by the suffering on the mountain that I had to travel very slowly. The men did not suffer very much; one man had his toes frozen.
>
> After crossing the mountain from Snake river, found the snow from one

[45]Frederick H. Burr Journal, 9 April 1858.

[46]For references to the message, see pp. 290, 307, 308. The story of the ambush is told on pp. 273, 274.

> to two feet deep, until I arrived at Pherni's fork of Bear river;[47] after leaving that point it soon disappeared.
>
> On the seventh my rations were exhausted. Some of my horses were so much jaded, that I left one man and four horses on Bear river, with some Indians, whose arrival I am hourly expecting. With the balance I pushed forward, and arrived at this camp on the tenth.
>
> The weather, on my return, was very unfavorable, either raining or snowing twenty-six days out of thirty.

The undaunted Virginian on 10 April 1858 finished an extraordinary midwinter journey that covered over sixteen hundred miles and four months. Capt. Jesse Gove, 10th Infantry, reported his arrival at Camp Scott in a letter to his brother in New Jersey: "To-day a Mr. B. F. Ficklin, who started in November last for the Flat Head country for horses, arrived here, having left his party about twenty miles from here. They have had a hard time since they left. They went as far as the British line. His men have been without food for three days, and I have been detailed with ten men to take them provision."[48] The following day, Capt. Albert Tracy on picket duty said, "Ficklin came in yesterday, passing my line with some thirty ponies—all in fair condition."[49] The condition of the horses makes it doubtful that they were the same animals the agent brought over the Continental Divide.

Five days later, Ficklin gave his report to the commander of the Utah Expedition, who sent it to the War Department on 17 April. "The service required of Mr. Ficklin was important," Colonel Johnston said, "and appears to have been faithfully performed under circumstances of great privation and exposure." Although the energetic agent "failed in accomplishing the object of the journey," he continued, "it will have the effect to direct the attention of the Flathead and other Indians on the head waters of the Missouri to this department as affording a market for their horses."[50]

The day before he transmitted the Virginian's report to Washington, the colonel unwittingly revealed the name of the man "with some Indi-

---

[47]Probably Smiths Fork at present Cokeville, Wyoming.

[48]Hammond, ed., *The Utah Expedition, 1857–1858: Letters of Capt. Jesse A. Gove, 10th Inf., U.S.A., of Concord, N.H., to Mrs. Gove, and special correspondence of the New York Herald*, 215, 216.

[49]Auerbach and Alter, eds., "The Journal of Albert Tracy," 11 April 1858.

[50]Johnston to Army Headquarters, 17 April 1858, Sen. Exec. Doc. 1, 1858, 68.

ans" Ficklin left on Bear River. On 16 April, he ordered Capt. J. H. Dickerson, assistant quartermaster, to "employ John W. Powell as Guide, at five dollars per day."[51] Johnston failed to say what qualifications Powell possessed to merit what was in those days a very handsome salary.

[51]Johnston to Dickerson, 16 April 1858, U.S. War Dept., "Utah Army," letters sent 1857–1861.

Chapter 12

A Time to Every Purpose

Ebin Robinson rode up hurriedly and informed me that Ezra Barnard and Baldwin Watts had come from Fort Limhi with the news that Indians had attacked the herdsman, driven off the stock, killed my brother James and George McBride, and wounded several others. I rang my school bell and called to the children to come back and get their books as there would be no more school.

— *Jacob Miller*

The virtually bloodless Utah War saw many acts of individual heroism on both sides, but few compare with the unheralded performance in March 1858 of Mormon express riders Ezra Barnard and Baldwin Watts, who delivered the news of the attack on Fort Limhi to Salt Lake Valley. Two weeks before, Barnard had injured his foot when his horse slipped on the ice during the incursion into the Beaverhead area to claim Thomas Smith's horse. But as the mission's most experienced plainsman, he had insisted on going. Having no spare horses, the pair had no margin of survival when they outraced Bannock pursuers at the Flathead Trail's Camas Creek crossing. On Snake River, where one horse broke down, Barnard rode the only good mount while Watts struggled through the snow on foot, leading the lame animal. For forty-eight hours they had nothing to eat, but they averaged nearly fifty miles a day to reach Barnard's Fort on Malad River in six days and Great Salt Lake City in eight.

For northern Utah settlements, the news they broke was devastating. Most of the sixty-seven men, women, and children now in peril on Salmon River came from homes north of Great Salt Lake, where families and friends still lived in close-knit communities bonded by intermarriage. Few in Davis and Weber counties were untouched by grief over the death of the two missionaries or fear for the safety of those still alive far to the north. Only four months before, Jacob Miller had said

JACOB MILLER
On leave for the winter, the Farmington schoolteacher and acting Salmon River Mission scribe dismissed his class on learning of his younger brother's death and rode with the military expedition to rescue surviving Fort Limhi settlers.
Courtesy of the Church Archives, The Church of Jesus Christ of Latter-day Saints.

goodbye to his younger brother at Fort Limhi and returned to their home in Farmington to teach school during the winter. Now he knew that twenty-year-old James Miller was dead.

For the Mormon theocracy and its destiny, the raid on Fort Limhi would have far-reaching consequences. Three days before the news arrived, Brigham Young sent the same short but intriguing message to his agents in Washington, D.C., and Liverpool: "We have our eyes on the Russian Possessions."[1] Overnight the option to move north in the event that the Kingdom of God failed to sustain by arms its contest with the American republic was unexpectedly eliminated. Gone, too, was the hope to prevail in its latest bid to adopt an independent position. Instead the Mormon chieftain faced only a compelling need to settle at once his dispute with the nation whose military expedition was camped on the territory's eastern border under a commander eager to move against the Mormon stronghold as soon as spring opened the canyon approaches to Salt Lake Valley. The unwelcome news Watts and Barnard

[1]Young to Bernhisel; and Young to Calkin, 5 March 1858, Brigham Young Papers. The draft letter to Asa Calkin reads, "We have our eyes on the Russian possessions but this must not alter your course in regard to former instructions concerning the emigration" (that is, to send English converts north of the Great Lakes).

handed Brigham Young on 8 March would force a drastic change in strategy and a more conciliatory attitude toward the forces Mormon leaders had been ferociously denouncing for months.

Young had already begun casting about for an alternative escape route. On 23 February he had directed the bishop at Fillmore in central Utah "to send out some old men and boys to the white and last mountains to the west of the settlements where we can raise grain and hide up our families and stock in case of necessity."[2] Now, in a revealing letter written two days after the news from Limhi reached Salt Lake, he directed William G. Young to establish a settlement in Ibipah Valley, a small oasis on the western edge of the Great Salt Lake Desert, and start farming operations immediately. "Let old men and boys be principally selected for this mission. We think this course will gratify the Indians who should be kindly treated and honorably dealt with by every person in any wise connected with the mission as well as all other men. Please to move in this matter immediately. No one that is called to go in the Standing Army must be selected for this mission."[3]

Something Had Transpired: Young Offers an Olive Branch

Shortly after news of the Limhi catastrophe arrived, Thomas L. Kane, the influential Mormon friend, wound up his talks with Mormon leaders at Brigham Young's mansion, known as the Lion House. For twelve days the self-styled peacemaker had tried to win their acceptance of President Buchanan's unofficial offer of a pardon or approval of Kane's proposal to extend a peace offering in the form of food to the hungry U.S. soldiers in the mountains. He had received a respectful hearing, but privately Mormon leaders mocked his efforts to defuse the crisis. The "6 pages of fools cap" Apostle Wilford Woodruff wrote "giving a rea-

---

[2]Young to Brunson, 23 February 1858, cited in Stott, *Search for Sanctuary: Brigham Young and the White Mountain Expedition*, 48. Following 8 March, Young managed to convince himself there was a refuge "larger than any of the Eastern States, that no man knows anything about" in today's central Nevada. He believed "there is room in that region for 500,000 people to live scattered about," and on 7 April he ordered Col. William Dame (commander of the militia that committed the Mountain Meadows massacre) to find it. As Clifford L. Stott observed in his perceptive work, "Young grossly misjudged the capabilities of this land and its suitability for settlement. " Ibid., 87, 107.

[3]Young to Young, 10 March 1858, Brigham Young Collection.

son of our hope and faith and the cause of our defending ourselves" do not survive, but a fellow apostle's response to Kane's peace proposals does. "It turns out that Col Tho. Kane's message is an unofficial one, he designs [to be] our good & is a warm friend, but he wants us to spare the lives of the poor soldiers camping about [Fort] Bridger," wrote George A. Smith in early March. "Mr. Buchanan would like us to feed them, and not destroy them until he can get sufficient reinforcements to them to destroy us—this is as near I can learn the design of the President of the United States." Smith summarized the Mormon leadership's reaction to Kane's conciliatory overtures with one word: "Bah!"[4]

But after receiving the news of the disaster at Fort Limhi, on the evening of 8 March Young "spoke out for the first time on a matter which I had not touched upon," Kane wrote the president. "He confessed to me that he had regarded the 'sending of that salt' in the light of an overture."[5] Young had asked, "Wasn't that to be taken as a waiver of my position expressed to Van Vliet?"[6] Later, when the Mormon leader escorted Kane to his boarding house, he did not tell him about the Salmon River disaster but "bade me good night & Godspeed with an effusion that was deeply touching."[7]

At his rooms, Kane welcomed a number of old friends, he told Buchanan, and realized at once "something had transpired which occasioned a stir in the community." For the first time he heard that "news had been received of a massacre of the Saints at Salmon River." Kane fancied it "a small affair" since only two men had been killed and several others wounded, and he could not understand why all the excitement. But when "Brigham Young called upon me the next day to see me off

[4]Kenney, ed., *Wilford Woodruff's Journal*, 5:173; and Smith to Dame, 3 February [March] 1858, William H. Dame Papers.

[5]Kane to Buchanan, 15 March 1858, Thomas L. Kane Collection, Utah War Correspondence. On hearing that U.S. forces were "much in need of salt," Young on 26 November had sent about eight hundred pounds on pack mules to the stalled Utah Expedition at Fort Bridger, apparently as a taunt for failing to reach Salt Lake Valley. Colonel Johnston refused to honor the gift with a reply, his adjutant said, because he would accept nothing from the Mormons as long as they took a hostile position to the U.S. Johnston was also indignant at Young's suggestion that he test the salt for poison.

[6]Ibid. In September 1857 Quartermaster Capt. Stewart Van Vliet had entered Great Salt Lake City to arrange a camp location and supplies for the U.S. Army expedition that President Buchanan had sent to Utah to enforce federal authority. Young told him the army would not be allowed to enter unopposed. After the officer left, Young declared martial law and branded the American army "an armed, mercenary mob."

[7]Ibid.

according to promise," he said, "I thought his manner dry, and he alluded to the matter too tersely to please me."[8]

Unknown to Kane, Young received more troubling information on Tuesday morning. "News arrived from the Weber that Ben Simons was in Echo Kanyon with 250 Indians," wrote Nauvoo Legion cavalry commander John R. Winder. "Rather Suspicious," he concluded. Young quickly composed a letter to Simonds assuring him "that I am your sincere and undeviating friend" and asking the Indian partisan to give his "love and assurance of unshaken friendship to Little Soldier and the brave men of your camp." But by Tuesday evening Young had called out one hundred infantrymen, and on Wednesday, 10 March, he dispatched them to Weber Canyon.[9]

Believing his peace mission had failed, Thomas L. Kane rode north for Camp Scott via Ogden on 9 March, escorted by the noted Orrin Porter Rockwell and other bodyguards.[10] As they passed through the settlements, he heard "'Salmon river' here, 'Salmon river' there to such an extent" that he "several times questioned myself if his [Young's] views were perhaps affected somewhat by the popular excitement." That night, as the ardent peacemaker bedded down in Weber Canyon, about forty-five miles from Great Salt Lake, Brigham Young dictated a letter to him that would soon end the Utah War of 1857–1858.

YOUNG TO KANE, 9 MARCH 1858,
SEN. EXEC. DOC. 1 (35-2), 1858, 87, 88.

Great Salt Lake City,
March 9, 1858—*Tuesday*, 8 *o'clock p. m.*

DEAR SIR: We have just learned through the southern Indians, that the troops are very destitute of provisions.

Mr. Gerrish, a merchant, formerly of this place, and who is now supposed to be detained in Colonel Johnston's camp, has quite a herd of cattle here, and for which he would doubtless like a market. We know of none that would be equal to the army of the United States, now encamped within our borders. We have, therefore, concluded to send this herd, consisting of

[8]Ibid.

[9]John R. Winder Diary, 9, 10 March 1858; and Young to Simons, 10 March 1858, Brigham Young Papers.

[10]There were no good roads through the Wasatch Mountains to Fort Bridger, but in winter the Weber Canyon route was often favored over the main emigrant trail, which left Weber River at present Henefer and crossed Big Mountain to enter Salt Lake Valley by Emigration Canyon.

nearly two hundred head of cattle, a portion of which are tolerable good beef. In addition to the foregoing, we shall send out fifteen or twenty thousand pounds of flour to the army, to which they will be made perfectly welcome, or pay for just as they choose. All of which will be forwarded in a few days, so soon as the necessary arrangements can be made and the snow will admit. If, after your arrival, you learn that Colonel Johnston will not receive the flour, we will be obliged if you will be at the trouble of communicating the fact to those who attend you, that we may be saved the trouble.

I send this by my son, Joseph A., and George Stringham.

Trusting that you are rapidly regaining your health, and that success may attend you, I remain, most respectfully.

BRIGHAM YOUNG.

Colonel THOMAS T. KANE

Just as he broke camp the next morning, "with great gratification" Kane "saw two horsemen come up." Brigham Young's oldest son, twenty-three-year-old Joseph A. Young, and George Stringham, twenty-one, had ridden all night to overtake him before he reached Camp Scott. The two men dismounted from their horses, "which had been badly hurt by falls on the ice," Kane said, and handed him the Mormon leader's message. On 14 March Kane delivered the letter to Colonel Johnston, who rejected Young's offer out of hand. "Whatever might be the need of the army under my command for food," the officer told the exhausted mediator, "we would neither ask nor receive from President Young and his confederates any supplies while they continue to be enemies of the government."[11]

Even so, at Camp Scott Utah's second governor, Alfred Cumming, and President Buchanan, to whom Kane sent a copy with his report, both saw the food offering for what it was—an olive branch—and they moved to make the most of it. On 5 April Cumming and Kane left the Army camp to visit Utah settlements where he was "universally greeted with such respectful attentions as are due to the representative of the executive Authority of the United States in the Territory."[12] At about the same time, Buchanan granted "the inhabitants of Utah, who will submit to the laws, a free pardon for the seditions and treasons heretofore by them committed" and named Lazarus W. Powell, former governor of Kentucky, and the renowned Texas Ranger captain, Ben McCulloch, as

[11]Johnston to Kane, 15 March 1858, Sen. Exec. Doc. 1 (35-2), 1858, 88.

[12]Cumming to Johnston, 15 April 1858, Sen. Exec. Doc. 1 (35-2), 1858, 72, 73.

peace commissioners. The president hoped they could "bring these misguided people to their senses."[13]

BRIGHAM YOUNG: VACATE THE FORT AND COME HOME

Even before Kane left the Lion House on 8 March, Brigham Young had launched a military expedition to rescue the sixty-seven men, women, and children on Salmon River. That day an expressman left Nauvoo Legion headquarters in Great Salt Lake City and rode overnight to deliver orders to Benjamin Franklin Cummings at Ogden. Early next morning, the original Fort Limhi missionary "got orders to prepare myself to go to Salmon River on horse back to start the next morning at 10 A.M. [I] did what I could to get ready." So it happened on 10 March that as Thomas Kane was reading Brigham Young's offer to make peace, "Frank" Cummings and his company of ten were riding north to Fort Limhi "with instructions to go through as quick as we could."[14] In his saddlebag the New Englander carried another letter from Young, addressed to Thomas S. Smith, president of the Northern Indian Mission.

YOUNG TO SMITH, 8 MARCH 1858, BRIGHAM YOUNG COLLECTION.

Presidents Office
Great Salt Lake City
Mar. 8th. 1858

Col. Thos. S. Smith
Dear Brother:-

Bros. Watt[s] and Barnard have just arrived through whom and by your letter of Feb.y 28th we learn the disastrous intelligence from your fort. We regret that any have been killed and trust that the wounded will all recover. We think that you had better vacate the Fort and come home, giving to the

---

[13]Floyd to Powell and McCulloch, 12 April 1858, Sen. Exec. Doc. 1 (35-2), 1858, 160–62. Buchanan warned that if Utahns rejected the pardon, "they must expect no further lenity, but look to be rigorously dealt with according to their deserts." Through the secretary of war, the president instructed the commissioners "to give extensive circulation" to the pardon but directed them not "to enter into any treaty or engagement with the Mormons." Despite the enduring misconception that he intended to destroy polygamy, Buchanan assured the Mormons that "the movement of the Army to Utah has no reference whatever to their religious tenants or faith." For Buchanan's pardon and instructions to the peace commissioners, see Hafen and Hafen, eds., *The Utah Expedition*, 329–37.

[14]Biography and Journals of Benjamin Franklin Cummings, 9, 10 March 1858. For the adventures of this advance party, see Chapter 1.

Indians such property as you cannot secure by safely cacheing or bring away. Do not destroy anything [but] leave your improvements Fort &c with friendly Indians, get back your stock if you can without fighting the Indians for it, but I would not delay any more time than possible for this object.

We send Brother Andrew Cunningham with one hundred men to aid you, in getting away.

Your friend and brother
Brigham Young

Thomas Smith's initial report that mountaineers at Soda Springs had conspired with the Indians and instigated the attack prompted other emergency measures to protect the most exposed northern settlements. "Your peculiar situation being so much exposed to depredations by Indians, Mountaineers, and others who are undoubtedly egged [on] by the soldiers," Brigham Young told bishops Peter Maughn in Cache Valley, John P. Barnard at Barnard's Fort, James Frodsham at Deep Creek, and "and the brethren near them" that "we consider it wisdom for you to come within our settlements; intending to discontinue all of our settlements north of Box Elder." The order to abandon their outlying locations included a word to the wise. "This is our counsel to you, and if you feel disposed to follow it we shall feel under more obligation to aid you in defending your families and property from being interrupted."[15]

In November 1857 Andrew Cunningham had established a new settlement on the Blackfoot River, near present Blackfoot, Idaho, as a way station on the trail to Fort Limhi in the event the Mormons moved north. On 6 March 1858, two days before news of the Fort Limhi attack reached Great Salt Lake City, he had been appointed one of two colonels in the new Standing Army of Israel.[16] To take his place as head of the Blackfoot settlement, Brigham Young that same day had told William Miller to round up its members, who had wintered in Utah, and "go and take charge of this mission."[17] Now, just six days later on

---

[15]Young to Maughn, 9 March 1858, Brigham Young Papers. The settlers, including the last three families left in the Malad Valley, retreated to Call's Fort. See Huchel, History of Box Elder County, 384.

[16]For Cunningham's appointment as colonel in the Standing Army, see General Orders No. 1, Nauvoo Legion Adjustant General's Office, 6 March 1858, Utah Militia Records, Series 2210, Box 1, Fld. 44. George D. Grant was the other colonel.

[17]See Young to Miller, 6 March 1858, Brigham Young Collection. There were no plans to abandon the Blackfoot River station prior to the attack on Fort Limhi.

12 March, Cunningham led an expedition north to save Fort Limhi settlers and salvage resources at both places, which would be permanently shut down. In the lead were two mounted companies of fifty each with horse-drawn wagons to haul baggage and supplies from these sites back to Utah. The colonel also carried further instructions from Brigham Young that reflected his continued determination to show the Indians "who are their friends."

YOUNG TO CUNNINGHAM, 10 MARCH 1858,
BRIGHAM YOUNG COLLECTION.

Presidents Office
Great Salt Lake City
Mar. 10 1858.

Col. Andrew Cunningham
& Thos. S. Smith
Dear Brethren: —

In reflecting upon your present difficulties with the Indians, we have considered it wisdom for you to avoid as much as possible having any difficulty with them even at the sacrifice of the stock in their possession. We would prefer for you to say to the Indians if they have not got enough of the Mormon's cattle to come and get some more, but that we would rather give them our cattle than to have them steal them. If you get to talk with the Indians and can exchange with them your wheat for cattle or otherwise make satisfactory arrangements with them I have no objections but do insist that they shall be conciliated and not molested in consequence of this late affair by pursuing this course it will certainly have its influence after awhile and they will learn who are their friends. If they choose to come into our settlements tell them to do so and we will be their friends.

Your brother in Christ,
Brigham Young

CALIBER OF MORMON TROOPS

A day behind Cunningham came a hurriedly-called company from Davis County, which left Farmington on 12 March, commanded by a recently appointed captain in the Standing Army of Israel, twenty-five-year-old Horton D. Haight, a native New Yorker from Farmington, Utah. The fall before, Haight had ridden with Major Lot Smith in Mormon military operations against the U.S. Army. He had also accompanied Brigham Young to Fort Limhi in May 1857 and knew the trail. Serving as first and second lieutenants in the fifty-four-man company were Hyrum Judd, thirty-three, and Edwin Walker, twenty-nine, both Mormon Battalion veterans of the War with Mexico.

Except for Haight's company, which was armed and equipped by subscription, the soldiers supplied their own weapons, usually a rifle and revolver, from forty to one hundred rounds of ammunition, personal gear, and at least three bushels of grain per man. Most reported with two horses, planning to ride one animal while breathing the other.

The Mormon companies drawn from the Standing Army of Israel and the Nauvoo Legion resembled large posses more than formal military outfits, largely from the lack of uniforms. The troopers dressed as best they could with too little to keep them warm. They wore endlessly patched homemade clothes, some buckskin shirts or pants, and boots that were usually handmade or repaired. After ten years, store clothing had become dear in the Great Basin where people were instructed to make their own. The weapons they carried varied almost as much as their dress, although most men boasted rifles instead of muskets, even a few early repeaters like the one they called a "15-shooter." A few probably carried revolvers manufactured at a new Great Salt Lake arsenal on Arsenal Hill, site of the present state capitol. Many of these weapons, like much of the other equipment, were borrowed from someone else.

The caliber of the Mormon troops more than compensated for shortcomings like these. They were youthful and adapted to their western environment, as strong as the horses they rode. Despite their tight organization and conditioned obedience, they exhibited a distinct lack of piety in speech and manners, especially among the American-born and particularly among the men and boys raised in the West. An echo from the Missouri-Illinois period of their faith's history was the practice of cursing the enemies of Zion, an avenue of creative expression that easily carried over to broken wagons or balky oxen. Still, they would come together on the trail every morning and again at night in a bond of common faith, heads bared to the wind and bowed, while one of their number committed their mission and safekeeping to a deity who almost seemed to ride in the midst of them Himself, more rough and ready than the rest.

JACOB MILLER: HORSES WERE WALLOWING UP TO THE SIDES IN SNOW

Every man from the Weber, Davis, and Lehi military districts knew the ordeal that lay ahead when he left with Cunningham's force, but few made excuses to stay home. To make a winter journey of nearly eight hundred miles into the northern Rocky Mountains and back would test the endurance of the hardiest frontiersman under the best of circumstances. But this spring conditions would be far short of ideal. After a mild February, winter would return with a vengeance in March to assault the expedition with blowing snow in the mountains and rain in the valleys over most of the next thirty days. From Farmington, Jacob Miller, brother of slain James Miller, was one of the three Salmon River missionaries in Haight's outfit.[18] He had wanted to bring his younger brother's body home for burial, but had been unable on short notice to find a metal casket. But he did take his pocket journal and wrote an account of the expedition.

JACOB MILLER JOURNAL, MARCH 1858.

There was a hurrying of horses from the range and preparing of baggage wagons with supplies. In two days from the call, the company was under way with Ebin Robinson and myself of the number.

Heavy rain set in and we reached Ogden completely drenched. March 13th we reached Box Elder through the mud. Sunday 14th, cold wind and snow storm from the north west held us at Box Elder. Next day, though the storm continued, we pushed on over rough roads and through the mud, fording Bear River and camped on the Malad. We were wallowing through snow and mud to Deep Creek on March 16th.[19]

March 17th. It snowed all last night and continued next day. We slept on the ground in the snow which piled on our beds so that we had to shake it off, it got so heavy. It was my turn to stand guard the last part of the night. We had a stampede of the horses, but as each of the guard was holding his saddle horse by the lariat while it was grazing, the stampede was soon checked.

---

[18]The other two were Ebenezer Jay Robinson and Jesse Tuttle Clark.

[19]Deep Creek was located 16.5 miles north of Barnard's Fort, just south of today's Malad, Idaho. Fort Limhi missionary Joseph Parry camped there on 23 December 1855 "with a few families of Saints who had settled here a few months previously. They were extremely poor and could not help us with any provisions. Among them was my old friend, James Frodsham, who had charge of the colony." See Huchel, *A History of Box Elder County*, 383.

> Progress today was very tedious getting over the mountains. The wind with the storm had covered the trail of Cunningham's company which had passed the day before. The cavalry, breaking road for the baggage wagons were soon sent back to dismount and load their horses from the wagons to lighten up. At the top of the divide, there were a number of ravines to cross which were so filled with drifting snow that the horses were wallowing up to their sides in snow, and the wagons to their axles. We had to unload and carry the loads on our backs across the ravines.
>
> We tied ropes to the sides of the wagons. Some 20 or more men who could stand on the packed snow of last winter would aid the wallowing horses to pull the empty wagons through the ravines. Other men would be holding six or more horses each, and some were moving the baggage forward on their shoulders. Others were at the wagons hitched to one empty wagon to move a few rods, then after resting, try, try again.
>
> After getting over the ravines, we reloaded and went down the mountain to a tributary of the Portneuf and camped, feeling it was good to be here. Tonight while on guard, I was comparing today's efforts with the one of last Spring in March, pulling over the mountain from Malad [River] to Bannock [Creek], when with the teams of six wagons on one wagon and several men holding it from turning over, we made our way through the deep snow and over sliding ground to the mountain top. Then we returned and took two more wagons up.
>
> Teams were taken back to the other wagons and part of us spent the night on the divide in such a heavy cold wind that it was necessary to brace our wagon bows and lock and block the wheels. Next day, we doubled the other three wagons up and moved down to the head of Bannock Creek, making a journey of nine miles in the two days.
>
> We made our way through snow, rain and cold March winds and mud. We reached the fort on the forenoon of March 25, 1858.

Jacob Miller and Haight's company arrived at Fort Limhi two days after the expedition's main body to find that Colonel Cunningham had lost no time in carrying out his orders to shut down the mission. But as settlers hurried to collect their belongings and pack wagons, he ignored his leader's instructions to placate the natives. On the afternoon of his arrival, he dispatched a company down the river to arrest several Shoshones who had taken part in the attack and bring them back to the fort for interrogation. When the natives refused to make restitution for any of the animals they had allegedly stolen, the colonel "put them under guard" for the night in the fort. The next day he led some eighty men to the Indian camp eight miles downstream and recovered by force three cows and some six or eight ponies. The rest of the livestock had long since vanished.

In the meantime, Jacob Miller found the place where his brother lay but made no attempt to remove or mark it. "His body and that of George McBride were left as they were buried in the South Fort," he said. "The ground had been packed over the graves and stock fed over them to blind them from the Indians."[20]

"FRANK" CUMMINGS'S LUCK RUNS OUT

Fifteen days earlier, Benjamin Franklin Cummings had received orders to lead a company of ten north on horseback to alert Fort Limhi settlers that help was on the way. In the rush north his dependence on speed and surprise had paid off. Now on 25 March Cunningham handed the New Englander another dangerous mission. He ordered him "to start the next morning for Salt Lake with an express, to be accompanied by 9 men," to deliver a report on progress of the rescue to Brigham Young.[21] Cummings picked only men he knew and trusted. They were George W. Hill, Thomas Bingham, William Bailey Lake, Baldwin H. Watts, Benjamin Cutler, George Washington Barber, Thomas Bloxham, John R. Blanchard, Jr., and Thomas Workman. Five were Fort Limhi veterans.[22]

Cummings and his chosen few loaded some supplies on pack mules and at 10 the next morning took off. In two days they rode some eighty miles and camped on 27 March under threatening skies on present Birch Creek. Darkness and snow fell together, and the storm grew heavier and continued all night. Soon after starting next day, in new snow and freezing temperatures, they discovered some Indians camped along the creek, "who told us that old Boo-e-Wat an Indian had gone over to Muddy lake the day before and had 3 horses belonging to the brethern," Cummings said. The animals were those the "friendly" Bannock, also known

[20]Jacob Miller Journal, 25 March 1858.

[21]Biography and Journals of Benjamin Franklin Cummings, 25 March 1858.

[22]The veterans were Cummings, Hill, Bingham, Lake, and Watts. Barber came to Fort Limhi in 1856 as a hired hand.

as Harvey, had slipped past the stockade at night two weeks before, as reported on 13 March by David Moore. The natives thought Cummings and his party "would overtake him."[23]

The following day, however, they passed Mud Lake on the south and camped on Camas Creek without seeing any sign of Harvey. They continued on 29 March to the big bend of Snake River, near present Roberts, Idaho, where "they found some Indians who had just arrived before us who informed us that Booe-Wat [*sic*] was on his way there and would soon arrive," Cummings said. They waited for him to come, but not for long. Then Watts and Bloxham borrowed ponies from the natives and rode back on the "upper road," probably the Flathead Trail, which crossed Camas Creek above Mud Lake, "fearing that they might get wind of our presence and secrete the stolen horses."[24] Two hours later, the fearless pair returned with the stolen horses belonging to David Moore, Richard Margetts, and William Taylor.

Cummings and his men were still not satisfied. When Boo-e-wat himself arrived, they demanded that he "pay us for some of the cattle he had killed." At this the Bannock became very angry and "peremptorily refused saying he had no more horses," Cummings said. As Harvey showed "some disposition to fight we thought it wisdom not to insist any longer as we had no authority to take any property by force."[25] They left the angry native early that afternoon and took up their journey, stopping two hours later only long enough to feed the horses and leave a note at an agreed upon spot to inform Cunningham of their progress. But as the case would show, such "trail post offices," if convenient, were hardly ever private.

Unaware their mail would be read by unfriendly eyes, they forded Snake River next day "at windy point," probably near present Idaho Falls, and rested at noon "at fort Lookout," a reference to the Blackfoot way station established by Cunningham the fall before. They then continued on to Portneuf River where "they found that several head of our cattle had been taken towards Soda Springs."[26] After making this dis-

[23]Biography and Journals of Benjamin Franklin Cummings, 27 March 1858.

[24]Ibid., 29 March 1858.

[25]Ibid.

[26]Salmon River Mission Journal, 30 March 1858.

covery, they camped after dark "on the bench above the ridge." Through the rain that fell that night, they could see "the light of some Indian lodges" along the river.[27]

B. F. Cummings: We Turned and Fired on Them

The advance guard of the Limhi evacuation started as early as it was light enough to see and rode past the Indian camp "to see if we could find any of our horses or cattle."[28] Seeing none, they traveled south over the bench to Bannock Creek, a winding stream between sage-covered hills. Here the party stopped about 9:30 for breakfast before heading up the creek toward the divide between the Columbia River and Great Basin drainages with its scouts B. H. Watts and Thomas Bloxham some distance in front. At 2:45, they saw "several Indians near the west mountain also traveling south." Suddenly three of the natives raced "up a canyon as fast as their horses could travel." At the same time, six Indians approached the party from the other side of the creek and a "smoke was raised on the west mountain." When the six came closer, Cummings called out and asked them to "come over and have a talk." But they ignored him and instead crossed the stream above them at a place called Cedar Point, where they took positions and waited. As Watts and Bloxham drew within range, the Indians fired, "but missed them both."[29]

The express company had ridden into an ambush. Caught in the open and fired on from higher ground, they headed for the opposite side of the creek seeking any cover they could find. Cummings described what happened next.

Biography and Journals of Benjamin Franklin Cummings, 31 March 1858.

We rushed from the point into the open ground but were followed by the Indians who rode all around us firing continually upon us; their ponies being very fast and ours so badly jaded that we could hardly get them out of a slow trot. It appeared their design [was] to ride ahead of us and take advantage of every point of mountain, hill or brush that might offer and to

[27]Biography and Journals of Benjamin Franklin Cummings, 30 March 1858.
[28]Ibid., 31 March 1858.
[29]Salmon River Mission Journal, 31 March 1858.

> use us up. We turned and fired on them but they took good care to keep at a good distance then but as soon as we were on our horses they were closing upon us again knowing that our horses could not move so as to give us any advantage. We sought the creek for shelter and while crossing W B Lake was shot and died. We saw that we could do nothing for him. As the Indians were getting into the brush on the creek close to us I thought it was not wisdom to stop there still long enough to give them a chance to make many dead shotts [*sic*] at us so we went on up the creek to find a convenient place to hide ourselves from their fire which we succeeded in doing about a quarter of a mile above. John Blanchard had his horse shot through just back of his leg while on him, about the same time that brother Lake was shot. We succeeded in hiding ourselves from the fire of the Indians under a bank of the creek but could not get our animals down; but held them by the briddle [*sic*] exposed to the fire of the Indians. They shot Geo Barbers mule dead and B. Watts horse so that he could not stand & shot br Lakes horse through so that he could not travel. We fired on the Indians several times and as we afterwards learned killed one and as we supposed from the appearances we shot a horse through but did not kill him. The Indians continued the siege on us for about 2 hours and then withdrew having got our pack animals, they having fed away so far that they got in between us and them and drove them away.

After the Indians left, yet fearing more would come, the party waited until nearly dark, then slipped away, "thinking that it was so near night that they would not attempt to follow and attack us in the night," Cummings said. "We now had six horses for nine of us to use and about six pounds of flour to do us to the settlements.[30] Left behind on the snow was the body of thirty-two-year-old Canadian William Bailey Lake, the stocky husband of three wives and four children, stripped, scalped, and filled with arrows.[31] A single shot to the back of his head had killed the Fort Limhi missionary as he rode up from the creek bottom.

The rest of the company moved all night, "keeping a sharp lookout for a surprise." At 9 the next morning they cooked the last of their flour and continued down Malad River to Barnard's Fort, now abandoned. Also vacated was Call's Fort on Bear River, where they arrived at 11 that

---

[30]Biography and Journals of Benjamin Franklin Cummings, 31 March 1858.

[31]A polygamist, Lake married Sarah Jane Marler in 1850. In March 1857 he married Louisa Ann Garner and Lovina Jones, both age thirteen, on the same day. He was the brother-in-law of Pleasant Green Taylor, who married two of Lake's sisters as well as his widow, Sarah Jane. Taylor also married two sisters of Lewis Shurtliff. By the four sisters of Lake and Shurtliff, Taylor fathered thirty-three children.

night. Taking possession of an empty house, they roasted and ate some small potatoes left by the former inhabitants and rested a few hours before renewing their journey at 6 A.M. Three hours later, they reached Box Elder, now Brigham City, where they learned that Mormon authorities had ordered reluctant followers to leave their homes and farms and move the opposite direction "as trouble was anticipated from our enemies." Cummings rode sixty miles over the next twenty-four hours to reach Great Salt Lake City on 3 April where he reported to Brigham Young "all the particulars of our trip to Salmon River and delivered the dispatch from Col. Cunningham."[32]

Fort Limhi Abandoned

Not far behind Cummings and his express party came sixteen heavily burdened wagons guarded by nearly two hundred men. There were no lamentations at Fort Limhi when the train, rather than wait till the next morning, took an early start at 4 P.M. on 27 March for Salt Lake Valley. Ahead was an uncomfortable journey of nearly four hundred miles. But few in the camp expressed sorrow at leaving the settlement they had labored to build. "We left Fort Limhi in the hands of the Indians," said Charles Middleton.[33] Henry Harmon's wife provided a further reason to rejoice at their departure. Next day, after traveling nine or ten miles, the train lay by as Susan Marler Harmon gave birth to daughter, Susan Elizabeth. Later, the "snow lay very deep" on the divide between today's Lemhi River and Birch Creek, Moore said, but "Capt. [Christopher] Layton with several of the troops assisted the teams with ropes to get through the snow drifts."[34]

Near the mouth of Birch Creek on 1 April Colonel Cunningham decided the party was no longer in danger. Leaving twenty-five men from his force, he "took the balance of the troops and went ahead." If the company lost most of its military protection, it gained a new member next morning when Emily Jane Clark, one of Israel Clark's wives, delivered a daughter, Harriet Louisa. Afterward the train pushed ahead to

[32]Biography and Journals of Benjamin Franklin Cummings, 1–3 April 1858.

[33]Charles F. Middleton Journal, 28 March 1858.

[34]Salmon River Mission Journal, 30 March 1858.

camp at the Camas Creek crossing. Reaching the big bend of Snake River, the wagons traveled down the right bank eighteen miles over the next two days and forded the river at the spot they called "Windy Point,"[35] referred to by Middleton as "the new ford."[36]

On 5 April at the abandoned Blackfoot River settlement that Cunningham had established the fall before, they found ten men he had left there "to show us some caches of flour, potatoes, etc., to aid us on our way," Moore said. The next day he announced a more significant discovery: "Some of our company saw several of our cattle's tracks on the Portneuf [River] bottom."[37] Less welcome was the sighting on 7 April at Cedar Point on Bannock Creek, where "McGary found a note left by Col. Cunningham stating that his company had found [Bailey] Lake's body and had taken him to Utah."[38] (Tenderly P. G. Taylor, a member of the colonel's force, had drawn the arrows from his brother-in-law's body and placed him on a bed of snow in his wagon for the journey home.) Still scattered about was other evidence of the expressmen's fight with the Indians a week before. "One horse & one mule dead," counted Middleton, "also a saddle & leggings belong[ing] to B. H. Watts."[39]

All Began to Be Changed: Israel Moves South

The heavily laden train crossed the rim of the Great Basin on 8 April and labored down a snow-filled canyon to camp after dark on the Malad River. The following day it moved twenty miles in sub-freezing weather before stopping for the night on Henderson Creek, within four miles of the Utah-Oregon border. It was too cold that night to post a guard, but most train members were comforted to know they were almost home with families and friends in northern Utah. Then such hopes were rudely dashed. News came early next morning that caused "much excitement in camp." On hearing it, David Moore wrote, "Our guard [is] leaving for home and some of our missionaries also going along with

[35]Ibid., 1–4 April 1858.

[36]Charles F. Middleton Journal, 4 April 1858. The distance traveled downstream from Snake River's big bend places this ford at or near Idaho Falls, location of the later Montana Trail crossing at Eagle Rock.

[37]Salmon River Mission Journal, 6 April 1858. The discovery was significant because it placed the cattle on the route to Soda Springs and Fort Bridger.

[38]Ibid., 7 April 1858. William Bailey Lake was buried in the North Ogden Cemetery.

[39]Charles F. Middleton Journal, 7 April 1858.

them."[40] Suddenly no one knew for sure where his home was or whether his family was safe. Said Charles F. Middleton: "We learned that all north of Salt Lake City had to move south."[41]

Ironically, Brigham Young's decision to evacuate northern settlements and send his followers, men, women, and children, streaming south like refugees fleeing before an invading army was a direct consequence of the Indian raid on the Oregon settlement the train had just left. With the option to move north now erased, Young had fallen back on the "Sebastapol Plan," the scorched-earth strategy the theocracy had devised to implement if their confrontation with the United States went badly.[42] As early as August 1857, Young had threatened that if the army came to Utah, "I shall cut every shrub and tree in the Valley, every pole, every inch of board, and put it all into ashes. I will burn the grass and the stubble and lay it waste, and make a Moscow of every settlement, and then I guess we will make a Potter's field of every Canyon they go into." His congregation, "at the tops of their voices, shouted, 'Yes'" when he asked if they were ready to flee into the mountains. "How do you think they will feel to come here and not find a house, or a barn, or a stick, or a board, nothing under the heavens in the shape of a building or of fuel or of lumber? Don't you think the new Governor would feel nice to come here and reign as Governor over a dreary, uninhabited, blackened waste?"[43]

Now, only ten days after news of the Indian attack reached him, on 18 March Young again proposed to "'Burn up' and flee" as an alternative to armed resistance. In this way, he believed, "the folly, and meanness of the President will be the more apparrant [*sic*] and he and his measures more unpopular." In addition to northern settlements, said Hosea Stout at Salt Lake, "It was decided to send 500 families from this city immediately to be selected from among those who had never been driven from their homes and from that class to take the poorest and most helpless."[44]

---

[40]Salmon River Mission Journal, 10 April 1858.

[41]Charles F. Middleton Journal, 11 April 1858.

[42]Stott, *Search for Sanctuary: Brigham Young and the White Mountain Expedition*, 56–61.

[43]A Discourse by President Brigham Young, Aug. 16th 1857, Reported by Geo. D. Watt, Brigham Young Papers. I am indebted to Will Bagley for his transcription of this unpublished jeremiad.

[44]Brooks, ed., *On The Mormon Frontier: The Diary of Hosea Stout, 1844–1861*, 2:654–55. Also see Young, "A series of Instructions and Remarks by President Brigham Young at a Special Council, Tabernacle, March 21, 1858."

So it was that from Henderson Creek, "all began to be changed," Lewis Shurtliff, a member of the returning party, observed. "The farm houses and farms were all right but no one could be found." The displaced veterans of Fort Limhi believed they were returning to Utah to join in the battle that would open the kingdom's march to universal dominion, and some of them, like Abraham Zundel, hardly knew what to think. He was "most bewilderd for we had made up our Mind to fight it out on the line but the Lord knows best about these things."[45]

The great move south was in full motion by 11 April, when the company reached Hot Springs, nine miles north of Ogden, and broke up. Just a day later, the territory's new governor, Alfred Cumming, arrived at Great Salt Lake, escorted into the city by Thomas Kane and dignitaries from Davis County. The next head of state was dismayed at what he saw. As his predecessor had predicted, the sight of suffering women and children fleeing for life before advancing U.S. soldiers had an impact more powerful than all the muskets Zion could muster.

For the home-comers from Salmon River, who had completed an arduous sixteen-day winter journey of nearly four hundred miles, the order to move imposed a severe and unwanted trial. It meant reloading their families and belongings into wagons and finding a place in the flood of people, animals and wagons streaming over the Mormon corridor toward the Spanish Trail to Los Angeles. No one knew when, if ever, they would return to their homes. "We were much surprised" at this move, said an unhappy David Moore, "and we were ill prepared for such a trip, not having much of any teams or even provisions for the summer."[46]

MILTON HAMMOND: THE MORMONS . . . HAS GAINED THE VICTORY

Typical of many was the hardship endured by Milton Hammond, who started his family south on 2 May with "15 hundred [pounds] on my wagon" and only one yoke of oxen to pull the load. Struggling through rain and mud for five days, he reached Spanish Fork in Utah

[45]Abraham Zundel Diary, 21, original at LDS Archives.

[46]Salmon River Mission Journal, 11 April 1858.

Valley, where he encountered Utah's new governor, Alfred Cumming. Like many others of his faith, he was not impressed by the rotund Georgian who had replaced Brigham Young. "He resembles a whiskey barrel more than the Governor of an intelegent community," he said. Hammond then drove to Summit Creek, some twenty miles south of Provo, where over the next five weeks he constructed a crude shelter "by digging into the bank south of the spring and covering it with brush" and planted wheat, potatoes, and "seeds of different kinds."[47] Finally word came that ended the Utah War of 1857–1858 and allowed the former Fort Limhi missionary and similar sufferers in the great move south to go home.

JOURNAL OF MILTON D. HAMMOND.

> Tuesday 15th of June 1858. News has arrived that the general Government has sent an investigateing commity to examine into the Utah difficulty. They bring the President's message which is a lie from beginning to end. They met with Pres. Young last Friday and Saturday. Come to his terms and agreed to not have many more troops come here. Those that were here expects to build a station either in Rush or Cash Valleys but they agree to let the settlements alone and consequently the Mormons, being directed by our Heavenly Father, has gained the victory without fireing a gun over the greatest nation (according to their own statements) on the earth.[48]

If one conflict was settled, another in the meantime had already begun. Hardly had the Fort Limhi settlers arrived home when Mormon leaders leveled charges against the white men they believed responsible for the raid on the northernmost outpost of their faith. Furthermore, in inciting the Indians to attack the Salmon River Indian Mission, they charged, the accused had acted on behalf of the United States Army.

---

47 Milton D. Hammond Journal, May 1857.

48 Peace commissioners Lazarus W. Powell and Ben McCulloch met with Brigham Young on 11 and 12 June 1858. They reported "discontented" Mormons in Provo said they would have stayed home "had they not been threatened with forcible ejection. We were also told that at least one-third of the persons who had removed from their homes were compelled to do so." Powell and McCulloch concluded Mormon leaders "congregated the people in order to exercise immediate control over them, and thus prevent their secession from the church." After much speechmaking, Young and his associates declared "their desire to live peaceably under the Constitution and government of the United States" and accepted the president's terms unconditionally. The commissioners believed that once the people learned the military was in Utah to protect them, "all true, loyal, and patriotic citizens will rejoice that a portion of the army is in their midst." See Powell and McCulloch to Floyd, 3 July 1858, Sen. Exec. Doc. 1, v. 2, pt. 2 (35-2), 1858, 172–74.

Chapter 13

From a Camp of U.S. Troops

I did not say or do anything myself, neither did any man under my command, to induce any Indians to interfere with the Mormons in any manner, on the contrary, I took every opportunity to tell all Indians and whites whom I met with on my trip, especially the Fathers of Saint Ignatius mission, that Colonel Johnston did not desire, and would not permit, any interference from Indians.

— *B. F. Ficklin*

Benjamin Franklin Ficklin was still composing his report on the winter stock-buying expedition he had led to the Flathead country when on 13 April 1858 the acting secretary of Utah Territory accused him of instigating the attack on Fort Limhi. William H. Hooper, who held his office *pro tem* under a questionable appointment by Brigham Young,[1] surprised arriving Governor Alfred Cumming at Great Salt Lake that day with written charges that the Virginian and other federal officers, including U.S. Indian agent Garland Hurt, had purposely instigated the Indian attacks on Salmon River and other Mormon settlements.[2] A dismayed Cumming, "with feelings of profound regret," sent Hooper's letter to Col. A. S. Johnston calling for an immediate investigation of these accusations at Camp Scott.

In his first report of the attack, Thomas Smith on 28 February had told Brigham Young that "Mountaineers & Indians" plotted the Fort Limhi raid "last summer at Soda Springs" and John W. Powell "helped

[1]Young in 1856 named Hooper to replace Almon W. Babbitt, also a Mormon, who was killed, supposedly by Cheyenne Indians, in August that year. The federal law creating Utah Territory specified that the U.S. president would nominate and with the advice and consent of the Senate appoint the governor, secretary, chief justice and associate justices, attorney, and marshal. The act made no provision for the governor to make *pro tem* appointments.

[2]Hurt always denied the charge and insisted instead that it was the Mormons who tried to forge an alliance with the Indians in opposing the U.S. Army expedition in 1857. He said that he urged the Utah tribe to reject such overtures, offering himself "as a hostage for the peaceful intentions of the troops." See Bigler, "Garland Hurt, the American Friend of the Utahs," 164.

the Indians drive off the cattle."[3] But Smith at that time had not implicated Ficklin's party, then camped on the Beaverhead. Shoshone Chief Snag exposed this connection on arriving at the fort from the Upper Missouri three weeks after the attack. Smith carried Snag's story to Great Salt Lake City, where he arrived about 8 April with Andrew Cunningham. Having failed to sustain the theocracy's sovereignty on the field, Mormon authorities seized the ammunition provided by a friendly native leader to throw their federal opponents on the defensive.

In Collusion with the Indians: The Opening Salvo

Hooper fired the first shot with his missive to Cumming. Said he:

> On the 25th February last a descent was made upon the herds of one of our most northern settlements by two hundred and fifty Shoshones and Barraks [Bannocks]. Two settlers were killed and five wounded; two hundred and twenty head of cattle and thirty-five horses were driven off. These Indians had been living, hunting, and fishing in the vicinity of this settlement from its commencement. Innumerable acts of kindness had been extended to them by the citizens, nor had there ever existed the slightest misunderstanding between them until (as a Shoshone chief, Snagg, states) a small detachment of "soldiers" or men from the camp of the soldiers at Bridger came to Beaver Head to buy stock; and that from the camp of this detachment a white man named J. H. Powell [*sic*] came to the lodges of the Barraks [*sic*] and Shoshones two days previous to the massacre herein referred to, and incited the Indians, giving them his aid and participation in the affair.
>
> The chief Snagg further states that subsequent to the massacre a quarrel occurred among the Indians, whereupon Powell left, and, after appointing a meeting with the [Bannocks] at Soda Springs, or Bear River lake, from where he would conduct them with their stolen stock to the camp of the troops, accompanied the detachment to Bridger. This information I derived from parties present at the scene of the difficulties and is confirmed by affidavits on file with the probate court of this county.[4]

Following Hooper's letter by only one day, the church-owned *Deseret News* at Great Salt Lake loosed a canister bombardment of rumors and unfounded allegations. The weekly paper charged the commander of the

[3]Smith to Young, 28 February 1858, Brigham Young Papers. See Chapter 10, pp. 229–31.
[4]Sen. Exec. Doc. 1 (35-2), 1858, 74–76.

Utah Expedition, the U.S. Army, and other federal officials, including Agent Garland Hurt, of inciting Indian attacks against peaceful white settlements, the worst kind of evildoing.

"Another Murder By Indians," *Deseret News,* 14 April 1858, 35/1–2.

On Bannock creek, March 31, Elder B. F. Cummings and a small party, on their way from Salmon river, were suddenly and furiously fired upon by a party of Indians in ambush, who killed br. Bailey Lake and robbed the company of eleven horses.

Whether the massacre and robbery by Indians at Fort Limhi on Salmon river, Feb.25; the killing of cattle and stealing of horses in Scull [*sic*], Rush and Tooele valleys; the late killing and robbing on Bannock creek; the threatened Indian foray from Uinta valley; and the current rumor that the Army have offered the Indians $150 for every "Mormon" they will bring into Col. Johnston's camp, can be PROVED in court of law to be a part of the "civilized mode of warfare" to be pursued by Government officers against the "Mormons" is uncertain, for witnesses may absent themselves, hold back the truth, or be excused from testifying, on the plea they would criminate themselves.

But it is certain that no trouble had heretofore occurred at Fort Limhi, and that a certain J. H. [*sic*] Powell was most actively engaged with the Indians in the massacre and robbery perpetrated at that Fort; and it is reported that soldiers from Col. Johnston's camp wintered at Beaver Head, a short distance east of Fort Limhi. It is certain that the Indians in and around Scull, Rush and Tooele valleys had mostly been friendly until quite recently, and that they openly avowed it to be their design to take the stolen animals to the U.S. army. How came they to think of doing that? It is also certain that until the U.S. troops entered this Territory, Government had never advanced a single dollar to the Utah Superintendency to be expended in making presents to the Indians, though many of the Superintendent's accounts for presents made by him have been allowed;[5] but now that an Agency is established, that is as yet unacquainted with the interests of the settlers of this Territory, Government can furnish thousands upon thousands of dollars for presents to the

---

[5]The complaint that the U.S. Office of Indian Affairs dispersed funds from appropriations for Indians in Utah only on receipt and approval of vouchers for prior expenditures reveals the hand of Brigham Young, former governor and *ex officio* superintendent of Indian Affairs of the territory, in preparing this article. An 1862 report on Young's accounts for 1856–1857 offers a rich source for further study. For example, none of the vouchers he submitted during the time of his visit to Fort Limhi in May 1857 indicate such expenses were incurred in Oregon Territory, which was outside his jurisdiction. Indian farmer John D. Lee, who signed many such vouchers, later said, "Brigham Young never spent a dollar on the Indians in Utah, while he was Indian Agent." See Lee, *Mormonism Unveiled; or The Life and Confessions of the Late Mormon Bishop, John D. Lee,* 257.

wild men of the mountains, and it will soon be known whether this is not designed for the express purpose of introducing their humane, Christian and civilized mode of warfare, through inciting Indian depredations against American citizens. It is quite authentically reported that the runaway Indian Agent Garland Hurt has passed most of the last winter in Uinta valley, and has been busily engaged in inciting the Indians against the "Mormons."[6] And of late the rumor is rife that our enemies have offered the Indians $150 for every "Mormon" they will deliver to them.

It must be conceded that the above facts, circumstances and reports, transpiring at this particular juncture of affairs, strongly impel the conclusion that some person or persons connected with Col. Johnston's command are in collusion with the Indians. Such collusion is more particularly forced upon the mind, when it is known to be in perfect keeping with the policy of several "powers that be," towards the "Mormons;" and that the mildest term in use in the army, when speaking of us, is "the damned Mormons."

But when has one of Col. Johnston's command been killed or their animals run off by Indians incited to by the citizens of this Territory?—Never, for Gov. Young and the "Mormons" have ever counseled the Indians to remain strictly neutral, as all truth-telling red and white men, cognizant of the facts, will substantiate.[7] It is not a difficult matter, for a good arithmetician, to count the toes upon a naked foot, when it is put out.

Thomas S. Smith: Powell Came to the Camp of the Indians

Thomas S. Smith finally joined the orchestrated assault on 15 April, the day after the *Deseret News* article appeared. Unaware of the growing controversy, Ficklin that same day handed Colonel Johnston the report of his four-month expedition to the lands of the Flatheads to acquire cattle for the Utah Expedition at Camp Scott.[8] True to character, Smith

[6]U.S. Indian Agent Garland Hurt escaped from the Spanish Fork Indian Farm on 27 September 1857 and reached the army with help from his friends among the Utahs. He accompanied Colonel Johnston's command to Fort Bridger. On reports that a Mormon force of some three hundred would intercept U.S. Army Major Randolph Marcy at Green River on his return to Camp Scott with replacement animals from Fort Union, Hurt in January 1858 volunteered to scout for the Army in the Uinta Basin. On returning to Camp Scott in April, Hurt learned that Marcy had come back by a different route. Ironically, on 4 December 1857 Hurt was first to report Mormon involvement in the massacre by Mormons and Southern Paiute Indians of some 120 Arkansas emigrants to California in September 1857 at Mountain Meadows in southwestern Utah.

[7]It would be difficult to square this statement with available evidence today to the contrary.

[8]For Ficklin's report, see Chapter 11.

was more factual and straightforward than the territory's only newspaper in describing the attack on his mission and its aftermath in a sworn affidavit before Elias Smith, the probate judge of Great Salt Lake County.

THOMAS S. SMITH AFFIDAVIT,
15 APRIL 1858, BRIGHAM YOUNG COLLECTION.

Territory of Utah
Great Salt Lake County

Personally appeared before me, Elias Smith, Probate Judge of Great Salt Lake County in the Territory of Utah, Thomas S. Smith, who being legally sworn says that on the twenty-fifth day of February, A.D. One Thousand Eight Hundred and fifty eight, a band of Shoshone and Banak [*sic*] Indians numbering about two hundred and fifty made a descent upon the Cattle herd belonging to the settlers of Fort Limhi on Salmon River in Oregon Territory, and drove off two hundred and twenty oxen and cows, also thirty five horses, killing two men, George McBride and James Miller, and wounding five others. Deponent further says that with the aforesaid Indians was a white man named J. W. Powell, who instigated and took part in the massacre and drive, that subsequent to the massacre a portion of the Indians engaged in it came in to Fort Limhi and told deponent that a quarrel had occurred among the Indians about the stolen cattle that the Indians divided and that Powell left their camp and notified the Banaks to meet him with the stolen stock at Soda Springs or Bear R. Lake and that he would conduct them into the Camp of the U.S. Troops at Ft. Bridger. Deponent further says that two days previous to the massacre said Powell came to the camp of the aforesaid Shoshones and Banaks direct from a camp of the U.S. Troops, and that previous to that time the Shoshone and Banak Indians were on terms of unquestioned friendship with the settlers at Ft. Limhi and all white people. Deponent further says that at the time of the massacre a small detachment of U.S. Troops was at Beaver Head, a distance of about one hundred miles from Ft. Limhi; that it was from this camp Powell came to the camp of the Indians; that the purpose of the detachment in coming to Beaver Head was to purchase stock.

Thomas S. Smith

Sworn and subscribed to before me in Great Salt Lake City,
County and Territory aforesaid, this 15th day of April AD, 1858.
In testimony whereof I have hereunto set my hand
and Seal of Court.
Elias Smith

Governor Cumming on 15 April dispatched these charges to Colonel Johnston at Camp Scott with a report about the "respectful attentions" he had received on his arrival with Thomas Kane in the Mormon settlements. "Ex-Governor Brigham Young paid me a call of ceremony as soon as I was sufficiently relieved from the fatigue of my mountain journey to receive company," he beamed. Moreover, Young had "evinced a willingness to afford me every facility which I may require for the efficient performance of my administrative duties." Cumming fancied that Young's course of action would meet "the approval of a majority of this community."[9] He would learn over the next three years just how true this would always be.

At Camp Scott, soldiers and federal officials alike greeted the governor's letter with skepticism and promptly went on the defensive. The Utah Expedition commander on 21 April replied that he was gratified Cumming had been "received and recognized as Governor of Utah." Colonel Johnston stiffly presumed that the Mormon soldiers "now occupying the canyons and other positions on or near the route to Salt Lake City" would immediately be disbanded as a "manifestation of a desire on the part of the people of the Territory to be reconciled to the government" and asked to be "informed when that will take place."[10] As for charges against Garland Hurt, Johnston had investigated them and satisfied himself that the agent to the Utah tribe had "faithfully discharged his duty" and had only given "good advice to the Indians." With a letter from Hurt to the governor, the colonel also sent one by Jacob Forney, Utah's new head of Indian Affairs, and affidavits by Ficklin, John W. Powell, and Craven Jackson. These documents "show that no act of hostility or annoyance has been committed on Salmon river, or Bannack Creek or any other place by the Indians in Consequence of the instigations by any one connected with the army," he said.[11]

Garland Hurt: Ready to Confront my Accusers

None of the accused directed his denial to acting territorial secretary William H. Hooper, the one who charged them with inciting Indian trouble on the Mormon frontier, because all considered his appointment to this office by Brigham Young to be unlawful. Garland Hurt's

[9]Cumming to Johnston, 15 April 1858, Sen. Exec. Doc. 1 (35-2), 1858, 72–73.

[10]Ibid., Johnston to Cumming, 21 April 1858.

[11]Ibid.

short, scornful response made this clear. He had often opposed Brigham Young's Indian policy and sought to win native loyalty for the United States, but nothing in his work since coming to Utah in 1855 implied that he would incite the natives against white settlers.[12] The self-reliant Hurt, known to the Utah tribe as "the American," bristled that the governor appeared to take such an accusation seriously.

HURT TO CUMMING, 21 APRIL 1858,
SEN. EXEC. DOC. 1 (35-2), 1858, 77–78.

CAMP SCOTT, UTAH, *April* 21, 1858

Sir: I have been shown your official letter to Colonel A. S. Johnston, with accompanying documents. I do not feel myself answerable to Mr. Hooper, in any capacity, for my official conduct, but, as your excellency has deemed it proper to take cognizance of these charges, I feel it due to myself to say that every material allegation and insinuation therein contained is false and unfounded, and he or they who originated them knew them to be so. If evil disposed persons who have heretofore tampered with the Indians would turn their attention to some lawful and useful avocation, and leave the Indians to my control and direction, I am not unwilling to guaranty [*sic*] the good conduct of those with whom I have been associated. At the proper time and place I shall be ready to confront my accusers, and expose their malicious chicanery.

Very respectfully, your obedient servant,

GARLAND HURT,
Indian Agent.

His Excellency A. CUMMING, *Governor.*

JACOB FORNEY: I CAN SPEAK CONFIDENTLY FOR THE TRIBES

Democrat Jacob Forney, who succeeded Brigham Young as Utah's superintendent of Indian Affairs, was a political appointee. He was new to the territory and possessed no experience in working with the western tribes. The Pennsylvanian was also a heavy buyer of whiskey from the Camp Scott sutler.[13] He may have purchased surprising quantities of

[12]See Bigler, "Garland Hurt, The American Friend of the Utahs." Hurt believed that Young's professed policy that it was cheaper to feed Indians than fight them made the natives overly dependent and aggressive while impoverishing white settlers. He tried instead to establish farms to teach the Indians how to feed themselves.

[13]For Sutler W. A. Carter's record of Forney's whiskey purchases from December 1857 through May 1858, see Judge William A. Carter Papers, B-864 thru H63-41/70 and H72-42.

intoxicants for friends, who did not want William Carter to put whiskey after their names in his books. If it was for his own consumption or for trade with the natives, however, his word might be of questionable worth. Even so, he forthrightly denied these charges and presumed to speak with confidence for the tribes under his control. He, too, addressed his letter to Cumming, the former superintendent of Indian Affairs at St. Louis.

FORNEY TO CUMMING, 21 APRIL 1858,
SEN. EXEC. DOC. 1 (35-2), 1858, 78.

CAMP SCOTT AT FORT BRIDGER, U. T

April 21, 1858.

Dear Sir: My attention was to-day called to an "editorial" in the "Deseret News" of the 14th of this month. The article in question does injustice to the Indians with whom I have had intercourse, and very great injustice to those who are intrusted [*sic*] with the management of Indian affairs in this Territory. The policy adopted and strictly adhered to, in all my intercourse with Indians thus far, has been to avoid inciting them against the Mormons, either person or property. It is the manifest design of the person or persons who have fabricated the reports in question to impress upon the public that presents have been lavished upon the Indians, to incite them against the Mormons. I can speak confidently for the tribes inhabiting this portion of the Territory, that no such bribes were necessary to secure their loyalty to the government.

So far as the Indian department in this Territory is concerned, and legitimate representatives of the government, the article is false and slanderous.

Your excellency knows more about my actions among the Indians than any one else.

I am, very respectfully, your obedient servant.

J. FORNEY,
Superintendent Indian Affairs, U. T.

His Excellency A. CUMMING, *Salt Lake city, U. T.*

Most important of the documents that Johnston dispatched to the governor were the affidavits of three men who knew, or claimed to know, the most about events at Fort Limhi—B. F. Ficklin, John W. Powell, and Craven Jackson, Powell's mountaineer associate. In almost the same words, each said the Mormon settlers precipitated the attack themselves by giving arms and ammunition to the Nez Percé, the enemies of the Bannocks and Shoshones, who visited the mission in December 1857.

There could be but one source for this story, for only one of this trio was on hand when the Nez Percés came to the fort that December and witnessed the later attack. He alone knew why it happened. He was John Powell, portrayed as a liar by Thomas Smith. Moreover, there is no evidence from any other source, Mormon or Indian, that the Mormons gave anything other than food to the Nez Percé visitors from the northwest.[14]

B. F. Ficklin: Mormons Furnishing . . . Nez Percés Arms and Ammunition

The first of these affidavits by Ficklin is as noteworthy for what it did not say as for what it said. It added nothing to the superficial report of his activities that he submitted on his return and or any detail about events of which he had firsthand knowledge. While it correctly placed him far to the north when the attack took place, it did not mention that he was probably on the Beaverhead himself, not in the Flathead region, at or just before the time Powell decided to cross the mountains and visit the Bannock encampment north of the Mormon mission. On the other hand, Ficklin gave detailed information on subjects of which he had no personal knowledge, such as the movements of Mormon express riders, the relief expedition, and the ambush on Bannock Creek. He further revealed for the first time that he had discovered and copied the message B. F. Cummings left at Camas Creek after reclaiming the Fort Limhi horses from the Bannock, Boo-e-wat.

Ficklin to Porter, 21 April 1858, Sen. Exec. Doc. 1 (35-2), 1858, 79.

Fort Bridger, U. T., *April* 21, 1858.

Sir: I find in the "Deseret News" of April 14, that a government party camping at Beaver Head are accused of being the cause of the massacre of some Mormons on Salmon River, about March 1. The only party in that

[14]There were widespread rumors that Mormons were trading arms and ammunitions to the tribes during this period, but the author has seen only isolated cases of the practice at Fort Limhi that were usually in violation of mission rules. On 30 July 1857 John Preece traded "50 gun caps" in return for "a skin" during the absence of Thomas Smith, the only one authorized to trade with the Indians. According to the Salmon River Mission Journal, a meeting was held "in which Bro Priest [*sic*] acknowledged his wrong was forgiven and all made right."

section during the winter was under my charge. I left this camp December 9, 1857, with instructions from the commissary to contract for beef cattle for the use of the army; instructions from the quartermaster to procure horses, also, for the command; and instructions from Colonel Johnston to act on the defensive with any party of Mormons which I might meet: also, was furnished by the quartermaster with letters of introduction from Governor Cumming to the different Indian agents, and Father Hoken [Hoecken] of the Saint Ignatius mission in the Flathead country. I did not *say* or *do* anything myself, neither did any man under my command, to induce any Indians to interfere with the Mormons in any manner; on the contrary, I took every opportunity to tell all Indians and whites whom I met with on my trip, especially the Fathers of Saint Ignatius mission, that Colonel Johnston did not desire, and would not permit, any interference from Indians. On March 11 I was in the Flathead country, three hundred miles distant by the route traveled in the winter. The attack on Salmon River Fort, by Bannacks and Snakes, was induced by the Mormons furnishing a party of Nez Percés arms and ammunition to make war on them, (the Bannacks and Snakes.)

The party of Mormons under B. F. Cummings attacked on Bannack's creek, March 31, had a rencontre[15] with some Indians on March 28, on Camas creek, and took from them three horses, in corroboration of which I enclose you a copy of a letter from B. F. Cummings, picked up on the road.

Respectfully submitted.

B. F. FICKLIN.

Major F. J. PORTER,
Assistant Adjutant General, Army of Utah.

Subscribed and sworn to before me, April 21, 1858.

D. R. ECKELS,
Chief Justice of Supreme Court, Utah Territory.

Monday, 29, 4 p.m.—All well. We have just taken three of the brethrens' horses from Boor-wat [*sic*], to wit: Brother Moore's and Margattese's, and one supposed to belong to William Taylor. We caught them on the way from Camash creek to Snake river. We tried to get him to pay for the cattle he has killed, but he refused, and got very angry, and as we did not feel authorized to resort to force we left them.

B. F. CUMMINGS.

COL. CUNNINGHAM AND COMPANY.

[15]French for rencounter, a hostile meeting.

JOHN W. POWELL: SIX INDIANS ATTACKED THE MORMONS

On the day before the raid on Fort Limhi, John W. Powell met missionary William Perry at the Indian encampment near the lower settlement and told him that "he [Powell] had been up all night talking to the Bannocks to keep them from coming to burn our hay stacks and that we had better be careful of our horses and cattle." Next morning, before the hills and both sides of the river became "black with Indians," David Moore went to Thomas Smith "to know his feelings" about the warning. Smith brushed the Canadian off with the comment that "he thought it was some of Powel's [*sic*] lies."[16] Now faced with the charge that he had incited the raid, the mountaineer reminded his accusers that he had indeed told them it was coming, but otherwise his sworn defense only seemed to validate Smith's opinion of his character.

In his affidavit, for instance, Powell laid a cover of false or misleading half-truths over his own role, while deliberately withholding vital information about the raid and its causes. He reported the December 1857 confrontation at Fort Limhi between Chief Eagle from the Light's Nez Percés and the Bannocks and Shoshones, but forgot to mention that he played a prominent role in that altercation. Nor did he make clear that it happened two months before the attack, more than enough time for the clash to lose much of its bearing as the immediate cause of the February incursion. Powell further reveals that he was the sole source of the accusation, repeated by all three affiants, that the mission had supplied arms and ammunition to the Nez Percés.

AFFIDAVIT OF JOHN W. POWELL BEFORE D. R. ECKELS, 21 APRIL 1858, SEN. EXEC. DOC. 1 (35-2), 1858, 80, 81.

UTAH TERRITORY, *Green River County*.

John W. Powell, being duly sworn, upon his oath deposeth and saith: That he came into the Territory aforesaid in July, 1856; his life has been threatened by the Mormons, but, with the exception of the loss of property, he has never been injured by them. He left the Territory of Utah in August, 1856, with an outfit of Indian goods, for the purpose of trading with the Bannack and Shoshonee [*sic*] Indians. He was at Fort Limhi, on Salmon river, in February, 1858; there he found six Bannack and some Shoshonee

[16]Salmon River Mission Journal, 24, 25 February 1858. Also see Chapter 10, p. 220.

lodges. These Indians stated that a war party of Nez Percés Indians had been at the Mormon fort in search of them, the Bannacks; that the Mormons had furnished this war party with arms and ammunition; had fed them on the products of their (the Bannacks') lands; that subsequent to this the horses belonging to the Bannacks and Shoshonees were stolen by the Nez Percés; that they had never received any compensation from the Mormons for the land occupied by them; and they were on this account enraged at the Mormons, and would drive off their stock. The Bannacks inquired of him if the government of the United States would accept of their services and allow them to join them in fighting the Mormons; he told them that the United States was strong, and would not allow them to join them in their difficulties with the Mormons. The Indians then determined to attack the Mormons. He warned the Mormons, and told them to guard their stock; he was not engaged in the affair in any manner. Six Indians attacked the Mormons, killed two, and wounded others, drove off all of their cattle and some horses. He states that Brigham Young had endeavored to bribe these Indians who attacked the Mormons to join him in fighting the troops of the United States. He also says that he has seen cattle in possession of the Mormons which he knows to have been stolen from emigrants. This is all he knows in relation to the Indian and Mormon difficulty at Fort Limhi; and further saith not.

JOHN W. POWELL.

Subscribed and sworn before me, April 21, 1858.

D. R. ECKELS,
Chief Justice of Superior Court, Utah Territory.

CRAVEN JACKSON: HE WAS STOPPED BY THE MORMONS

A little known mountaineer with an unfortunate first name turned in the third affidavit. Otherwise, he made few impressions on the historical record, possibly because he was illiterate and, unlike many of Montana's early denizens, left no other writings or reminiscences.[17] Craven Jackson swore in someone else's writing that he spent the past winter on the Beaverhead with the Bannocks. His admitted relationship with the tribe and residence at the mountaineer wintering place reveal an association

[17]Few references during this period give him a first name. In 1854 John Owen recorded that he "hired a man named Jackson." Granville Stuart said that he wintered with Dempsey and "Jackson" on Henrys Fork, near Fort Bridger, in 1858–1859. Johnny Grant and others mention a mountaineer named Jackson briefly, but offer few details about him other than that he was an American. The 1860 census lists Craven Jackson and family residing at or near Fort Bridger.

with Powell, who was bonded by marriage to the Bannocks, as well as with Ficklin and his party. Jackson said the Indians had told him all he knew about events at Fort Limhi, but his presence at Fort Bridger at this early date revealed that he had arrived with Ficklin and Powell. His sworn statement shows an intimate knowledge of the region and its people. It does not explain, however, why he entered the controversy, when none of Ficklin's men, who were closer to the events in question than he was, chose to do so.

AFFIDAVIT OF CRAVEN JACKSON BEFORE D. R. ECKELS, 21 APRIL 1858, SEN. EXEC. DOC. 1 (35-2), 1858, 81, 82.

UTAH TERRITORY, *Green River county.*

Craven Jackson, being duly sworn, upon his oath, deposeth and said: That he came into the Territory aforesaid in the month of December, 1854, from Oregon Territory; that since that time he has visited the Mormon settlements every fall for the purpose of buying provisions and Indian goods; that during these visits he was well treated; that he has been trading since he has been in this country with the Bannack and Shoshonee Indians, principally with the former; that during the past winter he has been residing with these Indians at Beaver Head, in Nebraska Territory, on the headwaters of the Missouri river; that these Indians have complained for some two years past very much about the Mormons settling on their lands and building a fort on Salmon river. They represented to the deponent that when the Mormons first arrived they promised to pay the Indians for the land, but that this promise has never been fulfilled; that last winter they told him that these Mormons had furnished fire-arms and ammunition to their enemies, the Nez Percés Indians, for the purpose of fighting them, (the Bannacks,) and that when they (the Bannacks) went to the Mormons for the same purpose, that they were refused any assistance; and that after these Nez Percés Indians had been furnished with fire-arms that they came and stole all of their horses, and that not knowing who else to call upon for restitution, and having it out of their power to overtake the Nez Percés, they stole and drove off all of the Mormon stock from their fort, killing in the attempt two of the Mormons, and wounding several others. The deponent does not know these facts of his own knowledge, but the above statements were made to him by the Indians with whom he was living. Beaver Head is about 120 miles from Fort Limlie [*sic*], the Mormon fort on Salmon river; and deponent further states, on oath, that last fall he started to go to Salt Lake City for the purpose of purchasing his goods, &c., as was his custom, but that he was stopped by the Mormons at their fort on the Malade river, in Salt Lake Valley, and was not allowed to go into the settlements, but was sent back;

that while he was at the Malade fort he purchased two oxen from a Mormon named John Barnard; that the said Barnard told him that he had bought these cattle from the Digger Indians, who live about the settlements, and who range as far as the Humboldt river, and that these Indians had stolen them from the emigrants on the road to California; these two were one yoke of oxen, out of five yoke which had been brought in at the same time; they were branded "T" on the left hip. The Indians told the deponent that said John Barnard had fifteen more, which had been stolen from the emigrants. Deponent says further, on his oath, that he has never taken any part or participation in any difficulties between the Indians and the Mormons, but has endeavored to prevent such difficulties; and further saith not.

his
CRAVEN + JACKSON.
mark

Subscribed and sworn to before me, April 21, 1858

D. R. ECKELS
Chief Justice of Superior Court, Utah Territory.

Soon after Johnston mailed copies of these affidavits to Army headquarters, two bitter Mormon critics came to the colonel's defense. W. M. F. Magraw,[18] superintendent of the Fort Kearney, South Pass, and Honey Lake Wagon Road project, interrupted by the Utah War, and renowned mountain man, James Bridger,[19] now acting as an Army scout, refuted the charge that Johnston had incited the Utah and Bannock Indians, "the former through the agency of Dr. Hurt, Indian agent, the latter through Mr. B. F. Ficklin." They said the commander of the Utah Expedition had met with Shoshone chiefs Washakee and Little Soldier and made clear that he would brook no involvement by their followers in the conflict, "that they must keep outside and look on." Colonel

[18]Magraw lost the federal mail contract between Utah and the east to Mormon Hiram Kimball in 1856. His letter to President Pierce that year, alleging theocratic wrongdoing in Utah, was among documents James Buchanan gave Congress to justify sending an Army expedition to the territory in 1857. For Magraw's career, see MacKinnon, "The Buchanan Spoils System and the Utah Expedition: Careers of W. M. F. Magraw and John M. Hockaday."

[19]Bridger and Brigham Young had not gotten along since their first encounter on Green River in late July 1847. Bridger denied charges he planned Indian attacks on the Mormons as early as July 1848 ("Such a thought never entered my Head"), but he complained to Young he had received "A Number Coins of Base or Bogos Money" from Mormons such as Jack Redding. See Bridger to Young, 16 July 1848, Brigham Young Papers. "Old Bridger is death on us," Young said. See 7 May 1849, Journal History. A Nauvoo Legion force tried to arrest Bridger in 1853, but "old Gabe" escaped. Mormons later claimed to have purchased Fort Bridger from his partner, but the mountaineer insisted to his last day that he had never sold the trading post on Blacks Fork but left because the Mormons wanted to kill him.

Johnston's position on the two occasions they knew about, "and his policy, as expressed to us on more than one occasion forbids even the supposition that he is in any way guilty of the charge," the two men said. Nor could he have been "in any way connected with the Utah's or Pannack's difficulties, complained of by the Mormons."[20]

The Cover Up

Johnston no doubt welcomed such help, but the former secretary of war of the Republic of Texas was no greenhorn himself when it came to defending his honor on the fields of public opinion and manipulating the press of his day. A number of officers and civilians in his command served as covert reporters for eastern newspapers, sending their stories under aliases, and it is safe to assume the colonel knew most of them. One, a storekeeper's clerk named Osborne, wrote for the *Washington Union* and, despite his humble army position, enjoyed ready access to Johnston. Osborne also cultivated a Tenth Infantry captain from New Hampshire, who doubled as a special correspondent for the *New York Herald*. Capt. Jesse A. Gove was also very ambitious and highly susceptible to flattery.

Seeing how close Osborne was to the commanding officer, Gove confided to his friend that he, too, wrote for an eastern newspaper. Soon after, Osborne visited Johnston and afterward told Gove what they had talked about. The captain in turn passed the good news to his wife. "Osborne mentioned [to Johnston] that we had some fine officers," he told her. "'Yes', says Col. J., 'I regard Capt. G. as one of the best officers in service, and one of the brightest ornaments of the army,'" Gove blushed on paper. "My dear, this is private," he wrote, "but who would not be proud of such an opinion."[21] On 22 April, the day before Johnston mailed copies of affidavits and letters to Army headquarters refuting Mormon charges on the Fort Limhi attack, B. F. Ficklin happened to stop by Gove's tent. He advised the officer "very privately" a mail delivery would go out next day and offered as the carrier to "take a letter to the 'widow Gove.'" The impressionable captain hurriedly penned one to his wife and a "communication to the Herald."[22]

---

[20]Magraw and Bridger to Porter, 28 April 1858, Sen. Exec. Doc. 1 (35-2), 1858, 82–84.

[21]Hammond, ed., *The Utah Expedition, 1857–1858: Letters of Capt. Jesse A. Gove, 10th Inf., U.S.A., of Concord, N.H., to Mrs. Gove, and special correspondence of the New York Herald*, 148–52.

[22]Ibid., 154.

Published on 12 June, Captain Gove's story was a lengthy account of "Captain" Ficklin's journey to the Flathead country, "one of the most extraordinary on record" and defense of Colonel Johnston and the Army. He enclosed the 14 April *Deseret News* and delivered an emotional counterattack against the Mormons. "Did they not stampede our animals, burn the grass within our very camp, drive off our cattle, destroy our supplies by burning our trains?" he asked. "The Mormons now endeavor to disguise their treachery to the government and their rebellion against the laws of their country, by attributing to Col. Johnston the hostility of the Indians by collusion, when it is a known fact, and susceptible of the clearest proof, that Col. Johnston has taken but one course with the Indian bands in this Territory, and that was to remain neutral." His defense of "Captain" Ficklin included references to the note B. F. Cummings left at Camas Creek for Andrew Cunningham that Gove could only have gotten from Ficklin himself.[23]

Nor did Johnston's manipulation of a vain subordinate end there. Gove wrote his wife on 29 April that his friend Osborne told him, "Col. J. was to send off a secret express, and that he could get my letters in for the Herald." The captain was on picket duty, but the stores clerk obligingly brought him a pencil and paper so he could write his story. Osborne then intimated that he would like to show the finished piece to Johnston. Feigning reluctance, Gove agreed, but only if Osborne told the Colonel "privately" that he had written it out of a "sense of duty to him, and the complicated position of the army in reference to the civil authorities," but did not tell him that he [Gove] knew the colonel had seen it. Later that afternoon, Gove wrote, Osborne told him "the baby was born." He said, "Col. J. was highly pleased that any officer should be so good a friend to him as to set the public right in these matters, the more so as it was farthest from his suspicion that I had so much interested myself in his behalf."[24]

Said the self-promoting captain, "So the colonel is in blissful ignorance of the fact that I am aware that he saw the letter, and I intend to keep him so."[25]

If less than blissful, also left in ignorance were those who hoped for a painstaking investigation into the causes of the 25 February 1858 raid.

[23]Ibid., 231–48. [24]Ibid., 156–57. [25]Ibid.

The alleged inquiry by the Utah Expedition's commanding officer was shallow at best and little more than a hurried attempt to protect himself and favored underlings at worst. On 20 April Johnston received Governor Cumming's letter of 15 April, enclosing William Hooper's charges and the 14 April *Deseret News* article. He replied to it with affidavits and letters from five principals at Camp Scott the very next day. Notably absent from his investigation was testimony by any of the ten men who comprised Ficklin's party or anyone else with knowledge of the attack. The latter would include Robert Hereford and Jacob Meeks, who accompanied Ficklin on his return from the Flathead country.[26]

But not everyone was willing to allow the guilty to go unpunished for lack of evidence. After moving south, Salmon River missionary Milton Hammond returned in July to Farmington, "grown up in weeds and grass which made the place look lonesome," and went to work to restore his farm. As he was going after the last load of hay on 13 August, he "met one of the Indians (Pasecun) in the road as he had been one of the worst Indians in the fuss." Recognizing the missionary, the native "put whip to his horse and would not stop." Hammond ran for his own horse and some help and "followed him to the city where we found him and took him prisoner and kept him prisoner until Pres. Young's mind was obtained concerning him."[27] But as far as the record shows, nothing came of that either.

In the absence of a serious investigation and with a subsequent cover-up, it can never be known for certain who, if anyone, touched off the February 1858 raid on Fort Limhi that destroyed Idaho's early white settlement after less than three years. But evidence has come to light since then that calls for a closer look at this event and supports a credible circumstantial case against the likely culprit and his motives.

---

[26]The only mountaineers from the Upper Missouri or Bitterroot Valley who turn up on the Sutler's account book at Camp Scott, prior to July 1858, are John Powell, Robert Hereford, and Jacob Meeks. See Judge William A. Carter Papers, December–July 1858.

[27]Milton D. Hammond Journal, 13 August 1858. Perhaps Pasecun was Pash-e-co, a warrior who may have led the Ward massacre and who later participated in the attack on Salmon River. Indian agent C. H. Miller considered this "celebrated prophet of the Western Snake tribe . . . one of the most dangerous and desperate men now living west of the Rocky Mountains." Miller reported, "He is extremely hostile to the Mormons. This noted partisan was the chief cause of the expedition against the Mormon settlement of Salmon River." See Trenholm and Maurine, *The Shoshonis: Sentinels of the Rockies,* 184–85.

Chapter 14

CONSPIRACY OR COINCIDENCE?

[Chief Snag said] a small detachment of "soldiers" or men from the camp of the soldiers at Bridger came to Beaver Head to buy stock; and that from the camp of this detachment a white man named J. H. Powell came to the lodges of the [Bannocks] and Shoshones two days previous to the massacre herein referred to, and incited the Indians, giving them his aid and participation in the affair. [Snag] further states that subsequent to the massacre a quarrel occurred among the Indians, whereupon Powell left, and, after appointing a meeting with the Bannacks at Soda Springs or Bear River lake, from whence he would conduct them with their stolen stock to the camp of the troops, accompanied the detachment to Bridger.

— William H. Hooper

The words of Shoshone Chief Ti-o-von-du-ah, widely known as Snag, remain after a century and a half the most reliable description of what happened at Fort Limhi in February 1858 and its aftermath. His story squares with known events at that time as well as evidence that has since surfaced. The respected leader of the native inhabitants of Salmon River's east fork, known then as the Sheepeaters and today as the Lemhis, gave his account less than three weeks after the attack to Thomas S. Smith, whose record as head of the Salmon River mission speaks for his straightforward honesty. On returning to Great Salt Lake, Smith affirmed Snag's statement by affidavit before the probate court. It pointed the finger directly at John W. Powell as the immediate culprit and implied that he conspired with Ficklin and party.

If the old Shoshone chief answered the questions of who and what, Johnny Healy, Powell's friend, later revealed one of the probable motives for the mountaineer's instigation of the raid. He said Powell lived with the Bannocks, "who regarded him as their head man," and was "an enemy of the Mormons." The mountaineer became their foe, Healy said, when Fort Limhi refused to protect him during the December 1857 controversy between the Bannocks and Nez Percés over stolen horses.[1] After the mission failed to take sides in the quarrel, he said, "Powell and the Bannocks made war upon the Mormons and actually forced them to leave or abandon Lemhi."[2] A rumor circulating about that time that the Mormons had threatened to kill Powell hardly improved the mountaineer's attitude.[3]

Sources of Disaffection

It took more than Powell's sway over the Bannocks, however compelling, to touch off the attack. Contrary to William Hooper's claim that there had never been "the slightest misunderstanding," relations between native inhabitants and the white settlers from Utah had grown increasingly unstable over many months. The mood of the Bannocks had become especially unfriendly. The causes of the tribe's disaffection were strikingly similar to sources of conflict between Mormon colonists and their neighbors elsewhere in the Rocky Mountains.

When the missionaries first came to the valley of Salmon River's eastern fork in June 1855, Shou-woo-koo, also called Le Grand Coquin (pronounced by the Mormons as "Rocky-e-kay"), had welcomed them warmly. The huge Bannock chief said he was "very glad that they had come to open up farms and show the Indians how to work" and told the Mormon arrivals that "they were welcome to any land that they might select for farming purposes."[4] Two and a half years later, the over six-foot-four inch "Big Rogue" led the raid on the mission herd.

The Bannocks' change of heart likely began during their first summer as the missionaries erected walls, literal and cultural, between themselves and their new neighbors. Natives watched in wonder as the newcomers labored to cut trees and haul logs from the hills to build the first fortification ever seen along the river. The square of upright timbers was a picket fence that defined separation and distrust between the newcomers and inhabitants. A further sign of aloofness came when the Mor-

[1]Healy wrongly identified the Nez Percés as Pend d'Oreilles.

[2]Healy, "J. W. Powell and Fort Lemhi Told by Johnny Healy."

[3]See "A Harmful Rumor," Chapter 9, pp. 201, 202.

[4]Salmon River Mission Journal, 12 June 1855.

mons, although polygamists themselves, spurned the invitation of tribal leaders to marry Indian women on the mistaken belief the proposal was a test of their morality. "In this they failed to bring any into transgression," Moore said.[5] Two years later, when Brigham Young came, they were surprised to learn that they were supposed to take Indian wives. But by then, as Young predicted and they soon found out, it was too late.

There is no evidence the missionaries ever promised to buy the land, as claimed by Powell and Jackson, but in 1857 there were signs of increasing native unrest over the spreading plowed fields and fences. While Snag led many of his Shoshone followers to the waters of baptism, Bannock conversions were comparatively few. An ominous sign came in May 1857, when the Bannock headmen pointedly ignored Young's visit. When Milton Hammond came back that October with a new company to expand the settlement, he noticed the cooling in relations between the colony and its neighbors. "The Indians did not seem to be possessed of a very good spirit," he said.[6] Nor would it improve the spirit of native peoples, whose survival depended on the river's bounty, to see eight wagons, heavily loaded with barrels of pickled salmon, roll out that month behind thirteen yoke of oxen to tables in Salt Lake Valley.

Further aggravating volatile relations was the approach of U.S. soldiers ordered to put down the Mormon theocracy's armed bid for independence. Rather than join their white cousins of Israel in opposing the U.S. Army, as Mormon emissaries urged them to do, the natives in most parts of the Rocky Mountains adopted a wait-and-see attitude before siding with either party in a dispute they did not understand.[7] Although accused of inciting raids on Mormon settlements, Colonel Johnston and U.S. Indian agents actually sought to discourage such hostilities. But up to this time, federal officials had enjoyed little success in exercising influence over the Bannocks of southeastern Oregon.

---

[5]Ibid., 23 June 1855.

[6]Milton D. Hammond Journal, 22 October 1858.

[7]For Mormon attempts to "instruct the Indians that our enemies are also their enemies & . . . that they must be our friends and stick to us, for if our enemies kill us off, they will surely be cut off by the same parties," see Wells to Dame, 13 August 1857, Palmer Collection; Wells to Evans, 13 August 1857, David Evans Papers; Adjutant General, Nauvoo Legion, to Col. W. B. Pace, 13 August 1857, Utah Militia Records; and Brooks, *The Mountain Meadows Massacre*, 35. For the lack of interest among the tribes in a Mormon alliance, see Dimick Huntington Journal, August–October, 1857.

More serious than any of these sources of unrest, however, was the blindness of Brigham Young's emissaries to cultural differences among the tribes, a common failing among religious denominations. Unlike mountaineers, who learned and adopted the ways of chosen tribes, Mormon missionaries persisted in seeing all natives as one people, a remnant of Jacob in the New World, called "Lamanites," ignoring the evidence before their eyes that all Indians were not the same. The more fervent the believers, it seemed, the slower they were to be taught by experience. And in their zeal to lead the natives to baptism, they too often failed to learn a vital lesson of survival in the wilderness—"the friend of my friend is my friend; the friend of my enemy is my enemy."

Illustrating this truth, yet again, was the controversy over stolen horses that broke out in December 1857 when Thomas Smith, with the best of intentions, tried to resolve the dispute peacefully and keep the goodwill of all sides, Nez Percé, Bannock, and Shoshone. If the Nez Percés had not come back in the night and stolen the animals in question, and likely some whose ownership was never in doubt, the mission head might have achieved a measure of success. But after that, even Snag would find it difficult to recover the trust of his people, many of whom blamed him for betraying them to the Mormons and Nez Percés. Indian resentments could run deep, and the rupture with some of the chief's followers and the Bannocks was now beyond repair.

B. F. Ficklin: Motive and Opportunity

Into an increasingly volatile social environment came a single-minded man hardly suited by temperament to prevent an explosion on the headwaters of the Missouri and Columbia rivers. Charged by the commander of the Utah Expedition to contract for the delivery of cattle and horses to Camp Scott at the earliest possible date, Benjamin F. Ficklin was combative, resourceful, and completely dedicated to his mission. Whether he knowingly conspired with Powell to seize the herd at Fort Limhi will never be known for certain, thanks to an apparent cover-up and the lack of any investigation worthy of the name. But events in which he had taken an active part added up to a compelling motive for him to do so.

As a survey crew chief on the federal government's first venture to open a wagon road over the Rocky Mountains, Ficklin had seen the project disrupted by Mormon military opposition to the lawful arrival of U.S. soldiers, escorting a new governor to an American territory. This battle-scarred veteran had seen the remains of Army supply wagons on Big Sandy and Green rivers, burned by Nauvoo Legion Major Lot Smith's mounted command. As a U.S. marshal, he had taken custody of two Mormon prisoners, Major Joseph Taylor and his adjutant, William Stowell. Soon after, he had witnessed a heartrending consequence of Mormon resistance: thousands of dead animals that made a thirty-mile stretch of the Oregon Trail from Hams Fork to Fort Bridger look like "one vast slaughter yard," where "from 10 to 15 mules and horses could be seen in a pile."[8] On 9 December, when he headed north from Camp Scott, Ficklin had little reason to doubt that a rebellious territory had thrown off the federal yoke.[9]

If Ficklin had the motive, he also had ample opportunity to conspire with men as impulsive and reckless as himself in instigating the attack. On 10 January 1858, he and his party of civilian volunteers arrived at the mouth of Ruby River, then known as the Stinking Water, at present Twin Bridges, Montana. There he met stock trader Robert Hereford, who would later accompany him to Camp Scott.[10] Richard Grant had already abandoned his cabin at this place and flown north with his family to escape a feared Mormon invasion. But among the mountaineers still camped there was a fellow Virginian whom Ficklin would meet for the first time: John W. Powell, a name the stock contractor would not mention in his report.

After leaving his party at Ruby River, Ficklin made two separate visits to Flathead and Bitterroot valleys, contrary to the perception he gives in his report. During his first trip, which lasted from 10 January to about 6 February, he "failed in the object of his visit Which was for the purchase of Stock" because the traders were too afraid of the Mormons to

[8]William A. Carter Diary, 18 November 1857.

[9]Ironically, Ficklin and Col. Albert S. Johnston would both join the seceding southern states four years later and fight against the government whose authority they undertook to maintain in 1857.

[10]This mountaineer winter camp was located just above the place where the Beaverhead and Big Hole rivers join to form the Jefferson River, one of the three forks of the Missouri. For its residents, see Stuart, *Forty Years on the Frontier,* 1:125–26.

drive their animals to Camp Scott.[11] Richard Grant, Henry Brooks, Michael Ogden, and others in Flathead Valley gave him no encouragement. Nor did John Owen in Bitterroot Valley, who planned to send his livestock to Walla Walla for safety. Owen said that Ficklin left his fort on 29 January and went back to the Beaverhead via Deerlodge Valley, a journey of some two hundred miles. Even allowing several days for a side trip to Flathead Valley, he could easily have covered this distance within nine days and reached his camp by 6 February.

If the agent had indeed plotted with Powell to seize the Fort Limhi herd, he would have done so between this date, when he rejoined his party on the Beaverhead, and the day he left to go back to Bitterroot Valley. John Owen said he was "much surprised to see Mr Ficklin ride up after dark" on 23 February. To reach Fort Owen by this day, Ficklin would have left his party on the Beaverhead on or about 16 February. There is no direct evidence that a conspiracy occurred at all, but if the two men did put their heads together to plan a raid on Fort Limhi, they would have done so during the ten days from 6 to 16 February 1858.

Within that period, some curious events occurred. On 9 February, three days after Ficklin's estimated return to his party on the Beaverhead, an Indian came to Fort Limhi from that very place to report "a company of ten soldiers were camped over there and that they had two Mormon prisoners."[12] That night the Indian slipped into the mission corral and stole Thomas Smith's horse. On 11 February a company of ten under Pleasant Green Taylor rode over the Continental Divide to recover the stolen animal. On 13 February the Mormon party reached the creek that "Dempsa [Robert Dempsey] the mountaineer is camped on and found the Indian and horse about 3 miles above Dempse camp and about 12 miles from Beaver Head Valley."[13] They seized the horse and rebuked the native. He in turn "put on his war cap, took his spear, mounted a small pony and put off saying he was going to tell the soldiers."[14] The soldiers he was talking about could only be Ficklin and party.

[11] Dunbar and Phillips, eds., *The Journals and Letters of Major John Owen*, 1:190.

[12] Salmon River Mission Journal, 9 February 1858.

[13] Milton D. Hammond Journal, 13 February 1858.

[14] Salmon River Mission Journal, 13 February 1858.

On about 16 February, Ficklin left this camp for Bitterroot Valley, while Powell soon after headed for the Bannock gathering near Fort Limhi. The day of the attack, 25 February, found Ficklin at Fort Owen, more than two hundred miles from the scene in the company of Flathead Agent John Owen, a respected witness, if one was needed, as to his whereabouts on that fateful day. The day before, Ficklin rode up Bitterroot River a short distance to visit Frederick Burr. What the two talked about is not known, but Ficklin, an inveterate letter deliverer, may have carried a message to Burr from his partner, John W. Powell, advising on where to meet that summer. "I went to look for Powell," Burr said that summer at the bend of Portneuf River, near present McCammon, Idaho.[15] During August the two mountaineers camped together on Bear River at the mouth of Smiths Fork, near present Cokeville, Wyoming.

In the meantime, Ficklin left Bitterroot Valley on 25 February, not 3 March, as he later reported, unless he spent an entire week in Flathead Valley, which is not likely. If he really "expected to start immediately" from Deerlodge with two hundred beef cattle he had agreed to buy from Johnny Grant, he would be sorely disappointed. He found instead that Richard Grant's oldest son had suffered second thoughts about the wisdom of the sale, especially since learning that Ficklin expected him to drive the cattle to Camp Scott. Grant had no desire to go in harm's way over a trail possibly controlled by the Mormons, who already had allegedly threatened to kill him. Known less for valor than his ability to stay alive, the mountaineer "positively refused to do it." Frustrated and angry, Ficklin returned to his camp at the confluence of the Big Hole and Beaverhead rivers, where he saw the "new grass beginning to grow finely" on Jefferson River before he started back to Camp Scott on 12 March.[16] He retraced his earlier trail via Soda Springs as empty handed as when he had come up it two months before.

JOHN W. POWELL: ACTIVE PARTICIPANT

Although circumstantial evidence points his way, it may never be known for certain whether Ficklin took part in an unauthorized scheme

[15]Frederick H. Burr Journal, 18 July 1858.

[16]Sen. Exec. Doc. 1 (35-2), 1858, 71.

to seize Fort Limhi's cattle. But there is far less doubt about the connection of John W. Powell to the raid and events that led up to it. Just two days after Pleasant Green Taylor's company returned on 14 February with Thomas Smith's horse, Bannock chief Shou-woo-coo, "Le Grand Coquin," arrived at the mission from the Beaverhead with his band, to which John Powell was joined by marriage. The gigantic native "went into the corral and examined it all around."[17] "Old Rocky Kay," as he was known to the missionaries, "did not seem very friendly," said Milton Hammond on 20 February.[18] And only two days later, Powell himself "passed down by the Fort from Beaver Head."[19]

From the Missouri River headwater where Ficklin's party was camped, a deadly storm had moved over the great divide toward the Mormon mission, and Thomas Smith hurried to take shelter. On the day Powell joined the Bannock encampment, 22 February, members of the second settlement moved up to the protection of the stockade. And as the native temper grew more threatening, William Perry, near the newly abandoned cabins downstream, had a talk with the mountaineer, who seemed alarmed that the whirlwind he had seeded was spinning out of control. The day before the raid, Powell claimed "he had been up all night talking to the Bannocks to keep them from coming to burn our hay stacks and that we had better be careful of our horses and cattle."[20]

In his affidavit, Powell admitted he was at Fort Limhi on 25 February 1858 but swore that he was "not engaged in the affair in any manner."[21] Yet Milton Hammond on 26 February, a day after the attack, said "some of the boys say that they see Powell the mountaineer in the fuss."[22] Thomas Smith also reported the sighting on 28 February to Brigham Young: "Powel a mountaineer was with the Indians and helped them to drive off the cattle."[23] The mountaineer also said that when he arrived at the Indian encampment on the river, it numbered only six Bannock and some Shoshone lodges. Moreover, said he, only six warriors

[17]Salmon River Mission Journal, 16 February 1858.

[18]Milton D. Hammond Journal, 20 February 1858.

[19]Salmon River Mission Journal, 22 February 1858.

[20]Ibid., 24 February 1858. To Powell's credit, his warnings to the Mormon missionaries suggest he was after their cattle and not their lives.

[21]Sen. Exec. Doc. I (35-2), 1858, 80, 81.

[22]Milton D. Hammond Journal, 26 February 1858.

[23]Smith to Young, 28 February 1858, Brigham Young Papers.

made the attack that killed two men, wounded five others, and made off with more than two hundred cattle and oxen and some thirty-five horses. But many eyewitness accounts put the number of attackers from 150 to nearly twice this number. The evidence leaves no reasonable doubt that Powell testified falsely. There only remains the question of why, if he was not involved, did he perjure himself?

After the raid, Powell told the Bannocks "to meet him with the stolen stock at Soda Springs or Bear R. Lake and he would conduct them into the Camp of the U.S. Troops at Ft. Bridger," according to Chief Snag and other natives.[24] This story rings true because the Bannocks' known proclivity for attacking small emigrant parties along the Snake River stretch of the Oregon Trail would make them afraid to appear at a U.S. Army camp with stolen cattle in their possession. To escape punishment, they would need a Powell or Ficklin to vouch for their respectable conduct. That Powell instructed the natives to meet him on Bear River reveals he did not go with them and the livestock.

Instead, Snag said, Powell left following the attack and, after arranging to meet the Bannocks at Soda Springs or Bear River Lake, accompanied Ficklin's detachment to Fort Bridger. As this report indicates, Powell returned to the Beaverhead by the way he had come to rejoin Ficklin's party, which explains the agent's knowledge of the raid. Ficklin left for Camp Scott on 12 March. That allowed just enough time for Snag to travel from the Beaverhead to Fort Limhi, where he arrived 16 March to tell the most coherent story of what happened.

Soon after Cummings posted his letter to Andrew Cunningham on 29 March, Ficklin and Powell reached the Camas Creek junction of the Flathead Trail and Mormon road from Fort Limhi, near Mud Lake, where they discovered the message. Their party now included Craven Jackson, Robert Hereford, and Jacob Meeks. In his denial, Ficklin did not say what day he found the note, but later told the "secret" *New York Herald* correspondent, Capt. Jesse A. Gove, that it was on 31 March.[25] If true, this would have placed him still in the mountains on the day Cummings and party seized the horses from the Bannock Boo-e-wat, and a

[24]Thomas S. Smith affidavit, 15 April 1858, Brigham Young Collection.

[25]Hammond, ed., *The Utah Expedition, 1857–1858: Letters of Capt. Jesse A. Gove, 10th Inf., U.S.A., of Concord, N.H., to Mrs. Gove, and special correspondence of the New York Herald*, 243.

full hundred miles from the ambush on Bannock Creek two days later, when Bailey Lake was killed. Yet even allowing nine days for his epic struggle in the snow on the Continental Divide and jaded horses, Ficklin should have arrived at the trail crossing sooner than he claimed. On 21 April he admitted that he knew all about the ambush on Bannock Creek. He knew about the encounters on both days because he was not far from the scene and had later contact with the native participants.

Mystery of the Vanishing Herd

There remain many unsolved mysteries from the attack on Fort Limhi. By far the most puzzling, still today, has to do with what became of the livestock. Given that some two hundred-fifty cows and oxen, plus thirty-five or forty horses, cannot just vanish into thin air, even on the northern Rocky Mountain frontier, the still unanswered question is, what happened to the herd? Where did the Indian raiders take these animals and why? If a conspiracy did exist, the answer would surely expose it. Find the beef, and one will find out who was behind the raid and why. But after a century and a half, the problem is still easier stated than resolved.

All eyewitnesses agree that, on the day of the attack, the Indians drove the herd downstream to the mixed Bannock-Shoshone encampment about eight miles north of the fort and some ten miles south of present Salmon, Idaho. There, said Chief Snag, a quarrel broke out between the Bannocks and the Shoshones who took part in the attack (not all of them did participate) over how to divide the herd. A Shoshone woman was killed in this argument before the Bannocks, the "principal actors in the difficulty," took most of the animals and left. Of the smaller number given to their less warlike relatives, repentant Sheepeaters voluntarily brought in more than forty head, while starving tribe members "killed a great many."[26] This still left over a hundred cattle and some thirty-five horses unaccounted for. Which way did they go?

From the mountain *cul-de-sac* where the Indians divided the herd, there was only one possible exit for livestock. To the north was 6,995-foot Lost Trail Pass at the head of Salmon River's North Fork that led into

[26]Biography and Journals of Benjamin Franklin Cummings, 21 March 1858.

Ross' Hole at the south end of Bitterroot Valley on the Lewis and Clark Trail. Not only would this have been a hazardous and difficult winter crossing, it also would have led to hostile territory for no discernable purpose. To the east stood the Beaverhead Mountains, crested by the Continental Divide and crossed only at 7,300-foot Lemhi Pass, opposite Fort Limhi, also on the trail of Lewis and Clark. Rancher Stephen Mahaffey, former owner of the Fort Limhi property, told the author in 1967 that he had moved cattle over this pass in mild winters. Such a crossing would have led to the Flathead Trail on the Missouri drainage, then south to another Continental Divide passage at Monida. February 1858 was unseasonably warm, but heavy snows in March, which blocked Granville Stuart and delayed Ficklin, would also have stopped the Bannocks and the herd at this pass.

The herd could only have gone south. Of two possible routes in this direction the best was the Mormon road from Fort Limhi to Fort Hall that joined the Flathead Trail near Camas Creek. But this would have taken the animals past the fort and, if lookouts there saw or heard cattle and horses go by, they did not report it. Even if the natives had slipped the herd past undetected in the dark, which seems unlikely, it is inconceivable they would not have left evidence of their passage. Yet none of the Mormon parties that traveled between Snake River and the fort during March reported seeing cattle tracks on this stretch, to the author's knowledge. They included Barnard and Watts on their heroic ride for help, B. F. Cummings's first party, Andrew Cunningham's rescue expedition, Cummings's returning mail party, and returning settlers. Only at Portneuf River at present Pocatello were tracks seen revealing that "several of our cattle had been taken to Soda Springs."[27]

This indicates that the Bannocks took the herd by the other route south, a well-traveled Indian trail that followed Salmon and Big Lost rivers on the line of U.S. 93 from present Salmon, Idaho, to the Snake River plain and the Oregon Trail's Jeffrey-Goodale Cutoff between Fort Hall and Fort Boise. If its upper stretch was mountainous and less suitable for cattle, its overall distance to Portneuf River was about the same as the Fort Limhi road. Moreover, it placed a mountain range between

[27]See Salmon River Mission Journal, 30 March and 6 April 1858. The route to Soda Springs followed the river south on the line of present I-15 to meet Hudspeth's Cutoff at McCammon, Idaho, then backtracked this California Trail shortcut on the line of today's U.S. 30 to Soda Springs on Bear River.

the natives and the fort and steered clear of Mormon parties on the same route. An arm of this horse trail left Salmon River at present Ellis, Idaho, to follow the Pahsimeroi and Little Lost rivers to Snake River. An estimate of how long it would take to move the cattle over this route to Portneuf River would make the tracks that Cummings saw on 30 March, showing that "our cattle had been taken toward Soda Springs," relatively fresh.[28]

Soon after, when Ficklin reached Snake River not far upstream, his animals were "so reduced by the suffering on the mountain," he later said, that he was forced to travel very slowly.[29] He did not describe his route to Soda Springs or say when he arrived there. But if he followed the same path he took going north, his party should have reached Bear River's big bend and Soda Springs at about the same time as the Indians. Even allowing a few days either way, it is not possible that Bannocks, Ficklin, and Powell could have been unaware of each other's presence at "beer springs" on the Oregon Trail. That the number of cattle had been sharply reduced by this time was shown by David Moore's report that returning settlers saw "several" of their cattle's tracks on Portneuf bottom.[30]

Now mounted on fresher horses, Ficklin pushed on from Soda Springs to cover the distance to Camp Scott, some 150 miles, at a rapid clip. On arriving on 10 April he learned for the first time that the crisis that had threatened four months before was now over. When he left, U.S. soldiers were under orders to treat armed Mormons as enemies. Now armed Mormons were escorting the territory's governor, Alfred Cumming, and Thomas L. Kane to Great Salt Lake City in response to Brigham Young's bid for peace. In December Ficklin had ridden over four hundred miles north into an uncharted region on a hazardous winter search for cattle to make up losses to Mormon raiders and ensure the survival of the U.S. Army's Utah Expedition and its dependents. Now he found out that Young, in an uncharacteristically generous offer, had just proposed to send two hundred cattle and up to twenty thousand pounds of flour to the Army, free of charge.

---

[28]Salmon River Mission Journal, 30 March 1858.

[29]Sen. Exec. Doc. 1 (35-2), 1858, 71.

[30]Salmon River Mission Journal, 6 April 1858.

It was hardly surprising that Ficklin took five days to write his deliberately vague report after arriving at Camp Scott. Some of his horses were so jaded, he said, that he left "one man and four animals on Bear river, with some Indians, whose arrival I am hourly expecting."[31] He failed to say who the Indians were, but his troubles with used-up horses seemed over by the time he arrived at Fort Bridger. "Ficklin came in yesterday, passing my line with some thirty ponies—all in fair condition," noted Capt. Albert Tracy on 11 April.

The Bannock warrior, Boo-e-wat, had headed for Camp Scott with three stolen horses from Fort Limhi before Cummings overtook him on 29 March at Mud Lake and recovered the animals. It is not unreasonable to question how many of the horses in "fair condition" that Ficklin delivered two weeks later came from the Mormon mission. Moreover, while he did not identify on 15 April the man he left on Bear River, whose arrival he expected "hourly," Colonel Johnston filled in that blank the following day, 16 April. He ordered the quartermaster that day to employ John W. Powell at the same generous rate of pay enjoyed by Ficklin himself.[32]

All of the above leaves unsolved the mystery of what happened to the vanishing herd. The best answer the author can offer is that out of fewer than two hundred head taken by the Bannocks, not enough animals outlasted native hunger during the season when game was scarce either to make a noticeable difference at the officers' mess or be conspicuous in army herds along Hams or Henrys forks. Certain it was that an unexpected addition of fresh beef to the rations then being doled out at the encampment would have caused rejoicing and comment. But to the author's knowledge there was no such celebration. So, if the question of "Where's the beef?" remains a mystery, the most likely answer was "in Bannock stomachs."

The Ficklin-Powell Duel

If Chief Snag's testimony and the timing of events appear to implicate Ficklin and Powell in a conspiracy to steal the Fort Limhi herd,

[31]Sen. Exec. Doc. 1 (35-2), 1858, 71.

[32]Porter to Dickerson, 16 April 1858, "Army of Utah," letters sent 1857–1861.

there remains the possibility that Ficklin was faithful to his orders but misled by his fellow Virginian. Frederick Burr gave this theory credence years later when he described Powell, his old partner, as "selfish, reckless, and able to despoil his best friend if he could."[33] It might also cast some light on the cause of a dispute between Ficklin and Powell so heated that the two determined to fight a duel to the death to settle it. Both were impetuous and hotheaded, and it took the district court for Green River County to put a stop to it.

Judge Delana R. Eckles on 16 May 1858 ordered the U.S. marshal to arrest both men on the charge of "threatening and agreeing to fight in mortal combat." Each pleaded not guilty the following day, but the new territorial chief justice thought otherwise. After hearing the case he found both men guilty and bound them to "keep the peace and be of good behavior towards all the good citizens of the said Territory" for three months. Their friends put up $2,000 in surety for each: Charles Mogo, Ch. Maurice Smith, and William Kearny for Powell, and Grier Tallmadge and H. F. Morrell for Ficklin. The judge further imposed court costs on both and levied an additional fine of $25 on Ficklin, the apparent instigator, for his contempt of court during the proceedings.[34]

Perhaps the greatest unanswered question is why Mormon authorities did not press their initial attack and demand a full investigation of the part Ficklin and Powell played, if any, in the attack on their faith's Northern Indian Mission. If they had wanted a thorough inquiry, they could have required Thomas Smith to file his complaint in one of the district courts before judges appointed by President Buchanan. Instead they avoided these benches, as they had done since their creation in 1850 under the national territorial organic act, and entered his affidavit before a probate court in which Utah lawmakers had vested both civil and criminal jurisdiction, ruled by a Mormon judge. Since the arriving district judges held that such powers violated the federal law, the court selection ensured that they and other non-Mormon appointees would ignore the charges.[35] Reasons not to pursue the issue included distrust of "gentile" justice born of experience in Missouri and Illinois.

---

[33]Burr to Stuart, 12 October 1868, Frederick H. Burr Journal and Letter.

[34]Minute Book and Naturalization Record, Dec. 7, 1857, to May 22, 1858, Book 4, Series 10035.

[35]Not until passage of the Poland Act in 1874 did Congress strip probate courts of the powers so liberally bestowed by Mormon lawmakers.

Although outspoken Apostle George A. Smith privately raged about the army's alleged use of Indian allies to a Mormon newspaperman, charging President Buchanan with "savage barbarity in employing the Indians to murder, butcher, roast and eat his countrymen," the LDS church dropped the matter.[36] It is reasonable to believe that Mormon authorities had no desire to provoke counter investigations into a number of atrocities that occurred in Utah Territory before and during their military showdown with the United States the year before. Foremost of these took place in September 1857, when Mormon militia and Southern Paiute Indians murdered some 120 Arkansas emigrants, men, women, and children, at a peaceful spot on the Spanish Trail to Los Angeles known as Mountain Meadows, near present Cedar City, Utah.[37]

Whatever the reason, the attack on Fort Limhi never received the investigation it deserved, and the episode soon faded from public notice as new alarms in the continuing confrontation between the western theocracy and its parent republic commanded official attention. Also forgotten was the strategic importance the northern outpost held for a time during the Mormon bid for independence in 1857 and 1858. But the men and women who faced the challenges of survival at the isolated Salmon River colony in the midst of the native peoples they knew as "Lamanites" would always remember the part they played in this great adventure. The many journals and biographies they left to their children and posterity speak of their pride in establishing the settlement in the northern Rocky Mountain wilderness, far from home and friends. Yet not all of them looked at the experience uncritically, and some took from it lessons that seem as true today as they proved to be then.

---

[36]Smith to Stenhouse, Provo, 7 June 1858, Historian's Office Letterbook, LDS Archives, 521.

[37]For the story of this crime, see Bagley, *Blood of the Prophets: Brigham Young and the Massacre at Mountain Meadows*.

GILBERT BELNAP

The independent-minded Canadian blamed grasshoppers and communal agricultural practices for Fort Limhi's downfall. A defender of the oppressed, the former revolutionist and marshal became LDS bishop at Hooper, Utah. *Courtesy of the Church Arhives, The Church of Jesus Christ of Latter-day Saints.*

Epilogue

> *I care not how much regard men have for their leader, nor the respect they have for the holy priesthood, when their means of subsistence are cut off and those dependent on them for their means of support are reduced to want, mankind are so organized by their Creator that they will make an extra exertion to free themselves from their distressed situation, for one hour of virtuous liberty on earth is worth a whole eternity of bondage.* — *Gilbert Belnap*

Millennial hopes rose almost as high as heaven itself in the year of the Lamanite, 1855, when the first party of Mormon missionaries left their homes in raw settlements in northern Utah to gather the "Remnants of the House of Jacob," the American Indians, in the northern Rocky Mountains. After twenty-five hundred years, the time had come for God's Kingdom to usher in the Second Coming of the Son of Man, as envisioned by the prophet Daniel, and fulfill its destiny to supersede all earthly realms, including the American republic. As a prelude to this longed-for day, the children of Israel in the wilderness must hear the gospel of their forebears, become as one, and join their white cousins in building New Jerusalem in Jackson County, Missouri. A nation would be born in a day.

Most of the twenty-seven men who established Fort Limhi and those who came after them demonstrated their dedication to this millennial purpose by their labor that first summer. In 1902, John V. Bluth, clerk of the Weber Stake of Zion and early Salmon River mission historian, interviewed survivors of this endeavor. "Those now living, and to whom access has been had for this account, say that they never worked so hard in their lives as during this summer in order to prepare themselves for winter, both as to needed supplies and as to the necessary protection and shelter from the hard winter and Indians," he said. "In addition to their labors in plowing, planting and building, they also aided the Indians in their fishing."[1] But faith and works together failed to sustain the dream after an American president ordered the U.S. Army to assert federal authority in Utah Territory, and the people that the Mormon proselytizers had sought to redeem turned against them and forced the abandonment of the Kingdom's northernmost colony.

Gilbert Belnap: We Were Like the Puritans

As the returning colonists dispersed in April 1858, a disappointed David Moore finished his record of the Indian mission, "which cost us some 200,000 dollars worth of Means & Labour besides the lives of three of our missionaries." For this heavy cost, he laid the blame squarely on the "plans and wicked devices of the Mountaineers and U.S. Troops & since made known by different Indians as well as whites."[2] Another Canadian, however, saw more fundamental shortcomings. Gilbert Belnap pointed his finger at the grasshopper plague and the communal economic doctrines imposed by Mormon leaders in the mountain West, where land belonged to God and was parceled out as inheritances that recipients could keep as long as they were faithful.[3]

Autobiography of Gilbert Belnap.

If the kingdom of God can be established in the tops of the mountains, and the Gospel preached to all nations, and Zion can be redeemed, and the poor can be gathered together in order that they may receive in common the blessings of the holy priesthood, and a whole people be sustained by such continuous draining of their substance, then I am willing to acknowledge that I understand not the course of human events. Two important causes have conspired against the interest of Fort Limhi. The first season the entire crop was cut off by the grasshopper and the second harvest was but small. The manner in which agriculture has been conducted served to dishearten the energetic and persevering.

In a measure we were like the Puritans in their first settlement in America as we held all things in common so far as related to the cultivation of the ground and the proceeds thereof. Previous to the year of 1611 during the settlement of Virginia no right of private ownership of property was estab-

---

[1]Bluth, "The Salmon River Mission," 3:11, September 1900, 807.

[2]Salmon River Mission Journal, 11 April 1858.

[3]See Bigler, *Forgotten Kingdom: The Mormon Theocracy in the American West, 1847–1896*, 37–39, 53–55.

> lished. The fields were cleared and cultivated by the joint labor of the whole and the proceeds were deposited in public stores and stored in common. This plan of proceeding presented but little inducement for industry. The idle trusted entirely to what was distributed from the common stores. This course has been too closely pursued to prove beneficial to us. If the plan adopted by Sir Thomas Dale in 1611 to remedy these evils had been adopted by us better results would have been manifest. Another assignment would have been necessary to satisfy the increasing demand of industry. In order to facilitate the settlement of a new country some plan must be entered into to attach men to the soil and induce them to regard it as their future homes.

Ironically, at the time of the Salmon River mission, the plan Belnap called for was already in place under the nation's land laws. In 1854 Congress extended this system to include Utah and provided for appointment of a surveyor general to survey the lands of the territory "preparatory to bringing the same into market."[4] But President Franklin Pierce's choice for this position, David H. Burr, former congressional cartographer and Frederick H. Burr's father, encountered such violent opposition that he fled from Utah in 1857. His letters to the U.S. General Land Office were among the documents President Buchanan sent to Congress in 1858 to justify dispatching U.S. troops to assert federal authority in the territory.[5] Not until 1869 would Utah's farmers gain ownership of the fields they harvested.

Meanwhile, those who served at Fort Limhi restored their losses and went on to new endeavors, some to win distinction, while some others who played a hand in the mission's downfall encountered retribution, divine or otherwise.

Few would match Gilbert Belnap's adventurous life or service to Mormonism. After his return from Fort Limhi, Brigham Young renewed his polygamous marriages to his wives Adaline Knight and Henrietta McBride, whose brother George would die the next February defending the Fort Limhi herd, on 17 July 1857 in the Endowment House. He served in Lot Smith's cavalry in late October 1857, and according to family lore Belnap joined a raiding party that "quietly placed lassoes

[4]See "An Act to Establish Territorial Government for Utah," *Acts, Resolutions and Memorials, Passed at the Several Annual Sessions of the Legislative Assembly of The Territory of Utah, from 1852 to 1870 Inclusive*, 25.

[5]See House Exec. Doc. 71 (35-1), 1858, 114–24.

around the tents in which U.S. soldiers were sleeping" and demolished the tents, "leaving the soldiers in the rain with no place to sleep." The next fall after his return from the relief of Fort Limhi and the move south, Belnap learned of a soldier at Camp Floyd named Belnap. "Wondering if the soldier could possibly be his brother Thomas, Gilbert loaded his wagon with produce and headed for Camp Floyd." Here Belnap was reunited with the brother he had not seen since leaving Canada in 1837. Naturally, according to this legend, Thomas Belnap had been bivouacked in one of the tents his brother's unit had torn down.

Elected sheriff of Weber County in August 1862, Belnap served four consecutive two-year terms, and his son and grandson later held the same office. He became the first presiding elder (and later bishop) at Hooper, Utah, in 1868 and served for twenty years. "He hated sham, dishonesty and oppression, was plain and outspoken and as brave as he was true to his convictions," wrote an LDS church historian. Gilbert Belnap died at Hooper on 26 February 1899, the husband of two wives and father of seventeen children.[6]

The Wild Life: John W. Powell

Described as "an educated gentleman" who had chosen "the wild life to civilization,"[7] the most likely instigator of the raid on Fort Limhi was born in Loudoun County, Virginia, in 1836. John W. Powell left the Old Dominion in 1853 at age seventeen and headed west to Great Salt Lake. There he met Frederick Burr and the two became occasional partners. The next year they drove a herd of four hundred cattle north to Bitterroot Valley where they arrived that fall and took up permanent residence in the mountains. Powell married a Bannock woman, learned the tribe's language fluently, and lived with the Bannocks, who regarded him as their headman. He was "light and young and active," but also combative, selfish, and hair-triggered.[8]

After his role in the Fort Limhi attack, Powell followed a varied career as trader, trapper, prospector, interpreter, lawman, and guide. In 1859

[6]Belnap Family Organization, Biography of Gilbert Belnap; and Jenson, ed., *Latter-day Saint Biographical Encyclopedia*, 2:747–48.

[7]Healy, "J. W. Powell and Fort Lemhi Told by Johnny Healy."

[8]Ibid. Also see Helming, *John W. Powell: An Historical Biography of a Notable Western Montana Mountain Man.*

he saved the notorious Boone Helm from starvation near Fort Hall before finding out that Helm was "the worst kind of desperado." His kindheartedness toward Montana's "most hardened, cool and deliberate scoundrel" made it necessary for the Virginia City Vigilantes five years later to choke off Helm's villainous career with a rope.[9] Powell was later elected Missoula County coroner, appointed deputy U.S. marshal, and named honorary member of the Historical Society of Montana. But his reckless nature was destined to prove his undoing.

"POWELL FELL ON HIS KNEES," *HELENA DAILY HERALD*, 17 MAY 1879.

A fatal shooting affray took place at Dewey's Flat twelve miles from this place, on Wednesday, the 7th last, between John Reeder and John W. Powell. The circumstances were as follows: Powell had a steer he wanted to kill and he went to A. M. Lebo, owner of a meat market, and obtained permission to use his slaughter house and tools for the purpose. Powell killed his steer, dressed it, hung it up in the slaughter house and came down town. Soon after Reeder who is an employee of Lebo's, went to the slaughter house with a band of cattle, inquired who owned the steer, and being told that it was Powell's got on his horse and rode down town. At the door of Walker & Manning's saloon he inquired if Powell was in. On being told that he was, Reeder alighted, went into the saloon and told Powell he wanted him to take his steer and entrails out of the slaughter house. Powell replied: "I won't do it, you s——." Reeder then struck Powell with the lash of a whip, when the latter put his hand behind him as if to draw a revolver. Reeder said, "You are heeled," and turned, got on his horse, went to the meat market, secured his 45 calibre gun, and stationed himself at the corner of the meat market. Powell, who was not "heeled," walked across the road to Madison's saloon, procured a gun, and started for the meat market. When about 60 feet distant Reeder called him and ordered him to lay down his gun. Powell said "shoot" and then jumped behind a Mr. Walker, who, frightened, ran away. Powell fell on his knees and received the fatal shot. The ball went through the left arm, into the left side and out of the right breast, making a terrible wound, killing him instantly.

The [coroners] jury disagreed as to whether the shooting was felonious or in self-defense.

John W. Powell's memory lives on today in the name of 10,300-foot Mount Powell, west of Deer Lodge, Montana, seat of Powell County,

[9]For Powell's account of this episode and Helm's execution, see Langford, *Vigilante Days and Ways: The Pioneers of the Rockies*, 78–81, 383–87; and Dimsdale, *The Vigilantes of Montana or Popular Justice in the Rocky Mountains*, 162–67.

both named in his honor. In 1993 Grace Helming of Wisdom, Montana, placed an attractive headstone on his grave at the town of Dewey on Big Hole River between Wise River and Divide. The mountaineer left at least ten children by three wives, all of whom were full or part Indian.[10]

Benjamin Franklin Ficklin

The man who lit the fuse, deliberately or not, that touched off the attack on Fort Limhi was one of western America's most colorful, if unchronicled, characters. Like Powell, "Ben" Ficklin was impetuous, energetic, and overconfident. By the time he led ten volunteers to the Flathead country to acquire cattle for the U.S. Army at Fort Bridger, he had already filled his thirty years with adventure. At Virginia Military Institute the free spirited Charlottesville native "never had his equal for mischief and pranks," but was also known as "the soul of honor, and the most popular man in the Corps." Expelled for firing a 12-pounder cannon on campus, he volunteered in the Mexican War and won promotion and reinstatement at V.M.I. by action on the battlefield. As the practical joker of his class, he made graduation memorable for its members in 1849 by "placing his diploma on the point of his bayonet and marching out of the hall."[11]

Following the 1857 Utah War, Ficklin joined the freighting firm of Russell, Majors & Waddell and probably conceived the idea of the Pony Express from St. Joseph, Missouri, to Sacramento, becoming superintendent of the mail service at Salt Lake City in 1860. An ardent southerner, he served during the Civil War as Virginia's quartermaster general, fought with "conspicuous gallantry" in the Battle of Malvern Hill, and became a Confederate purchasing agent in Europe and blockade-runner.[12] He was reportedly even detained as a possible conspirator in the Lincoln assassination but was released for lack of evidence. Later, he operated the Apache-infested San Antonio–San Diego mail route and other lines.

---

[10]For the best source of information on Powell, see Helming, *John W. Powell: An Historical Biography of a Notable Western Montana Mountain Man*. Also see Thrapp, *Encyclopedia of Frontier Biography*, 3:1168–69.

[11]Ficklin to Anderson, undated, but written by a descendant about 1910. Ficklin Collection.

[12]Ibid.

Ficklin, who owned Thomas Jefferson's estate at Monticello for a time, was known to care "nothing for wealth for himself—gave away as fast as he made money, often very unwisely." Of him his niece said: "Although so much of his life was passed in roughing it, as it were, he was one of the gentlest, most refined men I ever knew. His voice was low and sweet, and he was fastidious to a fault in his ideas of a lady's manner and dress. He never married; nor do I know that he ever had any serious affairs, though he frequently teased my sister and myself by telling us he was about to enlist in the married state. We considered him our special property, and did not wish a better-play fellow in his visits to us."[13]

Forty-four years of "braving every danger of land and sea" ended 12 March 1871 when he died "from getting a fish bone in his throat at the home of a friend in Georgetown, D.C."[14]

Lewis W. Shurtliff

Lewis Shurtliff escaped his religious obligation to marry Catherine, the Shoshone chief's daughter, and just before he married Louisa Moore, the two revisited the spot on the river where they had first met. There "we found two rose trees had grown and twined their slender branches together." They saw this as a sign of "future happiness" and "as the sun cast its last rays of light" upon the valley of Salmon River's east fork, they vowed "to love each other." But after the rosebushes had "come to perfection one of them faded and died," which caused the newlyweds "to look forward to the future with some anxiety."[15] The second omen sadly came true when Louisa Shurtliff died soon after their fourth child was born at Ogden in 1866. Not for six years would her husband remarry. And when he finally did, unlike his father, he limited his matrimonial accomplishments at the level of one wife. Lewis Shurtliff and Emily Wainwright had five children.

In the meantime one of the most high spirited and adventurous members of the Salmon River mission went on to become one of northern Utah's most respected leaders. Shurtliff became an LDS bishop at Plain

[13]Ibid.

[14]Ibid. The author is indebted to historian William P. MacKinnon and V.M.I. archivist Diane B. Jacob for the above information.

[15]Life and Travels of Lewis Warren Shurtliff.

City; a probate judge; president, Weber Stake of Zion; president of Ogden's first street railway firm; a top manager of Pioneer Electric Power; vice president of Utah Loan and Trust; a senator in the first Utah legislature after statehood in 1896; and an admired supporter of "every worthy cause."[16]

Chief Snag and Catherine

Less fortunate was Ti-o-von-du-ah, better known as Snag, nephew of Sacagawea of the Lewis and Clark expedition and friend of white people in general and the Mormon mission in particular. His son visited Utah and delivered letters from there to Fort Limhi. Snag became chief of the Shoshone group then called Sheepeaters, now the Lemhis, after the Blackfeet killed Sacagawea's brother, Cameahwait. He was baptized at Fort Limhi on 11 November 1855. Other family members joined the Mormons the following year, but not his daughter Catherine, who nearly became the wife of Lewis Shurtliff. She lived for a time with Frederick H. Burr before he left for California in 1857. She went back to him later that year on his return to Bitterroot Valley.

During Brigham Young's 1857 visit to the mission, James W. Cummings, Young's clerk, reported that the chief had been "wounded in the thigh by an accidental discharging of a pistol which causes a running sore out of which several pieces of bone have worked."[17] The injury never healed properly and made Snag lame.

Four years after the mission's abandonment, prospectors in July 1862 found gold on Grasshopper Creek, a Beaverhead tributary, less than fifty miles east of Fort Limhi on the Missouri River side of the Great Divide. A gold mining town, Bannack City, sprang up overnight. In addition to the law-abiding miners and evildoers of every stripe who rushed to the site, Chief Snag and his band camped on the outskirts of the lawless boomtown.

An Indian scare in June 1863 made it a bad time for Snag with others of his band to visit Bannack. After the notorious road agent Haze Lyons fired on Ten-doy, known as Bonapart (who escaped shouting,

[16]Whitney, *History of Utah,* 4:551.

[17]Cummings, "Travel of President Brigham Young to Oregon 1857," 11 May 1857.

"Good Indian", a local citizen warned the chief and his son to "ride off for their lives." Thomas Dimsdale described what followed:

> The son ran out and jumped on his horse. Old Snag stood in front of the door, on the edge of the ditch, leaning upon his gun, which was in a sole leather case. He had his lariat in his hand, and was talking to his daughter, Jemmy Spence's squaw, named Catherine. Buck Stinson, without saying a word, walking to within four feet of him, and drawing his revolver, shot him in the side. The Indian raised his right hand and said, "Oh! Don't." The answer was a ball in the neck, accompanied by the remark, enveloped in oaths, "I'll teach you to kill whites." And again he shot him through the head.

Snag was dead when the first citizen "attracted by the firing ran up."[18] Ten-doy became Lemhi chief the next day.

According to another account, Cyrus Skinner, another known scoundrel, "with savage brutality," scalped the old chief "who had always been friendly to the people."[19] Over the next eight months Stinson and Skinner, both road agents and killers, fell victim to the Vigilantes who imposed "popular justice" on a lawless region. "By a sudden twist of his head at the moment of his elevation," Dimsdale said with a note of satisfaction, the hangman's noose slipped under Stinson's chin at Bannack, "and he was some minutes in dying."[20] A Vigilante posse caught and hanged Skinner on Clark Fork in January 1864.

His murder avenged, Snag was later memorialized by his scalp, which reportedly was displayed for many years in a Salt Lake City bank. History granted not even this remembrance to Catherine.

George Washington Hill

George W. Hill was a born evangelist, and his outgoing personality and talent for understanding native languages and culture made him irresistible to Indians. The Ohioan had displayed his unusual gifts as an Indian missionary at Fort Limhi where he had talked Shoshones and Bannocks into the waters of baptism by dozens at a time. Called again at

---

[18]Dimsdale, *The Vigilantes of Montana or Popular Justice in the Rocky Mountains,* 51, 52. There are various widely differing accounts of Snag's shooting, but all agree that Stinson committed the unprovoked murder. Dimsdale's version appears to be the most accurate.

[19]Langford, *Vigilante Days and Ways: The Pioneers of the Rockies,* 180.

[20]Dimsdale, *The Vigilantes of Montana or Popular Justice in the Rocky Mountains,* 149.

age fifty-one as a missionary to the northern tribes, Hill in 1873 outdid even this amazing performance. At a time of cultural crisis among many Native American tribes, as well as renewed Mormon millennial expectations, he attracted so many Indians to the outskirts of a northern Utah town that the citizenry as a whole suffered a nervous breakdown.

In 1875 Hill located an Indian farm on Bear River, five miles from Corinne, then called "the Gentile capital of Utah," on the new transcontinental railroad west of Brigham City. As the word went out, potential Shoshone converts came from as far away as Fort Hall and the Wind River country of Wyoming to seek food and teaching in the arts of agriculture and hear the persuasive Ohioan. But the native gathering on the outskirts of their town, which soon grew to some two thousand, frightened the citizens of Corinne. Adding to such fears were rumors that Hill told the Indians that "the Bear River Valley belonged to them, and if the soldiers attempted to drive them away not to go, as their guns would have no effect upon them."[21]

The volatile mix of mysticism and misunderstanding exploded on 9 August 1875 when Corinne's newspaper announced the town was about to be massacred. Women and children holed up in the local hotel while men broke into a government arms shipment at the railroad depot for weapons to defend the place. A call for troops from the U.S. Army post at Fort Douglas brought soldiers to the rescue, but by the time they came, the Indian scare was over. Their captain told Hill to move his Indian camp away from the town and stop frightening people.

One of western America's most fruitful Indian missionaries, George Washington Hill lived to age sixty-nine when he left a wife, nine children, and an unequaled record in his faith for converting Indians in their own languages.

THOMAS SASSON SMITH

As Hill was a born Indian missionary, Thomas Smith's commonsense leadership qualities made him a natural western colonizer for his faith. Even before establishing the Salmon River settlement, he had been a

[21]Report of W. H. Danilson, Annual Report of the Commissioner of Indian Affairs, 1875, House Exec. Doc. I (44-1). This apparently referred to the Mormon undergarment, which, the natives were allegedly told, was bullet proof.

member of the Iron Mission sent to southern Utah in 1850 to start an iron-making industry near Cedar City. The poor quality of southern Utah iron ore and coal eventually defeated this effort, despite persistent efforts over more than two decades. Six years after Salmon River mission's abandonment, he was named to head the Cotton, or Muddy Mission, to grow cotton on the Muddy River, near present Overton in southern Nevada, fifty miles east of Las Vegas. His final and most successful colonizing venture came in 1883, when at age sixty-six he founded Mormon settlements on the upper Snake River in today's southern Idaho where he died in 1890.[22]

Benjamin Franklin Cummings

During the millennial enthusiasm and expectation of 1855 and 1856 and subsequent armed confrontation with the United States, B. F. "Frank" Cummings fulfilled assignments of high importance for an expansionist Mormon theocracy in the American West. A capable but retiring man by nature, he had acted as president of a major settlement, represented Brigham Young in negotiations with Hudson's Bay Company for the purchase of Fort Hall, and as an officer of the Nauvoo Legion led a battalion of Mormon infantry north to Soda Springs to block an attempt by U.S. troops to enter Salt Lake Valley from the north, among other tasks. To all of these duties he applied the qualities for which he was known. He was "the possessor of a fine mind, was a deep thinker, and had the power to express himself in clear and forceful language."[23]

Afterward, Cummings settled into a routine generally typical for most of the 116 men, women, and children who served at Fort Limhi from 1855 to 1858.[24] Life was more predictable during the following decades of political confrontation between the Mormon Kingdom and the United States as a revolutionary religious movement gradually evolved into a bastion of conservative American values. As a carpenter and millwright, he operated a sawmill, worked in a church factory, and farmed.

[22]See Rice, "Thomas Sasson Smith and Fort Lemhi," 80–85.

[23]Jenson, *Latter-day Saint Biographical Encyclopedia,* 3:621.

[24]For a complete list of those who served as missionaries, hired hands, or family members, see Appendix A: Comprehensive List of Missionaries, Family Members, and Hired Hands Who Served at Fort Limhi from May 1855 to April 1858.

Then, with a new millennial expectancy on the horizon, Cummings in 1878 was sent to reclaim the former members of his faith in Iowa and Nebraska, who had left the Utah church. The 1847 Utah pioneer died at Salt Lake City in 1899.

To prepare for a projected Second Coming in 1890–1891, other aging alumni of Fort Limhi, like George Hill, were sent once more to redeem the "remnants of Jacob" now on reservations. Amos Wright journeyed 1,200 miles with Mormon apostles Moses Thatcher and Lorenzo Snow in 1883 to meet "chiefs of the Crows, Flathead, Blackfeet, Sioux and Shoshone Indians" in Montana, Idaho, and Wyoming. He also claimed that he baptized the renowned Shoshone Chief Washakee, a conversion target of many Christian faiths.[25]

The Ruins of a World

"Before the advent of the Mormons into the Salmon River country in 1855, the area was so unlivable that no one but an occasional trapper risked staying to exploit the resources, and even they did not stay for any length of time," wrote Limhi mission chronicler Kate B. Carter in 1963, ignoring the fishers and hunters who had made their homes on the bounteous river since time immemorial. Paraphrasing Washington Irving, Carter described the Salmon River country as "a land where no man permanently resides; a vast uninhabited solitude, with precipitous cliffs and yawning ravines looking like the ruins of a world." But she acknowledged, "this huge expanse of land was known to be a stronghold of the redman who, for many centuries, had claimed the wild animals of the forest, the fish in the streams, and the rugged terrain as 'his country.'"[26]

Salmon River was Indian country before the first white settlers arrived in 1855, and it would be Indian country, if not for long, when they abandoned their hard-won homes in 1858. Not for sixty years would Mormon settlers return to the valley of Salmon River's east fork, now named Lemhi River in a misspelling of the earlier and almost forgotten colony. Those who preceded them are now remembered, when

[25]Anderson, Winifred (Gwen), My Father Said . . . A Story of the Life of Amos R. Wright, 18. Apparently unsure which was right, Washakie requested baptism by missionaries of several faiths before he died.

[26]Carter, The Salmon River Mission, 1.

A remnant of Fort Limhi's mud corral today marks the northernmost limit of the Mormon theocracy's expansion during the 1850s. *Photo by author.*

remembered at all, for such commonplace deeds as establishing the first white settlement, excavating the first irrigation ditch, or building the first fence in present Idaho. But they did much more than these ordinary achievements, however praiseworthy. For they advanced into Oregon Territory the standard of God's Kingdom and upheld it for three years in a hostile environment, nearly four hundred miles from the Chief Stake of Zion in Salt Lake Valley.

The remains of Fort Limhi today represent the northernmost limit of the Mormon theocracy's expansion from 1847 to 1859 as it audaciously challenged the legitimacy of the American republic's authority to govern and moved to fulfill its destiny of universal dominion. This ruin of mud is the only physical evidence of the sacrifice and suffering of the men and women who came to the farthest edge of the frontier with the best of intentions, hoping to build their homes and redeem the original inhabitants, whose dream died in an inescapable clash of cultures. The crumbling adobe wall of the corral that "Big Rogue," Chief Shou-woo-coo, examined so carefully early in 1858 is all that is left to commemorate the end of their Kingdom's bid for sovereignty in 1857, but it also marks the beginning of its transformation from a revolutionary millennial movement into a respected institution of American society.

Appendix A

A Comprehensive List of Missionaries, Family Members, and Hired Hands Who Served at Fort Limhi from May 1855 to April 1858

Thomas Marsh Abbott
James Riley Allred
Ira Ames, Jr.
George Washington Barber
William Bard
Ezra Jacob Wyckoff Barnard
John Porter Barnard, Jr.
Mormon Lachonias Barnard
William H. Batchelor
Gilbert Belnap
Thomas Bingham
Jonathan Slocum Bowen
Joseph Leonard Bowen
Clifton Smith Browning
John W. Browning
William L. Brundage
William Burch
William Burgess, Jr.
Thomas Butterfield
Cyrus Edward Clark
Elizabeth Angeline Tuttle Clark
Emily Jane Pearson Clark
Israel Justus Clark
James Israel Clark
Jesse Tuttle Clark
Henry Alanson Cleveland
Henry Rogers Cleveland
Reuben Collett
Sylvanus Collett
Thomas Corless
Benjamin Franklin Cummings
Charles Dalton
Eunice Daniels Dalton
John Luther Dalton
Thomas Day, Jr.
Owen T. Dix
Crandall Dunn
Francillo Durfee
Cynthia Harrington Bowen Durfee
Emma Durfee
John Galliher
Mary Adelia Hardy Gheen
Stephen Harris Gheen
George Roberts Grant
Eliza Jane Bowen Hadlock
Eliza Maranda Hadlock
Hathron Chauncy Hadlock
Sally Louisa Hadlock
Milton Datus Hammond
Joseph Henry Harker
Henry Martin Harmon
Susan Marler Harmon
Martin Henderson Harris
Alexander Hood Hill
George Washington Hill
James Hood Hill

*William Bailey Lake
Nathaniel Leavitt
Everet Lish
Mrs. Everet Lish
Richard Bishop Margetts
William Norton Marler
*George McBride
James McBride
Charles Aron McGary
Charlotte McGary
Wallace Marshall McIntire
Charles Franklin Middleton
Frederick Andrus Miller
Jacob Miller
*James Thadeas Miller
Francis Marion Molen
David Moore
Susan Vorce Moore
Henry Nebeker
Joseph Parry
William J. Perkins
Alice Stowell Perry
Cynthia Earnestine Perry
William Howard Perry
William Stephen Perry
John Preece
Andrew Quigley, Jr.
Ebenezer Jay Robinson
Oliver Lee Robinson
Orson Hyde Rose
William Montgomery Shaw
Isaac Monroe Shepard
Elsemina Emergene Shurtliff
Hascaline Shurtliff
Haskell Albert Shurtliff
Haskell Vincent Shurtliff
Lewis Warren Shurtliff
Louisa Catherine Smith Moore Shurtliff
Mary Ann Shurtliff
Ann Smith
Catherine Van Velsor Smith
Elizabeth Smith
Helen Maria Fox Smith
Henry Smith
Jesse W. Smith
Jesse William Smith
Thomas Sasson Smith
William Smith
David Henderson Stephens
Jane Narcissus Shurtliff Taylor
Levi Taylor
Pleasant Green Taylor
William Riley Taylor
James John Walker
Baldwin Harvey Watts
Pardon Knapp Webb
Fountain Welch
James David Wilcox
Amos Russell Wright
Abraham Zundel

*Killed by Indians

Appendix B

Members of Brigham Young's Company to Fort Limhi in April–May 1857, as Recorded by James W. Cummings, Clerk of the Camp

1st Ten
1. Prest. Brigham Young
2. Lucy A. Young
3. Clara Young
4. Zina Young
5. Joseph A. Young
6. Brigham Young, Jr.
7. John W. Young
8. [Brigham Heber] Young
9. Oscar Young
10. Henry S. Jacobs
11. Andrew Moffitt
12. Perry Decker
13. Joseph Elder
14. Pres. Heber C. Kimball
15. Sarah Ann Kimball
16. William H. Kimball
17. Lucy Kimball
18. Charles Kimball
19 George Bartholomew
20. Bemas H. Quigley
21. Prest. Daniel H. Wells
22. Arza Hin[c]kle[y]
23. Stephen Taylor
24. Patriarch John Young
25. Sarah Young
26. David Fairbanks
27. John M. Chidester
28. Isaac Chase
29. Orson Hyde
30. Joshua Whitney
31. Louisa Chase

2nd Ten
32. Robt. T. Burton
33. Lot Smith
34. Leonard Rice
35. Howard Egan
36. Patrick Lynch
37. William [George D.] Grant
38. James M. Barlow
39. William C. Dunbar
40. J. D. T. McAllister
41. James Ferguson
42. F. D. Richards
43. Heber J. Richards
44. J. L. Haywood [Heywood]
45. Mary B. Haywood [Heywood]
46. Lorenzo Snow
47. John Bankhead
48. John Reese
49. H. P. Jensen
50. John Neff
51. J. W. Cummings
52. Elijah F. Sheetes
53. William H. Dame

54. Thomas D. Brown
55. N. V. Jones
56. A. Carrington
57. Fred. Kesler
58. Ormus E. Bates
59. John Smith Patriarch
60. C. A. Huntington
61. Henry Heath
62. Saml. L. Sprague Dr
63. Saml. L. Sprague, Jr.
64. John W. Cooley
65. Jesse W. Fox

3rd Ten

66. Chauncey W. West
67. Mary West
68. Jesse C. Little
69. Emily H. Little
70. Charles Little
71. Abraham Hoagland
72. E. W. East
73. Lorin Far[r]
74. Nicholina Far[r]
75. Enoch Farr
76. Seth M. Blair
77. Texana Blair
78. Franklin Woolley
79. Olive Woolley
80. John W. Woolley
81. John Pack
82. Mary Jane Pack
83. George C. Pack
84. Thomas Dunn
85. Charlotte Dunn
86. Erastus Bingham, Sr.
87. Lucinda Bingham
88. Thomas Bingham
89. Verlum [Verulam] Dive[s]
90. John Doudle [Dowdle]
91. Jennet [Jeanette] Dive[s]

4th Ten

92. George Peacock
93. Warren Snow
94. Edwin Whiting
95. D. B. Funk
96. Sarah E. Snow
97. Elijah Everett [Elisha Averett]
98. John Lowery, Jr.
99. L. D. Bunce
100. Milo Andrus
101. Margaret Andrus
102. William T. Vannoy [Van Noy]
103. William S. Covitt
104. Thos. S. Smith
105. Henry Smith
106. [Pleasant] Green Taylor
107. Lewis W. Shurtliff
108. John Preece
109. John Leonard
110. Hector D. Haight
111. Dimick B. Huntington
112. Indian Chief Aropene &
113. Wispit his wife
114. L. E. Harrington
115. John Mercer
116. James C. Snow
117. Elias H. Blackburn
118. Henson Walker
119. John Holman
120. Stillman Riston
121. David Jones
122. Amos Wright

5th Ten
123. John Nebeker
124. E. B. Tripp
125. Martin H. Peck
126. David Evans
127. John Brown
128. Wm. Fotheringham
129. John S. Higbee
130. Wm. W. Rust
131. Phillip Garner
132. Lewis Hardie
133. Bates Nobles
134. Richard Ballantine [Ballantyne]
135. Charles Taylor
136. Thos. Rhoads
137. Francis [Frances] Burch
138. Elizabeth Burch
139. William Camp
140. Leonard I. Smith
141. James Craigun [Cragun]
142. Ann Evans

Appendix C

A Report of Brigham Young's Expedition to Oregon Territory

"Excursion to Fort Limhi"

Deseret News, Great Salt Lake City, U.T., 10 June 1857, 108/4–109/3.

His Excellency, Governor Young, Presidents Heber C. Kimball and Daniel H. Wells and Elders Orson Hyde and Franklin D. Richards with several others left this city on Friday, the 24th of April, to visit the settlement on Salmon river, to rest their minds, to invigorate their bodies, and to examine the intermediate country. The company reached Brigham City on the afternoon of the 25th, attended meeting there during the forenoon of Sunday, the 26th, were joined by Elder L. Snow and others of that city and several from Ogden City, East Ogden and Willow Creek, and in the afternoon passed on to Bear River ferry, crossed over, camped on the right bank and organized by unanimously electing Prests. B. Young, H. C. Kimball and D. H. Wells, Presidents of the company; Elders O. Hyde, F. D. Richards and L. Snow, Chaplains; Robert T. Burton, Captain; J. C. Little, Marshal; Warren S. Snow, Sergeant of the Guard; A. Carrington, Jesse W. Fox and T. D. Brown, Engineers; J. W. Cummings and T. D. Brown, Clerks; with a Captain to each of the five tens. The organized company comprised 115 men, 22 women and 5 boys, with 168 horses and mules, 54 wagons and carriages, and 2 light boats with deck planks for ferrying.

On the 27th and 28th the general course was a little west of North, up Bear river to the ford then deflecting westerly into Malad Valley, which opens onto Bear river, and up that valley, crossing several small tributaries to the Malad, also its left hand fork, and camping on the 28th near the head spring of the right hand branch of the right fork of the Malad where the Hudspeth Cutoff in the California road crosses. The Malad valley, from its southern extremity to the cross range of mountains between the main right and left forks, has a varying width of from 4 to 10 miles, has a generally fertile soil, a surface peculiarly well adapted to irrigation, is well grassed, tolerably well watered, rather scantily supplied with fuel and timber, and is bounded on the East and West by ranges of low mountains, the points and peaks of the western range being smoothly rounded and covered with grass nearly to their summits. Taken together it is much the best locality for settlement of any observed on the route beyond Bear river.

From the junction with the Hudspeth Cutoff the new track made by the settlers in going to Limhi leads northwesterly, and by a smooth, somewhat winding and gradual ascent in about six miles reaches the summit of the northern rim of the Basin, 133.4 miles from G. S. L. City. From this point the descent is rather rapid down the crest of a narrow and rocky spur ridge into Bannack valley, which has a general course N 10 W, averages about four miles wide, is tolerably well grassed in some portions, very sparsely timbered, opens onto Shanghi Plain, (the great desert region surrounding the Three Buttes) and is bounded on the east by the Basin rim and its spur ranges and on the west by a rugged range which blends with the Goose Creek mountains. The Bannack is a small stream with a sluggish current until it is joined by its right hand fork which considerably increases the volume and speed, after which it soon enters the Plain and runs a more westerly course in a narrow, steep-banked channel to its outlet into Snake river some three miles below the mouth of the Portneuf. A few small willows, birch, and alder fringe the Bannack.

From the mouth of Bannack valley the road enters upon the southern border of Shanghi Plain, and keeping a general course a few degrees east of North intersects the emigrant road from the States to Oregon some six miles S by E from Fort Hall, and follows that road across the bridges over the Portneuf and Ross Creek, when it leaves the old road to the right and strikes Snake river from one fourth to one half a mile below the mouth of Blackfoot Fork, and 193.3 miles from G. S. L. City. The Portneuf issues from the hills a few miles above the bridge, which is some six miles S. E. of Fort Hall, and at the bridge runs with a rapid current five feet deep by forty feet wide, being swollen by the melting of the snow. The narrow strip of bottom land upon this stream is rendered nearly useless by alkaline patches, sloughs, and the numerous spring runs that burst forth along the base of the upland banks. There is a narrow margin of good land along Ross Creek, and the first low hills east of the road are well clothed with grass, but timber would have to be obtained from the rugged mountains some twenty or more miles further east.

Reached Snake River by noon of May 1, when a wharf was built on the left bank and the boats at once prepared for ferrying, and by 10 p.m. the company and their vehicles were all safely crossed over, at an average of nine minutes to a wagon, including a rest of about half an hour. The animals were all safely swam on the morning of the 2d. This River, though very low for the time of year, is at the ferry about 130 yards wide and 8 feet deep in the center of the channel with a strong current, but has little bottom land so far as we traveled upon its bank above the ferry, a distance of 56.5 miles in a north-easterly direction, is plentifully supplied with islands, has the customary willow fringe with a few small, scattering cottonwoods, a few currant bushes just blossoming, still fewer dwarf cedar, and is crossed by several belts of black volcanic rock.

Among the pebbles and boulders thickly strewn on the banks of Snake River, sandstones and lime-stones of various qualities are the characteristic kinds, interspersed with numerous specimens of granite and a few of porphery.

The ford on Snake River is 13.5 miles above the ferry, at a point where three islands divide the river into four channels, but the water, though low for the season, was too high for crossing with wagons, as was also the Blackfoot Fork.

Should travel ever warrant the alteration, the ferrying point should be near the ford and a bridge be made across Blackfoot, thus shortening and otherwise bettering the route.

Meeting was held in the forenoon of Sunday, May 3, during which Elders L. Snow, F. D. Richards and O. Hyde and Prests. B. Young and H. C. Kimball made instructive and appropriate remarks upon union, conduct in traveling, &c.

The general course from leaving Snake River to where the road strikes Spring Creek [Birch Creek] is W by S for 43.2 miles, crossing a small sluggish stream called Kamas and passing by a small pond named Muddy Lake, into which the Kamas empties.

The circuitous route from near Fort Hall to Spring Creek is caused by the want of grass and water in the region of the Three Buttes, there being no other apparent hindrance to traveling across that portion of Shanghi Plain, except breaking a track through the sage which almost every where densely clothes it.

Spring Creek, where the road strikes it, was some 10 feet wide by 1 1/2 deep, with a gravelly bed and rapid current; is fringed with small willows, birch, and alders interspersed with a few small cottonwoods, and either sinks or forms a pond a few miles below. The valley here opens into Shanghi Plain, has an average width of some 5 miles, a general course N 30 W , is rather poorly grassed and is bounded on the East by a long, lime-stone spur range from the Rocky Mountains and on the West by the high, rugged, East flanking range of the Salmon River Mountains.

The ascent to [the] summit of Spring Creek Pass, a distance of 37 miles and 330 miles from G. S. L. City, is very smooth and gradual, as is also the descent, with the exception of a few smooth ascents and descents in the pass, caused by table land cross ranges connecting the Rocky and Salmon River Mountains.

From this pass the course is north-westerly down the right hand fork of Salmon river, from near the source of its headwaters in the Rocky Mountains, to Fort Limhi, a distance of 49 miles, and 379 miles from G. S. L. City. A few miles N.E. from the mouth of Little Muddy, a small affluent to the right bank of Deer creek which is the first branch of Salmon river intersected by the road, is a narrow gorge in the Rocky Mountains (which here are not very lofty and terminate abruptly on the bench land) through which it is said to be only some three or four miles from the waters of Salmon to the waters of Missouri river. The right hand fork of Salmon river, from its source in the Rocky and Salmon River mountains to its junction with the left hand fork, some 20 miles below Limhi, has but little bottom land and no valley, and may be said to run in merely an open kanyon. It has the usual willow, birch, and alder fringe, until within a few miles above Limhi, from which point small cottonwoods thickly cover the narrow bottoms. The left hand fork of Salmon river rises in Kamas valley in the Salmon River mountains at an estimated distance of 120 miles west of Limhi, and pursuing a north-easterly course joins the right hand fork and both run in a still narrower kanyon for some 20 miles when the river enters the mountains. The left fork of Salmon river is stated to be nearly twice the size of the right, which at Fort Limhi was some 25 yards wide and two feet deep, with a rapid current and gravelly bed.

The company reached Fort Limhi at 6 p.m. of Friday, May 8. This fort is a neat stockade inclosing a space 16 rods square, and has a large and securely fenced yard for animals, and a small grist mill not yet finished, though sufficiently so to be used. It is located on the bench land a short distance from the right bank of Salmon river, and has two good sized fields mostly plowed and sown, in which the crops look promising, considering the coolness and consequent lateness of the season. The big and red sided salmon are said to be very plenty here in their season, for which we were about a month too soon; but a few red sided salmon were purchased from the Indians. They are a fine flavored fish, and average about two and a half feet in length. A few Bannack Indians had pitched their lodges adjacent to the fort, among whom Governor Young distributed many presents of blankets, &c., on the 11th of May, which were very gladly received.

During the stay of four days and a half at Fort Limhi the weather was generally cool and cloudy, affording but little opportunity for observations for latitude and longitude, though two for latitude and one for time were obtained. The positions of the clouds precluded so good an observation for time as could have been wished, and other duties have hitherto prevented a discussion for the results, which have to be omitted till a future date.

Sunday, May 10, a meeting was held in the fort, and Prest. B. Young, Elders O.

Hyde, F. D. Richards and L. Snow, Prest. H. C. Kimball and D. H. Wells, Patriarch and President John Young, and President Thomas S. Smith severally addressed the congregation, and gave some excellent instructions. In the afternoon Snack [Snag], the head chief of this tribe of the Bannacks, and several other Indians came into the fort and had a smoke and a long and very friendly talk in which Arrapeen, head chief of the Utahs, and who accompanied the expedition, participated.

Sandstone of an excellent quality for grindstones and a very superior chalk are found a few miles below the fort, and coal is reported about 25 miles below, but the beds have not been examined.

There is a very good pass through the Rocky Mountains east of Fort Limhi, through which is it said to be only some 10 to 15 miles from the fort to Horse Prairie and the waters of the Missouri River.

Left Fort Limhi at noon of Wednesday, May 13, and arrived in G. S. L. City at 6:30 p.m. of May 26, having had a very pleasant trip out and back, and been absent 33 days.

The weather was very pleasant for traveling, except the evening, night, and day of May 7–8, during which it snowed quite rapidly at times, but soon melted; the evening, night and morning of May 14–15 which were rendered very disagreeable by a high, cold north wind causing the coldest weather any of the company had ever experienced at like date, and forming ice more than half an inch thick in buckets, and finishing up with a snow squall in Spring creek pass from 11 a.m. until noon of the 15th; and a heavy rain on Snake river from 7 a.m. of May 18 to 11:30 a.m. of the 19th, which thoroughly soaked the very dry soil to the depth of several inches, and made the road quite muddy until evening.

At Bear river, returning, Governor Young expressed his unalloyed gratification with the peace, good order, harmony and alacrity invariably displayed by each member of the company and welcomed them to the free use of two boats which he had built and transported to Snake river and back expressly for their use, a distance of 193 miles, also to the ferriage at Bear river without charge, which was quite a sum at the legal rates of toll for so large a company. A united and most heartfelt vote of thanks was returned to our President for his fatherly care and kindness, for his prudent mode of regulating the travel, noon halts, and camps, and for his most excellent example, counsels and instruction during the journey.

In the different settlements where the company halted they were very hospitably received and entertained, and at Brigham city, on their return, the whole company were seated at tables tastefully arranged and sumptuously furnished in the large basement room of the public hall, the upper rooms being not yet finished.

The road track is generally very good (being smooth and level for a mountainous country) with the exception of a few boggy places and bench land hills on Salmon river, the volcanic rock belts and sandy stretches on Shanghi plain, and the northern slope of the rim of the Basin.

With regard to the extensive region of country passed through beyond the Malad valley, suffice it to say that so far as was observed on the immediate line of travel, or could be seen to the right and left of the route and beyond Limhi, the whole of that extensive region is of but little worth save to answer the purpose of connecting territory which might otherwise be separated by a great gulf.

In this brief sketch of the journey and country but little allusion has been made to courses and distances, they being given in the accompanying table. The distances INCLUDE the turnings to and from noon halts and camps.

Courses and Distances from Great Salt Lake City to Fort Limhi on Salmon River

Localities.	Courses.	Distances	From G. S. L. City
Farmington		15.913	15.913
Ogden City		20.801	36.714
Box Elder		22.049	58.763
Bear River Ferry		11.773	70.536
Bear River Ford		9.095	79.631
1st Spring Creek		11.400	91.031
Barnard's Fort		2.585	93.616
Utah and Oregon Line		2.390	96.006
Henderson Creek		5.588	101.594
Willow Spring		4.270	105.864
Deep Creek	N. 20 W.	4.298	110.162
Muddy Creek		3.040	113.202
Lower Creek		7.484	120.686
1st Crossing Malad		1.401	122.087
Malad Fork		4.376	126.463
Head of Malad		1.135	127.598
Summit of Basin		5.820	133.418
Bannack Creek		3.772	137.190
1st Crossing of Bannack		1.989	139.179
Camp on Bannack		7.992	147.171
Crossing of Bannack	N. 10 W.	8.127	155.298
Right Fork of Bannack		9.564	164.862

Bannack Bench		3.394	168.256
Junction with Oregon & California Road		4.277	172.533
Portneuf River	N. 101-2W.	4.624	177.157
Ross' Branch		7.750	184.907
Snake River Ferry		8.400	193.307
Snake River Ford		13.474	206.781
Snake River	N. 271-2 E.	10.401	217.182
Cedar Point		7.292	224.474
Snake River		16.630	241.104
Leave Snake River	N. 14 E.	8.723	249.827
Kamas Creek	N. 46 W.	15.082	264.909
Muddy Lake	S. 881-2 W.	5.376	270.285
Summit Point	N.731-2W	4.227	274.512
Spring Creek		18.511	293.023
Camp on Spring Creek		9.525	302.548
1st Crossing of Spring Cr.		4.663	307.211
2d do.	N. 30 W.	2.076	309.287
3rd do.		3.868	313.155
Bear Creek		11.765	324.920
Summit of Divide		5.216	330.136
Deer Creek, 1st Crossing	N. 34 W.	5.668	335.804
2d Crossing Deer Creek		6.656	342.460
1st Fork Salmon River		7.121	349.581
2d do	N. 431-2 W.	0.341	349.922
Camp on Salmon River		5.951	355.873
Summit of Mountain Spr.		14.227	370.100
2d Creek Crossing	N. 12 W.	6.764	376.864
Fort Limhi		2.076	378.940

Compass courses and odometer readings and calculations by Territorial Surveyor General Jesse W. Fox. Two brass odometers were used, and it is highly creditable to the correctness of the instruments and the care and accuracy of Mr. Fox, that they differed only about one half a mile in the whole 379 miles, which is easily accounted for in the difference of driving, noon halting, and camping with two vehicles, over so long a distance in even the same company.—[Ed. 'News.']

Bibliography

Abbreviations

CtY	Yale University, Yale Collection of Western Americana, Beinecke Library, New Haven, Connecticut
CU-B	University of California, H. H. Bancroft Library, Berkeley, California
DNA	National Archives, Washington, D. C.
UAr	Utah State Archives, Salt Lake City, Utah
UHi	Utah State Historical Society, Salt Lake City, Utah
ULA	Utah State University, Logan, Utah
UPB	Brigham Young University, Harold B. Lee Library, Provo, Utah
USIc	Church Historical Department, Church of Jesus Christ of Latter-day Saints, Salt Lake City, Utah
UU	University of Utah, Marriott Library, Salt Lake City

Books and Pamphlets

Andersen, Winifred (Gwen) Dunn. *My Grandfather Said . . . A Story of the Life of Amos R. Wright.* Lehi, Utah: Free Press Publishing, 1956.

Arrington, Leonard J. *Great Basin Kingdom: An Economic History of the Latter-day Saints.* Cambridge: Harvard Univ. Press, 1958. Reprinted, S.L.C: Univ. of Utah Press, 1993.

___________. *Brigham Young: American Moses.* N.Y: Alfred A. Knopf, 1985.

___________. *History of Idaho,* 2 vols. Moscow and Boise: Univ. of Idaho Press and Idaho State Hist. Soc., 1994.

Bagley, Will. *Blood of the Prophets: Brigham Young and the Massacre at Mountain Meadows.* Norman: Univ. of Okla. Press, 2002.

___________. *Frontiersman: Abner Blackburn's Narrative.* S.L.C: Univ. of Utah Press, 1992.

___________. *A Road from El Dorado: The 1848 Trail Journal of Ephraim Green.* S.L.C: Prairie Dog Press, 1991.

Bigler, David L. *Forgotten Kingdom: The Mormon Theocracy in the American West, 1847–1896.* Spokane, Wash: Arthur H. Clark, 1998; paperback edition, Logan: Utah State Univ. Press, 1998.

___________, ed. *A Winter with the Mormons: The 1852 Letters of Jotham Goodell.* S.L.C: Tanner Trust Fund and Marriott Library, Univ. of Utah, 2001.

Bishop, Guy. *Henry William Bigler: Soldier, Gold Miner, Missionary, Chronicler, 1815–1900.* Logan: Utah State Univ. Press, 1998.

Black, Susan Easton. *Early Members of the Church of Jesus Christ of Latter-day Saints, 1830–1848,* 50 vols. Provo, Utah: Religious Studies Center, Brigham Young Univ.

Brooks, Juanita. *The Mountain Meadows Massacre.* Stanford, 1950. Revised Edition, Norman: Univ. of Okla. Press, 1962. New Edition, 1970.

__________, ed. *Journal of the Southern Indian Mission, Diary of Thomas D. Brown.* Logan: Utah State Univ. Press, 1964.

__________, ed. *Not by Bread Alone: The Journal of Martha Spence Heywood, 1850–1856.* S.L.C: Utah State Hist. Soc., 1978.

__________, ed. *On the Mormon Frontier: The Diary of Hosea Stout,* 2 vols. S.L.C: Univ. of Utah Press, 1964. Reprint Edition, 1982.

Burns, Robert Ignatius, S.J. *The Jesuits and the Indian Wars of the Northwest.* New Haven: Yale Univ. Press, 1966.

Campbell, Eugene E. *Establishing Zion: The Mormon Church in the American West, 1847–1869.* S.L.C: Signature Books, 1988.

Carter, Kate B. *The Salmon River Mission.* S.L.C: Utah Printing Co., 1963.

__________, comp. *Heart Throbs of the West,* 12 vols. S.L.C: Daughters of Utah Pioneers, 1939–51.

__________, comp. *Our Pioneer Heritage,* 18 vols. S.L.C: Daughters of Utah Pioneers, 1958–75.

__________, comp. *Treasures of Pioneer History,* 6 vols. S.L.C: Daughters of Utah Pioneers, 1952–57.

Carvalho, S. N. *Incidents of Travel and Adventures in The Far West.* N.Y: Derby & Jackson, 1857.

Cooley, Everett L., ed. *Diary of Brigham Young 1857.* S.L.C: Tanner Trust Fund, 1980.

Cradlebaugh, John. *Utah and the Mormons: Speech of Hon. John Cradlebaugh, of Nevada, on the Admission of Utah as a State. Delivered in the House of Representatives, February 7, 1863.* Privately printed, 1863.

Daughters of Utah Pioneers. *An Enduring Legacy,* 12 vols. S.L.C: Daughters of Utah Pioneers, 1978–89.

DeLafosse, Peter, ed. *Trailing the Pioneers: A Guide to Utah's Emigrant Trails, 1829–1869.* Logan: Utah State Univ. Press with Utah Crossroads, 1994.

Christensen, Scott R. *Sagwitch: Shoshone Chieftain, Mormon Elder, 1822–1887.* Logan: Utah State Univ. Press, 1999.

Crowder, David L. *Tendoy, Chief of the Lemhis.* Caldwell, Idaho: Caxton Printers, 1969.

Davies, J. Kenneth. *Mormon Gold: The Story of California's Mormon Argonauts.* S.L.C: Olympus Publishing, 1984.

Dimsdale, Thomas J. *The Vigilantes of Montana or Popular Justice in the Rocky Mountains.* Norman: Univ. of Okla. Press, The Western Frontier Library, 1953.

Dunbar, Seymour and Paul C. Phillips, eds. *The Journals and Letters of Major John Owen, Pioneer of the Northwest, 1850–1871,* 2 vols. N.Y: Edward Eberstadt, 1927.

Ecelbarger, Gary L. *Frederick W. Lander: The Great Natural American Soldier.* Baton Rouge: La. State Univ. Press, 2000.

Ekins, Roger Robin, ed. *Defending Zion: George Q. Cannon and the California Mormon Newspaper Wars of 1856–1857.* Spokane, Wash: Arthur H. Clark Co., 2002.

Esshom, Frank. *Pioneers and Prominent Men of Utah.* S.L.C: Western Epics, Inc., 1966.

Fales, Susan L. and Chad J. Flake. *Mormons and Mormonism in U.S. Government Documents.* S.L.C: Univ. of Utah Press, 1989.

Fox, Jesse W. *General Courses and Distance from G. S. L. City to Fort Limhi and Gold Diggings on Salmon River.* G.S.L.C: Deseret News Printing, 1862.

Franzwa, Gregory M. *Maps of the California Trail.* Tucson: The Patrice Press, 1999.

__________. *Maps of the Oregon Trail.* St. Louis: The Patrice Press, 1982; 3rd ed., 1990.

Furniss, Norman F. *The Mormon Conflict, 1850–1859.* New Haven: Yale Univ. Press, 1960.

Gardner, Hamilton. *History of Lehi.* S.L.C: The Deseret News, 1913. Revised Edition, Lehi, Utah: Free Press Publishing, 1950.

Gottfredson, Peter. *History of Indian Depredations in Utah.* S.L.C: Skelton Publishing, 1919. Reprinted as *Indian Depredations in Utah* with a foreword by Phillip B. Gottfredsen. Tucson: Fenestra Books, 2002.

Hafen, LeRoy R. and Ann W. Hafen, eds. *The Utah Expedition, 1857–1858: A Documentary Account of the United States Military Movement under Colonel Albert Sidney Johnston, and The Resistance by Brigham Young and the Mormon Nauvoo Legion.* Glendale, Calif: Arthur H. Clark Co., 1958.

Hammond, Otis G., ed. *The Utah Expedition, 1857–1858: Letters of Capt. Jesse A. Gove, 10th Inf., U.S.A., of Concord, N.H., to Mrs. Gove, and special correspondence of the New York Herald.* Concord: N.H. Hist. Soc., 1928.

Hanson, Klaus J. *Quest for Empire: The Political Kingdom of God and the Council of Fifty in Mormon History.* East Lansing: Mich. State Univ. Press, 1967.

Hartley, William G. *Kindred Saints: The Mormon Immigrant Heritage of Alvin and Kathryn Christenson.* S.L.C: Eden Hill, 1982.

Helming, Grace Piazzola. *John W. Powell: An Historical Biography of a Notable Western Montana Mountain Man.* Wisdom, Mont: privately printed, 1993.

History of Montana, 1739–1885. Chicago: Warner, Beers & Co., 1885.

Huchel, Frederick M. *A History of Box Elder County.* S.L.C: Utah State Hist. Soc., 1999.

Huntington, D. B. *Vocabulary of the Utah and Sho-sho-ne or Snake Dialects.* S.L.C: Salt Lake Herald, 1872.

Jenson, Andrew, ed. *Latter-day Saint Biographical Encyclopedia,* 4 vols. S.L.C: Andrew Jenson History Co., 1901. Reprinted S.L.C: Western Epics, 1971.

Johnston, William Preston. *The Life of Albert Sidney Johnston, Embracing His Services in the Armies of the United States, the Republic of Texas, and the Confederate States.* N.Y: D. Appleton and Co., 1878.

Josephy, Alvin M., Jr. *The Nez Perce Indians and the Opening of the Northwest,* abr. ed., New Haven: Yale Univ. Press, 1971.

Journal of Discourses, 26 vols. London: Latter-Day Saints Book Depot, 1854–86.

Kappler, Charles J. *Indian Affairs: Laws and Treaties,* 7 vols. Wash: Government Printing Office, 1904.

Kate and Sue McBeth, Missionary Teachers to the Nez Perce. Moscow: Univ. of Idaho Library, 1999. http://www.lib.uidaho.edu/mcbeth/

Kenney, Scott G., ed. *Wilford Woodruff's Journal,* 10 vols. Midvale, Utah: Signature Books, 1983.

Kip, Lawrence. *The Indian Council in the Valley of the Walla Walla.* San Francisco: privately printed, 1855.

Langford, Nathaniel Pitt. *Vigilante Days and Ways: The Pioneers of the Rockies.* N.Y., Chicago: A. L. Burt Co. Publishers, 1912.

Lee, John D. *Mormonism Unveiled; or The Life and Confessions of the Late Mormon Bishop, John D. Lee. Written by Himself.* St Louis: Bryan, Brand & Co., 1877.

MacKinnon, William P., ed. *At Sword's Point: A Documentary History of the Utah War of 1857–1858.* Spokane, Wash: Arthur H. Clark Co., forthcoming.

Madsen, Betty M. and Brigham D. *North to Montana: Jehus, Bullwhackers and Mule Skinners on the Montana Trail.* S.L.C: Univ. of Utah Press, 1980.

Madsen, Brigham D. *The Bannock of Idaho.* Caldwell, Idaho: Caxton Printers, 1983; paperback ed., Moscow: Univ. of Idaho Press, 1996.

___________. *The Lemhi: Sacajawea's People.* Caldwell, Idaho: Caxton Press, 1980.

___________. *The Northern Shoshoni.* Caldwell, Idaho: Caxton Printers, 1980.

___________. *The Shoshoni Frontier and the Bear River Massacre.* S.L.C: Univ. of Utah Press, 1985.

___________, ed. *Exploring the Great Salt Lake: The Stansbury Expedition of 1849–50.* S.L.C: Univ. of Utah Press, 1989.

Marcy, Randolph B. *Thirty Years of Army Life on the Border.* N.Y: Harpers, 1866.

Meikle, Lyndel, ed. *Very Close to Trouble: The Johnny Grant Memoir.* Pullman: Wash. State Univ. Press, 1996.

Miller, Joseph Royal and Elna Miller, eds. *Journal of Jacob Miller.* Mercury Publishing, 1967.

Moorman, Donald R. with Gene A. Sessions. *Camp Floyd and the Mormons: The Utah War.* S.L.C: Univ. of Utah Press, 1992.

Morgan, Dale L. *The State of Deseret.* Logan: Utah State Univ. Press and Utah State Hist. Soc., 1987.

Neff, Andrew Love. *History of Utah, 1847 to 1869.* S.L.C: Deseret News Press, 1940.

Paul, Rodman W. *The California Gold Discovery: Sources, Documents, Accounts and Memoirs Relating to the Discovery of Gold at Sutter's Mill.* Georgetown, Calif: Talisman Press, 1966.

Phillips, Paul C., ed. *Forty Years on the Frontier, as Seen in the Journals and Reminiscences of Granville Stuart, Gold Miner, Trader, Merchant, Rancher and Politician,* 2 vols. Cleveland: Arthur H. Clark Co., 1925; Univ. of Nebr. Press, 1977.

Poll, Richard D. *Quixotic Mediator: Thomas L. Kane and the Utah War.* Ogden, Utah: Weber State College Press, 1985.

Pratt, Parley P. *The Essential Parley P. Pratt.* S.L.C: Signature Books, 1990.

Roberts, B. H. *A Comprehensive History of the Church of Jesus Christ of Latter-day Saints,* 6 vols. S.L.C: Deseret News Press, 1930.

Robertson, Frank C. *Fort Hall: Gateway to the Oregon Country.* N.Y: Hastings House, 1963.

Ronan, Peter. *Historical Sketch of the Flathead Indian Nation.* Minneapolis: Ross & Haines, 1890; reprinted, Mont. Hist. Soc., 1965.

Schindler, Harold. *Orrin Porter Rockwell: Man of God, Son of Thunder.* S.L.C: Univ. of Utah Press, 1966. Revised Edition, 1983.

Sessions, Gene A. *Mormon Thunder: A Documentary History of Jedediah Morgan Grant.* Urbana: Univ. of Ill. Press, 1982.

Settle, Raymond W., ed. *The March of the Mounted Riflemen: First United States Military Expedition to Travel the Full Length of the Oregon Trail from Fort Leavenworth to Fort Vancouver, May to October, 1849.* Glendale, Calif: Arthur H. Clark Co., 1940.

Slater, Nelson, comp. *Fruits of Mormonism or A Fair and Candid Statement of Facts Illustrative of Mormon Principles, Mormon Policy and Mormon Character, by More than Forty Eye-Witnesses.* Coloma, Calif: Harmon & Springer, 1851.

Smith, Joseph, Jr. *History of the Church of Jesus Christ of Latter-day Saints. Period 1. History of Joseph Smith, the Prophet, by Himself,* 6 vols. S.L.C: Deseret News, 1902–1912.

Souvenir Program for the Dedication of the L.D.S. Idaho Pioneer Monument at Fort Lemhi. Pocatello, Idaho: Arrowhead Press, 13 May 1950.

Stevens, Hazard. *The Life of Isaac Ingalls Stevens,* 2 vols. Boston and N.Y: Houghton, Mifflin, 1900.

Stott, Clifford L. *Search for Sanctuary: Brigham Young and the White Mountain Expedition.* S.L.C: Univ. of Utah Press, 1984.

Thrapp, Dan L. *Encyclopedia of Frontier Biography,* 3 vols. Glendale, Calif: Arthur H. Clark Co., 1988, 1994.

Trenholm, Virginia Cole and Maurine Carley. *The Shoshonis: Sentinels of the Rockies.* Norman: Univ. of Okla. Press, 1964.

Warner, Mikell de Lores Wormall and Harriett Duncan Munnick. *Catholic Church Records of the Pacific Northwest, Vancouver,* 2 vols. St. Paul, Ore: French Prairie Press, 1972.

Weisel, George F., ed. *Men and Trade on the Northwest Frontier as Shown by the Fort Owen Ledger.* Missoula: Mont. State Univ., 1955.

Whitney, Orson F. *History of Utah,* 4 vols. S.L.C: Deseret News Press, 1892.

Young, Brigham. "A series of Instructions and Remarks by President Brigham Young at a Special Council, Tabernacle, March 21, 1858." UPB.

Articles and Periodicals

Auerbach, Herbert S. and J. Cecil Alter, eds. "The Journal of Albert Tracy." *Utah Historical Quarterly,* 13:1–3, 1945.

Bagley, Will. "Hensley's Salt Lake Cutoff," in DeLafosse, ed., *Trailing the Pioneers: A Guide to Utah's Emigrant Trails, 1829–1869.*

"The Bannock Mountain Road." *Idaho Yesterdays,* 8:1, 1964, 10–15.

Beal, Samuel M. "The Salmon River Mission Founding of Fort Limhi," *The Deseret News,* Church Dept., 1 January 1938.

Bigler, David L. "The Crisis at Fort Limhi, 1858." *Utah Historical Quarterly,* 35:2, 1967.

__________. "Garland Hurt, The American Friend of the Utahs." *Utah Historical Quarterly,* 62:2, 1994.

Bluth, John V. "The Salmon River Mission: An Account of Its Origin, Purpose, Growth and Abandonment." 2 pts., *Improvement Era,* 3:11, 12, September, October, 1900.

Brooks, Juanita. "Indian Relations on the Mormon Frontier." *Utah Historical Quarterly,* 12:10, 1944.

Campbell, Eugene A. "Brigham Young's Outer Cordon—A Reappraisal." *Utah Historical Quarterly,* 41:2, 1973.

Carter, D. Robert. "Fish and the Famine of 1855–56." *Journal of Mormon History* 27:2 (Fall 2001), 92–124.

Christy, Howard A. "Open Hand and Mailed Fist: Mormon-Indian Relations in Utah, 1847–52." *Utah Historical Quarterly,* 46:3, 1978.

Coates, Lawrence G. "The Spalding-Whitman and Lemhi Missions: a comparison." *Idaho Yesterdays,* 31:1-2, 1987.

Dibble, Charles E. "The Mormon Mission to the Shoshoni Indians." *Utah Humanities Review* 1:1, 1:2, 1:3 (January, April, July 1947), 52–72, 166–77, 279–93.

England, Eugene. "Lamanites and the Spirit of the Lord." *Dialogue: A Journal of Mormon Thought,* 18:4, 1985.

Erickson, Dan. "Joseph Smith's 1891 Millennial Prophecy: The Quest for Apocalyptic Deliverance." *Journal of Mormon History,* 22:2, 1996.

Flemming, L. A. and A. R. Standing. "The Road to 'Fortune': The Salt Lake Cutoff." *Utah Historical Quarterly,* 33:3, 1965.

Fletcher, Robert H. "The Day of the Cattlemen Dawned Early—in Montana." *Montana The Magazine of Western History,* ll:4, October 1961.

Flint, Thomas. "The Diary of Dr. Thomas Flint." *Annual Publications, Historical Society of Southern California,* Los Angeles, 1923, 116.

Fowler, Catherine S. and Don D. "Western Shoshonis." *Utah Historical Quarterly,* 64:32, 1971.

Harrington, Leonard E. "Journal of Leonard E. Harrington." *Utah Historical Quarterly,* 8:1, 1940.

Hartley, William G. "Dangerous Outpost: Thomas Corless and the Fort Limhi/Salmon River Mission." *Mormon Historical Studies,* 2:2, 2001.

Hayden, Carl E. "Lemhi Was The First." *The Deseret News,* 8 May 1960.

Healy, John T. "An Adventure in the Idaho Mines." ed. Clyde McLemore, *Frontier and Midland: A Magazine of the West* 18:2 (Winter 1937–38), reprinted as *Sources of Northwest History No. 26,* Mont. State Univ.

Henderson, W. W., ed. "The Salmon River Mission: Extract from the Journal of L. W. Shurtliff." *Utah Historical Quarterly,* 5:1, 1932.

Hill, George Washington. "An Indian Vision." *Juvenile Instructor,* 12, January 1877.

Lamont, Ruby. "The Salmon River Indian Mission." *The Deseret Weekly,* Salt Lake City, 18 April 1891, 42:17, 521–24.

MacKinnon, William P. "The Buchanan Spoils System and the Utah Expedition: Careers of W. M. F. Magraw and John M. Hockaday." *Utah Historical Quarterly* 31:2 (Spring 1963), 127–50.

__________. "125 Years of Conspiracy Theories: Origins of the Utah Expedition of 1857–58." *Utah Historical Quarterly,* 52:3, 1984.

Maillet, Louis R. "Historical Sketch of Louis R. Maillet." *Contributions,* Hist. Soc. of Mont., 4:1903.

Minto, John. "Reminiscences of Experiences on the Oregon Trail in 1844." H. S. Lyman, ed. *The Quarterly of the Oregon Historical Society* 2: 3 (September 1901), 209–30.

Morgan, Dale L. "The Administration of Indian Affairs in Utah, 1851–1858." *The Pacific Historical Review,* 17:4, 1948.

Nash, John D. "The Salmon River Mission of 1855," *Idaho Yesterdays,* Spring, 1967.

O'Neil, Floyd A. and Stanford J. Layton. "Of Pride and Politics: Brigham Young as Indian Superintendent." *Utah Historical Quarterly,* 31:3, 1978.

Purple, Edwin R. "Perilous Passage: a Narrative of the Montana Gold Rush, (1862–1863)." edited by Kenneth N. Owens, *Montana The Magazine of Western History,* 46:1, 1996.

Rice, Loretta R. Child. "Thomas Sasson Smith and Fort Limhi." *Upper Snake River Valley Historical Society Quarterly,* 1:4, Spring 1972.

Sessions, Gene A. and Stephen W. Stathis. "The Mormon Invasion of Russian America: Dynamics of a Potent Myth," *Utah Historical Quarterly,* 45:1, 1977.

Stuart, Granville. "A Memoir of the Life of James Stuart." *Contributions,* Hist. Soc. of Mont., 1:1876.

Warren, Charles S. "The Territory of Montana." *Contributions,* Vol. 2, Hist. Soc. of Mont;, reprinted Boston: J. S. Canner, 1966.

Whittaker, David J. "Mormons and Native Americans: A Historical and Bibliographical Introduction." *Dialogue: A Journal of Mormon Thought,* 18:4, 1985.

Woody, Frank H. "How an Early Pioneer Came to Montana and the Privations Encountered on the Journey." *Contributions,* Hist. Soc. of Mont, 7:1910.

__________. "A Sketch of the Early History of Western Montana, (written in 1876 and 1877)." *Contributions,* Vol. 2, Hist. Soc. of Mont.; reprinted Boston: J. S. Canner, 1966.

NEWSPAPERS

Alta California

Daily Independent, Helena, Mont.

Daily Herald, Helena, Mont.

Daily Union, Sacramento, Calif.

Deseret News, Great Salt Lake City, Utah Territory.

Deseret Weekly, Salt Lake City, Utah.

Latter-day Saints' Millennial Star, Liverpool, England.

New York Times

Salt Lake Tribune

San Francisco Evening Bulletin

Weekly Missoulian, Missoula, Mont.

Theses and Dissertations

Beal, Merrill D. "The Salmon River Mission." Ph.D. diss., Univ. of California at Berkeley, 1934.

Christensen, Scott R. "Sagwitch: Shoshoni Chieftain, Mormon Elder, 1822–1884." M.A. Thesis, Utah State Univ., 1995.

Green, Dean M. "The Lemhi Indians of Eastern Idaho, 1860 to 1907." M.S. thesis, Brigham Young Univ., 1958.

Miller, David Henry. "The Impact of the Gunnison Massacre on Mormon-Federal Relations: Colonel Edward Jenner Steptoe's Command in Utah Territory, 1854–1855." M.A. thesis, Univ. of Utah, 1968.

O'Neil, Floyd A. "A History of the Ute Indians of Utah until 1890." Ph.D. diss., Univ of Utah, 1975.

Peterson, Paul H. "The Mormon Reformation." Ph.D. diss., Brigham Young Univ., 1981.

Reinwand, Louis G. "An Interpretive Study of Mormon Millennialism during the Nineteenth Century with Emphasis on Millennial Developments in Utah." M.A. thesis, Brigham Young Univ., 1971.

Manuscripts

Belnap, Gilbert. Autobiography. UPB.

Belnap Family Organization. Biography of Gilbert Belnap. Copy in author's possession and available at http://www.mcoffice.com/belnap/gilbert.html.

Blackburn, Elias. Journals and Papers. UHi.

Billings, Alfred Nelson. Elk Mountain Mission Diary. USIc; UPB.

Borrowman, John. Journal, 1846–1860. UHi.

Brown, John. Autobiography. USIc.

Brown, Lorenzo. Journal, Vol. 1. UPB.

Burgess, William. Letter. USIc.

Burr, Frederick H. Journal, 1857–58, and Letter. CrY.

Carrington, Albert. Diary. UU.

Carter, Judge William A. Papers. Wyo. State Archives, Cheyenne.

Clark, Israel Justus. Autobiography and Diary, 1855–1878. UPB.

Clarke, William John, Jr. Journey to the El Dorado: Diary of William John Clarke, Jr. The Route from Camden Mills, Rock Island County, Illinois, to Johnson's Rancho Near Camp Far West, California, March 27, 1849–July 11, 1849. Typescript, Emigrant Journal Collection, Idaho State Hist. Soc. Original at Northeastern Nev. Genealogical Soc., Box 1903, Elko, Nevada.

Cummings, Benjamin Franklin. Biography and Journals. UPB.

Cummings, James W. Travel of President Brigham Young to Oregon, 1857. USIc.

Dalton, Charles. Journal, 1855–58. USIc.

Dame, William H. Papers. UPB.

Day, Thomas. Autobiography. UPB.

Evans, David. Papers. UHi.

Ficklin, Benjamin Franklin. Collection. Preston Library, Virginia Military Institute.

Haight, Horton D. "Captain Horton D. Haight's Company that served in the Salmon River Expedition, 1858." CtY.

Hammond, Milton D. Journal and Life Sketch. UPB, UHi.

Harker, Joseph. Journal. UPB.

Healy, Johnny. "J. W. Powell and Fort Lemhi Told by Johnny Healy." Mont. Hist. Soc.

Hill, George Washington. Autobiography and Journal, 1822–1856. USIc.

__________. Incidents in the Life of George Washington Hill. USIc.

Huntington, Dimick Baker. Journal, August 1857 to May 1859. USIc.

Journal History of the Church of Jesus Christ of Latter-day Saints. USIc.

Kane, Thomas L. Collection. Utah War Correspondence, 1–15 March 1858. UPB.

Lansdale, R. H. Journal, 1856–58. CtY.

McAllister, J. D. T. Diary. UPB.

Margetts, Richard Bishop. Diary, August 1857. USIc.

Middleton, Charles F. Journal. USIc. Typed copy of Salmon River Mission period in possession of the author.

Miller, Jacob. Journal. UU.

Miller, James T. Journal. UU.

Monroe, Marcellus. "Report of a Party of Observation." UAr.

Moore, David. Compiled Writings and Life History. UPB.

__________, and Jacob Miller. Salmon River Mission Journal. USIc; ULA. Edited version. CU-B.

Nash, John D. Letters. John D. Nash, Oakdale, Calif.; copies in possession of the author.

Nephi Mass Quorum of Seventies. Journal. UPB.

Nichols, L. H. "Dictation of David Moore." CU-B.

Pitchforth, Samuel. Journal, 1857–1868. UPB.

"Proclamation by the Governor," 15 September 1857. UU.

Robinson, Oliver Lee. Diary. UU.

Shurtliff, Lewis W. The Life and Travels of Lewis Warren Shurtliff. Idaho State Hist. Soc. and copy in possession of the author.

Simpson, Sir George. Incoming Correspondence. R3C IT5, Hudson's Bay Co. Archives, Provincial Archives of Manitoba, Winnipeg, Manitoba, Canada.

Smith, Thomas Sasson. Journal. MS 1423, USIc.

__________. Affidavit. Brigham Young Collection. UU.

Stephens, David Henderson. Diary. USIc.

Stuart, Granville. Collection. UPB.

Taylor, Brian L. Biography of William Bailey Lake. UHi.

Taylor, Pleasant Green. Autobiography and Family Record. Typescript in possession of the author.

Wells, Daniel H. to William H. Dame, 13 August 1857, William R. Palmer Collection, File 8, Box 87, Special Collections, Sherratt Library, Southern Utah Univ., Cedar City.

Winder, John R. Diary, 1857–1858. UU.

Young, Brigham. Collection. UU.

__________. Moorman Collection, Stewart Library, Weber State Univ.

__________. Papers. USIc.

Zundel, Abraham. Diary, 1856–58. USIc.

Public Documents

U.S. House. "Information in reference to the condition of affairs in the Territory of Utah." Exec. Doc. 25 (21-1), 1852, Serial 640.

U.S. House. "Annual Report of the Secretary of War." Exec. Doc. 1 (34-1), v. 1, pt. 2, n. 1, 1856, Serial 841.

U.S. House. "Indian Hostilities in Oregon and Washington." Exec. Doc. 93 (34-1), 1856, Serial 858.

U.S. House. "The Utah Expedition." Exec. Doc. 71 (35-1), 1858, Serial 956.

U.S. House. "Depredations and Massacre by the Snake River Indians." Exec. Doc. 46 (36-2), v. 8, 1860, Serial 1099.

U.S. House. "Maps and Reports of the Fort Kearney, South Pass, and Honey Lake Wagon Road." Exec. Doc. 63 (36-2), v. 9, 1860, Serial 1100.

U.S. House. "Accounts of Brigham Young, Superintendent of Indian Affairs in Utah Territory." Exec. Doc. 29 (37-2), 1862, Serial 1128.

U.S. House. "Annual Report of the Commissioner of Indian Affairs." Exec. Doc. 1 (44-1), v. 4, pt. 1, 1875, Serial 1680.

U.S. Senate. "Annual Report of Commissioner of Indian Affairs, 1857." Exec. Doc. 11 (35-1), v. 2, n. 29, 1858, Serial 919.

U.S. Senate. "Message of the President of the United States." Exec. Doc. 1 (35-2), 1858.

U.S. Senate. "Annual Report of the Secretary of War." Exec. Doc. 1, v. 2, pt. 2 (35-2), 1858, Serial 974.

U. S. Senate. "The Massacre at Mountain Meadows, and other massacres in Utah Territory." Exec. Doc. 42 (36-1), 1860, Serial 1033.

U.S. Attorney General. "Records relating to the appointment of Federal judges, attorneys, and marshals for the Territory and State of Utah, 1853–1901." DNA; UHi; UU.

U.S. Interior Dept. "Letters Received by the Office of Indian Affairs, 1824-81, Utah Superintendency, 1849-90." DNA; UHi; UU.

U.S. War Dept. Selected Letters from Col. E. J. Steptoe, 1854–55. DNA; UHi.

U.S. War Dept. "Army of Utah." Letters Sent 16 July 1857 to 15 July 1861. NA, MIC 112, UHi.

Utah Territory. *Acts, Resolutions and Memorials, Passed at the Several Annual Sessions of the Legislative Assembly of the Territory of Utah, from 1851 to 1870 Inclusive* (S.L.C: Joseph Bull, Public Printer, 1870). UAr; UHi.

Utah Territory. Militia Records. UAr.

Utah Territory. Minute Book and Naturalization Papers, 1st Dist. Court, Dec. 7 to May 22, 1858, UAr.

INDEX

The letter n following a page number indicates the information is found in one or more footnotes on the page.

The Author

David Louis Bigler is a native of Provo, Utah. A naval veteran of World War II and Korea, he graduated from the University of Utah in 1950 with a degree in journalism. He is the retired director of public affairs for U.S. Steel, now USX Corp. Since 1986 he has devoted himself to the full-time study of Utah and western history.

Mr. Bigler is past president, Oregon-California Trails Association; a founder and first president, Utah Westerners; former member, Utah Board of State History; former director, Friends of University of Utah Libraries; and member, Utah State Historical Society, Gold Discovery Park Association, and Sacramento Westerners. He is also a former officer or director of the Utah Manufacturers Association, Utah Mining Association, and Salt Lake Area Chamber of Commerce. He received an honorary Doctor of Letters degree in 1979 from Southern Utah State College, now Southern Utah University.

Mr. Bigler has written extensively on Western history. His essay on "Garland Hurt, the American Friend of the Utahs," won the Utah State Historical Society's Dale L. Morgan Award. He edited his great-uncle's diary, *The Gold Discovery Journal of Azariah Smith,* for the University of Utah Press. For the University of Utah's Marriott Library, he edited *A Winter with the Mormons: The 1852 Letters of Jotham Goodell,* part of the Tanner Trust series, "Utah, the Mormons, and the West." Westerners International presented its Best Book Award for 1998 to his *Forgotten Kingdom: The Mormon Theocracy in the American West, 1846–1896*. His second volume for the Arthur H. Clark Company, *Army of Israel: Mormon Battalion Narratives,* edited with Will Bagley, won the Mormon History Association's Best Documentary and the Utah State Historical Society's Military History prize in 2000.

KINGDOM IN THE WEST SERIES

The role of the Church of Jesus Christ of Latter-day Saints in the settlement of the American West has been a subject of controversy and fascination for one hundred and fifty years. *KINGDOM IN THE WEST: The Mormons and the American Frontier*, a series from The Arthur H. Clark Company, explores the story of the Mormon people and their part in the greater history of the American West. Using primary source documents, most of them never before published, the projected set of twenty volumes examines the Mormons' religious vision and political ambitions, revealing how they saw themselves and how they appeared to others. Each of the volumes thus far published has received awards from various historical organizations for excellence.

The series' first volume, *The Pioneer Camp of the Saints*, brought the Latter-day Saint people to the Great Basin via the Mormon Trail journals of Thomas Bullock. In Volume 2, *Forgotten Kingdom: The Mormon Theocracy in the American West, 1847–1896*, David L. Bigler provided a narrative overview of the Latter-day Saint movement in the American West. Volume 3, *Scoundrel's Tale: The Samuel Brannan Papers*, told the audacious story of Mormons in California and their larger ambitions in the American West. Volume 4, *Army of Israel: Mormon Battalion Narratives*, uses source documents to tell the story of one of the West's most amazing adventures, the Mormon Battalion. In Volume 5, *Defending Zion: George Q. Cannon and the California Mormon Newspaper Wars of 1856–1857*, Roger Robin Ekins collects writings from the *Western Standard* and the editorials and articles of the opposition press, painting a vivid picture of the debate over Mormonism as it approached the Utah War. Subsequent volumes will focus on Great Basin overland narratives, the handcart emigration, polygamy, Indian relations, and the Utah War.

Series subscriptions are welcomed. Manuscript proposals of a documentary nature may also be submitted. Address inquiries to the publisher:

THE ARTHUR H. CLARK COMPANY
P.O. Box 14707
Spokane, Washington 99214
(800) 842-9286